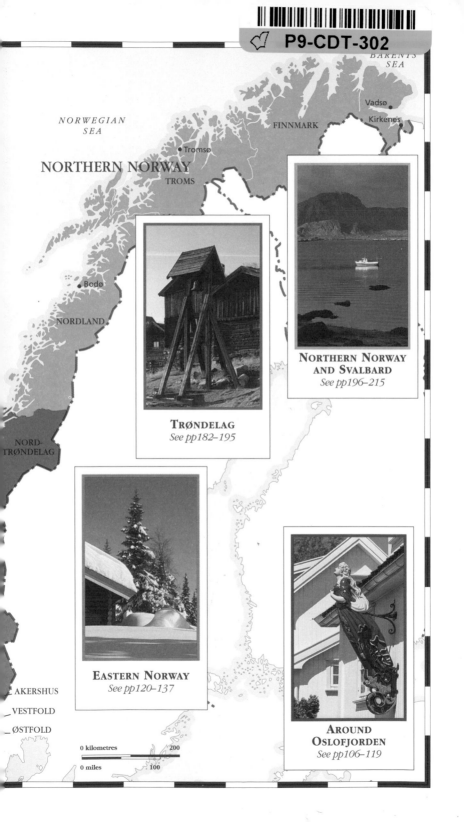

BARENTS SEA

NORWEGIAN SEA

Vadsø

Kirkenes

FINNMARK

Tromsø

NORTHERN NORWAY

TROMS

Bodø

NORDLAND

NORD-TRØNDELAG

AKERSHUS

VESTFOLD

ØSTFOLD

0 kilometres 200

0 miles 100

NORTHERN NORWAY AND SVALBARD
See pp196–215

TRØNDELAG
See pp182–195

EASTERN NORWAY
See pp120–137

AROUND OSLOFJORDEN
See pp106–119

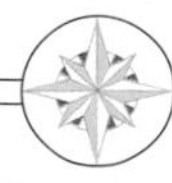

EYEWITNESS TRAVEL GUIDES

NORWAY

EYEWITNESS TRAVEL GUIDES

NORWAY

Main contributor:
SNORRE EVENSBERGET

DK PUBLISHING

LONDON • NEW YORK • MUNICH
MELBOURNE • DELHI

PRODUCED BY Streiffert Förlag AB, Stockholm

SENIOR EDITOR & DESIGN Bo Streiffert
PROJECT EDITOR Guy Engström

MAIN CONTRIBUTOR Snorre Evensberget

OTHER CONTRIBUTORS Alf G. Andersen, Hans-Erik Hansen, Tine Flinder-Nyquist, Annette Mürer

PHOTOGRAPHERS Jørn Bøhmer-Olsen, Frits Solvang, Rolf Sørensen

CARTOGRAPHER Stig Söderlind

ILLUSTRATORS Richard Bonson, Gary Cross, Claire Littlejohn, John Woodcock

ENGLISH TRANSLATION Fiona Harris

Dorling Kindersley Limited
EDITOR Jane Hutchings
SENIOR DTP DESIGNER Jason Little
PRODUCTION Sarah Dodd

Reproduced in Singapore by Colourscan
Printed and bound in China by
Toppan Printing Co. (Shenzhen Ltd)

First American Edition 2003
03 04 05 10 9 8 7 6 5 4 3 2

Published in the United States by DK Publishing, Inc.,
375 Hudson Street, New York, New York 10014

Published in Great Britain by Dorling Kindersley Limited

A CATALOGING IN PUBLICATION RECORD IS AVAILABLE FROM THE LIBRARY OF CONGRESS

ISSN 1542-1554
ISBN 0-7894-9339-X

THROUGHOUT THIS BOOK, FLOORS ARE REFERRED TO IN ACCORDANCE WITH EUROPEAN USAGE, I.E. THE "FIRST FLOOR IS THE FLOOR ABOVE GROUND LEVEL.

See our complete product line at
www.dk.com

The information in this Eyewitness Travel Guide is checked annually.
Every effort has been made to ensure that this book is as up-to-date as possible at the time of going to press. Some details, however, such as telephone numbers, opening hours, prices, gallery hanging arrangements and travel information are liable to change. The publishers cannot accept responsibility for any consequences arising from the use of this book, nor for any material on third party websites, and cannot guarantee that any website address in this book will be a suitable source of travel information. We value the views and suggestions of our readers very highly. Please write to: Publisher, DK Eyewitness Travel Guides, Dorling Kindersley, 80 Strand, London WC2R 0RL, Great Britain.

View of Geirangerfjorden

CONTENTS

HOW TO USE THIS GUIDE *6*

INTRODUCING NORWAY

PUTTING NORWAY ON THE MAP *10*

A PORTRAIT OF NORWAY *12*

NORWAY THROUGH THE YEAR *28*

THE HISTORY OF NORWAY *32*

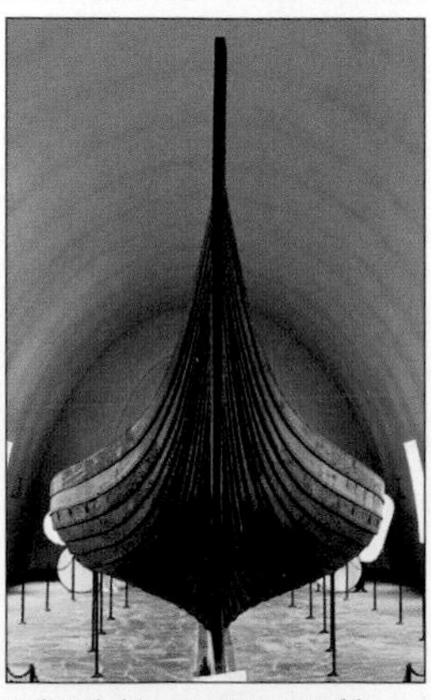

Gokstad ship, a 1,000-year-old Viking vessel ***(see pp84–5)***

◁ **Nærøyfjorden, an arm of Aurlandsfjorden, surrounded by steep-sided mountains**

Oslo Area by Area

Oslo at a Glance *44*

Central Oslo West *46*

Central Oslo East *62*

Bygdøy *76*

Further Afield *88*

Oslo Street Finder *98*

Bridal crown from Hallingdal *(see pp24–5)*

Norway Area by Area

Around Oslofjorden *106*

Eastern Norway *120*

Sørlandet and Telemark *138*

Vestlandet *154*

Trøndelag *182*

Northern Norway and Svalbard *196*

Travellers' Needs

Where to Stay *218*

Where to Eat *228*

Kransekake, a festive almond cake

Shopping in Norway *240*

Entertainment in Norway *246*

Sports and Outdoor Activities *250*

Skiers taking a break at a cabin in Trysil, Eastern Norway

Survival Guide

Practical Information *256*

Travel Information *264*

General Index *272*

Acknowledgments *285*

Phrase Book *287*

Oslo Transport Map *Inside back cover*

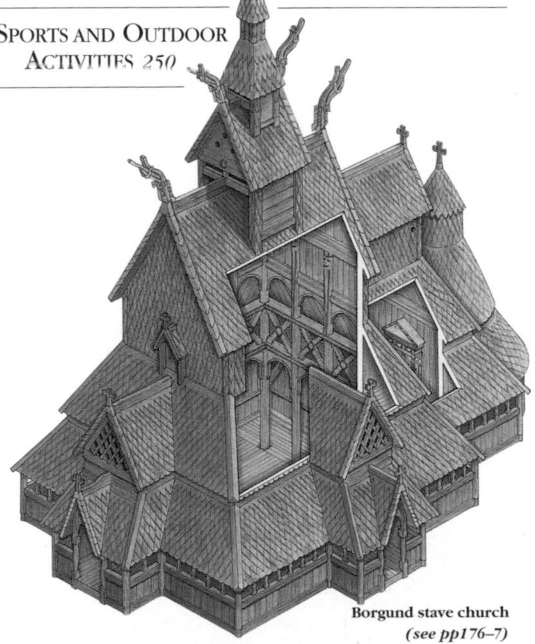

Borgund stave church *(see pp176–7)*

How to Use this Guide

This guide helps you to get the most from your visit to Norway by providing detailed practical information and expert recommendations. *Introducing Norway* maps the country and sets it in its historical and cultural context. The Oslo section and the six regional chapters describe important sights using maps, photographs and illustrations. Restaurant and hotel recommendations can be found in *Travellers' Needs*, while the *Survival Guide* has tips on everything from making a telephone call to using local transportation, as well as information on money, etiquette and safety.

Oslo

The centre of the capital is divided into three areas, each with its own chapter which opens with a list of the sights to be covered. A fourth chapter, *Further Afield*, covers the peripheral areas of Bogstad, Frogner and Toyen. All sights are numbered and plotted on each chapter's area map. Information on each sight is easy to locate as the entries follow the numbering used on the map.

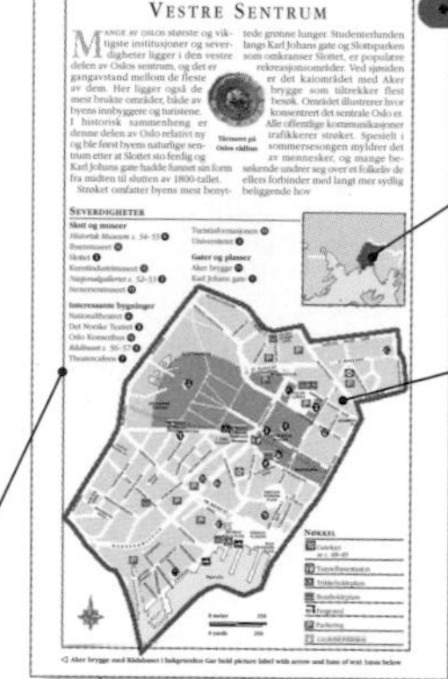

All pages relating to Oslo have red thumb tabs.

A locator map shows you where you are in relation to other areas in the city centre.

1 Area Map
For easy reference, sights are numbered and located on a map. The central sights are also marked on the Oslo Street Finder *maps on pages 98–103.*

Sights at a Glance lists the chapter's sights by category: Churches, Museums and Galleries, Historic Buildings, Parks and Gardens.

2 Street-by-Street Map
This gives a bird's eye view of the key areas covered in each chapter.

Stars indicate the sights that no visitor should miss.

Walking routes are shown in red.

3 Detailed Information
City sights are described individually. Addresses, telephone numbers and opening times are given, as well as information on admission charges, wheelchair access, guided tours and transport.

Story boxes talk about subjects of interest linked to the sights.

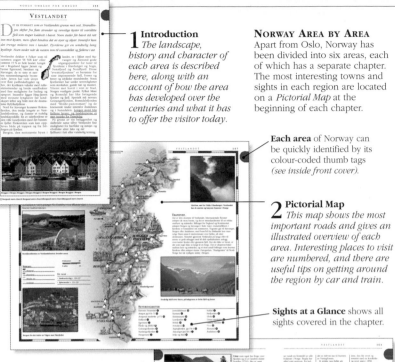

1 Introduction

The landscape, history and character of each area is described here, along with an account of how the area has developed over the centuries and what it has to offer the visitor today.

Norway Area by Area

Apart from Oslo, Norway has been divided into six areas, each of which has a separate chapter. The most interesting towns and sights in each region are located on a *Pictorial Map* at the beginning of each chapter.

Each area of Norway can be quickly identified by its colour-coded thumb tags *(see inside front cover)*.

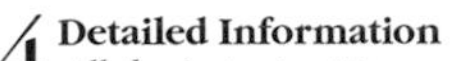

2 Pictorial Map

This map shows the most important roads and gives an illustrated overview of each area. Interesting places to visit are numbered, and there are useful tips on getting around the region by car and train.

Sights at a Glance shows all sights covered in the chapter.

4 Detailed Information

All the important towns and other places to visit are described individually. They are listed in order and follow the numbering on the Pictorial Map. *Within each town or city, there is detailed information on important buildings and other sights.*

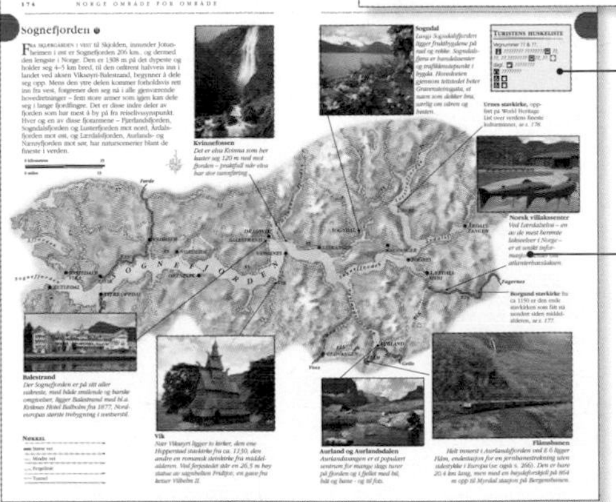

A Visitors' Checklist provides the practical information you will need to plan your visit.

5 Norway's Top Sights

National parks have maps showing places of interest. Three-dimensional illustrations reveal the interiors of historic buildings. Museums and galleries have colour-coded floorplans. Large towns have maps showing selected sights.

Introducing Norway

Putting Norway on the Map 8-11

A Portrait of Norway 12-27

Norway Through the Year 28-31

The History of Norway 32-41

Putting Norway on the Map

THE KINGDOM OF NORWAY is one of the largest countries in Europe, covering 324,219 sq km (125,148 sq miles). The most southerly point, Lindersnes, lies at about the same latitude as Aberdeen in Scotland, and the northernmost tip, near the North Cape, is at latitude 71°11'8" N. The coastline bordering the Skagerrak, the North Sea, the Norwegian Sea and the Arctic Ocean measures 20,000 km (12,400 miles). Much of the country is habitable thanks to the warming effects of the Gulf Stream. The country has around 4.5 million inhabitants, 500,000 of whom live in the capital, Oslo.

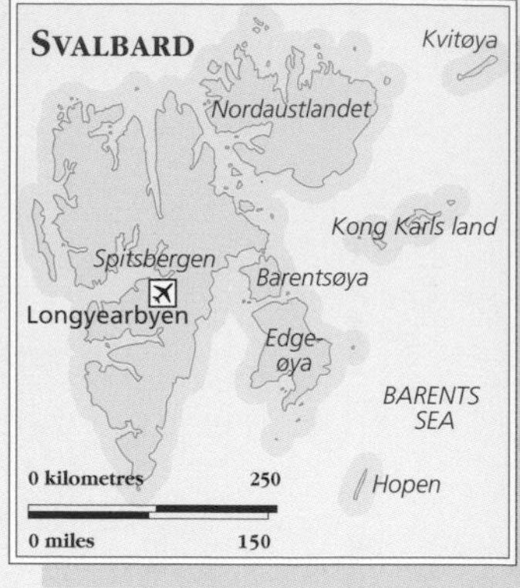

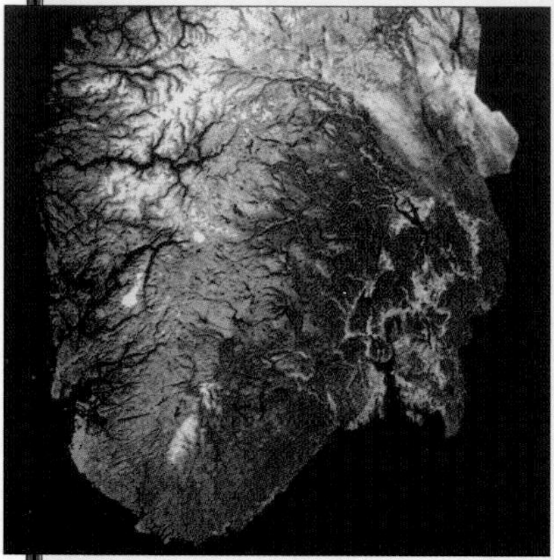

Satellite view of southern Norway

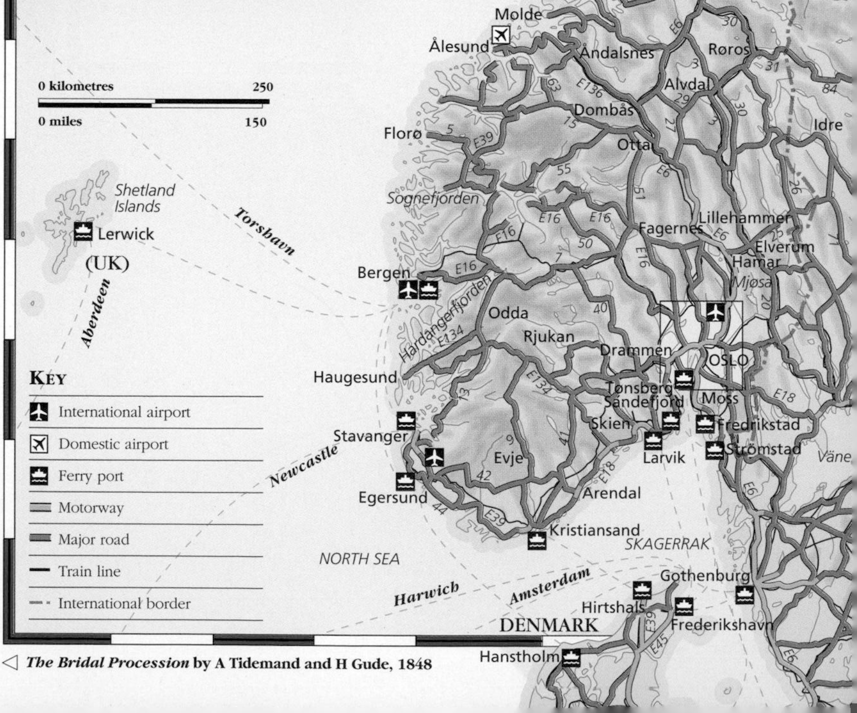

KEY

- International airport
- Domestic airport
- Ferry port
- Motorway
- Major road
- Train line
- International border

◁ ***The Bridal Procession*** **by A Tidemand and H Gude, 1848**

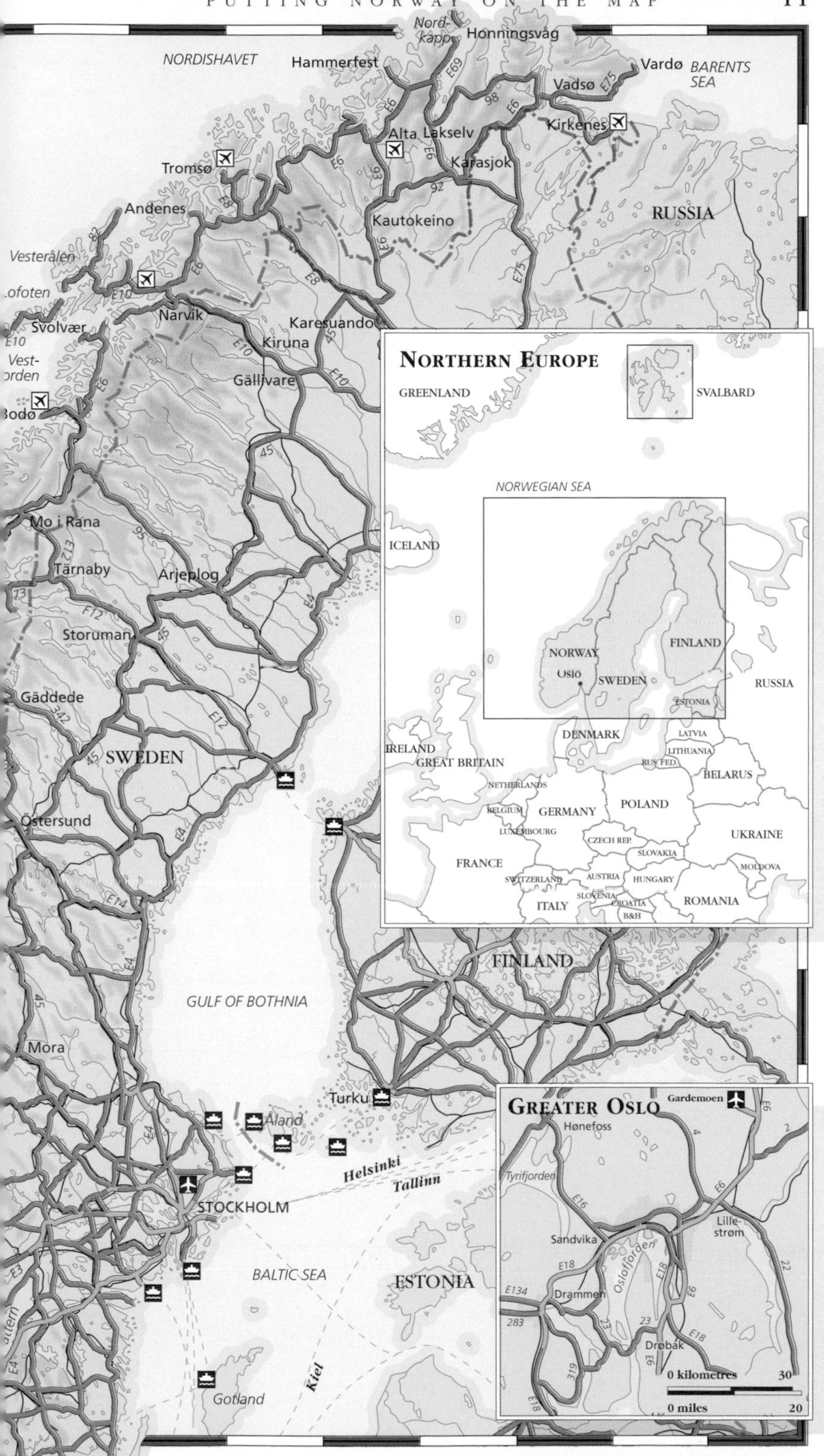
NORDISHAVET
Nord-kapp
Honningsvåg
Hammerfest
Vardø
BARENTS SEA
Vadsø
Kirkenes
Alta
Lakselv
Karasjok
Tromsø
Andenes
Kautokeino
RUSSIA
Vesterålen
Lofoten
Narvik
Svolvær
Karesuando
Kiruna
Vestfjorden
Gällivare
Bodø
Mo i Rana
Tärnaby
Arjeplog
Storuman
Gäddede
SWEDEN
Östersund
FINLAND
GULF OF BOTHNIA
Mora
Turku
Åland
Helsinki
Tallinn
STOCKHOLM
BALTIC SEA
ESTONIA
Kiel
Gotland
NORTHERN EUROPE
GREENLAND
SVALBARD
NORWEGIAN SEA
ICELAND
NORWAY
Oslo
SWEDEN
FINLAND
RUSSIA
ESTONIA
DENMARK
LATVIA
LITHUANIA
RUS. FED.
BELARUS
IRELAND
GREAT BRITAIN
NETHERLANDS
BELGIUM
GERMANY
POLAND
LUXEMBOURG
CZECH REP.
UKRAINE
SLOVAKIA
FRANCE
SWITZERLAND
AUSTRIA
HUNGARY
MOLDOVA
SLOVENIA
CROATIA
B&H
ITALY
ROMANIA
GREATER OSLO
Gardemoen
Hønefoss
Tyrifjorden
Lillestrøm
Sandvika
Oslofjorden
Drammen
Drøbak
0 kilometres 30
0 miles 20

A Portrait of Norway

Norway's magnificent scenery and untamed nature have long captivated visitors. Spectacular fjords indent the rugged coastline, mountains rise above tranquil valleys. This is a country where music, art and literature are part of its soul, where sports such as skiing and football are actively pursued, and current affairs are hotly debated. It is also the home of the Nobel Peace Prize.

Wrapped around northwestern Scandinavia like a protective bastion against the North Sea, Norway is one of the most scenically beautiful places in Europe. The country stretches an incredible 1,752 km (1,089 miles), from southernmost Lindesnes across the Arctic Circle to the North Cape. It is barely 430 km (267 miles) at its widest point, and only 6 km (4 miles) at its narrowest.

Geological processes such as the land rising, the Ice Age and erosion have created a remarkably varied landscape. Deep fjords penetrate the coastal mountain ranges, their glassy green waters extending far inland to waterside towns and settlements. More than 75,000 islands lie offshore, providing sheltered harbours and passageways for the numerous ferries, cruise ships and fishing boats that ply the coast.

A puffin

The capital, Oslo, is a vibrant city centred round a harbour and guarded by a castle. It is an eclectic place of traditional timber houses, stately Neo-Classical buildings and the latest in ultra-modern architecture, with a thriving café-life that spills outdoors in summer. Around Oslofjorden – a summer playground teeming with boats – evidence of Norway's Viking heritage abounds. The Vikings were a warrior-like maritime race whose voyages took them as far as America in one direction and the Caspian Sea

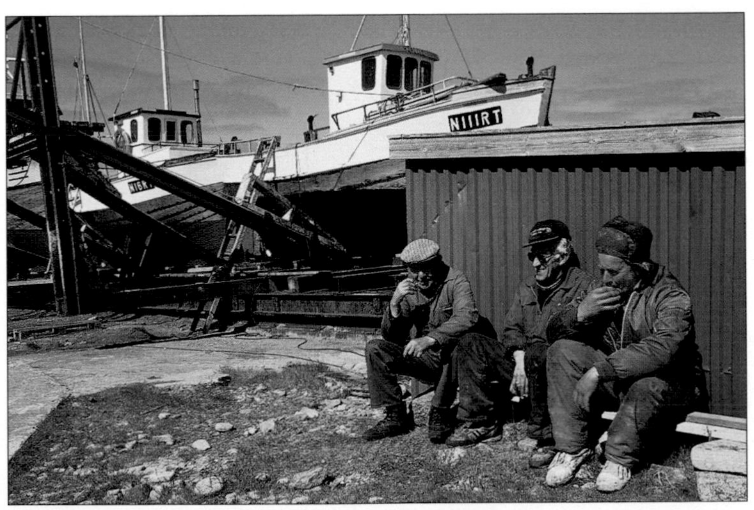

Fishermen at the former trading post of Sund in the Lofoten Islands

◁ **Woman dressed in a traditional *bunad* playing folk music on a Hardanger fiddle**

Pumping riches from the bottom of the sea on the Ekofisk oil field

in the other, and whose raiding parties inspired terror in the coastal communities of Northern Europe. Fascinating archaeological finds from this time, including 9th-century sailing vessels, are on show in museums such as Oslo's Viking Ship Museum.

Northeast of the capital, fertile farmland and forests give way to lofty mountains with peaks reaching 2,500 m (8,200 ft) and long, slender valleys with lakes and rivers. The south coast is lined with silver-sand beaches set against a backdrop of the 1,400-m (4,593-ft) high mountain plateau of Hardangervidda. Vestlandet, on the west coast, with the fishing port of Bergen and Norway's "oil capital", Stavanger, is picturesque fjord country.

Northern Lights

Pilgrims in days of old would make the treacherous journey north across the mountains to the sacred Nidaros Cathedral in Trondheim. Here lie the remains of the country's patron saint, Olav Haraldsson. The northernmost point in Norway, the North Cape, is a place of pilgrimage for modern-day travellers, its precipitous cliffs standing proud against the Barents Sea.

Northern Norway is the land of the midnight sun and shimmering Northern Lights. In the height of summer it basks in daylight around the clock; in winter the sun disappears altogether and its rearrival in the New Year is marked by joyous festivities.

Climate

It is possible to live so far north in Norway because of the warming effects of the Gulf Stream. On the west coast this results in warm winters and cool summers. The south and west of the country have the highest average temperatures: 22° C (72° F) in Oslo in July. The coldest temperatures can be found in the mountains, particularly Finnmarksvidda, where –51.4° C (–60.5° F) was recorded in December 1886.

Riches of the Land and Sea

Fishing, particularly herring, and the timber industry have formed the backbone of the Norwegian economy. This has always been a seafaring country, renowned for shipbuilding, and foreign trade has played an important role in its development. Industrialization gathered momentum in the 19th century; small sawmills and factories gave way to larger enterprises powered by hydro-electricity. In the 20th century, Norway made its fortune in offshore oil production, creating one of the world's richest countries. How the oil revenue should be spent has been the subject of much political controversy. The state of the environment is

National coat of arms

also a matter of fierce debate. Top of the list of concerns are pollution of the waterways, high energy consumption and which type of power stations should be built.

A Sami wedding party, Kautokeino, Finnmark

King and Government

Norway is a constitutional, hereditary monarchy. The current monarch is King Harald V, who succeeded to the throne in 1991. He is married to Queen Sonja, a commoner, and their two children, Crown Prince Haakon Magnus and Princess Märtha Louise, are also both married to commoners. Most Norwegians are traditionally fiercely proud of their royal family, who in turn are close to their people and are seen as modern, down-to-earth monarchs.

According to the constitution, the executive power rests with the king, but in practice it is the Council of State which governs. The Norwegian Parliament (Stortinget) has the decisive power when it comes to the management of the country. Elections to the 165-representative parliament are held every four years. Of the six principal parties jostling for power, the Labour Party held the majority from 1945–61; since then there have been both socialist and non-socialist governments.

The main political aims have been welfare, social stability and equality.

The marriage of Crown Prince Haakon Magnus and Mette-Marit in Oslo Cathedral, 2001

The Equal Opportunities Act of 1978 established a series of principles aiming to improve the balance of men and women in the workplace and ensuring equal pay for equal work. As a result, women entered political life in large numbers, and when Gro Harlem Brundtland formed her government in 1986, 44.4 per cent of the ministers were women, which caused an international sensation.

The People

Norwegians are hospitable people who will, more often than not, go out of their way to welcome a guest in their home and offer cake and a drink. This is a tradition that has its roots in the remote rural settlements of old when visitors needed sustenance after an arduous journey. Major investment in road-building, tunnels and bridges has meant that few communities are so isolated today, but old traditions live on.

The Norwegians are a deeply patriotic race, as can be seen on National Day (17 May), when young and old dress in folk costume (the *bunad*, *see pp24–5)* and parade through the streets. Yet this nationalistic outlook does not prevent them from accepting refugees and immigrants.

On the one hand Norwegians are regarded as a liberal, tolerant people, but on the other they still adhere to laws that hark back to a bygone era. The sale of alcohol, for instance, is restricted to government-owned shops known as Vinmonopolet.

Norway was a Catholic country until the Reformation in 1537, when the state church became Evangelical-Lutheran by royal decree.

Jubliant crowds on Holmenkoll Sunday for the ski-jumping highlight of the annual skiing festival

Language

Norway has had vigorous and at times heated discussions over the status of its two languages, *bokmål* ("book language"), which is a derivation of Danish, and *nynorsk*, an amalgamation of the many Norwegian dialects nationwide.

Both *bokmål* and *nynorsk* have had equal official status since 1885. *Nynorsk* is most widely spoken in the west of the country (Vestlandet) and in the central valleys to the south and east. Norway's oldest minority language, Sami, is spoken by some 20,000 people *(see p209)*.

A Nation of Avid Readers

Norwegians read more newspapers than anyone else in the world. On average, each household buys a remarkable 1.7 newspapers a day.

Sales of books are also high. The most popular volume today is Thor Heyerdahl's *The Kon-Tiki Expedition*, which has been published in nearly 70 languages and has sold millions of copies worldwide. Jostein Gaarder's *Sophie's World* was the world's best-selling book in 1996; Herbjørg Wassmo's *Tora-trilogy* has been translated into 22 languages, and several recent Norwegian crime novels have been published in as many as 30 countries.

Thor Heyerdahl's best-selling book, *The Kon-Tiki Expedition*.

Art, Music and Drama

The 19th-century passion for National Romanticism in Norway laid the foundations for what has become a rich heritage of visual arts, music and literature. Artists working at this time, such as Adolf Tidemand and Hans Gude, captured the countryside and its people in their paintings. Edvard Munch followed with his deeply emotional Expressionist works. In music, the violinist Ole Bull and the pianist and composer Edvard Grieg looked to Norwegian folk songs for inspiration. The playwrights Bjørnstjerne Bjørnson and Henrik Ibsen put Norwegian issues firmly centre stage in their dramas.

The importance of traditions is obvious in the country's many open-air museums. It seems that no town is complete without its own collection of rustic timber buildings representing local building style and crafts such as wood-carving and decorative painting (known as *rosemaling)*.

Folk music is rooted in the country's ancient songs and sagas, and musicians can often be heard playing the Hardanger fiddle, particularly at festivals. A multitude of school brass bands form a happy and harmonious part of the children's

National Day parade on 17 May and other festive occasions.

Sports and the Outdoors

Renowned as the cradle of skiing, during the 2002 Winter Olympics in Salt Lake City, USA, Norway won 11 gold medals and came third in the overall competition. The country has hosted two Winter Olympics: in Oslo in 1952 and Lillehammer in 1994.

Skiing is a popular winter pastime and with the first snowfalls, trails are prepared and people of all ages venture out on skis. Events such as the Holmenkollen Ski Festival attract thousands of spectators.

Football has a strong following with 1,800 clubs throughout the country. In other fields, the women's handball and football teams have had great successes, followed closely by the whole nation on TV.

The nature-loving Norwegians still spend much of their spare time outdoors, by the sea, sailing, fishing or walking in the forests and mountains, where a network of mountain huts *(hytte)* provides overnight accommodation.

Norway and the World

A member of NATO since 1949, Norway has remained a nation with a strong sense of "self". The

Skier taking a break at a hut in Rondane National Park during Easter holidays

referenda for joining the European Union (in 1972 and 1994) both resulted in a "no" vote; the latter with 52.2 per cent against and 47.8 per cent in favour. Opinion polls today indicate the same standpoint.

When it comes to international welfare and peace issues, however, Norway plays a central role. In relation to its gross national product, Norway is the world's largest donor. It has also sent nearly 60,000 soldiers to take part in United Nations peacekeeping missions, and awards the Nobel Peace prize every year.

Norway is becoming more dependent on the outside world, and there are concerns about the future and what will happen when its oil supplies run out.

It remains to be seen if the country's international involvement will increase after the next referendum on EU membership.

The annual award ceremony for the Nobel Peace Prize in the main hall of Oslo Town Hall

The Fjords

AMONG THE WORLD'S most spectacular geological formations, the Norwegian fjords are long, narrow inlets stretching deep into the surrounding mountains. At their innermost reaches, their depth often matches the height of the cliffs above, while shallower waters connect them to the sea. They were created by a gradual process of glacier erosion during the last Ice Age (around 110,000 to 13,000 BC) when enormous glaciers crept through the valleys, gouging steep-sided crevices into the landscape, often far below the surface of the sea. When the glaciers melted, sea water burst in and filled the hollows left by the ice.

Waterfalls *can be seen where glaciers and torrents of water once cut vertical precipices into the mountain sides.*

Where the fjords *meet the sea on the west coast of Norway, the tree-covered mountains rise steeply. Spruce and birch are the most common species. In the north, the cliff faces are often bare all the way down to the shore.*

The tree line in Vestlandet is usually at 500–1,000 m (1,640–3,280 ft).

The threshold between the fjord and the sea often has a depth of just one-tenth of the fjord at its deepest point.

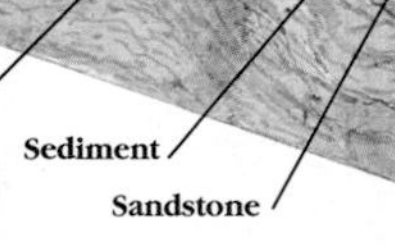

Sediment

Sandstone

Granite and gneissic rock

Fruit and vegetable *cultivation is a thriving industry at the inner reaches of the southern fjords. Here the climate is more favourable than by the coast.*

THE STRUCTURE OF A FJORD

This cut-away artwork shows a typical fjord, with a threshold of shallow water at the mouth falling steeply to great depths further inland, and inlets radiating from the main fjord. The sea bed, like the surrounding mountains, consists of granite and gneiss with sediment on top.

Glaciers *such as Jostedalsbreen* (see p178) *gouged out the fjords. Toward the end of the last Ice Age, the glaciers covered all of what was to become Sognefjorden. As the ice melted, the seawater forced its way into the basin.*

The mountain peaks *can reach as high as 1,500 m (4,900 ft) just a short distance from the shore. In inner Sognefjorden, the mountains rise to 2,000 m (6,560 ft).*

The inner arms of the fjord can extend 200 km (124 miles) from its mouth.

Small villages have developed in sheltered bays where the soil is good for fruit-growing and farming.

The inlets *can be very long and often branch into several tributaries. The glaciers carved through the rock wherever the surface was weak.*

A fjord's depth can be more than 1,200 m (3,930 ft)

Car ferries *criss-cross the fjords at many points. Although not as quick an alternative as road tunnels and bridges, they remain a popular choice for the scenic views they offer.*

Road Tunnels Under the Fjords

Communications along the Atlantic coast of Norway have always been a challenge, with fjords cutting long clefts into the land and the risk of avalanches and the mountains themselves creating other obstacles. In recent years great improvements to the infrastructure have been made possible thanks to the riches from the North Sea oil fields. Using modern engineering techniques, huge tunnels have been driven through mountain ranges and under fjords, making transport easier between the small communities.

The 24.5-km (15-mile) long Lærdal Tunnel ***(see p176)***

Landscape and Wildlife

NORWAY HAS AN IMMENSELY varied landscape. The plains and rolling hills of the southwest give way to rounded mountains cut by rivers and lakes where Arctic char, salmon and trout can be fished. Reindeer inhabit the high plateaus; elk, wolf and roe deer the forests. Further north the terrain becomes more rugged. This is the habitat of bear, lynx and Arctic fox. Polar bears can be seen on the islands of Svalbard *(see pp214–15)*. The coast is punctuated by fjords where seals and even whales may be spotted. Skerries and islands provide ideal nesting sites for some of the country's 250 species of birds. Out to sea the waters are rich in cod, coley, mackerel and herring.

***The brown bear** was once found throughout the country, but today lives in limited numbers in the far north.*

THE ATLANTIC COAST

The nesting cliffs of Runde, near Ålesund, Lofoten, Troms, Finnmark and Svalbard are home to several hundred thousand birds. Species include white-breasted guillemot, kittiwake, auk and puffin. Northern fulmar and northern gannet can also be seen in fewer numbers.

***Puffins**, "the parrots of the nesting cliffs", can be found in large numbers in northern Norway. The population varies according to feeding conditions.*

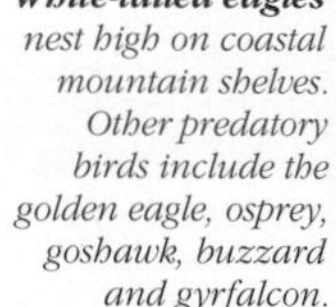

***White-tailed eagles** nest high on coastal mountain shelves. Other predatory birds include the golden eagle, osprey, goshawk, buzzard and gyrfalcon.*

THE FORESTS

Half of Norway's land area is forest, creating a natural habitat for elk and roe deer, hare, fox and squirrel. It is possible to witness a capercaillie mating game or the migration of woodcock, or even hear the call of the black grouse and the cry of the common crane from the marshes.

***The elk** is Norway's largest member of the deer family, which includes wild reindeer, red deer and roe deer. It is found throughout the country.*

***The lynx** prowls the area north from Trøndelag. Of the large predators, Norway also has bear and wolverine. The wolf, now an endangered species, inhabits the southeast.*

Sea Mammals

The killer whale is a relatively frequent visitor to the coast, especially to Tysfjord in northern Norway. Those people who take part in a whale and seal safari off Andøya *(see p201)* may be lucky to spot a sperm whale, which can be up to 18-m (60-ft) long. The Greenland whale occasionally appears off Svalbard. Porpoises swim close to the Norwegian shore and six species of seals live along the coast. Herds of walruses can be seen around Svalbard.

The killer whale *is one of the ocean's feared predators. It eats vast quantities of seals and fish, especially herring, and will attack other whales.*

The grey seal (fjordkobbe) *and the common seal* (steinkobbe) *are found off mainland Norway. Four other species can be seen on the islands of Svalbard.*

Fjords and Mountains

Red deer is the biggest game animal to be seen in the coastal areas and around the fjords. Reindeer rule the mountain plateaus, where the willow grouse lives in copses and willow thickets. The common ptarmigan is found on higher ground. The wolverine thrives in the mountains.

Wild reindeer *roam Hardangervidda, in the mountains of Dovrefjell and Rondane, and in the Bykle and Setesdal hills. The population fluctuates at around 70,000 animals.*

Musk oxen *can be found mainly in the Arctic, but a population has existed on the Dovrefjell plateau since 1932.*

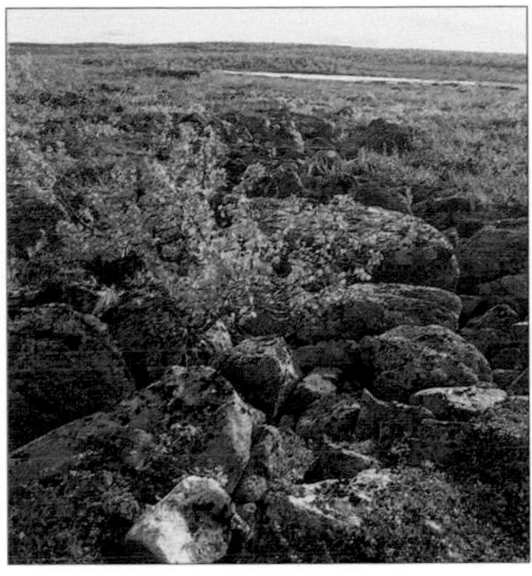

The Far North

Animals associated with the high mountains and forests, as well as Arctic species, are found in the far north of Norway. Wildlife on Svalbard is relatively limited, but Svalbard reindeer, Arctic fox and the polar bear in particular have adjusted well to the harsh environment. Bird life along the northern coast is particularly rich.

The Arctic fox*, or polar fox, was close to extinction in 1920 when it became an officially protected species. The population is growing, but is still very vulnerable.*

The common ptarmigan *has pure white winter plumage, apart from near its eyes and beak. It may nest as high as 1,650 m (5,400 ft) above sea level.*

Famous Norwegians

National romanticism made a huge impact on Norway in the 1850s. It was a time when patriotic feelings were running high. After the signing of the constitution at Eidsvoll and the ending of Danish rule in 1814 *(see p38)*, there was tremendous enthusiasm for all things Norwegian. The poetry of Henrik Wergeland (1808–45), a pioneer of National Romanticism, the paintings of Adolph Tidemann and Hans Gude, the musical compositions of Edvard Grieg, the virtuoso recitals of the violinist Ole Bull and the plays of Henrik Ibsen were all part of this search for a national identity. The movement looked to early Norse writings, such as Snorre Sturlason's (1179–1241) epic sagas of the kings, the *Heimskringla*, for inspiration, and to the 18th-century satirical writer and playwright, Ludvig Holberg.

Gustav Vigeland, Norway's foremost sculptor

Knut Hamsun, prose writer and winner of the Nobel Prize, 1920

Literature

The golden age of literature arrived with the Nobel Prize winner and dramatist, Bjørnstjerne Bjørnson (1832–1910), and the playwright Henrik Ibsen *(see p59)*. The most noted of Ibsen's 25 plays include *Peer Gynt*, *A Doll's House*, *The Wild Duck* and *Hedda Gabler*.

The country's greatest prose writer, Knut Hamsun (1859–1952), was awarded the Nobel Prize for *The Growth of the Soil* (1917), which exemplified his love of nature. Other works included his emótional novels *Hunger* and *Pan*, and a series set in northern Norway. Eight years later, Sigrid Undset (1862–1949) was awarded the Nobel Prize for her novels about the medieval heroine, Kristin Lavransdatter, and for her psychological masterpiece, *Olav Audunssøn i Hestviken.*

Another popular author is Cora Sandel (1880–1974) with her *Alberta Trilogy* about a young woman's journey to independence.

Two outstanding authors writing in *nynorsk (see p16)* were the social commentator Arne Garborg (1851–1924) and Tarjei Vesaas (1897–1970), who in *Huset i Mørkret (House in Darkness)* described occupied Norway in World War II. Children's authors Thorbjørn Egner *(Cardamom Town,* 1955*)* and Jostein Gaarder *(Sophie's World,* 1995*)*, are also acclaimed.

Painting and Sculpture

One of the first artists to let nationalistic sentiments influence his work was J C Dahl (1788–1857), "the father of Norwegian painting". He looked to his homeland for inspiration, as can be seen in *Stugunøset on Fillefjell* (National Gallery, Oslo). Others who followed in his footsteps included Adolf Tidemand (1814–76) and Hans Gude (1825–1903). Their painting, *The Bridal Procession in Hardanger (see pp8–9)* breathes national romanticism.

Of the painters from the 1880s and 1890s, Erik Werenskiold (1855–1938) and Harriet Backer (1845–1932) are among the best known (both are represented in the National Gallery in Oslo). In the early 20th century, Harald Sohlberg (1869–1935) with *Winter Night in the Mountains (see p53)* and Nikolai Astrup (1880–1928) with *Midsummer* came to the fore. Themes of love and death were explored by the expressionist Edvard Munch (1863–1944; *see p93*), whose work fills the Munch Museum, Oslo. The nation's first sculptor of international repute was Gustav Vigeland (1869–1943; *see pp90–92*). His large-scale figures dominate Vigeland Park, Oslo.

Music

Musicians associated with the National Romantic Movement include Halfdan Kjerulf (1815–68) and the violinist Ole Bull *(see p171 under Lysøen)*, with their patriotic overtones. Rikard Nordraak (1842–66), who wrote the music to the Norwegian national anthem, *Ja, vi elsker dette landet (Yes, We Love This Land)*, by Bjørnstjerne Bjørnson, had a decisive influence on the development of the composer Edvard Grieg (1843–1907; *see p171*). Grieg is a recognized interpreter of the Norwegian national character with his

Edvard Grieg, a pivotal figure in Norwegian music history

music for Ibsen's *Peer Gynt* and his folk songs and dances. His orchestral works, such as *Piano Concerto in A-minor*, and his ballads are performed all over the world.

Agathe Backer Grøndahl (1847–1907) was Norway's most distinguished female composer of her time and a highly gifted pianist. Harald Sæverud (1897–1992) won acclaim for compositions such as *Kjempeviseslåtten (Ballad of Giants)*. A cello concerto and the ballet *Stormen (The Tempest)* brought the composer Arne Nordheim (b.1932) to the attention of music lovers abroad.

In opera, Kirsten Flagstad (1895–1962) was one of the greatest Wagnerian singers of her time.

Foremost among today's musicians are the violinist Arve Tellefsen (b.1936) and Jan Garbarek (b.1947), the renowned jazz tenor and soprano saxophonist.

Fridtjof Nansen, explorer and Nobel Peace Prize-winner, 1922

Explorers

FRIDTJOF NANSEN (1861–1930) was the first person to cross the icy interior of Greenland in 1888. He was both a natural scientist and diplomat as well as an explorer. In 1893, he embarked on his ambition to reach the North Pole by drifting with the polar ice from Siberia to Greenland in his ship, *Fram* *(see p80)*. Two years later, at 78° 50' N, Nansen left the vessel to continue on skis, accompanied by Hjalmar Johansen. They reached 86° 4'N, a record at that time, but had to turn back to overwinter and finally arrived home after three years on the ice. Nansen later played an important role in the League of Nations, and as a leader of humanitarian aid projects. He was awarded the Nobel Peace Prize.

The crossing of the North West Passage by Roald Amundsen (1872–1928) in 1905, after spending three winters en route, was a remarkable feat. Six years later he set off for the South Pole with four companions. He was the first person to reach it, on 14 December 1911, after a tragic race against the English explorer Robert Scott. Scott arrived at the South Pole a month later, but on the return journey every member of his team perished. In 1926, Amundsen flew over the North Pole with the airship *Norge*. He died while on a rescue mission in the Arctic Ocean in 1928.

Thor Heyerdahl (1914–2002) led the *Kon-Tiki* expedition across the Pacific Ocean from Peru to Polynesia in 1947. His later expeditions included voyages in the reed boats *Ra I* and *Ra II* across the Atlantic. Heyerdahl's theories have thrown light on the settlement history of the Pacific.

Helge Ingstad (1899–2001) proved, through research along the east coast of Canada and excavations with the archaeologist Anne Stine Ingstad (1918–97), that there were Norse settlements in America 500 years before the arrival of Columbus.

Thor Heyerdahl with the reed boat, *Ra II*, crossing the Atlantic, 1970

Politics of Peace

NORWEGIAN POLITICIANS have played a prominent role in peace and humanitarian efforts worldwide. Former foreign secretary Trygve Lie was the first secretary general of the United Nations, from 1946–1953.

The former Norwegian prime minister, Gro Harlem Brundtland (b.1939), is now president of the World Health Organisation. Thorvald Stoltenberg (b.1931), a politician and diplomat who in 1990 was appointed the UN High Commissioner for Refugees, later became a peace negotiator in the Balkans. Terje Rød Larsen (b.1947) has, since 1994, been UN vice secretary general in the Middle East.

Gro Harlem Brundtland, president of the World Health Organization

The Norwegian Bunad

Silver filigree brooch, Nordland

NATIONAL DAY on 17 May draws crowds of Norwegians on to the streets dressed either in traditional folk costumes or in the national dress, known as *bunad*. The two outfits differ: folk costumes have long-standing traditions in the regions, whereas the *bunad* is a more recent version of the traditional outfits. The large migration of rural people to the towns has made the *bunad* a symbol of their identity and for many an important link with their roots. Its use for festive occasions is becoming increasingly popular.

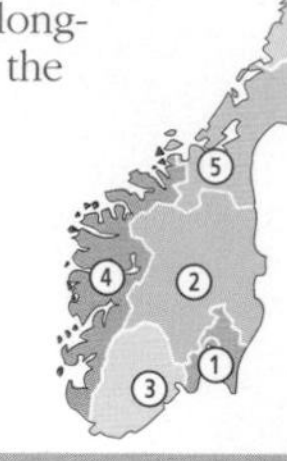

Bunad from Vestfold ①

The Vestfold *bunad* was recreated piece-by-piece. It was first presented in its final form in 1956. Vestfold's lively foreign trade probably led to the garments being made in lighter, imported materials, rather than thick homespun fabric, but these disintegrated more easily and no complete costumes have survived. There are two versions of the Vestfold *bunad (see left)*.

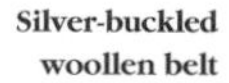

Silver-buckled woollen belt

Bonnet worn with the *bunad*

Hallingdal Bunad ②

The traditional *bunad* in Hallingdal consists of a black, sometimes layered skirt, a floral apron and a black cloth bodice embroidered with wool. It has a white shirt with white-work embroidery on the neckband and wristbands, just like the exquisite bridal *bunad (see left)*, which is on display in Hallingdal District Museum in Nesbyen.

Bridal crown in red woollen broadcloth

The bridal bodice in luxurious cream brocade

Åmli Bunad from Aust-Agder ③

The Åmli *bunad* is considered the last link in the development of a national folk costume. The ensemble has, since the 1920s, been based on original single garments used in Åmli and neighbouring rural settlements between 1700 and the mid-1800s. A striking part of this *bunad* is the shoulder piece, in red (or green) damask. It has three pairs of silver eyes which are cross-laced over the chest with a silver chain.

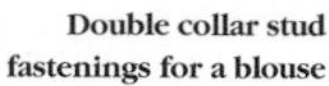

Double collar stud fastenings for a blouse

Embroidered linen headscarf with a fringe

Bridal Bunad from Voss ④

The most eye-catching part of the bridal *bunad* from Voss is the splendid crown, or *Vosseladet* as it is known. It is covered in red fabric embroidered with beads. Silver coins and filigree silver ornaments inset with semi-precious stones hang from the brim. Apart from the crown and a special black jacket, the bridal costume is largely the same as the normal Voss *bunad* worn for festive occasions.

***Agnus Dei* pendant worn with bridal gown**

Voss's bridal crown dating from the early 19th century

Bunads from Oppdal ⑤

There is one *bunad* that can be used in the whole of Trondelag, although many counties have their own version. The Oppdal *bunad* was reconstructed in 1963 from the fragments of old costumes. The multi-coloured woollen skirt is worn with a red, green or blue bodice. The man's *bunad* is based on an 18th-century garment. The breeches can be made of leather or black homespun.

***Agnus Dei* pendant worn by the women**

Man's waistcoat made from linen and wool

Bunads from Nordland and Troms ⑥

The Nordland *bunad*, created in 1928, was originally blue, but now also comes in green. It is based on a 200-year-old fabric from Vefsn. The bag or reticule is in the same colour and floral pattern as the skirt. The woman's *bunad* from Troms is inspired by costumes from Bjarkøy and Senja. The man's *bunad* is the same for Nordland and Troms.

A silver-clasped reticule for the woman

Traditional Sami Costumes

The colourful costume, an important part of Sami cultural identity ***(see p209)***

Sami costumes made from cloth can be traced back to the Middle Ages. They developed from earlier versions which were made from animal hide. Today, the three most distinctive outfits come from Kautokeino, Varanger and Karasjok.

The Kautokeino costume comprises a tunic top for the men, a pleated skirt for the women and a belt with silver buttons. Each item is richly decorated with bands of embroidery. The Varanger costume is also colourfully embellished, while that from Karasjok is remarkably simple and retains much of the cut of the ancient hide costume, the *pesk*. The women of Karasjok wear a beautiful fringed shawl.

The Home of Skiing

Norway is known as the "home of skiing" and, indeed, Morgedal in Telemark is considered by some aficionados to be the birthplace of the sport. The torch for the Winter Olympic Games in Oslo in 1952 and Lillehammer in 1994 was lit from ski veteran Sondre Norheim's fireplace in Morgedal. Norwegians excel in international skiing competitions, but it is as a leisure activity that skiing comes into its own. Long stretches of illuminated trails and floodlit pistes tempt both the young and the old on to the snowy tracks. Special family events and exercise competitions attract keen participants.

Poster for the 1952 Oslo Winter Olympics

The History of Skiing

Skiing is shown in ancient rock carvings and is mentioned in the Edda poems and Norse sagas. There is evidence of skiing for leisure and competition from the 1750s, with a rapid increase after 1850. Its popularity grew with Nansen's ski trek across Greenland in 1888 and Amundsen's journey to the South Pole in 1911. Since the first Winter Olympics in 1924, skiing in its various forms has been a key part of the programme.

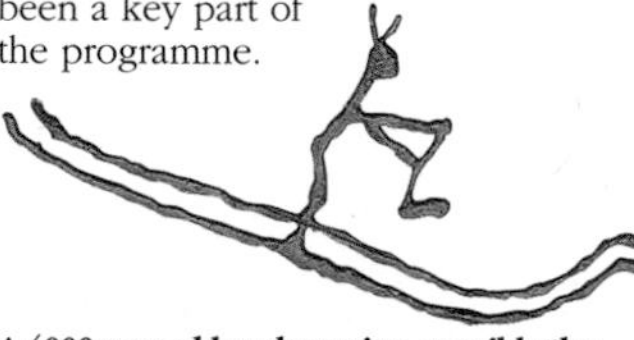

A 4000-year-old rock carving, possibly the oldest recorded depiction of a skier

The Birkebeiner rescue of young Prince Håkon, 1206 (painting by K Bergslien, 1869)

Roald Amundsen's expedition to the South Pole, 1910–12

Liv Arnesen, first lone woman to reach the South Pole, 1994

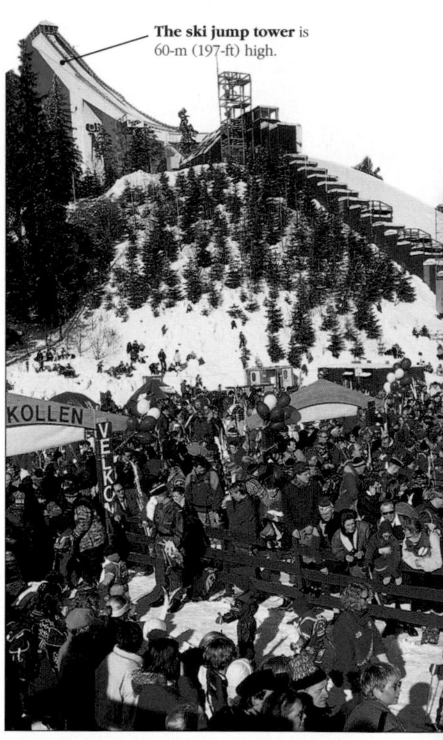

The ski jump tower is 60-m (197-ft) high.

Holmenkollen Ski Festival

The first skiing competition at Holmenkollen in 1892 combined an 18-km (11-miles) cross-country course with jumping. The longest jump was 21.5 m (70 ft). Today's record is more than 132 m (433 ft). A 50-km (31-miles) cross-country course was introduced in 1902. The trail event, *Holmenkollmarsjen,* and the Children's Day *(see above)*, are held in March.

Skiing traditions *are very important to the Norwegians. This is a popular modern ski, built according to an old cross-country model.*

The annual Birkebeiner race *every March from Rena to Lillehammer celebrates the rescue of baby Prince Håkon in 1206 by two Birkebeinere on skis. The race is 58-km (36-miles) long.*

The landing slope is 115-m (377-ft) long.

An electronic scoreboard keeps track of the results.

Cross-country trail *in "Marka", the area around Oslo which comprises 2,000 km (1,243 miles) of prepared wide tracks for skiers. There are narrow tracks, too, for those who prefer to ski alone. Ski huts dotted at intervals along the routes are popular meeting places for a rest and a sandwich.*

From Cross-Country to High Jump

It all began with cross-country, because skis were the most efficient means of getting around on the snow. Ski-jumping and Alpine skiing were introduced as sports for fun, games and competition.

Classic cross-country *was universal until 1987, when the faster "ski-skating" developed into a separate discipline.*

Telemark style*, such as the Telemark turn and landing, has been the model for cross-country and ski-jumping since 1860.*

Alpine skiing *developed in the Alps, but the word* slalom *is Norwegian* (sla*: hill;* låm*: track). Downhill skiing became a form of popular entertainment.*

Ski-jumping *has seen a rapid development with increasingly higher and longer ski jumps. The aerodynamic "Boklöv style" has been universally adopted.*

Norway Through the Year

There are four clearly defined seasons in Norway, but as the saying goes: "Every season has its charm." Norwegians enjoy being one of the world's top skiing nations, and even town-dwellers will don their skis as soon as the first snow falls in November or December. The winter sports centres have something to offer everyone, both beginners and experienced skiers, and are extremely popular, particularly at Easter. The arrival of spring brings long light-filled days. Norway celebrates National Day on 17 May with children's parades and festivities. The arts and cultural scenes begin to stir after their winter slumber.

Summer flowers and snow-clad mountains

In summer Norwegians head for the islands and skerries. There are boat festivals, fairs and games all the way along the coast. Autumn is the season for theatre-going, concerts, opera, dance, film premieres and art exhibitions.

Bergen Festival concert in the magnificent Grieg Hall

Spring

When the severe "King Winter" loosens his grip, the country bursts into life. The spring sun at the end of April heralds the last of the season's skiing trips in the mountains and encourages an urge to get out and about and experience life anew. The tourist season starts in earnest in May when the countryside is crisp and fresh, and the arts and cultural festivals are beginning to blossom. At this time of year activities such as dancing and musical events move outdoors. There are markets and shows to visit.

March

Sun Party at Svalbard *(1st week of Mar).* The world's northernmost celebration of the return of the sun.
Holmenkollen Ski Festival *(2nd week Mar, see pp26–7).*
The Birkebeiner Race *(3rd week of Mar).* Ski marathon from Rena to Lillehammer *(see pp27, 125 and 130).*
Winter Festival, Røros *(all month).* Excellent musical events in this old copper-mining town.
Røros Market *(late Mar).* A big trade fair.
Oslo Festival of Church Music *(early Mar)* features a variety of concerts.

April

Sami Easter celebrations and weddings *(end of Mar or early Apr).*
Vozzajazz Hordaland *(early Apr).* International jazz festival, one of the first of the season.
Bergen Blues and Roots Festival (Ole Blues) *(end Apr–early May).* Voted the best Norwegian festival by its participants.
Day of Dance *(29 Apr).* World Dance Day is celebrated all over the country with performances and dance stunts in the streets and squares by amateurs and professionals.

May

May Jazz, Stavanger *(1st half of May).* A fast-growing festival offering big stars and exciting new talent.
17 May, *("Syttende Mai"),* Norway's National Day, is celebrated nationwide with children's parades and a host of festivities.
Bergen Festival *(end of May/early Jun)* offers 10 days of music, drama and artistic events of international standing attracting large numbers of visitors.
Night Jazz Bergen *(end of May/early Jun).* Staged around the same time as the Bergen Festival, Night Jazz Bergen attracts large audiences to more than 70 different concerts featuring both Norwegian and international artists.

Norway's National Day, 17 May, on Karl Johans Gate, Oslo

SUMMER

The long, light summer nights are not for sleeping. Summer is the peak season for festivals and outdoor productions ranging from musicals to historical plays and classical dramas using nature as a backdrop.

In many parts of the country traditions centre around types of food, such as the Oslo Seafood Festival in August. Often they are combined with varying degrees of physical challenges. Tourist offices can recommend events off the beaten track.

JUNE

Salmon Fishing Season *(1 Jun–mid/end Aug).* Dates may vary slightly.
Day of Music, Oslo *(1 Jun).* Classical, jazz, pop and rock.
Norwegian Mountain Marathon *(1st week Jun).* A remarkable marathon in the spectacular mountains of Jotunheimen.
Summer Concerts at Troldhaugen, Bergen *(Sat, mid-Jun to mid-Aug).* The music of Edvard Grieg performed in his own home.
Stryn Summer Ski Festival Sogn og Fjordane *(mid-Jun).* Skiing in shorts.
Nordland Festival, Sortland, Vesterålen *(mid-Jun).* Deep-sea fishing.
North Sea Festival, Haugesund *(mid-Jun).* European sports-fishing competition.
Norwegian Wood, Oslo *(14–16 Jun).* Rock music festival *(see p248).*
St Hans *(24 Jun).* Midsummer is celebrated with bonfires and festivities.
Cultural Festival in Northern Norway Harstad *(around midsummer).*
Risør Festival of Chamber Music, Risør *(last week of Jun).* Top-class concerts in idyllic Sørlandet.
Extreme Sports Week, Voss *(last week of Jun).* Mountain biking, mountain climbing, extreme skiing, plus music.
Rauland National Folk Music Contest *(end of Jun/early Jul).* Folk musicians and dancers.
Vestfold Festival *(end of Jun/early Jul).* Ten-day festival of music, dance and theatre.

Skiing in summer

Salmon fishing in Ågårdselva, Østfold

JULY

Norsk Aften, Norsk Folkemuseum, Oslo *(daily from 1 Jul).* The "Norwegian Evening" offers guided tours in the stave church and museum area; folk dancing; traditional Norwegian food.
Kongsberg Jazz Festival *(early Jul),* with top musicians such as Joshua Redman.
Quart Festival, Kristiansand *(1st week of Jul).* Rock concerts both in and outdoors featuring Norwegian and international bands and artists.
Fjæreheia Grimstad *(from mid-Jul).* Agder Theatre's outdoor performances of Ibsen dramas and musicals.
Molde International Jazz Festival *(last week of Jul),* starring the world's best performers and first-class Norwegian artists.

Thousands of fans at the Molde International Jazz Festival in July

AUGUST

Telemark Festival, Bø *(1st week of Aug).* International folk music festival with something for all the family: song, dance, music, concerts, courses and seminars.
Bjørnson Festival Molde *(1st week of Aug).* International festival of literature. Bjørnson was one of Norway's greatest writers *(see p22).*
Notodden International Blues Festival *(1st week of Aug).* Concerts in clubs and outdoors. There is a "blues cruise" for those without a boat of their own.
Gålåvann Gudbrandsdalen *(3–11 Aug).* The Ibsen drama, *Peer Gynt*, is performed outdoors in beautiful surroundings.
Nordic Hunting and Fishing Days Elverum *(1st half of Aug).*
Stavanger Chamber Music Festival and **Oslo Chamber Music Festival** *(mid-Aug)* attract large numbers of visitors to the summer evening concerts.
Sildajazz, Haugesund *(1st half of Aug).* Colourful festival featuring 20 concert venues both inside and outdoors, children's and street parades, harbour market and pleasure craft.
Wooden Boat Festival, Risør *(1st half of August).* Exhibition of coastal culture, old and new wooden boats; outdoor concerts.
Norwegian Film Festival Haugesund *(end of Aug/early Sep).* More than 100 new films are shown during the eight-day festival. Buy a season ticket. Presentation of the Amanda awards.

Bearberries colouring the mountains red in the autumn

Autumn

Walking in the forests and mountains, picking berries and gathering mushrooms are ideal pastimes in autumn. As the evenings begin to close in, Norwegians retreat indoors and enjoy the many cultural events that are staged in theatres large and small. Autumn brings plenty to refresh the mind: new books are published and major art exhibitions open at this time of year.

September

The National Theatre (Nationaltheatret), Oslo *(1st half of Sep)*, alternates the start of the season each year with either the Ibsen Festival or the Contemporary Festival *(Samtidsfestival)* of new drama.

Seafood for All Bergen *(2nd half of Sep)*. Food from the ocean, with a public party in the city's fish market and an award for the best fish stall.

Chanterelle harvest

Young Jazz Ålesund *(end of Sep)*. Talented jazz musicians under the age of 30 perform in Norway's Art Nouveau town *(see p180)*.

October

Ultima Contemporary Music Festival, Oslo *(1st half of Oct)*, presents the latest in music, dance and dramatic art in co-operation with theatres and museums, including Black Box Teater, Oslo Konserthus, Henie Onstad Kunstsenter, and Filmens Hus.

Fartein Valen Days, Haugesund *(end of Oct)*. The composer Fartein Valen (1887–1952) is showcased with a series of lectures and concerts in churches, galleries and in his childhood home.

Oslo Horse Show *(mid-Oct)*. A popular family event held in Oslo Spektrum.

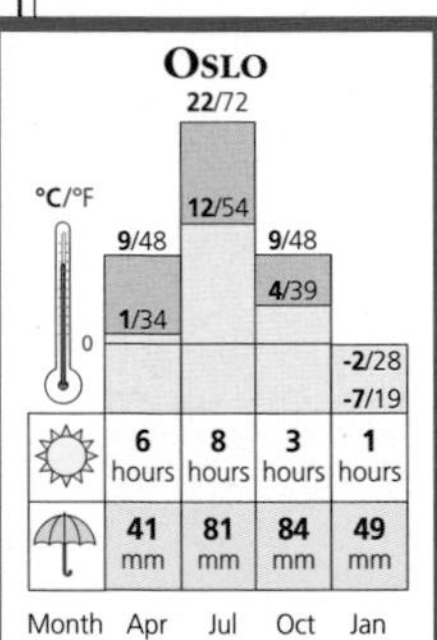

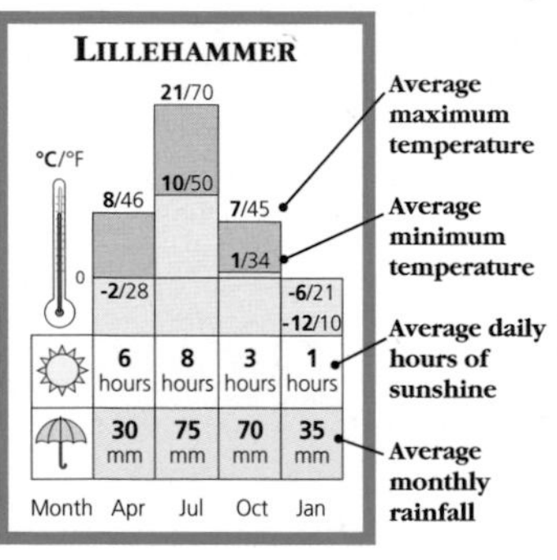

Climate

Western Norway has an Atlantic climate with warm winters and cool summers. The highest average temperatures are in Sørlandet and Vestlandet. Østlandet has an inland climate, with cold winters and warm summers. Vestlandet has the most rain; the north end of Gudbrandsdal and the depths of Finnmarksvidda have the least rain.

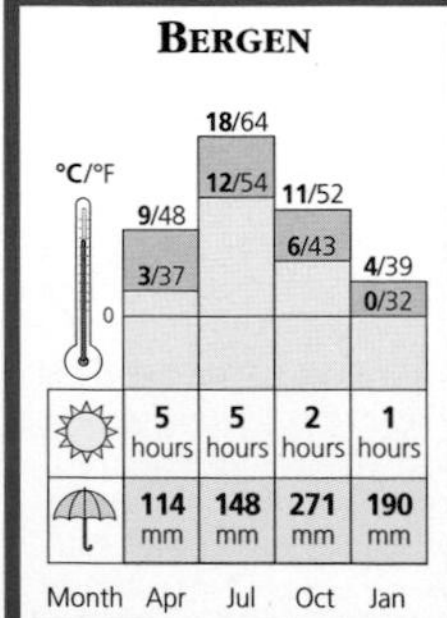

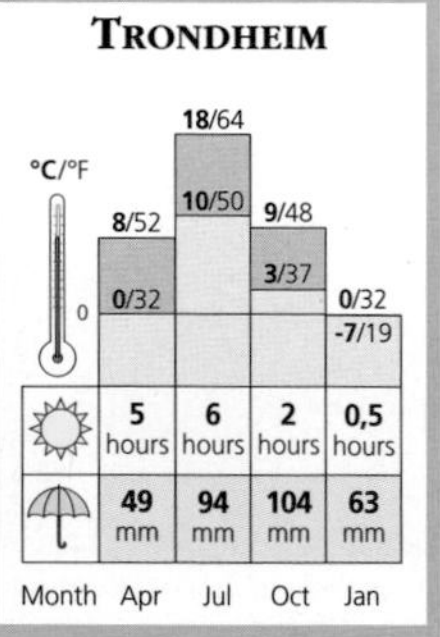

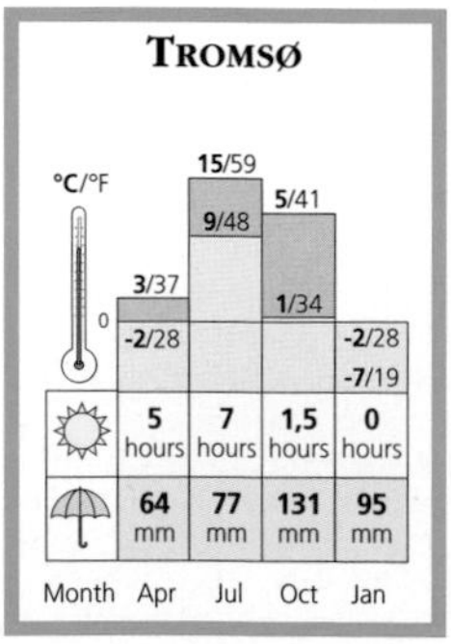

Tromsø

°C/°F

Month	Apr	Jul	Oct	Jan
Max	3/37	15/59	5/41	-2/28
Min	-2/28	9/48	1/34	-7/19
Sunshine	5 hours	7 hours	1,5 hours	0 hours
Rainfall	64 mm	77 mm	131 mm	95 mm

WINTER

THE CHRISTMAS SEASON gets underway when the Christmas trees are lit, the first Christmas snow starts to fall and colourfully decorated gingerbread cookie houses start appearing. Restaurants are fully booked for their Christmas buffets, with the Norwegian speciality, *lutefisk* (dried fish treated with lye), on the menu.

New Year sees the start of the skiing season, and the prospect of fresh tracks lures many on to the slopes.

NOVEMBER

Rakfisk Festival, Valdres *(1st weekend in Nov).* Fermented mountain trout is a delicacy, and visitors can choose from the best producers have to offer.
Museum of Children's Art, (Det Internasjonale Barnekunstmuseet), Oslo, has extended opening hours during the winter, on Tue, Wed, Thu and Sun morning. Paintings and drawings by children worldwide.
Lighting the Christmas Tree *(1st Sun of Advent).* Trees are lit in towns and villages and there is music, speeches and group singing, as well as the traditional walk around the tree.

DECEMBER

Christmas Concerts *(all Dec).* Well-known singers and entertainers give church concerts, often with local choirs and orchestras.
Christmas Markets *(Sun).* Folk museums such as the Norsk Folkemuseum, Oslo, and Maihaugen, Lillehammer, arrange special folk dancing displays and concerts, the sales of crafts and Father Christmas workshops.
Gingerbread Houses, Galleriet, Bergen *(all Dec).* The world's biggest gingerbread town according to the *Guinness Book of Records.* A remarkable show of 150 gingerbread houses, ships, aeroplanes and ski jumps skilfully made by children, young people and professionals.

Full moon over a wintery scene at Lillehammer

JANUARY

Ski-Kite, Møsvann, Telemark *(early Jan).* Skiing with the aid of a kite. Lessons at the Rauland Ski Centre.
Festival of Northern Lights, Tromsø *(end of Jan).* Visitors from around the world come to see the magnificent northern lights *(aurora borealis)*, which shimmer and dance across the sky on clear winter nights in northern Norway.

Traditional Christmas displays in a shopping centre

Giant snowman at the Snow Sculpture Festival, Vinje

Polar Jazz Svalbard *(end of Jan).* The world's most northerly jazz and blues festival. Four to five days of concerts and events staged throughout the Svalbard town of Longyearbyen.

FEBRUARY

Snow Sculpture Festival, Vinje *(1st week of Feb).* A sculpture park with a difference. With imagination and some expert helpers you can create your own masterwork in ice and snow – and admire other people's eye-catching handiwork.
Opera Week, Kristiansund *(early Feb).* Opera, ballet, art exhibitions and a number of other events are staged at Festiviteten.
Winter Market, Rauland *(end of Feb).* The Rauland winter market bursts full of handicrafts in all shapes, sizes and colours.

PUBLIC HOLIDAYS

New Year's Day (1 Jan)
Palm Sunday (Sunday before Easter)
Maundy Thursday
Good Friday
Easter Sunday
Easter Monday
Whit Sunday
Whit Monday
Labour Day (1 May)
National Day (17 May)
St Hans (24 Jun)
Christmas Day (25 Dec)
Boxing Day (26 Dec)

The History of Norway

When the Norwegian chieftain, Ottar, visited the court of King Alfred the Great in England 1,100 years ago, he was the first person to give an account of "Nor-weg", the homeland of the Northmen. The Viking Age was to follow, and centuries of strife and colonization, union, war and occupation. The country survived to achieve prosperity and international standing.

The first traces of human habitation in Norway are those of the Komsa and Fosna cultures, both more than 9,000 years old. Archaeological finds from the Stone Age to the Iron Age include crude implements and weapons, and realistic rock carvings of reindeer and fish. Later, symbols of sun wheels and boats appear. Iron Age burial mounds containing weapons and ornamental items, rune stones and ships have been uncovered.

Norway's first coin, struck in 995

The Viking Age *(see pp34–5)* marks a transition in the history of Norway. Viking warriors set forth on their voyages and brought home ideas that were to influence the country's political and cultural development.

Norway was united as one kingdom at the Battle of Hafrsfjord at Stavanger in 890 AD. Here Harald Hårfagre (Harald Fine-hair) defeated his enemies and secured sufficient power to establish a permanent army and maintain unity. Those who failed to fall into line left the country, became outlaws or were killed.

Some of those who left Norway settled in Iceland. They included Erik the Red (Eirik Raude), who in 985 laid the foundations for a settlement on Greenland. His son, Leiv Eiriksson, discovered America in AD 1000. This led to temporary Norse settlements on the northern point of Newfoundland.

After Håkon the Good, the popular younger son of Harald Fine-hair, conflict ensued over the kingship, until Olav Tryggvason (d. AD 1000), and Olav the Holy *(see p194)* united the kingdom and introduced Christianity. They tore down the pagan statues and built stave churches.

Over the centuries, Norway became a sovereign kingdom and built up an empire comprising the Faeroe Islands, Orkney Islands, Hebrides, Isle of Man and, after 1260, Iceland and Greenland.

From 1130, the conflict for leadership caused civil war until finally the line of Sverre Sigurdsson triumphed. Norway stood at the height of its power when his grandson, Håkon Håkonsson, was crowned king in 1247. After the death of Håkon V Magnusson in 1319, the order of royal succession did not work in Norway's favour. His grandson, Håkon VI, was the last king of an independent nation.

Timeline

9300 BC The first inhabitants, the Komsa hunters, fishermen and gatherers, live around Alta, Finnmark

c.4000 BC Growth of farming in Østfold

1800–500 BC Bronze Age people build large burial mounds on ridges, roadsides and on the coast, such as in Jæren

c.500 BC Early Iron Age. Iron extraction begins on Hardangervidda and in Aurland. The climate becomes colder

793 The Viking Age begins with a raid on the monastery on Lindisfarne in northeast England

Viking Age sculpture of Odin

890 Battle of Hafrsfjord: Norway is united under Harald Hårfagre

c. 1000 Leiv Eiriksson discovers Vinland in North America

1030 Olav the Holy is killed at the Battle of Stiklestad

1247 Håkon Håkonsson is crowned king

10 000 BC | 1500 | AD 500 | 750 | 1000 | 1250

◁ ***Håkon Håkonsson's coronation in Bergen, 1247, by Cardinal Vilhelm of Sabina*** **(Gerhard Munthe, 1910)**

The Vikings

Thor's hammer

For more than 300 years, from the 8th to the 11th century, the Vikings took the world by storm. As traders, settlers and plunderers, they set sail from their homes in Norway, Sweden and Denmark in search of land, slaves, gold and silver. They carried out raids throughout Europe, sailed as far as Baghdad and even reached America. Terrified Christian monks wrote of dreadful attacks on monasteries and towns. But the Vikings were more than barbarians. They were clever traders, outstanding seafarers, craftsmen and shipbuilders, and they lived in an open society that was democratic for its time.

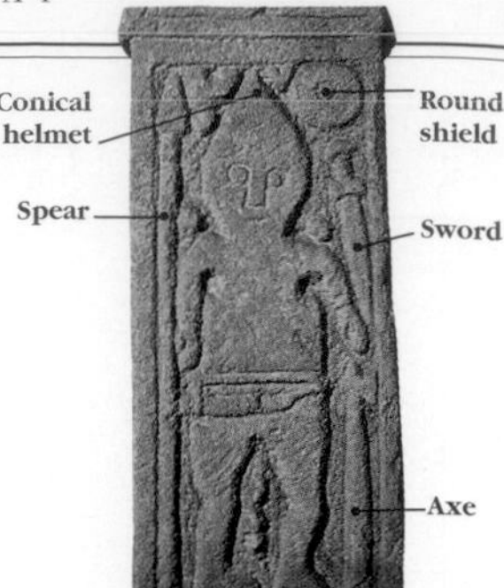

A Viking warrior *with his equipment in a carving on a 10th-century stone cross from Middleton, England.*

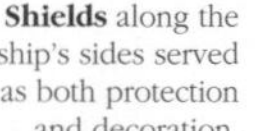

Shields along the ship's sides served as both protection and decoration.

Lindisfarne *is a small island off the north-east coast of England. Its monastery was raided by Vikings in 793. This gravestone shows an attacking band of Vikings.*

A tent provided the only shelter from the elements.

Leiv Eiriksson Discovers America

The Norse discoverers sailed in broad, robust ships that were heavier than the narrow longships used in battle. They had more room for a crew with goods and provisions. In his painting of 1893, Christian Krohg portrays the moment when Leiv points in wonder to the new continent, America. Leiv was the son of Erik the Red. He was known as the "lucky one".

Viking ships *were extremely seaworthy and could travel long distances. The ships had sturdy, shallow keels, which enabled them to be rowed up rivers and landed on shallow shores. They could also be pulled on rollers overland between the fjords and rivers.*

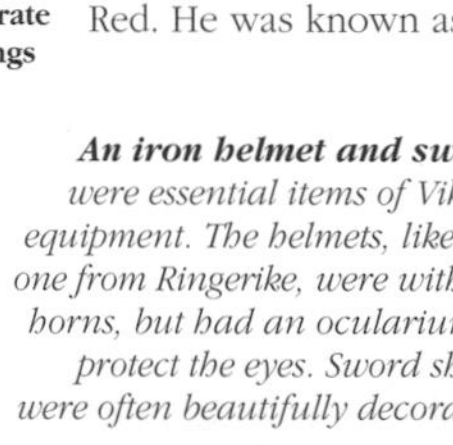

Snake's head

Elaborate carvings

Clinker-built hull

An iron helmet and sword *were essential items of Viking equipment. The helmets, like this one from Ringerike, were without horns, but had an ocularium to protect the eyes. Sword shafts were often beautifully decorated.*

Viking women *ran the household and the farm while the men were away. They were independent and self-sufficient.*

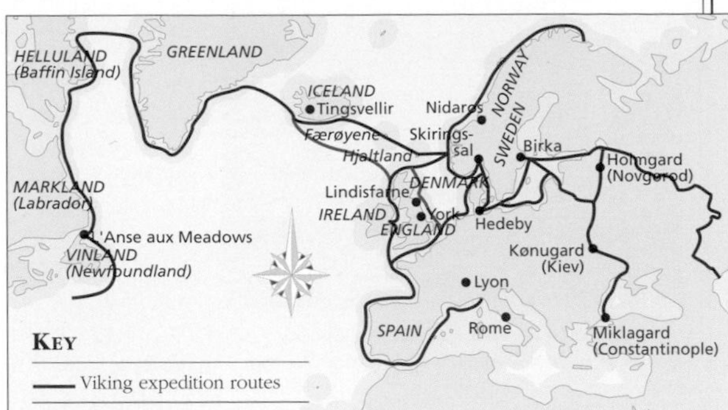

The tiller was on the ship's starboard side.

THE WORLD OF THE VIKINGS

The Vikings raided, traded and invaded far and wide. They reached Iceland in about 870 and sailed west to Greenland in 982. Leiv Eiriksson discovered America in about 1000. In the east, the Vikings travelled to Russia and sailed on rivers as far as the Black Sea and Constantinople. Others travelled along the west coast of Europe and into the Mediterranean.

The ruins *of a 9th-century Viking farm on the Shetland Islands. It had two rooms, a long hall and a kitchen. The inhabitants slept on benches along the sloping walls.*

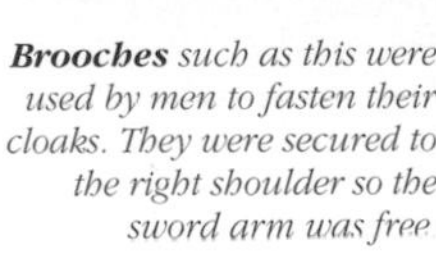

Brooches *such as this were used by men to fasten their cloaks. They were secured to the right shoulder so the sword arm was free.*

The important Viking gods *were Odin, god of wisdom, Thor, god of war and Frey, god of fertility. This statue depicts Frey. Norway converted to Christianity in the 11th century.*

TIMELINE

793 Vikings raid the English monastery of Lindisfarne

799 Viking raids begin in France

834 The ship *Oseberg* is used for a Viking burial

841 A large Viking fleet overwinters in Dublin

845 The sack of Hamburg and Paris

870 Vikings colonize Iceland

876 Vikings settle permanently in England

890 Battle of Hafrsfjord: the kingdom is united

911 Normandy is founded by the Viking chieftain, Rollo

912 Vikings reach the Caspian Sea

Viking ship c.980

948 Håkon the Good attempts to convert his countrymen

985 Erik the Red settles in Greenland

c.1000 Leiv Eiriksson discovers Vinland in North America

c.1000 Olav Tryggvason is killed at Svolder

1030 Battle of Stiklestad

1066 Battle of Stamford Bridge: Vikings are defeated by Harold II of England

800 | 830 | 860 | 890 | 920 | 950 | 980 | 1010

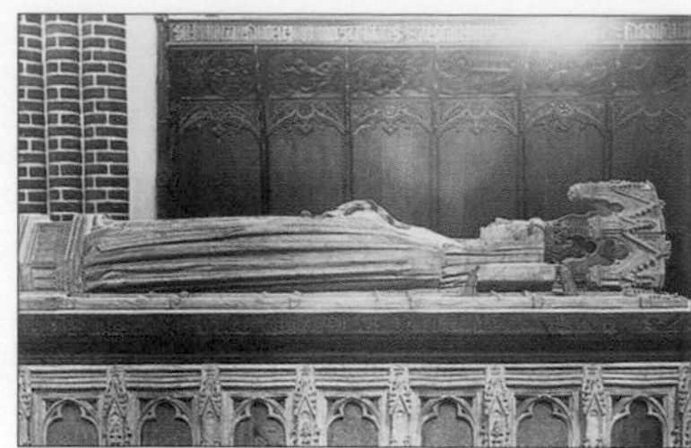

Sarcophagus in Roskilde Cathedral of Queen Margrete, ruler of Denmark, Sweden and Norway

The Kalmar Union

Håkon VI Magnusson married the Danish princess, Margrete. Their only child, Olav, became king of Denmark in 1375, and inherited the Norwegian throne on Håkon's death in 1380. This was the start of the 400-year-long Danish-Norwegian union.

When Olav died at the age of 17, Margrete became ruler of both countries, and of Sweden, too, in 1388. By adopting her nephew, Erik of Pomerania, as king of all three nations in 1397, she laid the foundation for the Kalmar Union, which was to last until 1523, when Gustav Vasa seceded from the Union and established a new dynasty in Sweden.

Union with Denmark

Margrete conducted a fair policy towards Norway. The country's position weakened in 1536 when Christian III declared that Norway would forever be a vassal state of Denmark.

Norway was unable to assert its authority in the union, because from the middle of 14th century the Black Death reduced the population by more than half. The Reformation forced Archbishop Olav Engelbrektsson, one of the few to campaign for Norwegian independence, to flee the country. Norway was ruled by feudal overlords as a dependency of Denmark. Its middle class was weakened by the power of the Hanseatic merchants from northern Germany who dominated trading life on the west coast.

Christian IV

The union with Denmark was not without its high points. Norwegian industry gradually began to pick up. Fishing expanded; forestry and the export of timber became a new resource. As the Hanseatic League declined, Norwegian traders were able to step in. Mining became an important industry, especially under Christian IV (1577–1648), who took a great interest in Norwegian affairs. He visited the country on 30 occasions, founded the city of Christiania and streamlined the administration. The country was granted a new church ordination and its own military system.

Christian established Norwegian control of the north of the country. But his on-going conflict with Sweden resulted in Norway having to cede land in the east to Sweden. His son, Frederik III, introduced absolute rule in the "double monarchy" in 1660. This meant rule by officials appointed by

Bærums Verk, one of the first ironworks in Norway, dating from 1610

Timeline

1349 Black Death reduces Norway's population by 50 per cent

1380 Håkon VI Magnusson, the last king of an independent Norway, dies

1397 Kalmar Union unites Norway, Denmark and Sweden under one king

1400 Hanseatic League, based in Bergen, reaches the height of its power, controlling imports and exports

1536 Christian III of Denmark declares that Norway will forever be a vassal state of Denmark

1537 The Reformation: Archbishop Olav Engelbrektsson is driven out of Norway

1558 Hanseatic grip weakens

Queen Margrete (r.1388–1412)

1350 | 1400 | 1450 | 1500 | 1550

Painting of the poets' nationalist society, *Det Norske Selskab*, in Copenhagen, by Eilif Peterssen (1892)

the king instead of rule by aristocrats. Increasingly, officials came from the Norwegian middle class, which worked in Norway's favour.

In the early 18th century, under Frederik IV, the wars with Sweden continued. They produced a national hero for Norway, the naval commander Peter Wessel Tordenskiold, who, in a surprise attack, obliterated the Swedish fleet.

The Swedish warrior king, Karl XII, twice tried to conquer Norway, but was killed during a siege on Halden in 1718.

Demands grew for Norwegian independence. This was due in part to a revival in interest in the country's history, brought about by a patriotic society of poets and historians, *Det Norske Selskab*, in Copenhagen. Calls for a national university in Norway were finally conceded to in 1811. Nevertheless, it was mostly affairs outside the country that led to the parting of the "double monarchy" in 1814.

Naval hero Peter Wessel Tordenskiold

IN NAPOLEON'S SHADOW

The Danish-Norwegian king, Frederik VI, allied himself with Napoleon in 1807. As a result, Britain blockaded Norwegian harbours and halted all imports and exports. Isolation became total when, for a time, there was also a war with Sweden. Then followed the years of great need in 1808 and 1812. Crops failed, fishing yields were poor and there was much hunger.

In Sweden, the former French marshal, Jean Baptiste Bernadotte, became crown prince in 1810 under the name Karl Johan. He joined the coalition against Napoleon and was able to persuade his allies – Russia, Britain, Austria and Prussia – that he would be able to force Denmark to relinquish Norway to Sweden when Napoleon was defeated. When Napoleon was finally routed at Leipzig in 1813, Karl Johan marched toward Denmark, and at the Treaty of Kiel in January 1814, Norway was surrendered to Sweden.

1624 Oslo burns down. Christiania is established north of Akershus Castle

1709 The Great Nordic War between Denmark-Norway and Sweden

1718 The Swedish king, Karl XII, is killed at Frederiksten Fortress during his second attempt to conquer Norway

1813 Karl Johan marches on Denmark

1814 Norway is ceded to Sweden at the Peace of Kiel

1600 | 1650 | 1700 | 1750 | 1800

Christian IV (1577–1648)

1645 Under the Treaty of Bromsebro, Norwegian territories of Jemtland and Herjedalen are ceded to Sweden

1660 Frederik III introduces absolute rule

1769 Norway's population totals 723,000 of whom 65,000 live in towns

1772 Patriotic society, *Det Norske Selskab*, is founded

1811 The University of Norway is founded in Oslo

A painting of *The National Assembly at Eidsvoll*, by O. Wergeland, 1885, hanging in the Storting in Oslo

The National Assembly at Eidsvoll

The Danish prince, Christian Frederik, was governor-general of Norway at the time of the Treaty of Kiel, which ceded Norway to Sweden. Both he and the Norwegian people opposed the agreement. An assembly of 21 of the most prominent men in Norway declared Christian Frederik to be the most suitable candidate for the throne of their country, but would not agree to his wish for an absolute monarchy. Instead, it was decided that the people should elect delegates to a national assembly. On Easter Sunday 1814, 112 representatives convened at Eidsvoll and on 17 May they adopted the Norwegian constitution. Christian Frederik was elected king of an independent, free Norway.

Meanwhile, Crown Prince Karl Johan of Sweden demanded that the Treaty of Kiel be implemented. There was a brief war. Karl Johan then accepted the Eidsvoll constitution and on 4 November 1814 the Storting (Norwegian Parliament) elected Sweden's elderly Karl XIII as king of Norway. He was followed in 1818 by Karl Johan himself.

Union with Sweden

The *riksakt*, the convention that was ratified by the Norwegian and Swedish parliaments, ruled that the two countries should have a common king and would stand united in war. Apart from this, they were equal and independent of one another. But there were no provisions in the *riksakt* for a Norwegian foreign service or a national flag. The demand for a flag was not resolved until 1898. The tug-of-war over the foreign service was one of the reasons that led to the dissolution of the union. Another area of dispute was whether the king should be entitled to appoint the governor-general in Norway

By the time of his death in 1844, Karl Johan had become popular in Norway, despite attempting to suppress displays of national identity. *Torvslaget* (Battle in the Marketplace) on 17 May 1829 in Christiania (Oslo) was one such occasion. Norwegians were celebrating National Day when troops attacked. The poet Henrik Wergeland, who was in the crowd, received a blow from a sword. He was subsequently inspired to write with fervour in praise of a free Norway. *Torvslaget* had added new meaning to the 17 May festivities.

The Battle in the Marketplace, Christiania, 17 May 1829

Timeline

1814 Norway's constitution is adopted on 17 May by the National Assembly

Henrik Wergeland

1829 Battle in the Marketplace: troops attack crowds on National Day, 17 May. The nationalist poet, Henrik Wergeland, is wounded

1837 First performance at Christiania Theatre

1844 Karl Johan dies; succeeded by his son, Oscar I

1810 | 1820 | 1830 | 1840 | 1850

1816 Norges Bank established

1818 Karl Johan is crowned king of Norway in Nidaros Cathedral

1819 The first edition of *Morgenbladet*, Norway's first daily newspaper

1848 Marcus Thrane founds Norway's first workers' union

1854 The first railway line is opened for passenger trains from Christiania to Eidsvoll

The Christiania–Eidsvoll railway line, completed in 1854

Economic Growth

An economic crisis in the first few years after 1814 was short-lived. Norges Bank was established in 1816, the country stabilised its currency and was free of debt by 1850. This period marked a watershed in the Norwegian economy. Industry was in the throes of change and growing rapidly. Shipping was experiencing a golden age, particularly between 1850 and 1880, with the transition from sail to steam. Norway built its first railway in 1854; the telegraph arrived in 1850 and the telephone in 1880.

Textile worker at the Hjula weaving mill, 1887

An economic downturn in 1848–50 caused mass unemployment and prompted Marcus Thrane to establish the first workers' union. By 1865, Norway's population had doubled from 900,000 in 1800 to 1.7 million, and it continued to rise. Emigration to America began in 1825 and gradually increased in intensity – between 1879 and 1893 a quarter of a million people crossed the Atlantic.

A Vote for Freedom

Political life toward the end of the period of union with Sweden was characterized by turbulence and the transition to democracy. Parliamentary rule was introduced in 1884, universal suffrage for men in 1898, and for women in 1913.

The long-standing conflict over demands for a separate foreign minister finally brought the union to its knees. In 1905, Norway's Michelsen government resigned because the king would not sanction the Storting's bill on the consular service. The king refused to accept the government's resignation on the grounds that: "A new government cannot now be formed." Michelsen used these words as a pretext to declare the union dissolved. As the king was outside the government and was unable to form a new one – which he was obliged to do under the constitution – he could no longer fulfil his role and was thus no longer the Norwegian king. Without a common king, the union ceased to exist. On 7 June, it was dissolved by the Storting, but Sweden demanded a referendum: 368,208 people voted in favour of secession; 184 against. The Swedish-Norwegian union ended peacefully.

Postcard marking the dissolution of the union with Sweden after a "yes" vote in the 1905 referendum

1871 Opening of the telegraph line to Kirkenes in Northern Norway

1879 Ibsen's play *A Doll's House* is published

1882 The height of emigration to North America

Christian Michelsen

1905 Under Prime Minister Christian Michelsen, the union with Sweden comes to a peaceful end

1860 | 1870 | 1880 | 1890 | 1900

1865 Norway's population exceeds 1.7 million people

1875 Norway's merchant navy becomes the third largest in the world

1884 Parliamentary rule is introduced after a bitter struggle

1889 Compulsory schooling introduced

1898 Universal suffrage for men

1900 Norwegian Employers' Confederation (NAF) is founded

1899 The Norwegian Federation of Trade Unions (LO) is established

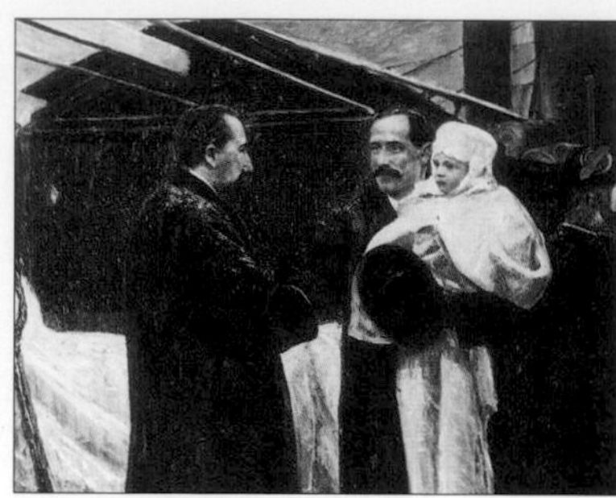
Prime Minister Christian Michelsen greeting Prince Carl and the infant Olav, 25 November 1905

A New Royal Family

After 400 years of Danish and Swedish rule, the Norwegian royal family had died out and the nation turned to Prince Carl, second son of the heir to the Danish throne, to be its head of state. His wife was the British princess, Maud, and they had a two-year-old son, Olav. Prince Carl adopted the name Haakon VII and was crowned in Nidaros Cathedral.

For the first period following the dissolution of the union, domestic policy concentrated on social reforms. Roald Amundsen's successful expedition to the South Pole in 1911 created an enormous wave of national pride. With the writer Bjørnstjerne Bjørnson leading the way, Norway made its presence strongly felt in peacekeeping efforts. In 1901, the Storting had been given the honourable task of awarding the annual Alfred Nobel Peace Prize.

Fridtjof Nansen, polar researcher

Norway remained neutral during World War I, but half of her merchant fleet was lost. Nevertheless, shipping and the export of iron ore provided good revenues and led to wild speculation in shares and a boom period. Toward the end of the war, a shortage of provisions caused difficulties.

Between the Wars

After the war, restrictions in many areas led to bankruptcies and industrial disputes. Farmers and fishermen who had invested heavily in new machinery and equipment in the boom-time were forced to sell up.

In 1930, as the Great Depression took hold in Norway, hardship increased. The banks failed and people lost their savings. Some 200,000 people were unemployed, and many industrial disputes resembled armed conflicts. Shipping fared better: the modern Norwegian merchant fleet had become the third largest in the world.

Between 1918 and 1935, Norway had nine different governments. Then Johan Nygaardsvold's Labour Party came to power and remained in office until 1945. Norway joined the League of Nations and participated in its activities under the guidance of the scientist and diplomat, Fridtjof Nansen.

The dispute between Denmark and Norway over the sovereignty of Greenland was brought before the International Court at The Hague in 1931, and Norway lost its claim.

Under Occupation

Norway declared itself neutral when World War II broke out in September 1939. Regardless, Germany invaded on 9 April 1940. Norwegian troops succeeded in sinking the German cruiser, *Blücher*, in Oslofjorden, and held back the German advance for 62 days before capitulating. On 7 June the king, the

Timeline

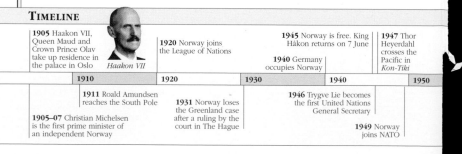

1905 Haakon VII, Queen Maud and Crown Prince Olav take up residence in the palace in Oslo

Haakon VII

1905–07 Christian Michelsen is the first prime minister of an independent Norway

1911 Roald Amundsen reaches the South Pole

1920 Norway joins the League of Nations

1931 Norway loses the Greenland case after a ruling by the court in The Hague

1940 Germany occupies Norway

1945 Norway is free. King Håkon returns on 7 June

1946 Trygve Lie becomes the first United Nations General Secretary

1947 Thor Heyerdahl crosses the Pacific in *Kon-Tiki*

1949 Norway joins NATO

1910 | 1920 | 1930 | 1940 | 1950

crown prince and the cabinet fled from Tromsø to continue the fight in exile in London.

Vidkun Quisling, with German backing, became prime minister of an occupied Norway, but he lacked popular support. There was mounting civil resistance. An underground military organisation *(Milorg)* was formed, eventually comprising 47,000 men, which was controlled by the government in exile. They passed intelligence to the Allies and conducted numerous covert operations against the occupying forces, the most renowned of which was at Rjukan, where resistance fighters destroyed a heavy water plant *(see pp150–1)*.

The Norwegian merchant navy played a major role in the war effort outside the country, but more than half the fleet was lost and 3,000 sailors perished. About 35,000 people were imprisoned during the occupation and 1,400 people, including 738 Jews, died in German concentration camps.

While retreating from Finnmark, the Germans forced the population to evacuate and scorched everything behind them. Germany capitulated on 7 May 1945; 8 May marked liberation day. A month later, King Haakon returned to Norway.

German troops marching along Karl Johans Gate in Oslo, 9 April 1940

A massive oil platform under construction in Gandsfjorden, Stavanger

Modern Norway

Rebuilding the country after World War II took place faster than expected. During the first year of peace, output reached the pre-war level. Politically, Norway was more stable than during the interwar years. At the elections to the Storting in 1945, the Labour Party achieved a clear majority and, except for a short break, remained in power until 1963. Einar Gerhardsen, the "father of Norway", was prime minister. Norway joined NATO in 1949 and EFTA in 1960. Many social reforms were introduced and Norway was on the road to becoming a welfare state.

Following the Gerhardsen period, parliamentary power shifted between Labour and the non-socialist coalition parties. The longest-serving prime minister was Gro Harlem Brundtland *(see p23)*. Since the 1970s the economy and welfare policies have been buoyed up by North Sea oil extraction and strong growth in the fishing industry. Two referenda on membership of the EU have ended in a "No", and Norway seems keen to keep its independent spirit.

1957 Haakon VII dies and Olav V succeeds as king

1970 Discovery of rich oil reserves in the North Sea, off the coast of Norway

1986 Gro Harlem Brundtland becomes Prime Minister

1994 Norway hosts the Winter Olympics in Lillehammer. Second EU referendum

1960 | 1970 | 1980 | 1990 | 2000

1967 National insurance is introduced

1960 Norway becomes a member of EFTA

1972 Norwegians vote "no" to membership of the EEC (EU)

1989 *Sametinget*, the first Sami parliament, opens in Karasjok

1991 Olav V dies. His son, Harald V, succeeds as king

Gro Harlem Brundtland

2000 Norway is elected as 2-year term member of the United Nations Security Council

Oslo Area by Area

Oslo at a Glance 44-45
Central Oslo West 46-61
Central Oslo East 62-75
Bygdøy 76-87
Further Afield 88-97
Oslo Street Finder 98-103

Oslo at a Glance

OSLO HAS CHANGED ITS NAME several times in its history – from Oslo to Christiania and then to Kristiania. In 1925 the capital reverted to its original title, Oslo. The city enjoys an unsurpassed location. Within its boundaries, it is possible to swim in Oslofjorden in summer and ski on well-maintained ski trails in winter. The centre of Oslo is home to museums and galleries, a royal palace, parks and public institutions, all of which can be reached on foot. Its harbour is guarded by a 14th-century castle. There is a wide choice of shops, and in summer cafés spill out onto the pavements and waterfronts. Most sights are within walking distance from the centre, apart from those on Bygdøy.

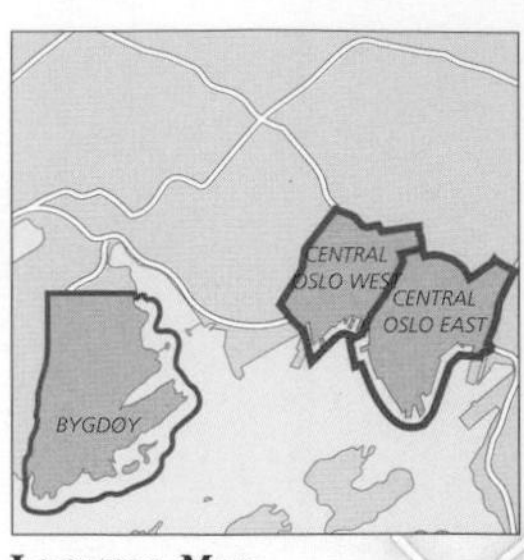

Locator Map

Aker Brygge, *situated on the waterfront, is a popular place to meet up for a drink, a meal or to shop. This former shipyard abounds with life. It is packed with shops and eating places* (see p57).

CENTRAL OSLO WEST

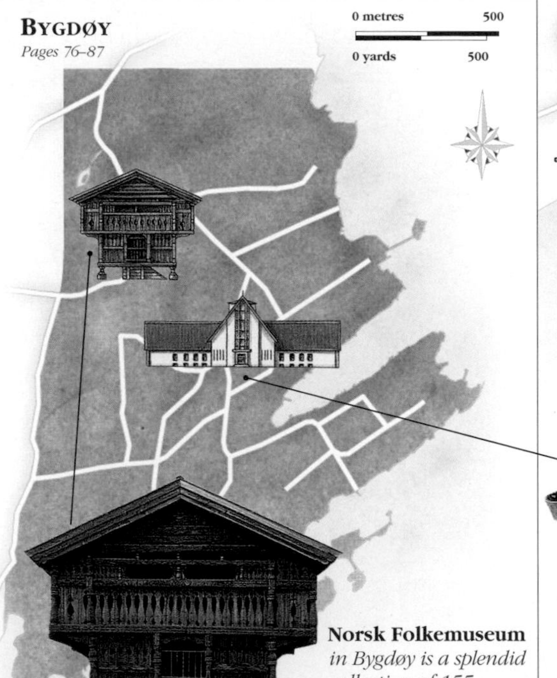

Norsk Folkemuseum *in Bygdøy is a splendid collection of 155 historic buildings from the Middle Ages onward* (see pp82–3).

Vikingskipshuset, *a museum housing three of the best-preserved Viking ships in the world, is one of Norway's cultural jewels* (see pp84–5).

◁ **Jubilant crowds parade along Karl Johans Gate to Slottet (the Royal Palace) on National Day, 17 May**

Visitors' Checklist

500,000. Gardermoen 45 km (28 miles) from the centre. Oslo Promotion: Brynjulf Bulls Plass 1, 23 11 78 80. 17 May on Karl Johan, Ultima Music Festival (first half Oct); Oslo Church Music Festival (first half Mar); Oslo Horse Show (mid-Oct).

Slottet *(the Royal Palace) is a Neo-Classical building on three floors. It was built as a royal residence in the reigns of King Karl XIV Johan and Oscar I, between 1825 and 1848* (see p51).

Karl Johans Gate *has been the city's main thoroughfare for more than 100 years. The lower part is pedestrianized; the upper section is used for parades* (see p50).

CENTRAL OSLO EAST

Stortinget *is constructed in yellow brick on a granite base. This is where Norway's National Assembly meets. It was completed and first used in 1866* (see p74).

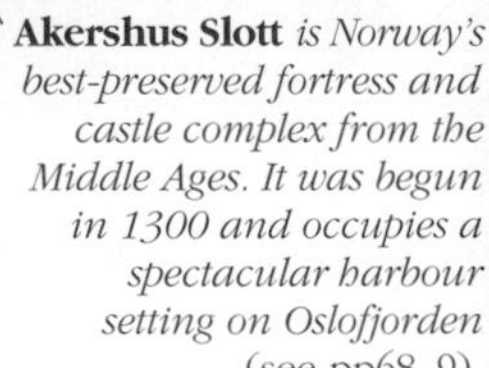

Akershus Slott *is Norway's best-preserved fortress and castle complex from the Middle Ages. It was begun in 1300 and occupies a spectacular harbour setting on Oslofjorden* (see pp68–9).

Central Oslo West

Many of the capital's largest and most important institutions and sights are situated in the western part of central Oslo, and most of them are within walking distance of each other. In a historical context, this area of the city is relatively new. It became the capital's centre when the Royal Palace was completed and Karl Johans Gate had been laid out in the second half of the 19th century.

The area includes Oslo's most popular swathes of green: Studenterlunden, alongside Karl Johans Gate, and Slottsparken, which surrounds the Royal Palace, are both used as recreational spaces. The bustling former wharfside at Aker Brygge, with its shops and bars, galleries and theatres, attracts the most visitors. This area of central Oslo is well served by all forms of public transport. During the summer, the streets teem with people, and cafés and restaurants open out on to the pavements in a way more normally associated with the capitals of southern Europe.

Clock on Rådhuset

Sights

Castles and Museums

Historisk Museum pp54–5 4
Ibsenmuseet 14
Kunstindustrimuseet 15
Nasjonalgalleriet pp52–3 3
Slottet (Royal Palace) 5
Stenersenmuseet 13

Interesting Buildings

Nationaltheatret 6
Det Norske Teatret 8
Oslo Konserthus 12
Rådhuset pp56–7 9
Theatercafeen 7

Tourist Information 10
Universitetet 2

Streets and Squares

Aker Brygge 11
Karl Johans Gate 1

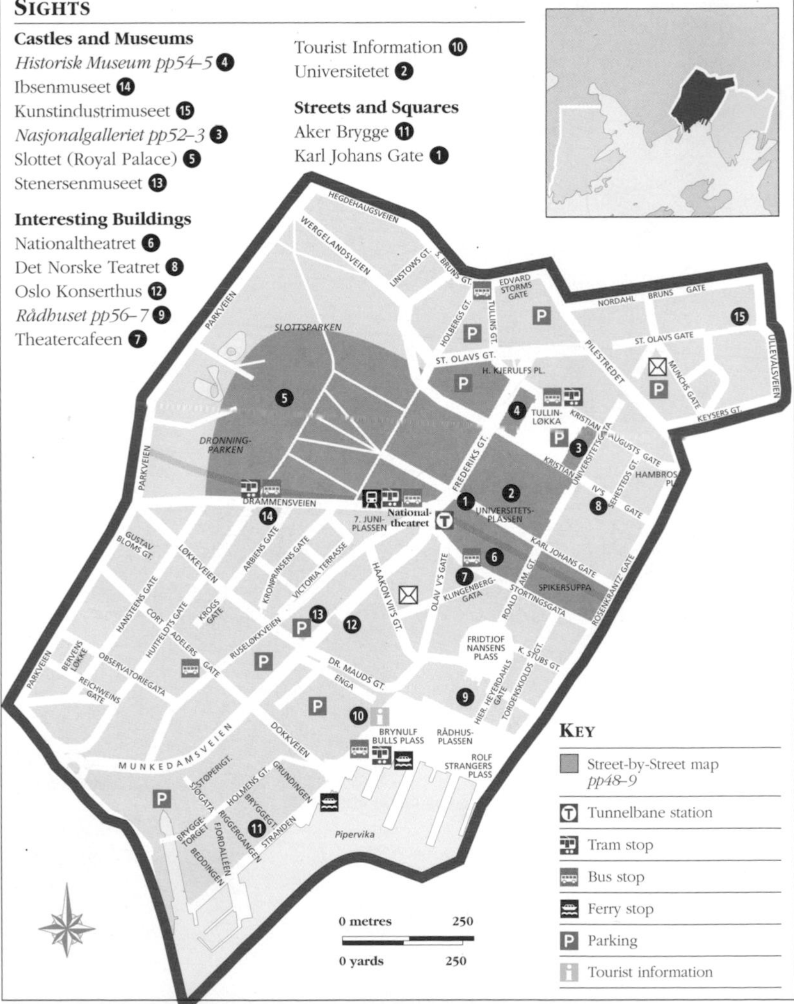

◁ **Aker Brygge, with Rådhuset in the background, bustling with life on a warm summer's day**

Street-by-Street: Karl Johans Gate

KARL JOHANS GATE IN THE HEART of Oslo is the best-known and busiest thoroughfare in Norway. Every day 100,000 pedestrians use the street, better known as Karl Johan. Many of Norway's foremost institutions are situated here, including the Royal Palace (Slottet), Stortinget (the Norwegian Parliament), the university and the National Theatre. The street is lined with department stores, specialist shops and places to eat. The Historisk Museum and Nasjonalgalleriet are only a couple of minutes' walk away. The upper part of Karl Johan, beside the park known as Studenterlunden, is the venue for parades. In winter it is transformed into a skating rink, which attracts young and old.

Slottet
The Royal Palace is situated on a hill at the end of Karl Johans Gate. It forms a natural and imposing focal point ❺

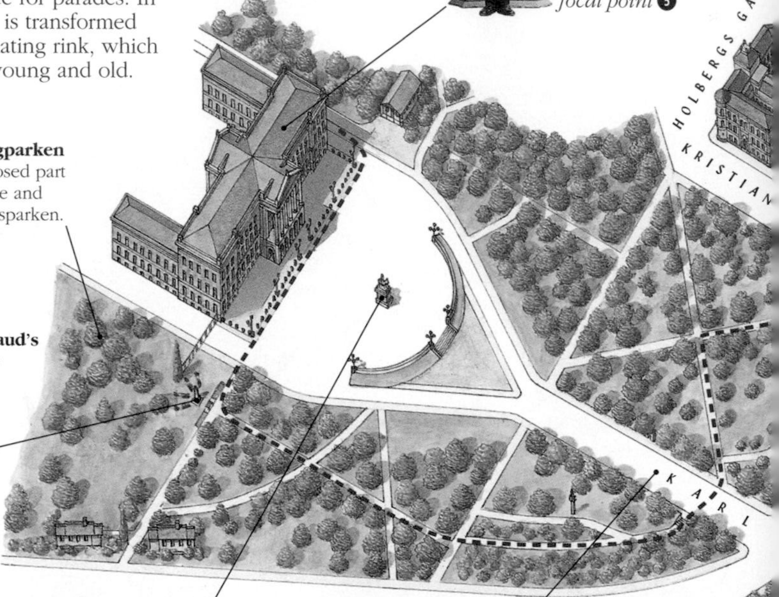

Dronningparken is an enclosed part of the large and open Slottsparken.

Queen Maud's statue was designed by Ada Madssen in 1959.

King Karl Johan depicted on his horse in Slottsplassen. He built the Royal Palace and gave Oslo's main street its name. The statue is by Brynjulf Bergslien, 1875.

Karl Johans Gate
Oslo's main thoroughfare is the focal point for both city life and national events such as the 17 May parades. It was planned by the palace architect, H D F Linstow, in 1840 and named after King Karl Johan ❶

STAR SIGHTS

★ **Historisk Museum**

★ **Nasjonalgalleriet**

KEY

- - - Suggested route

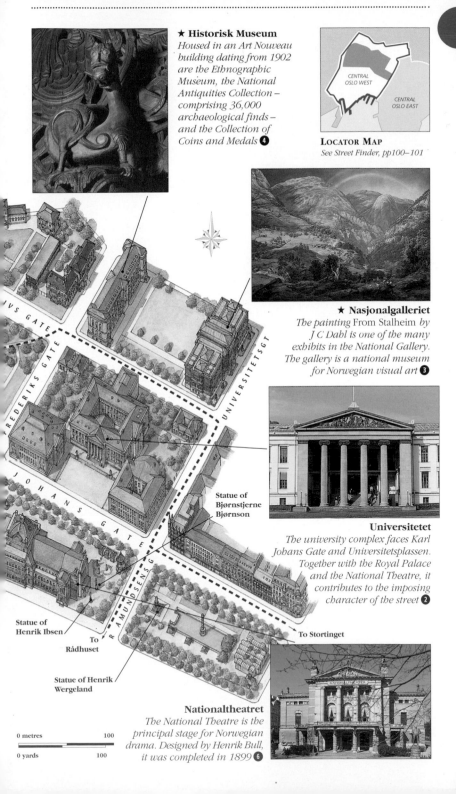

★ Historisk Museum
Housed in an Art Nouveau building dating from 1902 are the Ethnographic Museum, the National Antiquities Collection – comprising 36,000 archaeological finds – and the Collection of Coins and Medals ❹

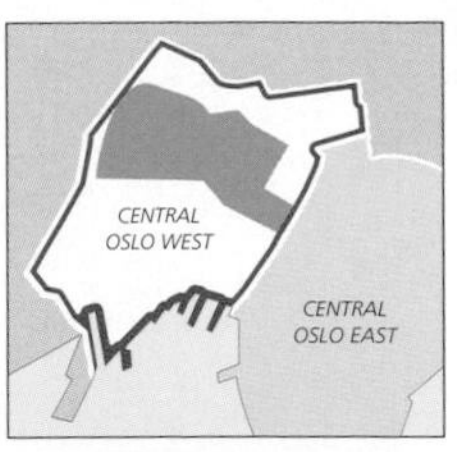

LOCATOR MAP
See Street Finder, pp100–101

★ Nasjonalgalleriet
The painting From Stalheim *by J C Dahl is one of the many exhibits in the National Gallery. The gallery is a national museum for Norwegian visual art* ❸

FREDERIKS GATE

UNIVERSITETSGT

KARL JOHANS GATE

RAMUNDSENS G

Statue of Bjørnstjerne Bjørnson

Universitetet
The university complex faces Karl Johans Gate and Universitetsplassen. Together with the Royal Palace and the National Theatre, it contributes to the imposing character of the street ❷

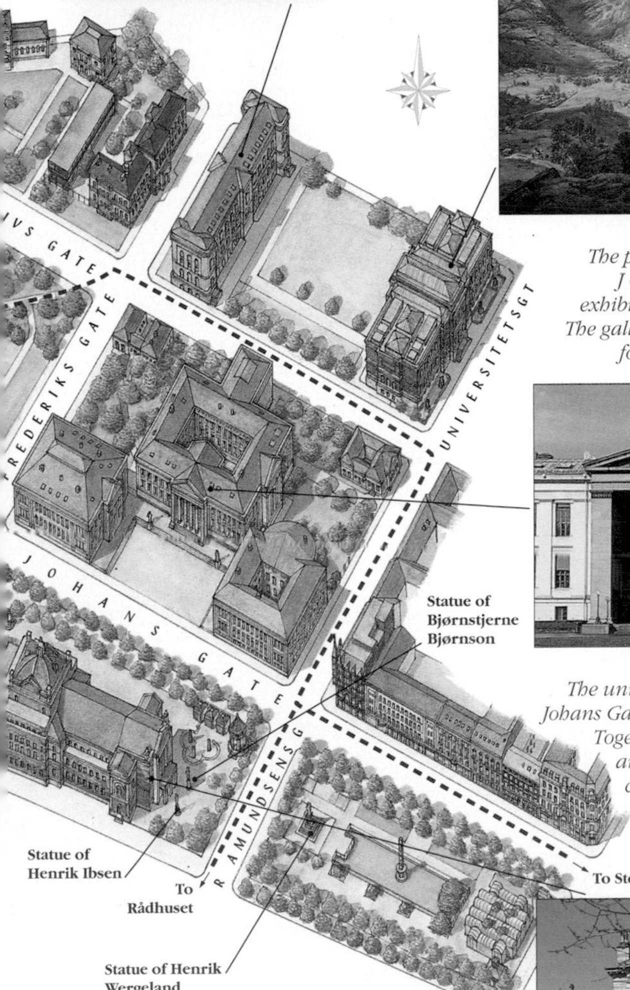

To Stortinget

Statue of Henrik Ibsen

To Rådhuset

Statue of Henrik Wergeland

Nationaltheatret
The National Theatre is the principal stage for Norwegian drama. Designed by Henrik Bull, it was completed in 1899 ❻

0 metres 100

0 yards 100

The upper part of Norway's foremost thoroughfare, Karl Johans Gate

Karl Johans Gate ❶

Map 3 D3. Ⓣ *Stortinget, Nationaltheatret.* *13, 15, 19.* *30, 31, 32, 33, 45.*

NORWAY'S BEST-KNOWN and busiest thoroughfare is Karl Johans Gate. It is named after the king of Norway and Sweden, Karl Johan (1818–44), and is known simply as Karl Johan by the people of Oslo. The street is flanked by stately, Neo-Classical buildings.

The upper section is the most imposing. Stortinget (the Norwegian parliament) is situated here and Slottet (the Royal Palace) takes pride of place at the western end of the street. Between these two buildings lie the university and Nationaltheatret, a park known as Studenterlunden, and a skating rink which is open to the public in winter (skates are available for hire). The lower part of Karl Johans Gate terminates at Central Station. Basarhallene (the market halls) at Kirkeristen can be found in this section.

Karl Johans Gate grew in importance after the Royal Palace, designed by the architect H D F Linstow, was completed in 1848. Linstow also planned Karl Johan.

In addition to the many public buildings, the street is lined with department stores, specialist shops and places to eat. Karl Johans Gate has been a popular meeting place since the 19th century. The citizens of Oslo used to stroll along Studenterlunden to see and be seen. Today, young people continue to meet on the "Strip". It is also the focal point for royal occasions and state visits. Undoubtedly the biggest day of the year on Karl Johan is Norway's National Day, 17 May, when thousands of children, accompanied by singers and musicians, parade toward the palace to be greeted by the royal family who come out on to the balcony.

In 2000 a system was installed to illuminate the façades along Karl Johans Gate and now lights switch on automatically each evening as darkness falls. The street teems with life until the early hours. Visitors are often surprised by the vibrancy of the nightlife in and around Karl Johans Gate, which is more on a par with some of the larger capitals of Europe.

Universitetet ❷

Karl Johans Gate 47. **Map** 3 D3. *22 85 50 50.* Ⓣ *Nationaltheatret.* *13, 15, 19.* *30, 31, 32, 45.*

THE UNIVERSITY DOMINATES the northeast side of Karl Johans Gate. The Neo-Classical building was completed in 1852, 40 years after Frederik VI decreed that Norway could finally have its very own university. He gave it his name, the "Royal Frederik University in Oslo", by which it was known until 1939.

Over the years, most of the teaching, other than the Faculty of Law and some of the administration, has moved to Blindern on the outskirts of Oslo. The university complex is situated directly opposite the Nationaltheatret. It comprises three buildings which encircle University Square. To mark its centenary in 1911, the university built a new auditorium, the Aula, in an extension to the main building. The Aula is renowned for its murals by the Norwegian artist Edvard Munch *(see p22)*, installed in 1916. The powerful background motif, *The Sun*, symbolizes light in the form of an explosive sunrise over the coastline. The main canvas on the right, *Alma Mater*, depicts a nursing mother representing the university, while that on the left, *History*, represents knowledge and wisdom. Edvard Munch regarded the paintings in the Aula as his major work.

Politicians and humanitarians from all over the world have, over the years, visited the Aula. It was used as the venue for the presentation of the Nobel Peace Prize until 1990 when the award ceremony was moved to Rådhuset (Oslo Town Hall).

On one day in mid-August every year, 3,000 students gather in University Square to register for a university place.

Oslo University's Aula with Edvard Munch's murals, 1916

Nasjonalgalleriet ❸

See pp52–3.

Historisk Museum ❹

See pp54–5.

Slottet (the Royal Palace) standing supreme on the hill at the top of Karl Johans Gate

Slottet ❺

Drammensveien 1. **Map** 2 C2. *22 04 87 00. Nationaltheatret. 13, 15, 19. 30, 31, 32, 45, 81, 83. guided tours only; end Jun–mid-Aug: 10am–4:30pm Mon–Thu & Sat, 1–4:30pm Fri & Sun; tickets in advance from post offices.*

THE ROYAL PALACE (Det Kongelige Slottet) occupies an elevated position overlooking the city centre and forms a natural focal point on Karl Johans Gate.

King Karl Johan decided to build a royal residence in Oslo on ascending to the Swedish-Norwegian throne in 1818. He commissioned the architect Lieutenant H D F Linstow to design the project.

Work on the interior, by the architects H F Schirmer and J H Nebelong, began in 1836. Peter Frederik Wergmann was responsible for the Pompeii-style wall friezes in the Banqueting Hall. The Palace Chapel and the Ballroom were designed by Linstow; the painter Johannes Flintoe decorated the Bird Room.

The palace was not completed until 1848, by which time Karl Johan had died. It was inaugurated by Oscar I amid great festivities.

The grand buildings did not become a permanent residence until 1905 when Norway finally became an independent nation. King Haakon and Queen Maud, the newly crowned monarchs, moved into what was then a poorly maintained palace. It has been gradually restored and upgraded over time and at the end of the 20th century underwent a further comprehensive restoration.

The palace is built of brick and plaster. It has three wings of three storeys each. Slottsparken, the gardens surrounding the buildings to the south and east, are not fenced off and are open to the public. Dronningsparken, to the west, is private property and is not open to visitors.

The palace has a splendid collection of fine art. In the summer of 2000, the public had the opportunity for the first time to view the collection and some of the interior, on guided tours. The tours are now a regular feature every year from the end of June until mid-August.

A statue of Karl Johan stands in front of the palace.

The palace's Banqueting Hall with Wergmann's Pompeii-style friezes

Nationaltheatret ❻

Johannes Dybwads plass 1. **Map** 3 D3. *22 00 14 00. Nationaltheatret. 13, 15, 19. 30, 31, 32, 45, 81, 83.* **Ticket Office** *9.30am–6.30pm Mon–Fri, 11am–5pm Sat. public hols. by arrangement.*

IT WAS NO COINCIDENCE that a play by the Norwegian dramatist Henrik Ibsen was on the programme when the National Theatre opened its doors in 1899. The theatre's first production was the socially critical drama, *An Enemy of the People.* Since then, Ibsen's work has become a central part of the repertoire, and his powerful plays have inspired many generations of actors.

The Baroque-style building was designed by Henrik Bull and is regarded as the country's most significant expression of the renaissance of brickwork in the 19th century. Its Baroque-like design is typical of theatre architecture throughout Europe toward the end of the 19th century. A fire caused extensive damage to the building in 1980 and the subsequent restoration work took five years to complete.

The ticket for a play also gives access to one of Norway's finest art collections. Throughout the building are paintings by Erik Werenskiold, Karl Fjell, Christian Krohg, P S Krøyer and busts by Gustav Vigeland, Per Palle Storm and other Norwegian artists. In front of the theatre stand sculptures of two of Norway's most renowned writers – Henrik Ibsen and Bjørnstjerne Bjørnson – each on a pedestal.

Nasjonalgalleriet 3

THE NATIONAL GALLERY HOUSES Norway's largest public collection of paintings, sculptures, drawings and engravings. Visual art up until 1945 is well represented, with particular emphasis on National Romanticism and Impressionism. The Edvard Munch Hall contains a number of the artist's most famous works. Another highlight is the collection of 15th and 16th-century Russian icons from the Novgorod School. Sculptures by Norwegian and foreign artists can be found in several of the exhibition halls. With 50,000 volumes, the National Gallery has the best art library in the country. The building was designed by H E and Adolf Schirmer and completed in 1882.

Façade Detail
The National Gallery is in the Neo-Renaissance style, which was much favoured in the capital in the 1880s.

A Little a-Port
Christian Krohg's Babord Litt *(literally "turn the helm a little to port") was painted in 1879 by this productive and much loved artist. His portrayals of contemporary life are considered high points in Norwegian art.*

★ The Scream
Skrik (The Scream), *by Edvard Munch, is one of the most frequently depicted works of art in the world. It was painted in 1893, and is regarded as a breakthrough for Expressionism.*

Reading room with the collection of engravings and hand drawings

Auditorium

Gallery Guide

On the ground floor there is a shop, library, reading room and a collection of antique sculptures. The first floor showcases Norwegian art and a number of European paintings. On the second floor there are engravings and drawings, as well as a selection of Scandinavian art.

Main entrance

Henrik Ibsen
Norway's renowned sculptor, Gustav Vigeland, designed this marble head of the playwright Henrik Ibsen.

Star Features

- ★ ***The Scream*** **by Edvard Munch**
- ★ ***Winter Night in the Mountains*** **by Harald Sohlberg**

Portrait of Mme Zborowska
This portrait by Amadeo Modigliani was painted in 1918. It is typical of the Italian artist's linear style with flat areas of colour. Modigliani is known for having created Subjective Expressionism.

VISITORS' CHECKLIST

Universitetsgaten 13. **Map** 3 D3. 22 20 04 04. *Nationaltheatret.* 13, 15, 19. 30, 31, 32, 45, 81, 83. *10am–6pm Mon, Wed & Fri; 10am–8pm Thu; 10am–4pm Sat; 11am–4pm Sun.* *public hols.* *by arrangement.* www.nasjonalgalleriet.no

The Repentant Peter
El Greco's portrayal of the apostle, Peter, is thought to have been painted between 1610 and 1614. The intensity of the painting and the daring choice of colour in the cape is typical of the artist.

2nd floor

★ Winter Night in the Mountains
Harald Sohlberg's Vinternatt i Rondane, *1914, is a major work of Norwegian Neo-Romanticism. It broke with the naturalistic tradition of landscape painting in Nordic art in the early 20th century.*

1st floor

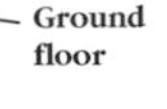

Ground floor

Library with reading room

Mount Stetind in the Fog
Peder Balke's Stetind i Tåke *1864, is one of the most important works of the National Romantic movement. Balke was a pupil of the landscape artist J C Dahl (1788–1857).*

KEY TO FLOORPLAN

- Norwegian painting and sculpture
- Antique sculpture
- Casts
- Scandinavian painting and sculpture
- Older European painting
- 19th- and 20th-century European painting and sculpture
- Exhibition of engravings and hand drawings
- Non-exhibition space

Historisk Museum ❹

THE THREE UNIVERSITY MUSEUMS, Oldsaksamlingen (National Antiquities Collection), Etnografisk Museum (Ethnographic Museum) and Myntkabinettet (Collection of Coins and Medals) are collectively known as the Historical Museum. They document Norwegian and international history from the first settlements to the present day. Rare objects from Viking and medieval times are on show and medieval religious art is particularly well represented. There is also a rich collection from the Arctic Inuit culture. The building was designed by Henrik Bull (1864–1953) and completed in 1902.

Inuit Mask
The mask from East Greenland represents a tupilak *– a figure which is animated through magic rituals and which brings ill fortune to its victim.*

★ Mary and the Child from Hedalen
The wooden sculpture of Mary and Jesus, dating from around 1250, illustrates the skills of Norwegian wood carvers in the 13th century. The majority of the original paintwork remains intact.

★ Portal from Ål Kirke
This intricately carved stave church doorway dating from 1150 is one of the few wooden objects from the early Middle Ages to be found in Europe. Some of the paint on the portal remains.

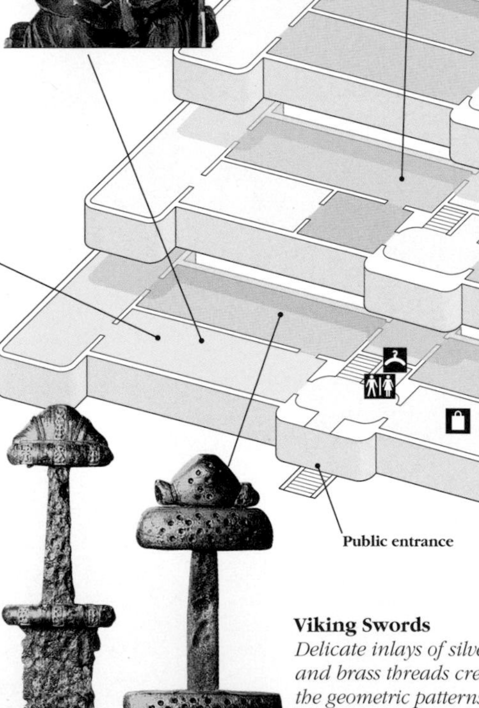

Viking Swords
Delicate inlays of silver and brass threads create the geometric patterns on these swords, which were discovered in Viking burial mounds.

STAR FEATURES

- ★ Mary and the Child from Hedalen
- ★ Portal from Ål Kirke

Wheel of Life
This Tibetan temple painting (thamka) *shows a demon as a symbol of evil clinging to life. The wheel is kept in motion by evil forces such as lust, anger and ignorance.*

VISITORS' CHECKLIST

Frederiks Gate 2. **Map** 3 D2. *22 85 99 12.* *Nationaltheatret.* *10, 11, 13, 17, 18, 19.* *30, 31, 32, 45, 81, 83.* *15 May–14 Sep: 10am–6pm daily; 15 Sep–14 May: 11am–6pm daily.* *public hols.* www.ukm.uio.no

GALLERY GUIDE

The Historisk Museum covers four floors. The National Antiquities Collection is on the ground floor. The first floor is shared by the Collection of Coins and Medals, and by the Ethnographic Museum, which also occupies the second and third floors. The collections are well arranged in airy rooms. Many of the exhibits are accompanied by information in Norwegian, English and German.

3rd floor

2nd floor

1st floor

Ground floor

KEY TO FLOORPLAN

- Stone, Bronze and Iron Age
- Viking Age
- Middle Ages
- Treasure Chamber
- Collection of Coins and Medals
- Indians in North and South America
- The Ancient World
- Arctic Ethnography
- African Ethnography
- Asian Ethnography
- Changing exhibitions
- Non-exhibition space

Chair from the Buli School of Masters in the Congo
This African carving of a woman carrying a chair dates from 1850. The woman's hairstyle and the scars from extensive tattoos indicate that she is the sister or the mother of a chieftain.

Theatercafeen ❼

Stortingsgaten 24–26. **Map** 3 D3. *22 82 40 50.* *Nationaltheatret.* *13, 15, 19.* *30, 31, 32, 45, 81, 83.* *11am–11pm Mon–Sat, 3–10pm Sun.*

IN OSLO, FRIENDS often meet for a meal at the classy Theatercafeen, a restaurant conveniently situated just across the street from the Nationaltheatret.

Ever since it opened in 1901, it has been a focal point for Norway's most celebrated artists, authors and actors, including Knut Hamsun, Edvard Munch, Herman Wildenvey and Johanne Dybwad, many of whose portraits line the walls. While most of these names belong to a bygone era, Theatercafeen still attracts many well-known contemporary figures to its tables.

The restaurant has its own classical orchestra which plays from the balcony.

Det Norske Teatret ❽

Kristian IVs Gate 8. **Map** 3 D3. *22 47 38 00.* *Nationaltheatret.* *30, 31, 32, 45, 81, 83.* *13, 15, 19.* **Box Office** *9am–8pm Mon–Fri, 9am–6pm Sat.*

NORWAY'S "SECOND National Theatre", Det Norske Teatret, was opened already in 1913, but was forever on the move until finally in September 1985 it was able to welcome audiences to its own new, ultra-modern home.

The theatre has two stages, Hovedscenen with 757 seats and Biscenen with 200 seats. There are rehearsal rooms, beautifully decorated foyers and a bistro. Hovedscenen is fitted with advanced technical equipment and movable units, so stage layouts and sets can be changed quickly.

Det Norske Teatret is the main venue for works in the *nynorsk* language *(see p16)*. The principal repertoire features Norwegian/Nordic drama, but both modern and classical plays are performed on a regular basis.

Rådhuset 9

IN 1918 THE COMPETITION TO DESIGN a new City Hall was won by Arnstein Arneberg and Magnus Poulsson. The building was opened in 1950 to mark the city's 900th anniversary, but it has taken many years for the people of Oslo to come to terms with this Modernist landmark in dark brown brick. The City Hall is the administrative centre of Oslo and contains the richly adorned ceremonial hall known as Rådhushallen in which the Nobel Peace Prize is presented in December each year. Prominent Norwegian artists were invited to decorate the interior, including Henrik Sørensen, whose painting, *Work, Art and Celebration*, fills an entire wall.

Rådhuset from the north, showing the main entrance and courtyard

★ Rådhus Hall
The ceremonial main hall covers 1,519 sq m (16,350 sq ft) of floor space. Henrik Sørensen's oil painting on the rear wall is the largest in Europe.

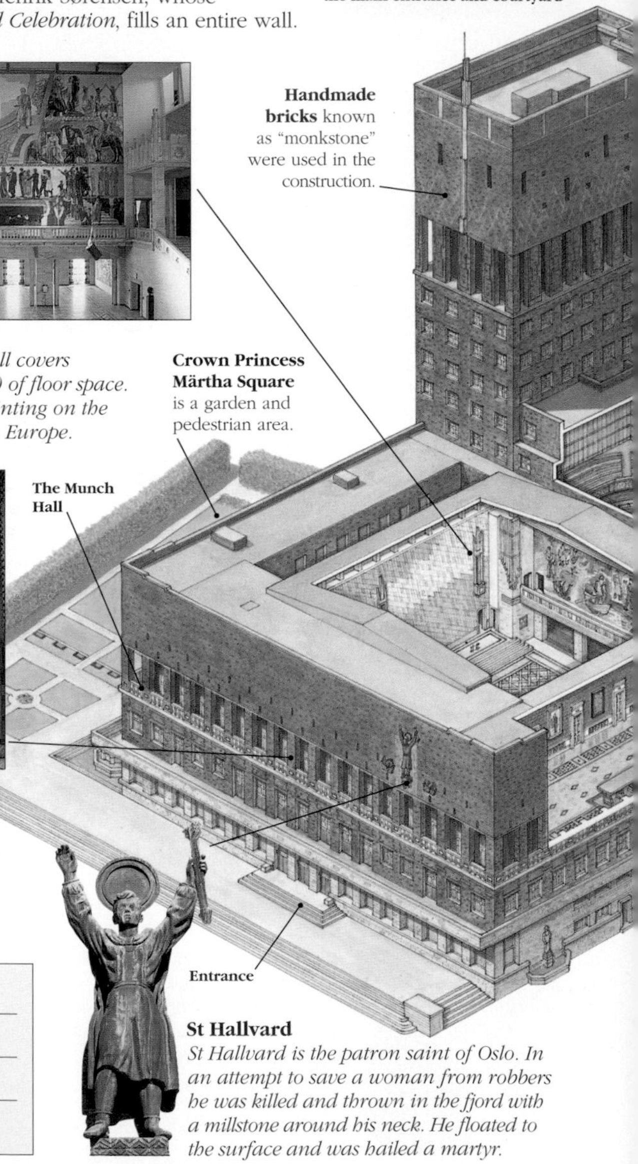

Handmade bricks known as "monkstone" were used in the construction.

Crown Princess Märtha Square is a garden and pedestrian area.

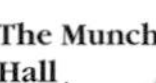

The Munch Hall

★ Feast Gallery
Axel Revoldt's fresco depicts the industrial and consumer society of the 1950s. It focuses on agriculture, shipbuilding, fishing and factories.

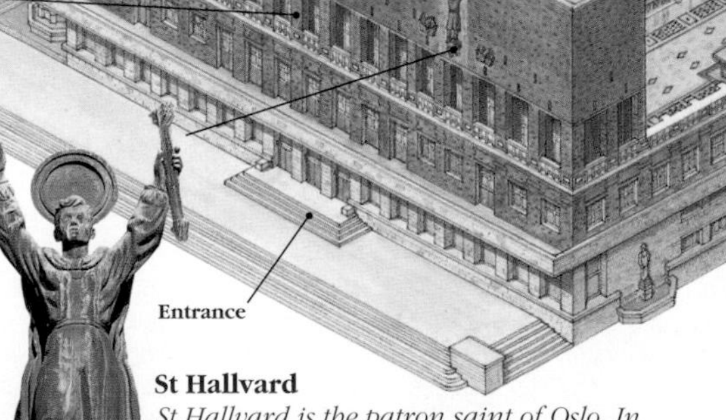

Entrance

St Hallvard
St Hallvard is the patron saint of Oslo. In an attempt to save a woman from robbers he was killed and thrown in the fjord with a millstone around his neck. He floated to the surface and was hailed a martyr.

STAR FEATURES

- ★ **Bystyre Hall**
- ★ **Feast Gallery**
- ★ **Rådhus Hall**

★ Bystyre Hall
The Hall of the City Council (Bystyresalen) lies at the heart of Rådhuset. The council's 59 representatives have regular meetings here.

VISITORS' CHECKLIST

Fridtjof Nansens Plass. **Map** 3 D3. *23 46 16 00. Nationaltheatret, Stortinget. 10, 12, 13, 15, 19. 30, 31, 32, 45, 81, 83. May–Aug: 9am–5pm daily; Sep–Apr: 9am–4pm daily. public hols. by arrangement.* www.oslokommune.no

The Eastern Tower is 66-m (217-ft) tall.

Albertine
The tragic character of Albertine was created by Christian Krohg in his written and painted works. Albertine was later recaptured by Alfred Seland in this relief sculpture on the eastern façade of the Rådhuset.

Banqueting Hall
The venue for grand dinners, the Banqueting Hall (Bankettsalen) is a light and airy room that is richly decorated and embellished with royal portraits.

Tourist Information ⑩

Vestbanebygningen, Brynjulf Bulls Plass. **Map** 2 C3. *23 11 78 80. Nationaltheatret. 10, 12. Apr–May: 9am–5pm Mon–Sat; Jun–Aug: 9am–7pm daily; Sep: 9am–5pm Mon–Fri; Oct–Mar: 9am–4pm Mon–Fri.* www.visitoslo.com

OSLO HAS two tourist information offices (Turistinformasjonen). The biggest, Oslo Promotion, is in Vestbanebygningen, a former station on the western railway. As well as offering general tourist information services *(see p256)*, it contains a café, bar, restaurant, newsagent and souvenir shop.

Vestbanebygningen is worth a visit in its own right. It was built in 1872 by the architect Georg A Bull, who also designed Østbanen, the eastern railway station, which is now part of Oslo Central Station. The last train left from Vestbanen in 1989, and the Tourist Information Centre opened here in 1991.

Aker Brygge ⑪

Map 2 C4. *Nationaltheatret. 10, 12.*

IN 1982 THE long-established shipyard, Akers Mekaniske Verksted, closed down, freeing up a potentially attractive area on Oslo's harbourfront. Aker Brygge has been transformed to provide a major shopping and entertainment centre with residential apartments and the city's biggest concentration of restaurants. Many of the old shipyard warehouses have been restored. Bold new architecture blends with the old and has attracted international acclaim as a successful example of inner-city redevelopment.

Aker Brygge is a delightful setting in which to enjoy a beer or a glass of wine at the quayside, or to splash out on a sumptuous dinner in a good restaurant. From here there is a panoramic view across the water to the fortress of Akershus *(see pp68–9)*.

Sculptures by Turid Eng (1984) at the entrance to Oslo Konserthus

Oslo Konserthus ⓬

Munkedamsveien 14. **Map** 2 C3. *23 11 31 00.* *Nationaltheatret.* *13, 15, 19.* *30, 31, 32, 45, 81, 83.* **Box office** *10am–5pm Mon–Fri; 11am–2pm Sat; and 2 hrs before performance.* *July.*

OSLO'S CONCERT hall, situated in the area of Vika, has been a leading venue for Norwegian cultural and musical life since its opening in 1977. The world's top artists and orchestras regularly perform here.

In the 1960s, the Swedish architect, Gösta Åberg, won the competition to design the new building. The exterior is clad in polished granite; inside the floors and walls are of white marble. The hall has been specially designed to stage orchestral works, with a podium large enough to accommodate 120 musicians. It can be transformed into a theatre for shows and musical productions with seating for an audience of 1,400.

The concert hall is the home of Oslo-Filharmonien (the Oslo Symphony Orchestra). The orchestra plays a central role in the musical life of the city. It is also regarded as one of the world's leading symphony ensembles, and its recordings have attracted international acclaim.

More than 300 events are held annually at the Konserthus, with audiences totalling more than 200,000 over the year.

Stenersenmuseet ⓭

Munkedamsveien 15. **Map** 2 C3. *22 49 36 00.* *Nationaltheatret.* *13, 15, 19.* *30, 31, 32, 45, 81, 83.* *11am–7pm Tue & Thu; 11am–5pm Wed & Fri–Sun.* *2:30pm Sun.*

ONE OF THE most recent museums to open in Oslo is the Stenersenmuseet, named after the author, art collector and patron of the arts, Rolf Stenersen. In 1936, he donated his collection to Oslo City Council. The paintings remained in store until 1994, when Stenersenmuseet was completed. It is located in Konserthusterrassen (beneath the Konserthus).

The Stenersen bequest is one of three collections on show in the museum. It includes paintings and a large number of graphics and drawings by Edvard Munch *(see p22)*, who was a friend of Stenersen. They span Munch's output from his early work, *The Sick Room*, to the later *Dance of Life*. In addition to Munch, Scandinavian art is well-represented with works by Kai Fjell, Jakob Weidemann and Per Krohg.

The other two collections feature paintings by Amaldus Nielsen (1838–1932) and Ludvig O Ravensberg (1871–1958).

Nielsen was a landscape painter who immortalized the southern Norwegian coast in his work. Ravensberg was known for his naive portrayals of Roman ruins of old Oslo. He was strongly influenced by Munch, who was his relative.

Ibsenmuseet ⓮

Arbins Gate 1. **Map** 2 C3. *22 55 20 09.* *Nationaltheatret.* *13,15, 19.* *30, 31, 32, 45, 81, 83.* *guided tours only.* *noon, 1pm, 2pm Tue–Sun.*

HENRIK IBSEN, Norway's revered playwright, produced the major part of his work while living in Munich (1864–92).

After his return to Oslo, in 1895, Ibsen and his wife took an apartment in Arbiens Gate, on the first floor on the corner facing Drammensveien. This was where he wrote his last plays, *John Gabriel Borkman* (1896) and *When We Dead Awaken* (1899). It was in this home that he suffered a stroke, which prevented him from writing,

Høstens promenade, **Ludvig O Ravensberg, Stenersenmuseet**

The Baldishol Tapestry, one of the most prized exhibits in the Kunstindustrimuseet

and he subsequently died in 1906, aged 78 years.

Great attention has been paid to the restoration and redecoration of the couple's large apartment. Even the colour scheme resembles that of Ibsen's day and his study contains the original furniture.

Every day he would set off from here to walk to the Grand Café in Karl Johans Gate where he held court until ill-health confined him to the apartment.

The museum is open for guided tours and lectures.

Kunstindustri-museet ⓯

St Olavs Gate 1. **Map** 3 E2.
22 03 65 40. Stortinget, Nationaltheatret. 60, and a short walk to 30, 31, 32, 45, 81, 83.
11am–3pm Tue–Fri; noon–4pm Sat–Sun. public hols.

THE MUSEUM OF Applied Art (Kunstindustrimuseet) is one of the oldest museums in Europe. It was established in 1876, and contains a fine collection of Norwegian and foreign crafts, fashion and design products from the 17th century to the present day.

The museum holds Norway's biggest collection of tapestries from the 16th and 17th centuries, including the national treasure, the Baldishol Tapestry, dating from 1200. This is the only surviving Nordic tapestry that uses the Gobelin technique from the Middle Ages, and is one of the few remaining European tapestries to exhibit Roman characteristics. The tapestry was found when Baldishol Church in the county of Hedmark was demolished in 1879.

The museum also contains silver, glassware, ceramics and furniture. On show in the Royal Costume Gallery (Kongelig Norsk Dragtgalleri) are clothes from the Norwegian monarchy. In the Department of East Asian Art there is an imperial Ming vase dating from the 15th century.

Since 1904 the museum has shared an imposing building with the National College of Art and Design. Their joint library is open to the public.

Goblet by Torolf Prytz (1900)

HENRIK IBSEN

Described as the father of modern drama, Henrik Ibsen (1828–1906) is Norway's most famous writer. He left a remarkable legacy of plays that revolutionized modern theatre and are still performed worldwide. They included *Peer Gynt*, for which Edvard Grieg *(see p22)* composed the music, *A Doll's House*, *Hedda Gabler*, *Ghosts*, *The Wild Duck* and *An Enemy of the People*. Ibsen was born in Skien *(see p142)* in southern Norway. He began writing while working as a chemist's assistant, but his first play, *Catilina*, was rejected. Undeterred, he took a job as a journalist in Bergen and later became director and playwright at Ole Bull's Theatre. From 1857–1863 he was director of the Norwegian Theatre in Oslo, but the theatre went bankrupt and he moved abroad. Over the next 30 years he wrote numerous dramas, concentrating on social issues and the pettiness of Norwegian society. They earned him literary fame and in 1892 he returned to Olso a national hero.

Portrait of Henrik Ibsen, dramatist

Oslo's inner harbour, home to the city's sightseeing boats, with Aker Brygge in the background ▷

Central Oslo East

THE CITY ORIGINATED more than 1000 years ago in what is now eastern Oslo. The first market was situated in Bjørvika, which today is a commercial port and traffic hub. The area is about to undergo a large-scale transformation, centred around a new waterfront opera house.

In 1624, the old city of Oslo was almost entirely destroyed by fire. The new city spread for the first time to the west of the Akershus fortress. Under the auspices of Christian IV, the area of Kvadraturen (Quadrangle) developed to the north of the fortress. The king renamed the new city Christiania in 1624. Many of its historic buildings are to be found in Kvadraturen itself, alongside places of interest such as the Norwegian Resistance Museum, the Museum of Contemporary Art and the Theatre Museum. Parts of the eastern area have a multi-cultural population and are characterized by a cosmopolitan mix of restaurants and ethnic shops.

Canon at Akershus Fortress

Sights at a Glance

Castles and Museums

Akershus Slott pp68–9 1
Astrup Fearnley Museet 10
Forsvarsmuseet 9
Høymagasinet 3
Museet for Samtidskunst pp70–71 7
Norges Hjemmefrontmuseum 2
Norsk Arkitekturmuseum 4
Postmuseet 12
Teatermuseet 5

Public Buildings

Børsen 11
Den Gamle Logen 8
Regjeringskvartalet 16
Stortinget 14

Theatre and Opera

Den Norske Opera 18
Oslo Nye Teater 15
Oslo Spektrum 19

Churches and Squares

Christiania Torv 6
Oslo Domkirke 13
Youngstorget 17

◁ **The solid walls of Akershus Slott seen from the south**

Street-by-Street: Kvadraturen

Oslo has been ravaged by fire on a number of occasions, the worst of which was in 1624, when almost the entire city was destroyed. The king, Christian IV, decided to build a new city to be known as Christiania. Development started at the foot of the Akershus fortress. The area, Kvadraturen (the Quadrangle), took the form of a rectangular grid. Although few of the original buildings remain, Kvadraturen is still characterized by its historic architecture. It has old market squares and museums, picturesque sights and traditional eating-places. The fortress bordering the harbour is the focal point. From the ramparts there is a splendid view across southern Oslo and the inner reaches of Oslofjorden.

Teatermuseet
The Theatre Museum is in the city's former town hall, dating from 1641. It highlights the history of drama in Oslo from the early 19th century 5

To Stortinget

AKERSGATA

CHRISTIANIA TORV

RÅDHUSGATA

To Rådhusplassen

AKER

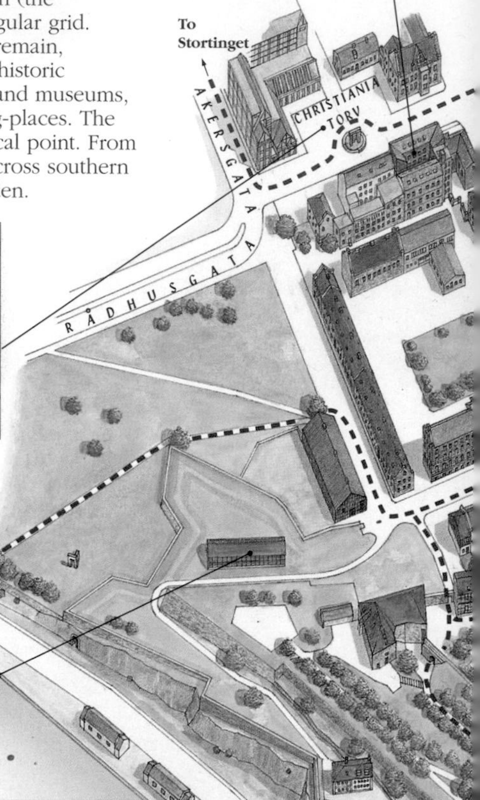

Christiania Torv
The city's first market square, Christiania Torv, has been renovated and is home to many new eateries. The fountain, Christian IV's Glove, *is by Wenche Gulbransen (1997)* 6

Høymagasinet
Originally a hay barn, the half-timbered Høymagasinet dates from 1845. It houses models illustrating the history of the city's buildings 3

Hjemmefrontmuseet
Norway's Resistance Museum is situated at the top of the Akershus fortress. It provides a comprehensive picture of the years of German occupation in 1940–45 2

Christian Radich, 1937, is often moored at Akershus. The sailing ship achieved worldwide fame for its part in the film *Windjammer* (1957).

0 metres 100

0 yards 100

Star Sights

- ★ **Akershus Slott**
- ★ **Museet for Samtidskunst**

Key

- - - Suggested route

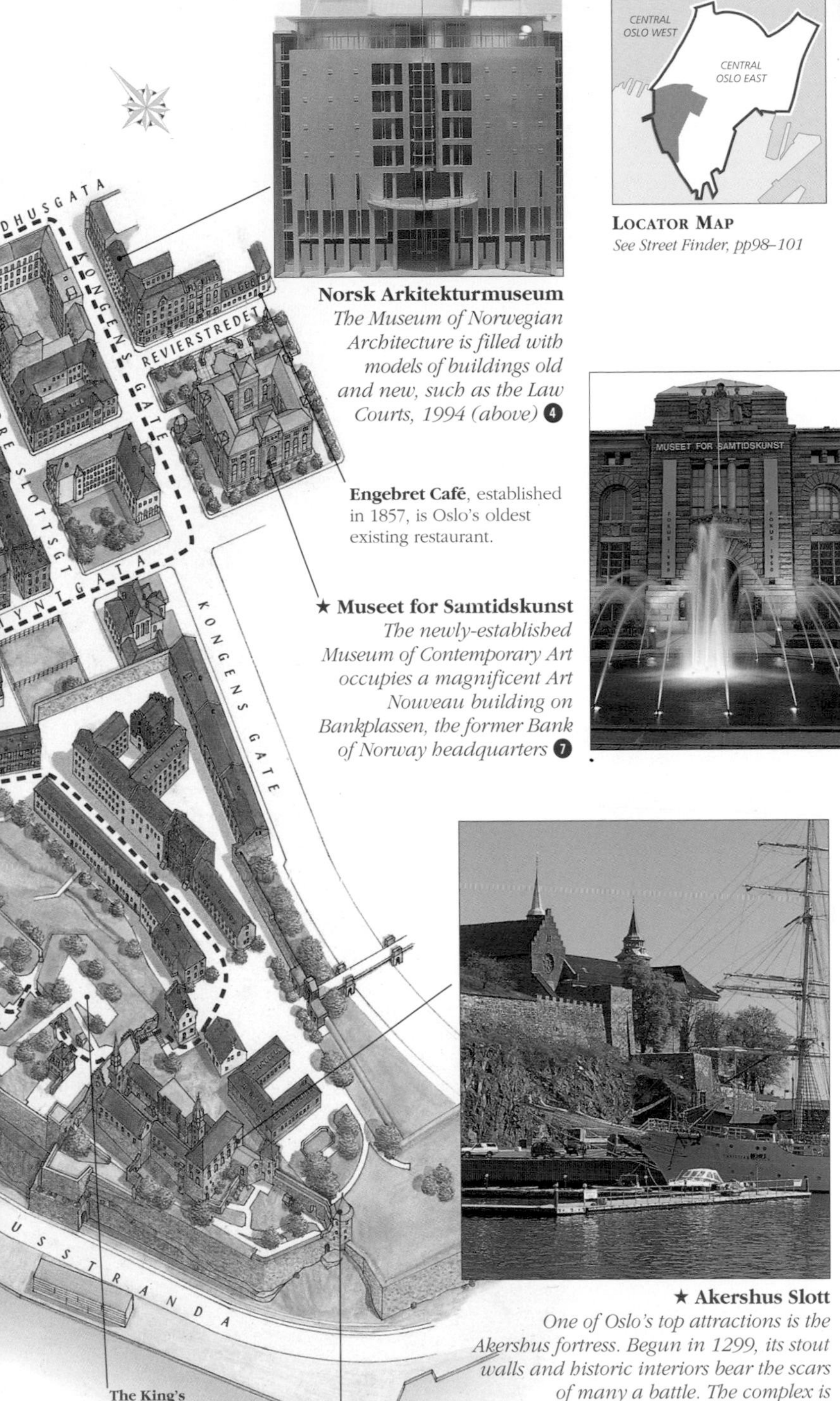

Locator Map
See Street Finder, pp98–101

Norsk Arkitekturmuseum
The Museum of Norwegian Architecture is filled with models of buildings old and new, such as the Law Courts, 1994 (above) ❹

Engebret Café, established in 1857, is Oslo's oldest existing restaurant.

★ Museet for Samtidskunst
The newly-established Museum of Contemporary Art occupies a magnificent Art Nouveau building on Bankplassen, the former Bank of Norway headquarters ❼

★ Akershus Slott
One of Oslo's top attractions is the Akershus fortress. Begun in 1299, its stout walls and historic interiors bear the scars of many a battle. The complex is strategically situated on a rocky outcrop with excellent views over Oslofjorden ❶

The King's Battery

Munketårnet

Akershus Slott ❶

See pp68–9.

Norges Hjemmefrontmuseum ❷

Akershus fortress area. **Map** 3 D4. 23 09 31 38. Stortinget. *10, 12 and a short walk from 13, 15, 19.* *60 and a short walk from 30, 31, 32, 45, 81, 83.* *1 Oct–14 Apr: 10am–3pm Mon–Fri; 11am–4pm Sat–Sun; 15 Apr–14 Jun: 10am–6pm Mon–Sat; 11am–4pm Sun; 15 Jun–31 Aug: 10am–7pm Mon, Wed, Fri, Sat; 10am–6pm Tue & Thu; 11am–5pm Sun; Sep: 10am–4pm Mon–Sat; 11am–4pm Sun.* *public hols.*

On 9 April 1940, German forces occupied Norway. While the Norwegians made a valiant attempt at halting their advance, the country succumbed 62 days later. For the next five years the Norwegian Resistance conducted a heroic campaign against the invaders and their exploits are well-documented in Norway's Resistance Museum. Taped speeches and film clips recreate the World War II years, and bring to life the comprehensive collection of documents, posters and memorabilia from that time.

The museum is in a 200-m (656-ft) long, 17th-century stone vault in Bindingsverkshuset (Half-Timbered House) at the top of Akershus Slott. It was opened on 8 May 1970, the 25th anniversary of the liberation. Next to the museum, there is a memorial to the Norwegians who were shot here during the war.

Model of old Christiania in Høymagasinet

Høymagasinet ❸

Akershus fortress area. **Map** 3 D4. 22 33 31 47. Stortinget. *10, 13 (Christiania Torv); 12, 13, 19 (Wessels Plass).* *60 (Akershusstranda).* *Jun-Aug: 10am–3pm Tue–Sun.*

A former hay barn at Akershus Slott is the location for Høymagasinet, a museum devoted to the history of Christiania from 1624 to 1840.

The year 1624 marked the devastating fire that left most of the old city of Oslo in ashes. The Danish-Norwegian king, Christian IV, decided to rebuild the city further west and named it Christiania. During the first 100 years reconstruction was slow, but it gathered speed in the 18th century. The history of the city over 200 years is illustrated with the help of models and other displays, in addition to a 25-minute long multimedia programme.

The museum also offers visitors short, guided walks through the streets of Kvadraturen *(see pp64–5)*, the original Christiania.

Norway's Resistance Museum depiction of the battles of April 1940

Norsk Arkitekturmuseum ❹

Kongens Gate 2. **Map** 3 E4. 22 42 40 80. Stortinget. *10, 12, 13, 15, 19.* *60 and a short walk from 30, 31, 32, 45, 81, 83.* *10am–6pm Mon, Tue, Thu & Fri; 11am–6pm Wed; noon–4pm Sat & Sun.* *public hols.*

Founded in 1975, the Museum of Norwegian Architecture features drawings, photographs and models covering 1,000 years of the nation's building history. On the 1st floor there is a permanent exhibition, *Houses of History*. The museum also arranges touring exhibitions of present and past architectural projects.

Norsk Arkitekturmuseum is located in old Christiania, in a building from the reign of Christian IV. The oldest part of the house dates from 1640. It underwent extensive renovation in 1993.

Teatermuseet 5

Christiania Torv 1. **Map** 3 D4. *22 42 65 09. Stortinget. 10, 12, 13, 15, 19. 60 and a short walk from 30, 31, 32, 45, 81, 83. 11am–5pm Wed; noon–6pm Thu; noon–4pm Sun. public hols.*

TEATERMUSEET (the Theatre Museum) is devoted to Oslo's dramatic arts from the early 19th century onward. Theatre, ballet, opera, musical revues and the circus are represented among the many paintings, photographs, models, posters, cartoons and costumes that are on display.

A significant part of the collection originates from the Christiania Theatre, which was built in 1837 and torn down in 1899. It was for many years the only theatre in town and plays by the Norwegian dramatists Henrik Ibsen and Bjørnstjerne Bjørnson were performed here for the first time.

The Theatre Museum occupies the first and second floors of the city's oldest town hall, Gamle Rådhus, which dates from 1641. There is a restaurant on the ground floor.

Wagnerian costume worn by the opera singer Kirsten Flagstad

Christiania Torv 6

Map 3 D4. *Stortinget. 10, 12, 13, 15, 19.*

THE SQUARE IS OLD, but the name is rather new. It was decided in 1958 that this part of Oslo's original market square *(torv)* should be called Christiania, after the old name for Oslo. For many years the square was plagued by heavy traffic. It underwent extensive renovation in the 1990s when traffic was diverted through a tunnel. Now free from vehicles, Christiania Torv is once more a pleasant place to visit. In 1997, a fountain created by the artist Wenche Gulbransen was erected in the square.

Christiania Torv, featuring some of Oslo's best-preserved buildings

Around the square are several historic buildings, among them the city's first town hall (now the Theatre Museum) and the Garnison Hospital, the oldest building in the capital and home to the Oslo Artists' Association.

Museet for Samtidskunst 7

See pp70–71.

Den Gamle Logen 8

Grev Wedels Plass 2. **Map** 3 D4. *22 33 44 70. Jernbanetorget. 10, 12, 13, 15, 19. 30, 31, 32, 41, 45, 60, 81, 83.*

IF WALLS COULD TALK those of Den Gamle Logen (The Old Lodge) would have a fascinating story to tell about the history of Oslo. The city council held its meetings here from the end of the 19th century until 1947. The lodge was also used as a court room during the legal proceedings against Vidkun Quisling *(see p41)*, who was sentenced to death for treason at the end of World War II.

Constructed by Freemasons in the 19th century, the design of the Old Lodge is based on drawings by Christian H Malling and Jens S Seidelin. It was opened in 1839.

The vast Neo-Classical banqueting hall is the central feature. Noted for its excellent acoustics, it was for a long time the city's foremost concert hall. But immediately after World War II, the lodge was taken over by the Oslo Port Labour Office and the splendid banqueting hall became a workers' canteen.

It reverted to its original use as a concert venue in the 1980s when Oslo Summer Opera moved in. The Old Lodge has since undergone extensive restoration and once again its beautiful rooms are being used for banquets and musical events. In the entrance there is a statue of Edvard Grieg, created by Marit Wiklund in 1993.

Den Gamle Logen concert hall at Grev Wedels Plass

Akershus Slott ❶

For 700 years the Akershus fortress has been standing guard over Oslo to ward off all attempts to invade the city from the sea. The castle occupies a spectacular setting on a hill at the head of Oslofjorden. King Håkon V began building in 1299, since when the fortifications have undergone numerous improvements and reconstructions. One of the fortress's greatest moments was to resist the siege of the Swedish king, Karl XII, in 1716. In the 19th century, the castle's defensive role declined in significance and it became an administrative centre for the armed forces. Today, Akershus Slott contains a variety of historic buildings, museums and defence installations. It is also the government's principal venue for state functions.

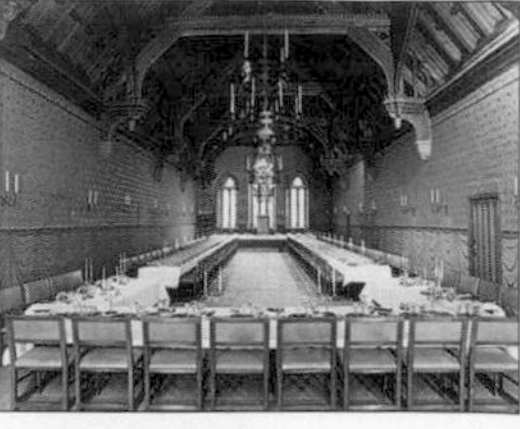

★ Olav's Hall
The North Hall was renovated in 1976 and named after King Olav V (1903–91).

Romeriks Tower

North Wing

The Romeriks Hall
The fireplace (1634–42) with the coat-of-arms of Governor-General Christopher Urne and his wife was found in another building in 1900 and restored to the castle.

Scribes Rooms
The rooms known as Skrivestuene were named after a timber-framed building called the Scribes Rooms House that once stood on this site. It was used by court administrators.

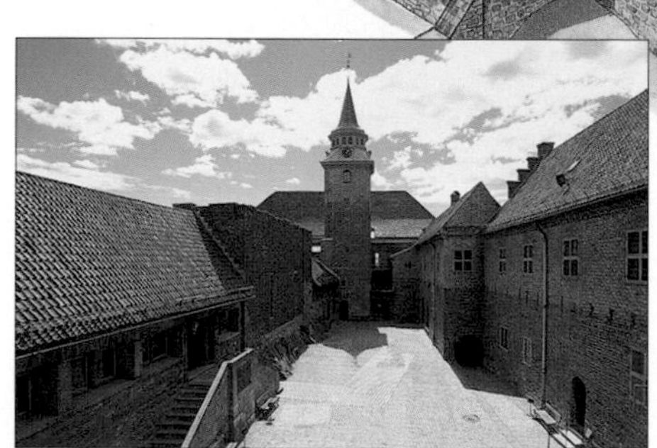

★ Courtyard
In the Middle Ages, the Courtyard (Borggården) was divided by a large tower, Vågehalsen, which was destroyed by fire in 1527. A Renaissance courtyard was created and the two towers, Romerikstårnet and Blåtårnet, were erected.

Star Features

- ★ Christian IV's Hall
- ★ Courtyard
- ★ Olav's Hall

Akershus Slott in 1699
A painting by Jacob Croning, who was attached to the court of the Danish-Norwegian Christian V. The king asked Croning to paint Norwegian scenes.

VISITORS' CHECKLIST

Map 3 D4. *23 09 39 17.* *Stortinget.* *10, 12 and a short walk from 13, 15, 19.* *60 and a short walk from 30, 31, 32, 45, 81, 83.*
Castle *2 May–15 Sep: 10am–4pm Mon-Sat; 12:30–4pm Sun.* *public hols.*
Fortress *6am–9pm daily.*

Remains of Vågehalsen, the medieval tower which once divided the courtyard.

The Blue Tower (Blåtårnet)

The tapestry, *Rideskolen*, was woven by E Leyniers, c.1650, to a design by J Jordaiens.

★ Christian IV's Hall
In the 17th century this hall formed part of the Danish king and queen's private apartments. In the 19th century it became a military arsenal. Now restored, it is used by the government for receptions.

South Wing

The Virgin Tower (Jomfrutårnet)

Royal Mausoleum
The mausoleum contains the remains of Sigurd Jorsalfar, Haakon VII and his wife Maud, and Olav V and Martha, among others.

The cellars were used as dungeons from 1500–1700. One of the dungeons was known as The Witch Hole. Later, prisoners were locked up in the fortress.

Museet for Samtidskunst 7

THE MUSEUM OF CONTEMPORARY ART is home to Norway's greatest collection of Norwegian and international modern art from the post-World War II period until today. Previously a department of the National Gallery, its opening in 1990 was heralded as a national event. It is now firmly established on the Norwegian arts scene and regularly hosts major international exhibitions. The permanent collection is so large that only part of it is on show at any one time. The museum may be new, but the building – the former head office of the Central Bank of Norway – is an example of Art Nouveau architecture from 1906. It is constructed in Norwegian granite and marble. The richly decorated Banking Hall provides an exciting contrast between old and new.

Winter Sun
Gunnar S Gundersen's Winter Sun *(1966) may be seen as an abstract impression of a landscape.*

★ Inner Room V
Per Inge Bjørlo's Inner Room V *(1990) is one of two permanent installations in the museum. It consists of metal plates and a sheet metal floor. The viewer is encouraged to step right into the installation.*

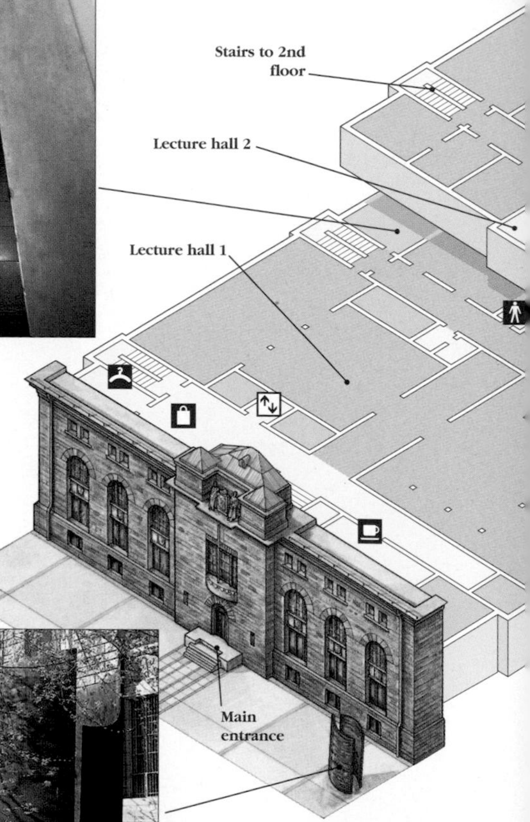

Stairs to 2nd floor

Lecture hall 2

Lecture hall 1

Main entrance

KEY

- Permanent exhibitions
- Temporary exhibitions
- Non-exhibition space
- Not open to the public

STAR FEATURES

- ★ ***Inner Room V*** **by Per Inge Bjørlo**
- ★ ***The Rubbish Man*** **by Ilya Kabakov**

Shaft
The museum's eye-catching landmark is Richard Serra's sculpture, Shaft *(1988). It stands at the entrance on Bankplassen.*

★ The Rubbish Man
Ilya Kabakov's installation (1983–95) is a "museum" of rubbish dedicated to the Man Who Never Threw Anything Away. Viewers can enter the room to experience the collector's mania and his passion for order.

Visitors' Checklist

4 Bankplassen. **Map** 3 D4. 22 86 22 10. *Stortinget.* *10, 12, 13, 15, 19.* *60.* *10am–5pm Tue, Wed, Fri; 10am–8pm Thu; 11am–4pm Sat; 11am–5pm Sun.* *public hols.* *free Thu.* www.museet.no

Tilted Form No. 3
Part of a series of six gouaches, Tilted Form No. 3 *(1987) is by the American Sol LeWitt, with variations on the same motif – the cube. This form of seriality is typical of the artist.*

Children's workshop

2nd floor

Skylight Hall

1st floor

Stairs to 1st floor

Ground floor

Banking Hall
The splendid Banking Hall (Banksalen) provides a challenging contrast to the contemporary art now adorning its halls.

Gallery Guide

The museum has three floors. The ground floor has temporary exhibitions in addition to one of the museum's two permanent installations. There is also a bookshop and a café. The first floor is devoted to temporary exhibitions. The second floor features a permanent installation and a children's workshop.

Without Title
Per Maning is known for his photographic portraits of animals, mainly dogs, seals and monkeys. This portrait shows a cow with its eyes closed (1990), against a typical Norwegian landscape.

Battle scene tableau on display at Forsvarsmuseet

Forsvarsmuseet ❾

Akershus Slott, Building 62. **Map** 3 D5. *23 09 35 82.* *10, 12, 13, 15, 19.* *60.* *Jun–Aug: 10am–6pm Mon–Fri; 11am–3pm Sat & Sun; Sep–May: 10am–3pm Mon–Fri; 11am–4pm Sat & Sun.* *public hols.*

The history of the Norwegian armed forces, from Viking times to the present day, is represented in Forsvarsmuseet (the Armed Forces Museum) at Akershus Slott. Two large brick buildings from the 1860s, once used as military arsenals, provide an appropriate historical setting.

Of the military items on display, there is a collection from the time of the union with Denmark in the 16th century, and the subsequent Nordic wars, through to the struggle for independence during the union with Sweden. The exhibits are arranged in time blocks, and include a number of life-like models and objects, such as a German tank and a V-1 bomb from World War II.

Astrup Fearnley Museet ❿

Dronningens Gate 4. **Map** 3 E4. *22 93 60 60.* *Jernbanetorget.* *10, 12, 13, 15, 19.* *30, 31, 32, 45, 60, 81, 83.* *11am–5pm Tue, Wed, Fri, 11am–7pm Thu, noon–5pm Sat & Sun.* *public hols.* *1pm Sat & Sun.*

The Astrup Fearnley museum shows both Norwegian and international art from the post-World War II period to the present day.

The majority of pictures on display belong to the museum's own collection. There are works by Francis Bacon, Lucian Freud and R B Kitaj, key figures in the School of London. Other international names in the collection include Anselm Kiefer, Gerhard Richter, Cindy Sherman and Damien Hirst. Norwegian art is represented with works by Knut Rose, Bjørn Carlsen, Olav Christopher Jenssen, Kjell Torriset and Odd Nerdrum.

Opened in 1993, the building is characterized by the use of modern materials and design. The exhibition halls are large and airy with high ceilings allowing plenty of space to show contemporary art to its full advantage. The two main halls are called *Impulsen* (The Impulse) and *Skulpturgården* (The Sculpture Court).

The museum was established as a result of funds and charitable trusts set up by the Astrup and Fearnley families who, since the 1800s, have made their mark on Norwegian business life and society. Hans Rasmus Astrup (1831–98) was a politician and a successful businessman who amassed a considerable fortune. Thomas Fearnley (1880–1961) was a shipowner, with an interest in the arts. He set up the Thomas Fearnleys Contribution and Gift Fund.

In addition to the larger shows, the museum also mounts smaller exhibitions of shorter duration.

Astrup Fearnley Museet showing art in a modern setting

Børsen (the Stock Exchange) featuring a Neo-Classical exterior

Børsen ⓫

Tollbugata 2. **Map** 3 E4. *22 34 17 00.* *Jernbanetorget.* *10, 11, 13, 15, 19.* *30, 31, 32, 45, 60, 81, 83.* *by arrangement.* *special tours can be arranged.*

One of the oldest institutional buildings in Oslo is Børsen (the Stock Exchange). Long before the construction of the royal palace and the parliament building it was decided that the trading of commodities should take place on a site of its own. Børsen was opened in 1828, the first of Oslo's grand buildings. Designed by the architect Christian H Grosch, the Neo-Classical façade with its Doric columns contrasts strongly with the more modern buildings nearby. The two side wings and a southern wing were added in 1910.

Originally, there was an enclosed courtyard containing a statue of Mercury. The statue was moved outside when the courtyard was redesigned to house the new Stock Exchange hall in 1988.

The entrance hall is dominated by Gerhard Munthe's mural painting from 1912, *Handelen og Sjøfarten (Trade and Shipping)*.

Børsen also has its own library, reading room, antique trade museum and a portrait gallery.

Postmuseet ⓬

Kirkegata 20. **Map** 3 E4.
23 14 80 59. Stortinget. 10, 12, 13, 15, 19. 30, 31, 32, 42, 60, 81, 83. 10am–5pm Mon–Fri; 10am–2pm Sat; noon–4pm Sun.

IN 1872 THE POST horn appeared for the first time as a symbol on Norwegian stamps and its use continues to this day.

A large number of post horn stamps are on show in Postmuseet (the Post Museum) alongside a fine collection of objects connected with the history of the post office over the centuries. Of particular interest is the display relating to the story of Gunnar Turtveit, a postman who in 1903 was buried beneath an avalanche near Odda. Fifty-six hours later he emerged having used his horn to dig himself out through the snow.

A model in the Postmuseet showing how mail was delivered

Richly-carved pulpit in Oslo Domkirke dating from 1699

Among the other exhibits, philatelists can feast on the wide-ranging collection of Norwegian stamps, including sketches, variants, printing errors and sample print runs. There is a good selection of stamped letters, too. Also on show are postmen's uniforms, weapons and a large collection of old message cylinders known as *budstikker*.

Oslo Domkirke ⓭

Stortorget 1. **Map** 3 E3.
23 31 46 00. Jernbanetorget, Stortinget. 10, 11, 17, 18. 13, 15, 19. 11am–4pm daily. 11 am & 7:30pm Sun; noon Wed in Eng, Ger or Fre.

OSLO DOMKIRKE (cathedral) is the principal church for the diocese of Oslo. The foundation stone was laid in 1694, and the church was built in several stages. The altarpiece and pulpit date from 1699; the interior was completed in the 1720s.

Since then there have been a series of reconstructions and renovations. In the mid-1850s the Baroque interior was remodelled in Neo-Gothic style. In the course of a subsequent restoration 100 years later, the baptismal font, altarpiece and pulpit were changed back to the pre-1850 style. When the sacristy was renovated in 1963, rich decorations from the 18th century were discovered.

Cathedral doorway

Among the adornments are stained glass windows by Emanuel Vigeland, a silver sculpture with a Lord's Supper motif by Arrigo Minerbi and bronze doors by Dagfin Werenskiold. The modern painted ceiling, depicting scenes from the Bible, was created by Hugo Louis Mohr between 1936 and 1950. In the course of this work, the original ceiling paintings were destroyed, an act which has since attracted much criticism.

The cathedral has 900 seats and was the venue for the wedding ceremony of Crown Prince Haakon and Mette-Marit in 2001.

In its tower hangs the great bell, weighing 1,600 kg (3,527 lb), and three smaller bells. The great bell has been recast six times.

Below the ground floor of the cathedral is a crypt.

Stortinget, home of the Norwegian parliament, centrally situated just off Karl Johans Gate

Stortinget ⓮

Karl Johans Gate 22. **Map** 3 D3. *23 31 31 80. Stortinget. 13, 15, 19. 30, 31, 32, 41, 45, 81, 83. guided tours only. Sat: 10am Nor, Eng & Ger, 11:30am Nor & Ger, 1pm Nor, Eng & Ger; 1 Jul–20 Aug Mon–Fri: 10am Nor & Eng, 11:30am Nor & Ger, 1pm Nor, Eng & Ger.*

NORWAY'S NATIONAL Assembly has its seat in the grand Stortinget (Norwegian Parliament building). The building was designed by the Swedish architect, Emil Victor Langlet, after a long and bitter debate and a series of different proposals. The foundation stone was laid on 10 October 1861. Construction took five years and in March 1866 the assembly met for the first time in its own building.

Stortinget is built of yellow brick on a reddish granite base. The style is a blend of Norwegian and Italian building traditions. It has been expanded and partly reconstructed on several occasions. The new wing toward Akersgata was added in the 1950s.

The assembly chamber, which seats the 165 members of parliament, resembles an amphitheatre, with the speaker's chair positioned below Oscar Wergeland's painting of the 1814 Eidsvoll assembly, which ratified the Norwegian constitution *(see p38)*. The painting dates from 1885, and depicts the men who helped to shape Norway's constitution.

The building has been richly embellished by Norwegian artists, including the painter Else Hagen who decorated the stairwell. A tapestry, *Solens Gang*, by Karen Holtsmark, hangs in the central hall. The sculptures in the stair hall are by Nils Flakstad.

Oslo Nye Teater ⓯

Rosenkrantzgate 10. **Map** 3 D3. *22 34 86 00. Stortinget. 13, 15, 19. 30, 31, 32, 45, 81, 83.* **Box Office** *9am–4pm Mon, 9am–7pm Tue–Fri, 10am–6pm Sat.*

THERE ARE THREE theatres in what is known as Oslo Nye Teater (the Oslo New Theatre): Hovedscenen (Main Theatre) in Rosenkrantzgate; Centralteateret in Akersgata; and Dukketeateret (Puppet Theatre) in Frognerparken.

Oslo Nye Teater, a modern and lively city centre theatre

Hovedscenen was established in the 1920s with the aim of providing a stage for new Norwegian and foreign drama. However, the repertoire was for many years dominated by comedy with leading revue artists. Recently there has been a move toward creating a more urbane and modern theatre with a bolder, fresher approach and an emphasis on younger actors who are just establishing themselves.

Regjerings-kvartalet ⓰

Akersgata 42. **Map** 3 E3. *22 24 90 90. Stortinget. 10, 11, 17, 18. 33, 37, 46.*

THE LARGE complex on Akersgata housing the various government departments is known as Regjeringskvartalet (the Government Quarter). It is dominated by a tall H-block in which the prime minister has a suite of offices on the top floors.

Regjeringskvartalet was developed in five stages during the years 1958–96. The architect for the four first stages was Erling Viksjø. Torstein Ramberg designed the fifth stage.

The complex has been the subject of great controversy. In

order to clear the ground, the historic, conservation-worthy Empirekvartalet (Empire Quarter) was torn down. This led to an intense debate about conservation in the 1950s. Today's politicians would probably not have authorized the demolition of such a distinctive area.

The 12-floor, concrete H-block was completed in 1958. A further two floors were added in 1990.

The building features decorative art by Kai Fjell, Tore Haaland, Inger Sitter, Odd Tandberg, Erling Viksjø, Carl Nesjar and Pablo Picasso. Nesjar and the Spanish master collaborated to transfer three drawings by Picasso on to the concrete façade on the Akersgata frontage.

Bust of E Gerhardsen, Prime Minister 1945–65, Regjeringskvartalet

Youngstorget ⓱

Map 3 E3. Ⓣ *Jernbanetorget.* *10, 11, 12, 13, 15, 17.* *30, 31, 32, 34, 38, 56.*

MANY OF THE Labour movement's most important institutions have their headquarters around Youngstorget, among them the Norwegian Labour Party and the Norwegian Trades Union Federation, *Landsorganisationen.* Other political parties such as *Fremskrittspartiet* (Progress Party) and *Venstre* (Liberals), also have offices in the area.

Youngstorget was laid out in 1846, and was for many years a cattle market. The square is named after the merchant Jørgen Young, who originally owned the area. In 1990 it underwent a substantial renovation. A copy of the original fountain from 1880 was installed and the market kiosks from 1876 were restored. There are shops, workshops and various places to eat and drink in the market.

Youngstorget with its market, opera house and trades union offices

Den Norske Opera ⓲

Storgaten 23. **Map** 3 E3. *23 31 50 00.* Ⓣ *Jernbanetorget.* *10, 11, 12, 13, 15, 17.* *30, 31, 32, 34, 38, 56.* **Box Office** *10am–6pm Mon–Fri; 10am–2pm Sat.* *by arrangement.*

OSLO ACQUIRED its first opera house in 1959. It was opened on the premises of what had been the long-established Folketeatret, built in 1932–5. The former theatre has never been ideally suited to opera and is due to be replaced by a spectacular new opera house that is being built on the waterfront at Bjørvika. It is expected to open around 2010.

Norway's foremost operatic star, the soprano Kirsten Flagstad (1895–1962), was the first director of the Norwegian State Opera.

Oslo Spektrum ⓳

Sonja Henies Plass 2. **Map** 3 F3. *22 05 29 00.* Ⓣ *Jernbanetorget.* *10, 12, 13, 15, 18, 19.* *30, 31, 32, 34, 38, 41, 45, 46.* **Box Office** *9am–4pm Mon–Fri; 10am–3pm Sat.*

THE 10,800 CAPACITY Oslo Spektrum is the main venue for large-scale sporting and cultural events and trade fairs. Designed by Lars Haukland, the complex was completed in 1991.

Major events such as the Norwegian Military Tattoo (September), the Oslo Horse Show, featuring dressage and show-jumping (October), and the Nobel Peace Prize concert (December) are held here. International pop stars, including Paul McCartney, Elton John and Sting, perform at the stadium. It is also the venue for national handball matches.

The façade is clad with a striking 200-m (656-ft) long mosaic designed by Rolf Nesch and crafted by Guttorm Guttormsgaard. Made up from 40,000 glazed bricks, it features an eye-catching mix of abstract shapes interspersed with human figures.

Oslo Spektrum, the city's main venue for sport, culture and trade fairs

GOKSTADSKIBET

BYGDØY

SITUATED ON THE INNERMOST reaches of Oslofjorden, Bygdøy is just a short distance from the city centre. Bygdøy means "the inhabited island", and it was an island until the end of the 19th century when the sound between Frognerkilen and Bestumkilen was filled in. It is one of the city's most exclusive residential areas and a popular tourist destination.

Bygdøy is home to a select group of museums which collectively reflect Norway's cultural history and national life, its seafaring traditions and intrepid voyages of discovery.

Sailors' memorial, Bygdøynes

Kongsgården covers half the island and is run as an independent farm. The area's connections with royalty go back to the 16th century when the Danish-Norwegian kings came here to hunt. Much of Bygdøy is still forested. There are groves, meadows and parkland, and a wealth of different plant species.

Several of Oslo's most popular bathing beaches, including Huk and Paradisbukta, are on Bygdøy.

SIGHTS AT A GLANCE

Museums

Frammuseet ❻
Kon-Tiki Museet ❹
Norsk Folkemuseum pp82–3 ❷
Norsk Sjøfartsmuseum ❺
Vikingskipshuset pp84–5 ❸

Interesting Buildings

Bygdøy Kongsgård ❾
Dronningen ❶
Oscarshall Slott ❿

Nature Reserve

Hukodden ❽

Churches

Sjømannskirken ❼

KEY

- Street-by-Street map *pp78–9*
- Bus terminal
- Parking
- Ferry terminal

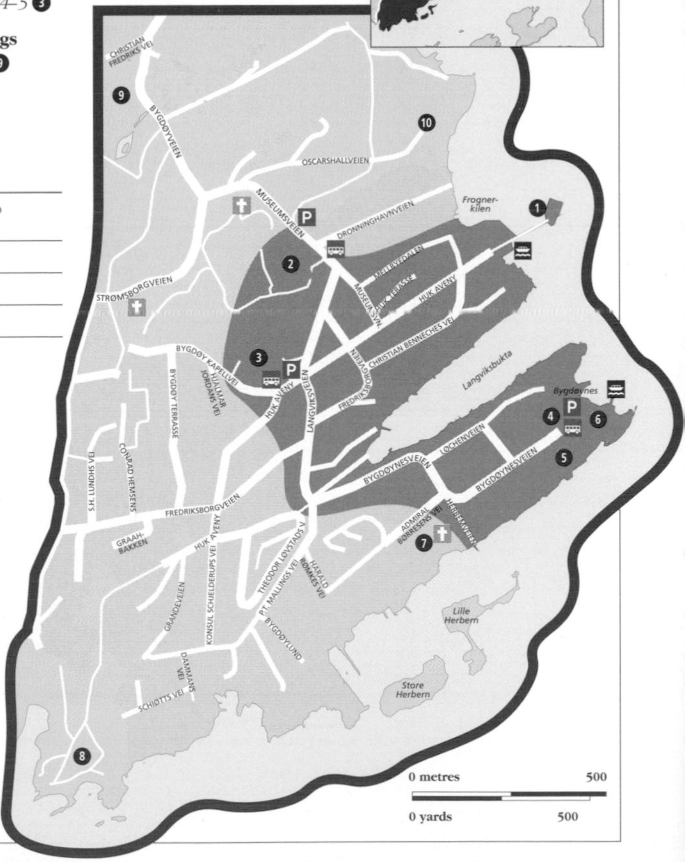

0 metres 500
0 yards 500

GETTING THERE

It is very easy to get to Bygdøy and its museums. Ferries leave from the quayside directly opposite Rådhuset several times an hour. The trip only takes a few minutes. Buses 30 B (Oct–Apr) and 30 also depart several times an hour from Jernbanetorvet and Nationaltheatret.

◁ **Gokstadskipet, a well-preserved burial ship on display in the Vikingskipshuset in Bygdøy**

Street-by-Street: Around Bygdøynes

Bird's nesting box, Norsk Folkemuseum

A VISIT TO OSLO would not be complete without a trip to Bygdøy and the peninsula of Bygdøynes. This is where locals and tourists alike go to enjoy the beautiful outdoors and to explore some of the most remarkable museums in Europe. Viking ships, polar expeditions and daring voyages across the Pacific Ocean on rafts such as the *Kon-Tiki* form the focal points for three of the collections. Stave churches and rural buildings have been reassembled to create the open-air Norsk Folkemuseum. Bygdøy is accessible by car, bus and ferry *(see p77)*.

★ Norsk Folkemuseum
Set in an idyllic landscape, the museum features 150 reconstructed townhouses, farm buildings and churches from Norway's past. Inside there are exhibitions of folk art and costumes ❷

Gamlebyen at the Norsk Folkemuseum is a collection of old, restored townhouses.

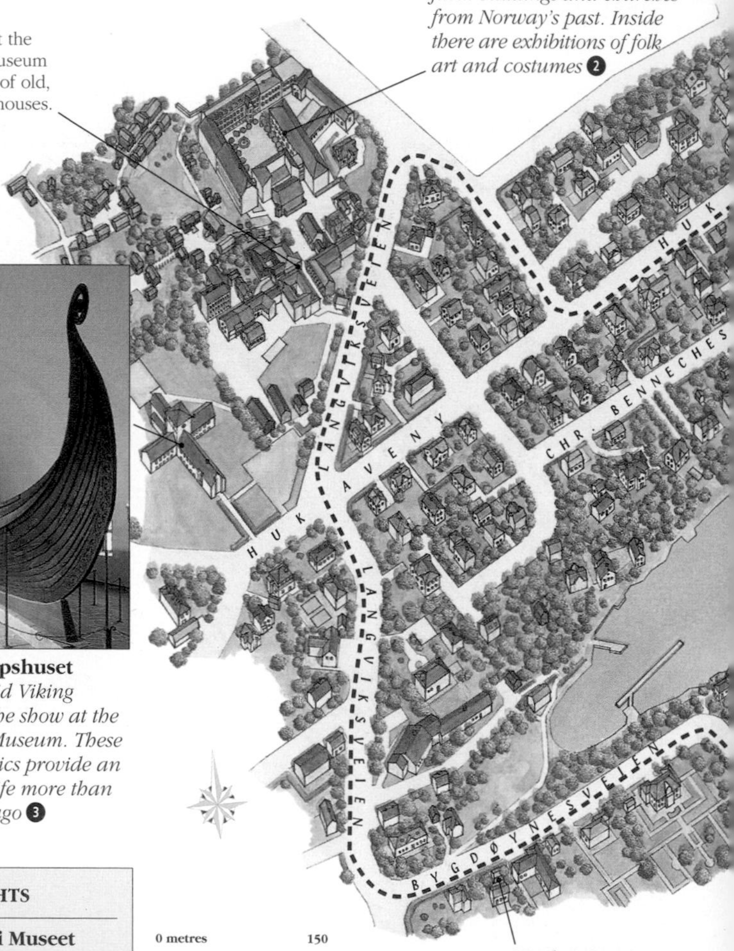

★ Vikingskipshuset
Three splendid Viking vessels steal the show at the Viking Ship Museum. These and other relics provide an insight into life more than 1,000 years ago ❸

Stately private homes and embassies are situated in the area along Bydøynesveien.

STAR SIGHTS

- ★ Kon-Tiki Museet
- ★ Norsk Folkemuseum
- ★ Vikingskipshuset

0 metres 150

0 yards 150

KEY

- - - Suggested route

Dronningen
Former restaurant Dronningen, now the headquarters of the sailing club, Kongelig Norsk Seilforning, forms a prominent landmark of Functionalist-style architecture on the fjord's shoreline ❶

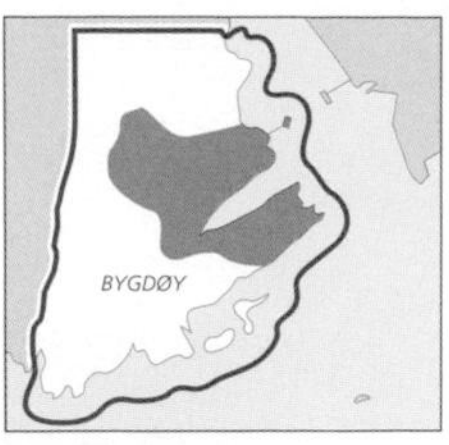

Locator Map
See Street Finder p99

★ Kon-Tiki Museet
The main attractions at the Kon-Tiki Museum are the balsa wood raft, Kon-Tiki *(1947), and the reed boat,* Ra II *(1970). Thor Heyerdahl won worldwide acclaim when he set sail across the oceans in these craft* ❹

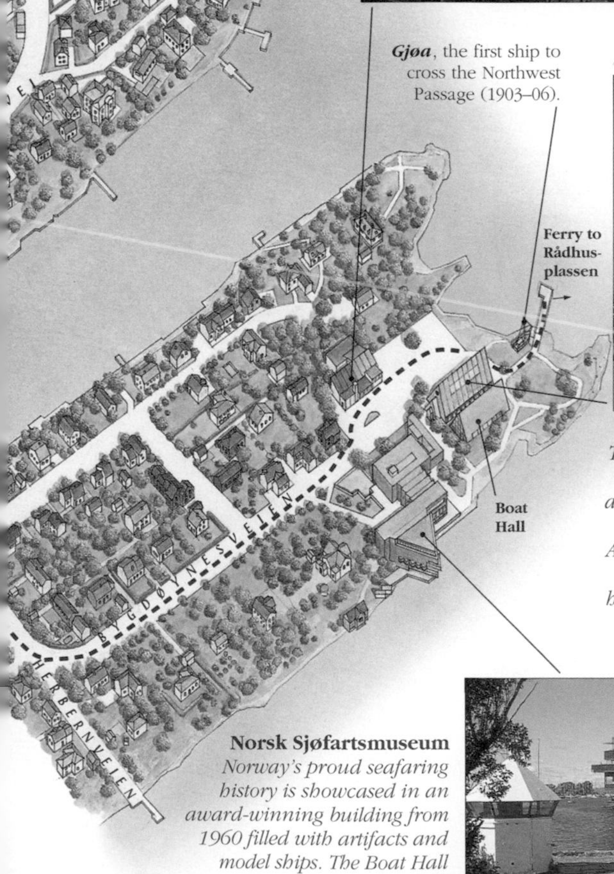

Ferry to Rådhusplassen via Bygdøynes

Gjøa, the first ship to cross the Northwest Passage (1903–06).

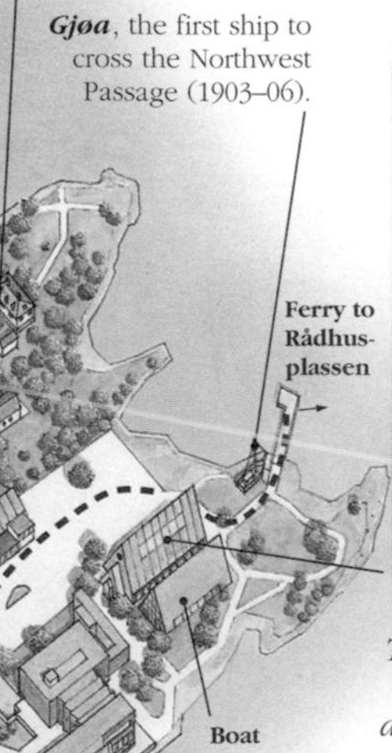

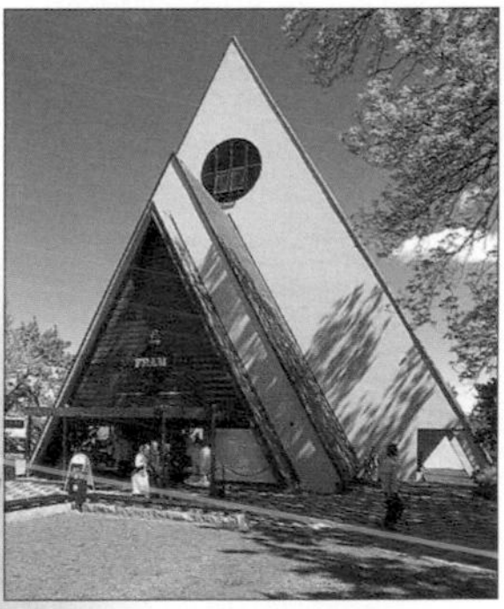

Ferry to Rådhusplassen

Boat Hall

BYGDØYNESVEIEN

HERBERNVEIEN

Frammuseet
The museum is dedicated to the polar ship Fram *(1892) and the expeditions made by Fridtjof Nansen and Roald Amundsen to the Arctic and Antarctic* (see p23). *Their heroic exploits are captured in the various displays* ❻

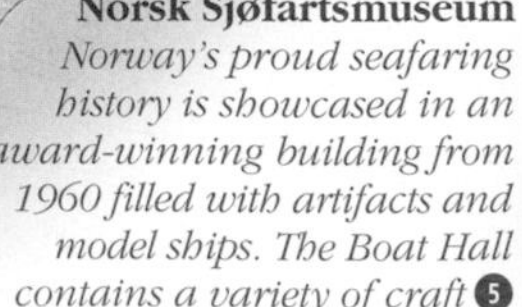

Norsk Sjøfartsmuseum
Norway's proud seafaring history is showcased in an award-winning building from 1960 filled with artifacts and model ships. The Boat Hall contains a variety of craft ❺

Dronningen, an architectural landmark on the Frognerkilen waterfront

Dronningen ❶

Huk Aveny 1. **Map** 1 C3.
22 43 75 75. 91 (May–Sep). 30 (a short distance away).

BEFORE AND AFTER World War II, Dronningen ("the Queen") was one of Oslo's most popular summer restaurants. The building, constructed in 1930, was one of the first to be designed in the Functionalist style in Norway. It is situated on Dronningskjæret in Frognerkilen. However, in 1983 it was converted to offices. The Royal Norwegian Yacht Club and the Norwegian Students' Rowing Club are based here.

Dronningen ("the Queen") was often associated with Kongen ("the King"), a restaurant and summer variety theatre on the opposite side of Frognerkilen. In 1986 it, too, was converted to offices.

Frognerkilen is a major sailing centre dotted with large yachting marinas.

Norsk Folkemuseum ❷

See pp82–3.

Vikingskipshuset ❸

See pp84–5.

Kon-Tiki Museet ❹

Bygdøynesveien 36. **Map** 1 C4.
23 08 67 67. 91 (May–Sep). 30. Apr–May: 10:30am–5pm daily; Jun–Aug: 9:30am–5:45pm; Sep: 10:30am–5pm; Oct–Mar: 10:30am–4pm. public hols.

THE WORLD watched with interest when Thor Heyerdahl (1914–2002) and his five-man crew sailed across the Pacific in the fragile balsa-wood raft, *Kon-Tiki*, in 1947. Over the course of 101 days the raft covered 8,000 km (4,970 miles) from Peru to Polynesia. The voyage proved that it would have been possible for South Americans to have reached Polynesia in bygone days on balsa rafts. The raft is the main attraction in the Kon-Tiki Museet. A number of objects connected with the voyage are also on show.

Text and montages in both Norwegian and English give a graphic account of how those on board must have felt to have been so close to marine life that it was possible to catch sharks with their bare hands. They describe how on one occasion they felt a massive whale shark pushing against the raft.

Heyerdahl embarked on a new expedition in 1970. He sailed a papyrus boat, *Ra II*, across the Atlantic from Morocco to Barbados to prove a theory that it was possible for West African explorers to have landed in the West Indies before Columbus. *Ra I* had broken up well into the voyage due to a design fault, but *Ra II* survived and is on display in the museum.

Seven years later, Heyerdahl steered the reed boat, *Tigris*, across the Indian Ocean to prove that the ancient civilizations of the Indus valley and Egypt had contact with each other.

Polynesian mask, Kon-Tiki Museet

The museum's exhibits include a large number of archaeological finds from Heyerdahl's expeditions to places such as Easter Island and Peru.

Its 8,000-volume library contains the world's largest collection of literature about Polynesia.

The balsa-wood raft, *Kon-Tiki*, in the Kon-Tiki Museet on Bygdøy

Norsk Sjøfarts-museum ❺

Bygdøynesveien 37. **Map** 1 C4.
22 43 82 40. 91 (May–Sep). 30. 15 May–30 Sep: 10am–6pm daily; Oct–May: 10.30am–4pm daily (10:30am–6pm Thu). some public hols.

THE MOST SOUTHERLY of the museums on the idyllic Bygdøy peninsula is Norsk Sjøfartsmuseum (the Norwegian Maritime Museum). It is located on the shore near the Frammuseet and Kon-Tiki Museet, and has its own quay and a marvellous view over Oslo's harbour and its approach from the fjord.

Norwegian maritime traditions, including the fishing industry, shipbuilding, shipping and marine archaeology, form the focal point of the collection. Norway's 1,500-year-old tradition of boat-building is a key part of its coastal culture.

The museum traces the development of shipping from the Middle Ages to present-day supertankers. The main theme linking the exhibits is man's use of the sea through the ages and how people have faced up to the challenges and dangers of this mighty element.

From the museum's main entrance, visitors enter the Central Hall containing a model of the Norwegian Navy's steam frigate, *Kong Sverre*, one of three of the largest and most powerful warships ever to be built in Nordic lands. Christian Krohg's painting, *Leiv Eiriksson Discovers America* *(see pp34–5)*, hangs on one of the walls. The exhibition halls feature an abundance of model ships through the ages in addition to relics from various maritime activities.

In the Boat Hall traditional fishing craft and working vessels are on show, and there is a display on the diversity of coastal culture. The schooner, *Svanen*, is often moored at the quayside when it is not at sea as a training ship for young people. Also standing outside the museum is the *Krigseilermonument*, which commemorates sailors killed in World War II *(see p77)*.

Figurehead in the Sjøfartsmuseum

The museum is the centre for a marine archaeological department, which protects any finds discovered along the Norwegian coast.

The well-stocked museum library contains a collection of drawings, marine literature, archives and photographs.

Boat Hall of the Sjøfartsmuseum, Frammuseet and the polar vessel, *Gjøa*

Frammuseet ❻

Bygdøynesveien 36. **Map** 1 C4.
23 28 29 50. 91 (May–Sep). 30. Nov–Feb: 11am–2:45pm Mon–Fri; 11am–3:45pm Sat & Sun. Mar–Apr: 11am–3:45 daily. 1 May–16 May: 10am–4:45pm daily. 18 May-15 Jun: 9am–5:45pm daily. 16 Jun–Aug: 9am–6:45pm daily. Sep: 10am–4:45pm daily. Oct: 10am–3:45pm daily. public hols.

NO OTHER SAILING vessel has been further north or south in the world than the polar ship, *Fram*. It was used for three Arctic expeditions by the explorers Fridtjof Nansen (1893–96), Otto Sverdrup (1898–1902) and Roald Amundsen (1910–12). On the third expedition, in 1911, Amundsen became the first person to raise a flag on the South Pole.

The schooner was built by Colin Archer, and was specially constructed to prevent it from being crushed by pack ice. On its first commission with Nansen's expedition to the North Pole, it was frozen in at 78º 50'N. The vessel's rounded form allowed it to be pressed up onto the ice, where it remained undamaged until the ice thawed. *Fram* also proved itself to be extremely seaworthy in the stormy Antarctic Ocean on Amundsen's historic expedition to the South Pole.

The museum opened in 1936 with the restored ship as its centrepiece. Expedition equipment, paintings, busts and photographs of the polar explorers are on show. Outside the museum is Amundsen's first polar exploration vessel, *Gjøa*.

The deck of the polar exploration vessel, *Fram*, at the Frammuseet

Norsk Folkemuseum ❷

Gol stave church

More than 150 buildings from all over Norway have been assembled in Europe's original and largest open-air museum, the Norsk Folkemuseum on Bygdøy. It was established by Hans Aall in 1894 at a time of widespread nationalist enthusiasm. The recreated farms evoke the pattern of everyday life in the valley, fjord and fishing communities of bygone times. Town buildings from all parts of the country have been reconstructed to create Gamlebyen (the Old Town). Traditional folk costumes are on show and Norwegian folk art, with its rich tradition of woodcarving, is well represented. An annual highlight is Julemarkedet (the Christmas market) in December.

King Oscar II's collection of buildings *(see p87)* became part of the Folkemuseum in 1907.

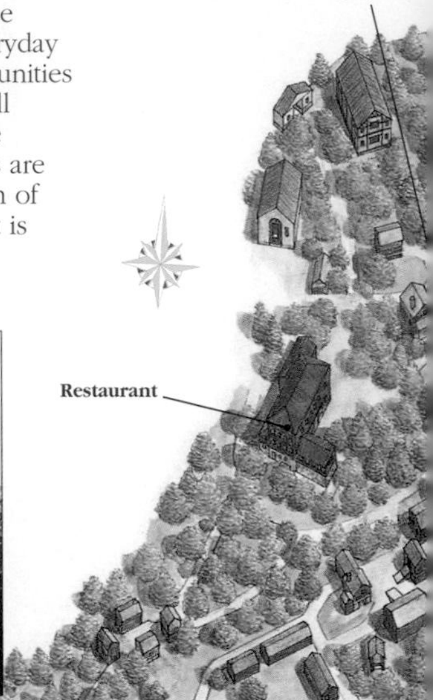

Festplassen
In the middle of the open-air museum is a square, Festplassen, surrounded by timber buildings from different parts of Norway. The square is used for dancing displays and other special events such as these Midsummer Eve celebrations.

Restaurant

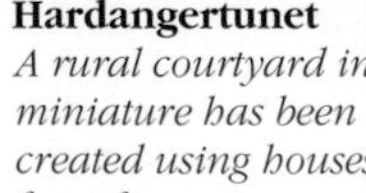

Hardangertunet
A rural courtyard in miniature has been created using houses from farms in Hardanger, Vestlandet.

Hallingdalstunet
This is an example of a rectangular courtyard commonly found in Hallingdal. The oldest building is the Hemsedal storehouse (1650–1700). The goatshed from Hol dates from the 18th century.

0 metres 50

0 yards 50

Star Features

- ★ **Gamlebyen**
- ★ **Gol Stave Church**
- ★ **Setesdaltunet**

Open-air theatre

Main entrance

Museum shop

★ Gol Stave Church
Adorned with paintings and carvings, the Gol stave church was built in Hallingdal in 1200. It is one of 30 preserved stave churches in Norway.

Visitors' Checklist

Museumsveien 10. **Map** 1 B3. 22 12 37 00. 91 (May–Sep) 30. 15 May–14 Sep: 10am–6pm daily; 15 Sep–14 May: 11am–3pm Mon–Fri; 11am–4pm Sat & Sun. 24–25 Dec, 31 Dec, 1 Jan, 17 May.
www.norskfolke.museum.no

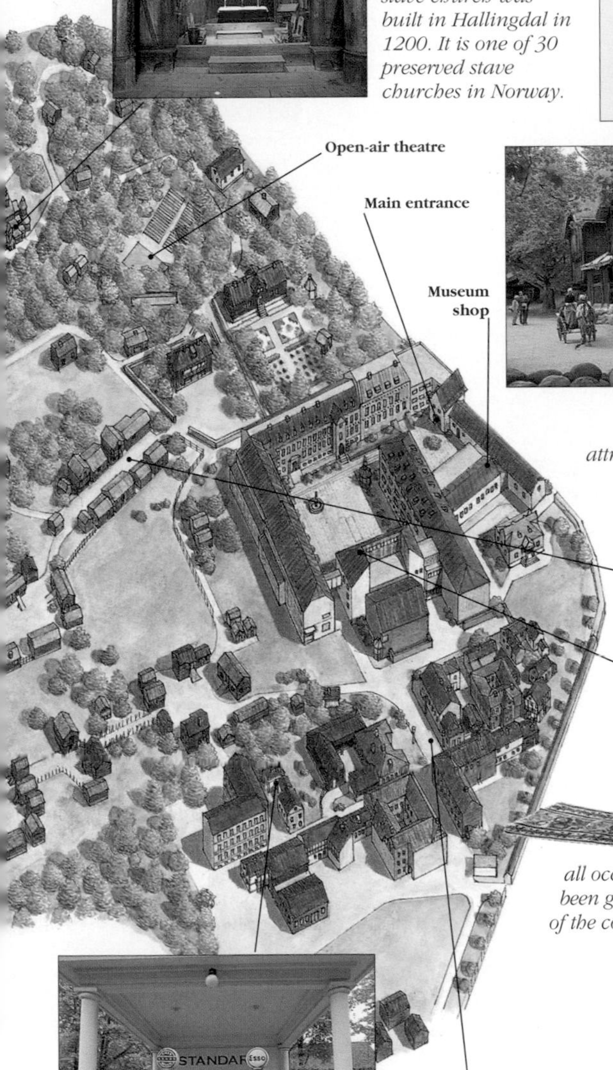

★ Setesdaltunet
Among the most popular attractions in the museum is a collection of buildings from Setesdal in southern Norway. Two of the open-hearth rooms have a fireplace in the centre.

Social Customs and Clothing
Folk costumes for all occasions throughout life have been gathered from different parts of the country to create this display.

Petrol Station
This reconstructed concrete petrol station is typical of the 1920s. The pumps and other equipment featured are all original.

★ Gamlebyen
Buildings from old Christiania (Oslo) and elsewhere have been reconstructed to form Gamlebyen. Townhouses from the Oslo suburb of Enerhaugen, which were demolished in the 1960s, are also on show.

Vikingskipshuset 3

Detail from the Oseberg wagon

Two of the world's best-preserved Viking ships from the 9th century and sections of a third can be seen in Vikingskipshuset (the Viking Ship Museum). Found in three large burial mounds on farmland, the ships are considered to be among Norway's greatest cultural treasures. The Oseberg and Gokstad vessels were discovered in Vestfold, and the Tune ship at Haugen in Tune, Østfold. They were used to transport the bodies of high-ranking chieftains on their last journey to the kingdom of the dead. Pieces of jewellery, weapons and implements were also found in the graves. The museum was designed by Arnstein Arneberg in 1914 to create a light, airy setting for the ships, which can be explored from relatively close quarters.

Exterior view of the steep-pitched Vikingskipshuset

★ Oseberg Ship
In 1904 archaeologists opened the grave where the Oseberg ship was found along with the remains of two women and a large number of artifacts. About 90 per cent of the 22-m (72-ft) long ship is of original wood.

Entrance hall

Main entrance

★ Gokstad Ship
The excavation of the 24-m (79-ft) long Gokstad ship took place in 1880. The remains of a 60-year-old man, a sledge, three small boats, a gangplank and 64 shields were uncovered. The vessel has 16 pieces of planking on each side compared to the Oseberg's 12 pieces.

Key to Floorplan

- Oseberg Ship
- Gokstad Ship
- Tune Ship
- Oseberg Collection
- Non-exhibition space

Star Features

- ★ Gokstad Ship
- ★ Oseberg Ship
- ★ Oseberg Wagon

Gallery Guide
The main attractions are arranged in the form of a cross. Nearest to the entrance hall stands the Oseberg ship and on the far side is the Oseberg Collection. The Gokstad ship stands alone in the left wing. The least well-preserved find, the Tune ship, is housed in the right wing. In the gallery above the entrance, reproductions of three wooden beds are displayed. To the left of the entrance is the museum shop.

★ Oseberg Wagon
The richly carved Oseberg wagon is the only one known to exist from the Viking period in Norway. It was probably used by women of high status. Similar wagons have been found in Denmark and Germany.

Visitors' Checklist

Huk Aveny 35. **Map** 1 A3. *22 43 83 79.* *91 (May–Sep).* *30.* *May–Sep: 9am–6pm daily; Oct–Apr: 11am–6pm daily.* *public hols.* *by prior arrangement with individual tour operators* (see p271).
ukm.uio.no/vikingskipshuset

Animal Head
This animal-head post and four similar ones were found in the Oseberg ship. It is not known what they were used for. This one is in the shape of a predator's head with a gaping mouth, and is an example of the Viking wood-carvers' skills.

Burial Chamber
The Tune ship dates from around 900 and was found in a burial mound on the farm of Haugen in Tune, Østfold. It was made of oak and had been rowed with 10–12 oars. Above the ship's stern lay the remains of a burial chamber.

The Oseberg Collection features the remarkable equipment buried with the two women, including a wagon, sledges, iron-clad chests and caskets.

Excavating the Ships

Unearthing the 1,000-year-old Viking ships from the burial mounds proved a difficult task. The Oseberg ship was buried in blue clay and covered with stones beneath a 6-m (20-ft) high burial mound. The grave was almost hermetically sealed. Ground movement had partly compressed the ship and caused it to break up. The Gokstad ship was also buried in blue clay but the forces of nature had allowed it to lie in peace, and the ship and its contents were well preserved. Robbers had plundered some of the grave furnishings.

Excavation of the Oseberg ship in 1904

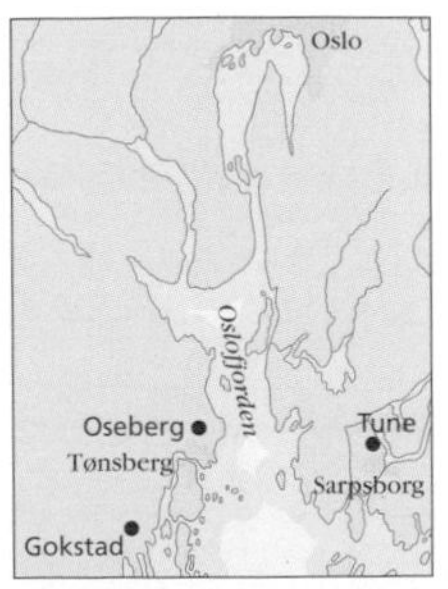

The Viking ship burial sites around Oslofjorden

Sjømannskirken, a church dedicated to the welfare of sailors

Sjømannskirken 7

Admiral Børresens Vei 4. **Map** 1 B4. *22 43 82 90. 91 to Bygdøynes (May–Sep). 30. 11am Sun.*

In 1954 Oslo Sjømannsmisjon (the Seamen's Mission) acquired a beautiful building on Bygdøy as a centre to help sailors and those working in Oslo harbour. The house was originally a private residence, built by Arnstein Arneberg (who designed the Viking Ship Museum) in 1915. It was consecrated as a church, and a large assembly hall and a sacristy were added in 1962. Until then, the Seamen's Mission had operated in very basic conditions; preachers used to conduct their sermons standing on herring barrels and fishing crates.

In 1985, the church was taken over by Den Indre Sjømannsmisjon (Internal Seamen's Mission). It contains the seamen's memorial, which was erected in 1966 to commemorate Norwegian sailors who died at sea.

Hukodden 8

Map 1 A5. *91 to Bygdøynes (May–Sep). 30.*

Most of Bygdøy's south side facing the fjord is public land with tranquil walkways along the shore and through the woods. On the southernmost tip of the peninsula lies Hukodden beach, teeming with bathers on fine summer days. It is easily accessible from the city by boat or bus. Despite its proximity to the city, the water quality is good for bathing. A beach restaurant is open in season.

From the furthest point on Huk there is a splendid view over Oslofjord, from Dyna lighthouse to Nesoddlandet in the south and to the islands in the west. The waterway is busy with ships and pleasure craft.

In the park area there are two modern sculptures, *Large Arch*, by Henry Moore, dating from 1969, and *Ikaros*, 1965, by Anne Sofie Døhlen. On a spit of land to the north of Huk there is a naturist beach, and beyond is the popular bathing spot of Paradisbukta (Paradise Bay).

Bygdøy Kongsgård 9

Map 1 A2. *22 43 75 93. 91 to Dronningen, then by bus. 30.* **Residence** *to the public.* **Tracks** *for walking. of the farm by prior arrangement.*

King Olav V (1957–91) used the royal estate of Bygdøy Kongsgård as a summer residence for many years. He treasured the tranquillity and idyllic surroundings of the 14th-century royal farm.

King Håkon V Magnusson had acquired the farm and given it to Queen Eufemia in 1305. It became a monastic estate in 1352, but was taken over by the crown in 1532. At the time of the Reformation in 1536 it became a royal *ladegård* (working estate).

King Karl Johan bought it from the state in 1837. Included in the deal was the main building erected in the 1730s. It was in the garden room here that King Christian Frederik received his farewell deputation on 10 October 1814. He had expected to become king of Norway but was forced to make way for Karl Johan *(see p38)*.

Oscar II took an interest in the estate, and in 1881 he established an open-air museum of old Norwegian

The furthest point of Hukodden offering panoramic views over the inner Oslofjord

wooden houses in the grounds. This collection later became the foundation of the Norsk Folkemuseum *(see pp82–3)*. King Oscar also built the Kongvillaene in Swiss Alps chalet style for employees of the court. Today only one of these villas remains, Villa Gjøa.

The main building, a stately wooden mansion painted in brilliant white, makes a lovely sight in summer when surrounded by green foliage.

Bygdøy Kongsgård covers a large area of northwestern Bygdøy. It comprises 200 hectares (500 acres) of forest and agricultural land. The area facing the sea is known as Kongeskogen (King's Wood). Here there are 9.5 km (6 miles) of public walking tracks. Today, Kongsgård is run as a tenant farm through the king's private estate.

Bygdøy Kongsgård, the former summer residence of King Olav V

The dining room in Oscarshall Slott with friezes by Adolf Tidemand

Oscarshall Slott ⑩

Oscarshallveien. **Map** 1 B2. ☎ *22 54 69 77.* 🚌 *30.* 🕐 *end-May–mid-Sep: 10am–4pm Tue, Thu & Sun.*

KING OSCAR I of Sweden and Norway (1799–1859) built a pleasure palace on a headland in Frognerkilen between 1847 and 1852, at the height of the era of National Romanticism. He named it Oscarshall and it became a favourite party venue for the kings of the Bernadotte dynasty. In 1863 the palace was sold to the state, since when it has been at the disposal of the ruling monarch. It was never intended to be a residence, but rather a showcase for the architecture, handicrafts, applied art and fine art of the time, and for many years it was open to the public.

After the dissolution of the union in 1905 *(see p39)*, Oscarshall was closed, and large parts of its artistic decoration were placed in the Norsk Folkemuseum. In 1929, plans were made to refurbish the palace as a residence for the crown prince, but they were later abandoned. Instead, the building was extensively restored and re-opened to the public.

Oscarshall is built in the style of an English castle. For inspiration, the architect, J H Nebelong, drew on Norman castle design and looked at the design of oriental white buildings with terraces and fountains. A Classical influence is evident in the proportions of the palace and in the strictly geometric shape of the rooms.

The drawing room is the largest room in Oscarshall with elegant windows and glazed doors opening on to the park. The entrance hall was inspired by a chapel from the Middle Ages with a circular stained-glass window on one of the end walls. The dining room is noted for its decorations by Adolph Tidemand (1814–76), a popular artist famous for his portrayals of everyday life in Norway *(see pp8–9)*. The king invited him to decorate the dining room with a series of 10 paintings inlaid in friezes around the upper walls. The pictures depict peasant life from childhood to old age.

The king's living room contains Gothic-style carved and moulded decorations and paintings based on the old Norwegian sagas.

Oscarshall Slott, Oscar I's 19th-century pleasure palace

ruhrgas
OSLO

Further Afield

Many of Oslo's attractions are to be found just outside the city centre, often in rural surroundings. They are easily accessible by public transport, and several are close enough to one another that they can be visited in a single day.

Viglandsparken *(see pp90–91)* is the showcase for the sculptures of Gustav Vigeland and nearby a museum is dedicated to his work. Edvard Munch's paintings can be seen in the Munch-museet, and an innovative collection of art by children has been assembled at the Barnekunstmuseum. Holmenkollen is the site of the famous ski jump. It is in areas such as Holmenkollen, Sørkedalen and Kjelsås, with their forests, lakes and wildlife, that it is possible to appreciate why the inhabitants of Oslo treasure the countryside on their doorstep. In summer it is never too far to go swimming, and in winter there are many ski tracks and slopes. Some areas, despite being near the centre, are so uncrowded that occasionally a solitary elk might be seen.

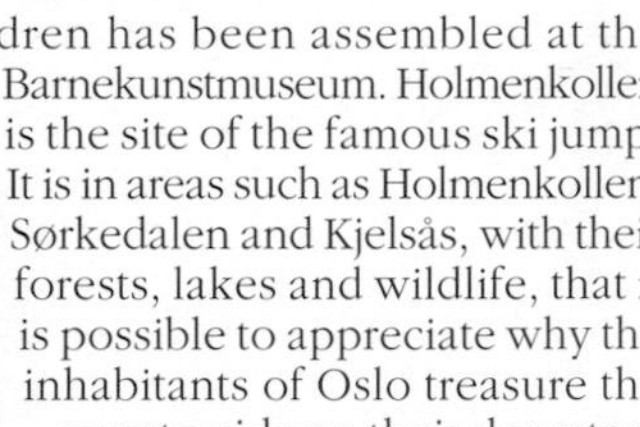

The Monolith, Vigelandsparken

Sights

Museums and Galleries
Bogstad Herregård 15
Botanisk Hage and Museum 6
Det Internasjonale Barnekunstmuseet 10
Emanuel Vigeland Museum 12
Geologisk Museum 7
Munch-museet 5
Oslo Bymuseum 2
Teknisk Museum 11
Vigelandsmuseet 3
Vigelandsparken pp90–91 1
Zoologisk Museum 8

Historic Districts
Gamlebyen 4
Grünerløkka 9

Recreation Areas
Frognerseteren 14
Holmenkollen 13

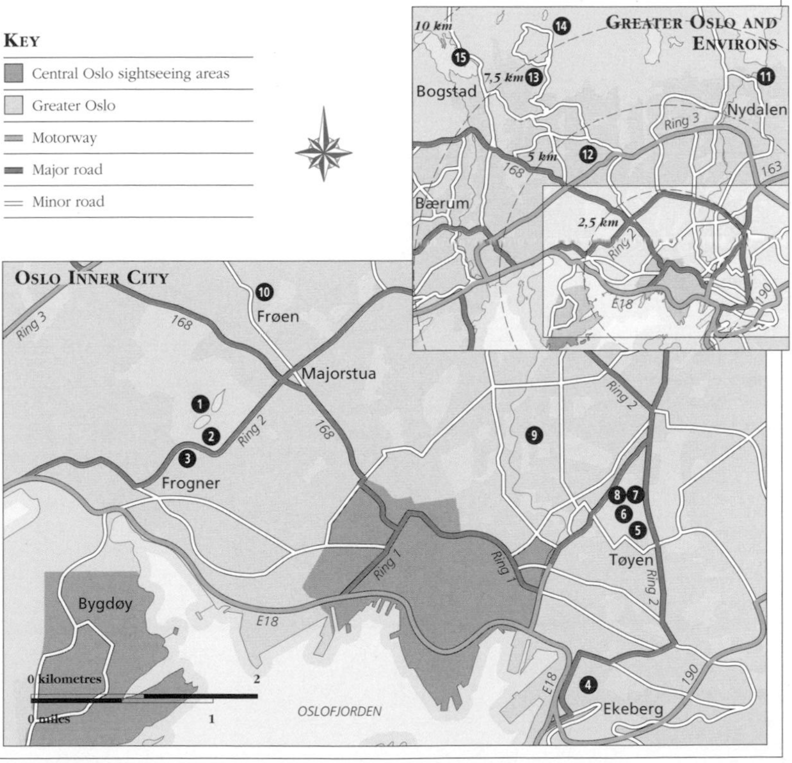

Key

Central Oslo sightseeing areas
Greater Oslo
Motorway
Major road
Minor road

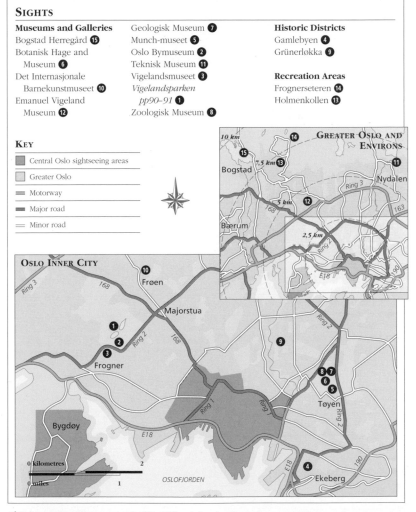

Greater Oslo and Environs

10 km
7,5 km
5 km
2,5 km
Bogstad
Nydalen
Bærum
Ring 3
Ring 2
168
163
190
E18

Oslo Inner City

Frøen
Majorstua
Frogner
Tøyen
Bygdøy
Ekeberg
Ring 1
Ring 2
Ring 3
168
190
E18
OSLOFJORDEN
0 kilometres 2
0 miles 1

◁ **Holmenkollen ski-jump tower, built in 1892 and since hosting various competitions**

Vigelandsparken ❶

The Little Angry Boy

OSLO'S LARGEST PARK is named after the sculptor, Gustav Vigeland, whose 212 sculptures depicting humanity in all its forms are artfully positioned along the central axis. The focal point is the soaring Monolith on a stepped plinth surrounded by groups of figures. Vigeland started work on the park in 1924. By 1950, seven years after his death, most of the pieces were in place. The sculptures were modelled in full size in clay by Vigeland himself, but the carving in stone and casting in bronze were carried out by others. The interplay between the sculptures, the green areas and the architecture is a breathtaking sight.

Sundial (Soluret), stands on a granite plinth decorated with the signs of the zodiac.

Wheel of Life
The Wheel of Life (Livshjulet), *which sums up the park's dramatic theme, was modelled in 1934. The wheel is a symbol of eternity and consists of a garland of men, women and children holding onto each other in an eternal cycle.*

★ Monolith
The 17-m (56-ft) tall Monolith *is the highest point in the park. It comprises 121 human figures, supporting and holding onto each other. On the plinth at the base of the column there are 36 groups of granite figures depicting the cycles of life and relationships.*

Vigelandsmuseet *(see p92)*, just outside the park, houses the artist's studio and an exhibition of his earlier works.

STAR FEATURES

- ★ Bridge
- ★ Fountain
- ★ Monolith

Triangle
The group of figures known as Triangle *was one of the last pieces to be placed in Vigelandsparken. It was erected in 1993.*

The Clan
The last large group of figures in the Vigeland complex, the Clan, *was finally put in place in 1988 as a gift from trade and industry.*

Visitors' Checklist

Kirkeveien. **Map** 2 A1.
22 54 25 30. *Majorstuen.*
12, 15. *20, 45.*
Park *daily (24 hrs).*
Vigelandsmuseet *May–Sep: 10am–6pm Thu–Sat, noon–6pm Sun; Oct–Apr: noon–6pm Tue–Sun.* **Kafé Vigeland** *10am–6pm daily.*
www.vigeland.museum.no

Bronze statuette, *Pike og øgle* (Girl and the Lizard), 1938

★ Fountain
The fountain shows six giants carrying an enormous vessel on their shoulders. Around the edge of the pool are 20 groups of figures. The surrounding fountain square is in mosaic.

Frogner ponds

Kafé Vigeland and Visitors' Centre

Oslo Bymuseum
(see p92)

Main Entrance
The monumental entrance consists of five wrought-iron main gates and two smaller pedestrian gates leading through to the sculptures.

★ Bridge
The granite bridge is lined with 58 bronze sculptures, modelled in the years 1926–33, and depicting the various stages of life. The lizard groups on each corner symbolize mankind's fight against evil.

Oslo Bymuseum ❷

Frognerveien 67. 23 28 41 70. 12, 15. 20, 45. *Jun–Aug: 10am–6pm Thu–Fri, 11am–5pm Sat & Sun; Sep–May: 10am–4pm Tue–Fri, 11am–4pm Sat & Sun.* *Occasional public hols and 1 Jan–15 Jan.*

HOUSED IN the Frogner Hovedgård, a handsome, well-preserved 18th-century manor house, is Oslo Bymuseum, a museum devoted to the city's 1,000-year history. The town's growth, commercial and cultural life come to life through models, room interiors, pictures, sculptures, photographs and displays. There is particular emphasis on the history of Oslo from the Middle Ages to the present day.

On the first floor, rooms dating from 1750 are on view in summer. Among the attractions are Bernt Anker's ballroom from the 1790s and landscape paintings of Oslo, then Christiania, in the 19th century.

With its origin in the Middle Ages, the former farm is in traditional style, with three buildings laid out around a square yard behind the museum. Its garden and old pastures together form Frognerparken, which also encompasses Vigeland Park *(see pp90–91).*

Vigelandsmuseet, showcasing the work of the sculptor, Gustav Vigeland

Vigelandsmuseet ❸

Nobelsgate 32. 22 54 25 30. 12, 15. 20, 45. *May–Sep: 10am–6pm Tue–Sat, noon–6pm Sun; Oct–Apr: noon–4pm Tue–Sun.* *some public hols.*

A MAJOR PART OF Gustav Vigeland's (1869–1943) artistic output can be seen in Vigelandsmuseet, just by Vigelandsparken *(see pp90–91).*

The collection contains 2,700 sculptures in plaster, bronze, granite and marble, 12,000 drawings and around 400 woodcuts and carvings. The original models for the Vigeland Park sculptures as well as casts for busts and other monuments are on display. Old photographs show the making of the sculpture park. The museum is the result of a contract drawn up in 1921 between the artist and Oslo City Council. Vigeland donated to the city all his existing and future works. In return the council built him a studio, which was later to be converted into a museum to exhibit his work.

Built in the 1920s, the studio-turned-museum is considered to be one of the finest examples of Norwegian Neo-Classicism. Vigeland himself chose the interior colour scheme.

Moving through the rooms, it is possible to follow the artist's development from his 1890s' expressive and thin-figure style to the heavier expression of the years between the two world wars. The artist's living quarters are also on view.

After Vigeland's death in 1943, his ashes were placed in the tower at his request.

A middle-class home of around 1900 in Oslo Bymuseum

Gamlebyen ❹

2 km (1 mile) E of town centre. *18, 19.* *34, 70.*

IN THE MIDDLE AGES, the town of Oslo was centred on Gamlebyen (the Old Town). From the 12th century until the great fire of 1624, nearly all development in this area lay between Ekebergåsen, Bjørvika, Grønland and Galgeberg. Many of the medieval ruins in Gamlebyen have been preserved, including those of Mariakirken (Maria Church), Kongsgården (the Royal Manor) and Clemenskirken (Clemens Church). A medieval park has been established next to the ruins of St Hallvard Cathedral. There are other reminders of the Middle Ages, including Oslo Ladegård og Bispegården (Oslo Manor and the Bishops' Residence).

For many years after World War II Gamlebyen suffered from heavy traffic. Recent regulations have tackled the problem and Gamlebyen is experiencing new prosperity. The future opera house and a new town development are taking shape in Bjørvika. Houses and commercial buildings are being restored. Meanwhile, excavations have revealed the remains of timber houses and townhouses and an array of decorative items and utensils.

Gamlebyen's medieval park among the cathedral ruins

Munch-museet containing Edvard Munch's extensive artistic output

Munch-museet ❺

Tøyengata 53. Tel 23 24 14 00. Tøyen/Munchmuseet. Bus 20, 60. Jun–15 Sep: 10am–6pm daily; 16 Sep–May: 10am–4pm Tue–Fri, 11am–5pm Sat & Sun. Closed 24–25 Dec, 1 Jan, 1 May, 17 May. www.museumsnett.no/munch

The largest collection of work by Edvard Munch (1863–1944) is housed in Oslo's Munch-museet. Prior to his death, Edvard Munch bequeathed all the paintings in his possession to the City of Oslo. A century after his birth, the Munch-museet opened. Designed by Gunnar Fougner and Einar Myklebust, the museum is situated next to Tøyenparken on Oslo's east side, where the artist grew up. It was completely renovated and enlarged in 1994, on the 50th anniversary of Munch's death.

The collection is extensive, comprising 1,100 paintings, 4,500 drawings and 17,000 prints. It contains the principal works from every period of the artist's productive life, including versions of *The Scream*, the worrying *Anxiety* (1894), the serene but melancholic *Young Woman on the Shore* (1896) and the sensuously claustrophobic *Kiss* (1897).

Some of Munch's major works may be on loan to museums elsewhere and not all pieces are displayed at the same time. But with 1,888 sq m (20,322 sq ft) of exhibition space and such a rich collection to draw on, the museum is never without material to provide a detailed account of the artist's life and work. Special exhibitions presenting new perspectives on his art are shown regularly.

Other examples of Munch's work can be seen in the Nasjonalgalleriet *(see pp52–3)*, Henie Onstad Kunstsenter *(see p114)* and Bergen's Rasmus Meyers Samlinger *(see p167)*.

Edvard Munch

Norway's most renowned visual artist and one of the forerunners of Expressionism, Edvard Munch (1863–1944) made his debut at the Autumn Exhibition in Oslo when he was just 20 years old. He painted a number of masterpieces shortly after his debut, including *The Sick Child*, connected to a personal experience – his sister's death when she was 14 years old. After studies in Norway he moved to Paris in 1889, and later to Berlin, where he further developed his highly individual style with themes of love and death in the *Frieze of Life* series.

Spiritual experiences and angst characterize his work as is evident in his best-known painting, *The Scream* (1894), in which a desperate figure can be seen screaming on a bridge. The agitated style of his works reveals a troubled life: in 1908 he suffered a mental breakdown and a year later he returned to Norway. By then he was accepted as a major artist and was commissioned to do works for public buildings, including the Aula of Oslo University *(see p50)*.

Munch's self-portrait, *The Night Wanderer*

Floral splendour in the Botanisk Hage at Tøyen in Oslo

Botanisk Hage and Museum 6

Sars Gate 1. *22 85 17 00.* *Tøyen/Munch-museet.* *20, 60.* **Museum** *11am–4pm Tue–Sun, 11am–8pm Wed.* **Botanisk Hage** *Apr–Sep: 7am–8pm Mon–Fri, 10am–8pm Sat & Sun; Oct–Mar: 7am–5pm Mon–Fri (until 8pm Wed), 10am–5pm Sat & Sun.* *some public hols.*

RIGHT ACROSS FROM Munch-museet is the Botanisk Hage, Norway's largest botanical garden. It is a popular excursion for Oslo's residents, who come both to admire the thousands of Norwegian and foreign plants and to escape from the hustle and bustle of the city.

One of the highlights is the Alpine Garden, with a waterfall and 1,450 species of mountain flora from Norway and abroad. In the Systematic Garden plants are grouped according to family and genus. The Medicinal and Herbal Garden contains medicinal plants, spices and cash crops. For those in wheelchairs or with impaired vision, the Aromatic Garden is a special attraction. Here, fragrant plants grow in raised beds and are accompanied by texts in Braille. In the Victoria House and Palm House are plants from tropical and temperate regions, including rare orchids, carnivorous pitcher plants, cacti, cocoa trees, fig trees and palms.

The Botanisk Hage is part of the Natural History Museum and since 1814 has formed the basis for research and education in botany at the University of Oslo.

In the middle of the Botanical Garden is a manor house, Tøyen Hovedgård, dating from 1780. The old greenhouses and three museum buildings form an attractive planted enclosure.

An extensive herbarium containing 1.7 million examples of herbs provides an important resource for the documentation and research of Norwegian flora.

Geologisk Museum 7

Sars Gate 1. *22 85 17 00.* *Tøyen/Munch-museet.* *20, 60.* *11am–4pm Tue–Sun, 11am–8pm Wed.* *some public hols.*

A CIRCULAR SHOWCASE of gemstones is the first eye-catching exhibit on entering the Geologisk Museum. The gems are mainly Norwegian in origin. The ground floor of the museum is devoted to a presentation of the geological processes at work in the Earth, including the formation of volcanoes, mountain ranges and rocks.

Norway as an oil-producing nation is the subject of a separate exhibition.

In an intriguing display about Oslofeltet (the Oslo Field), remarkable fossil-bearing rocks are on show alongside other geological items that would normally lie hidden deep below the crust of the earth or in the murky depths of the North Sea. Exhibits include fossils such as weird-looking trilobites, brachiopods, cuttlefish and various microscopic creatures.

Zoologisk Museum 8

Sars Gate 1. *22 85 17 00.* *Tøyen/Munchmuséet.* *20, 60.* *11am–4pm Tue–Sun, 11am–8pm Wed.* *some public hols.*

THE NORWEGIAN HALL of the Zoologisk Museum features displays of stuffed native animals in recreations of their various habitats, including fish and marine and freshwater creatures, mammals and birds. Ptarmigan and reindeer can be observed against a mountain backdrop; cranes and black grouse are on show, and the pre-mating antics of the wood grouse are demonstrated. There are beaver dams and a display of the bird colonies that nest on the sea-cliffs.

In the Svalbard Hall exhibits feature Arctic animals, such as

Arctic animals on display at the Zoologisk Museum

polar bears and seals. The Animal Geography Hall presents large and small creatures in different world zones, such as penguins in Antarctica, and lions, hippopotamuses and crocodiles in the tropical regions. Also, there are several butterfly montages.

In the Systematic Hall there are detailed displays of Norway's animal life, from single-celled amoebas to the largest mammals. A "sound bar" provides recordings of animal noises from the wild.

Grünerløkka, a renovated and old popular working class district

Grünerløkka ❾

1 km (half a mile) N of the centre. *30, 58. 11, 12, 13.*

THE FORMER WORKING class district of Grünerløkka has undergone something of a renaissance in recent years. It is made up largely of apartment blocks dating from the end of the 19th century, which were under threat of demolition. But repeated proposals to clear the area and build afresh have finally been shelved and instead the old housing stock is being restored. Small and inadequate apartments have been combined, and units are becoming larger and fewer, but the neighbourhood still retains the character of old Oslo. As a result, people from all walks of life have been attracted to Grünerløkka and the area has become particularly popular among young people.

With the influx of this vibrant new community, a large number of cosmopolitan shops, cafés and restaurants have opened, including the popular Sult *(see p234)*.

Collections in the Teknisk Museum appealing to all ages

Det Internasjonale Barnekunst-museet ❿

Lille Frøens Vei 4. *22 46 85 73.* *Frøen. 46. 25 Jun–8 Aug: 11am–4pm Tue–Thu & Sun; 15 Sep–24 Jun: 9.30am–2pm Tue–Thu, 11am–4pm Sun. 9 Aug–14 Sep and public hols.*

CHILDREN'S ART from 150 countries has been assembled in Barnekunst-museet (the International Museum of Children's Art). Exhibits include paintings, sculptures, ceramics, collages and textiles by children from around the world.

The museum was set up in 1968 in collaboration with the SOS Children's Villages, an international organization for children in need.

Although the museum is designed to give space to children's opinions and things that are dear to them, the works have been selected on the basis of quality just as in an adults' museum.

Visiting children can express themselves actively in the Music and Dance Room, the Doll Room and the Painting and Drawing Studio. Videos and films on children's art are shown and workshops held.

Barnekunstmuseet, a lively forum for children's art

Teknisk Museum ⓫

Kjelsåsveien 143. *22 79 60 00.* *12, 15. 22, 25, 37. to Kjelsås. 20 Jun–20 Aug: 10am–6pm daily; 21 Aug–19 Jun: 10am–4pm Tue–Fri, 10am–5pm Sat & Sun. some public hols*

TECHNOLOGY PAST and present is the subject of Norsk Teknisk Museum (the Norwegian Museum of Science and Technology), founded in 1914 in Kjelsås. Exhibits include Norway's first steam engine, its first car, imported in 1895, and its first aeroplane, in addition to early sewing machines, vacuum cleaners and other everyday objects.

The ground floor is dedicated to industry. The first floor covers transport and communications, telecom technology and information technology. Here it is possible to follow the development of steam power and the transition to mass production. Telecommunication is traced from the first warnings sent via beacons to the development of the telegraph and telephones, mobile phones and the internet.

An exhibition illustrates oil and gas exploration in the North Sea, and shows how the raw material is pumped to the surface, transported and refined. In an unusual display titled *The Forest as a Resource*, the importance of cellulose in revolutionizing the production of paper 150 years ago is also highlighted.

There are educational exhibits and a science centre, Teknoteket, with hands-on activities. A variety of family events take place at weekends.

Emanuel Vigeland Museum, featuring the artist's work and mausoleum

Emanuel Vigeland Museum ⓬

Grimelundsveien 8, 5 km (3 miles) N of centre. *22 14 57 88.* *Slemdal.* *46.* *noon–4pm Sun.*

On the western side of Oslo lies one of the most unusual museums in Norway. It is dedicated to the artist Emanuel Vigeland, younger brother of Gustav, the sculptor who created Vigelandsparken *(see pp90–91).*

Emanuel Vigeland (1875–1948) pioneered fresco painting in Norway. He also perfected the art of medieval stained glass techniques.

The museum building was originally Vigeland's studio; on his death it became his mausoleum and was opened to the public in 1959. On show is his lifework, *Vita*, a series of fresco paintings from 1927–47, in addition to portraits, drawings and sculptures. The frescoes have to be viewed in somewhat subdued lighting, because in the 1940s the subjects in *Vita* were considered too daring for public taste and it was thought that strong lighting would make them even more provocative. Today, few people would regard Vigeland's work as indecent.

Another oddity is the unusually low-ceilinged entrance area. This has been attributed to the artist's desire for humility in the face of the art one is coming to view.

Examples of Vigeland's stained glass can be seen in the windows of Oslo Domkirke *(see p73).*

Holmenkollen ⓭

6 km (4 miles) N of centre. *22 92 32 00.* *Holmenkollen.* **Skimuseet & Ski Jump** *Jan–Apr & Oct–Dec: 10am–4pm daily; May & Sep: 10am–5pm daily; Jun–Aug: 9am–8pm daily.* *by arrangement.*

Ski-jumping is almost always guaranteed to attract the crowds in Norway, and the impressive ski jump at Holmenkollen is no exception. The venue for the annual Holmenkollen Races and ski-jumping events is Norway's biggest tourist attraction, drawing more than 1 million visitors a year. The races have been held here since 1892. Crown Prince Olav participated in the jumping competitions in both 1923 and 1924.

The ski jump, which has been remodelled 14 times, was for many years regarded as the most important arena for Nordic skiing. The world championships have been held here on three occasions, as were many of the skiing events for the 1952 Winter Olympics, when 150,000 people turned out to watch the jumping competition. During the past few years the complex has also become the main arena for the Biathlon, involving cross-country skiing and marksmanship.

The public can visit both the ski jump and the jump tower all year round. The tower, in particular, offers a splendid view over Oslo and the inner Oslofjord.

The Skimuseet, at the base of the ski jump, opened in 1923. It focuses on more than 4,000 years of skiing history *(see pp26–7).* Displays illustrate various types of skis from different eras and regions of Norway, and follow the development of each of the skiing disciplines. The Olympics in Oslo in 1952 and Lillehammer in 1994 are also covered. In addition, Norway's prominent role in polar history receives special attention and the now antique-looking equipment used by Nansen and Amundsen can be admired.

In 1999, the museum was expanded to provide space to exhibit Norwegian paintings concentrating on the themes of snow and skiing.

The striking profile of the Holmenkollen ski jump

Frognerseteren on a winter's day, offering sweeping views over Oslo

Frognerseteren ⓮

7 km (4 miles) N of centre.
Restaurant *22 92 40 40.*
Frognerseteren.
Tryvannstårnet *22 14 67 11.*
Oct–Apr: 10am–4pm Fri–Sun, noon–4pm Mon–Thu; May: 10am–5pm daily; Jun: 10am–7pm; Jul–Aug: 9am–8pm; Sep: 10am–5pm.

About half an hour's walk from Holmenkollen hill is Frognerseteren, a favourite excursion spot from the city. Originally it was a pasture, which was first inhabited in the 1790s.

A traditional wooden lodge, built by the municipality at Frognerseteren at the end of the 19th century, houses a restaurant. From its terrace there is a spectacular view over Oslo, the fjord and surrounding areas. Below the building, a stone monument commemorates the 1814 Constitutional Assembly.

The road northward from Holmenkollen to Frognerseteren was opened in 1890 in the presence of Oscar II and the German Emperor Wilhelm II. It was named Keiser Wilhelms Vei. After World War II it was renamed Holmenkollveien.

Frognerseteren is the last station on the Holmenkollen Tunnelbane line. It is a popular starting point for walks in the Nordmarka woods throughout the year, giving access to the network of signposted footpaths and ski trails.

From the station, a 15-minute walk leads up to Tryvannstårnet, an observation tower 529 m (1,735 ft) above sea level. The actual tower rises a further 118 m (387 ft). A lift connects to the public gallery, 60 m (197 ft) above the hilltop. On a clear day it is possible to see Sweden far to the east and the Gaustatoppen mountain to the west. Close by, or so it seems, lies Oslo and the seaward approach to the city. Beyond are the extensive areas of forest that surround the capital.

Prime minister Peder Anker (1749–1824) and his family

Bogstad Herregård ⓯

Sørkedalen 826, 8 km (5 miles) NW of centre. *22 06 52 00.* *41.*
mid-May–mid Oct, only for guided tours: noon–4pm Tue–Sun.
1pm, 2pm Tue–Sat; 12.30pm, 1.30pm, 2.30pm, 3.30pm Sun.
(café and shop open noon–4pm Tue–Sun).

On a promontory on the eastern side of Bogstad Lake in Søkerdalen lies Bogstad Herregård, a farming estate which dates from the Middle Ages.

Bogstad originally belonged to the Cistercian Monastery on Hovedøya, an island situated in the innermost part of Oslofjorden. It then passed to the crown before being sold to the alderman, Morten Lauritzen.

The present manor house was erected in the late 18th century by Peder Anker (1749–1824) who later became prime minister. Most of the contents and the large art collection date from that time. The estate then passed to Baron Herman Wedel Jarlsberg. Oslo Municipality took over its forests and arable land in 1954 when the building, complete with contents, and the surrounding parkland became part of Norsk Folkemuseum.

The manor house is open to the public in the summer months, and in December it is the venue for various Christmas events.

In 1978 the wagonhouse and woodshed next to the driveway from Sørkedalsveien burned down and were later replaced by reproductions. Extensive restoration took place in 1999 when the barn was converted to provide banqueting facilities.

The park surrounding Bogstad Herregård was established around 1785 by the Norwegian garden designer Johan Grauer. For inspiration, Peder Anker had sent Grauer to England to study English landscape design. Grauer's park layout was one of the first Norwegian examples of the English landscape style.

Bogstad Herregård, a farming estate dating back to the Middle Ages

Oslo Street Finder

The map below shows the areas of Oslo covered by the *Street Finder*. The map references given in the guide for the capital's sights, restaurants, hotels and shops refer to the maps in the *Street Finder*. The first number of the map reference tells you which map to turn to. The letter and number that follow refer to the grid reference on that map. All the major sights are marked and should be easy to find. The symbols listed in the key below indicate other important points plotted on the maps, such as post offices, Tunnelbane (metro) stations, bus and ferry terminals, car parks and churches. On page 89 there is a small-scale map of Greater Oslo and Environs.

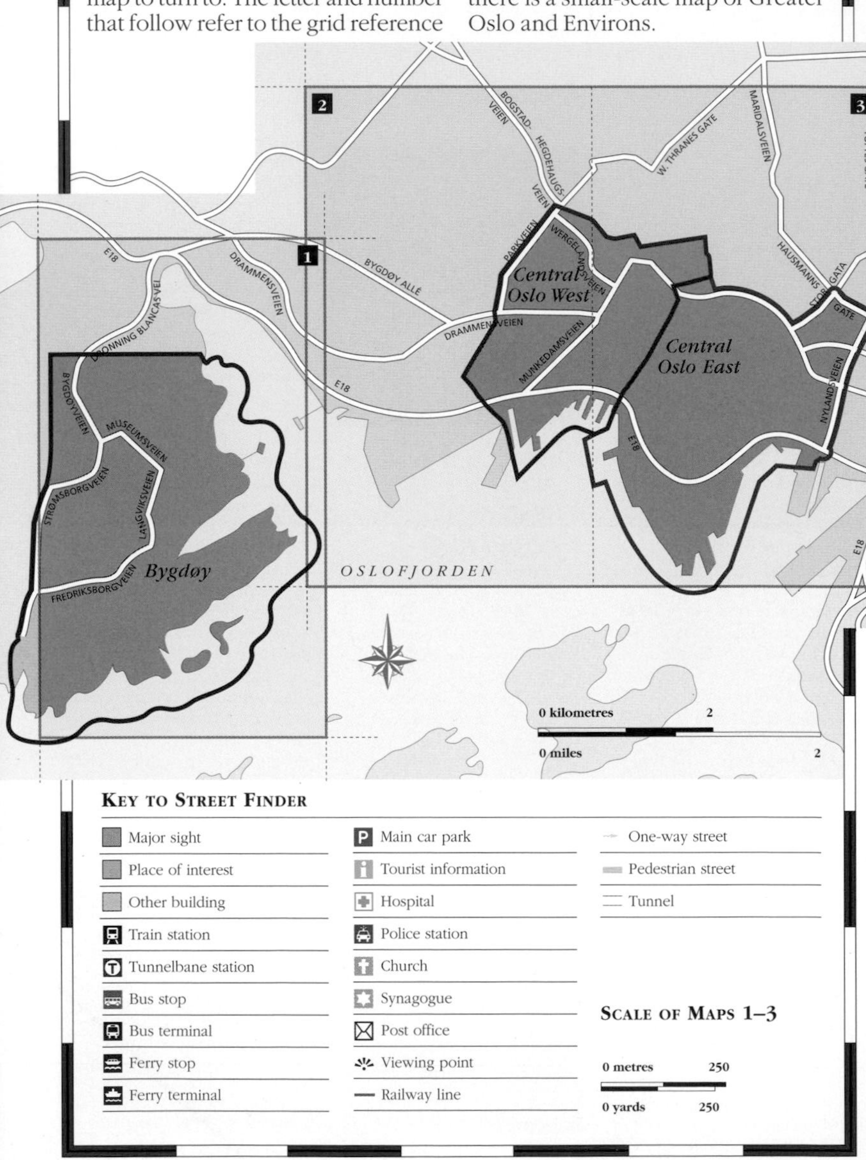

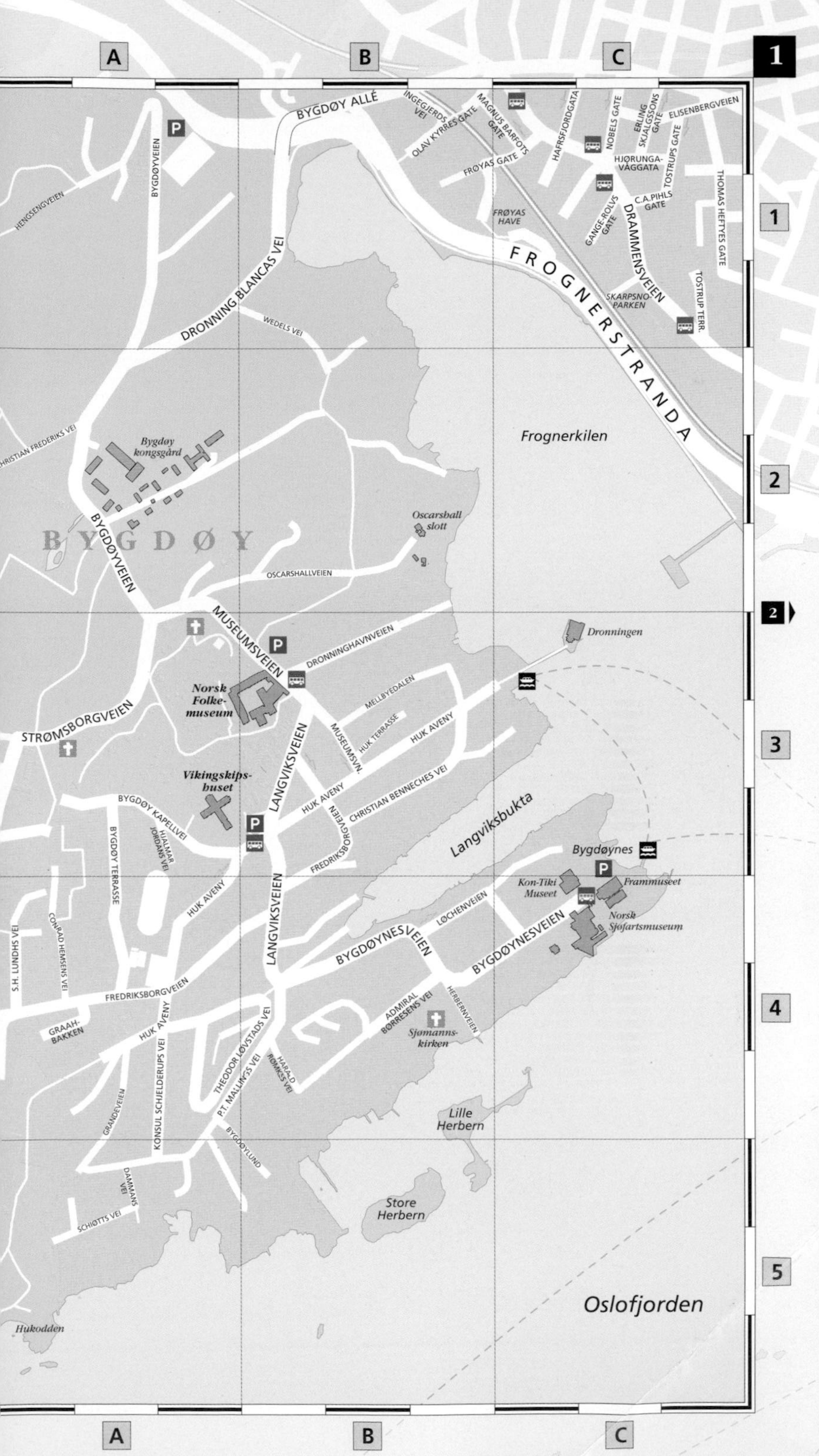

A
B
C
1
BYGDØY ALLÉ
INGEGJERDS VEI
OLAV KYRRES GATE
MAGNUS BARFOTS GATE
FRØYAS GATE
HAFRSFJORDGATA
NOBELS GATE
ERLING SKJALGSSONS GATE
ELISENBERGVEIEN
HJØRUNGA-VÅGGATA
TOSTRUPS GATE
C.A.PIHLS GATE
GANGE-ROLVS GATE
DRAMMENSVEIEN
THOMAS HEFTYES GATE
TOSTRUP TERR.
FRØYAS HAVE
FROGNERSTRANDA
SKARPSNO PARKEN
BYGDØYVEIEN
HENGSENGVEIEN
DRONNING BLANCAS VEI
WEDELS VEI
Frognerkilen
CHRISTIAN FREDERIKS VEI
Bygdøy kongsgård
Oscarsball slott
BYGDØY
OSCARSHALLVEIEN
MUSEUMSVEIEN
DRONNINGHAVNVEIEN
Dronningen
Norsk Folke-museum
MELLBYEDALEN
STRØMSBORGVEIEN
LANGVIKSVEIEN
MUSEUMSVN.
HUK TERRASSE
HUK AVENY
Vikingskips-huset
BYGDØY KAPELLVEI
CHRISTIAN BENNECHES VEI
FREDRIKSBORGVEIEN
Langviksbukta
Bygdøynes
Kon-Tiki Museet
Frammuseet
Norsk Sjøfartsmuseum
BYGDØY TERRASSE
HJALMAR JORDANS VEI
LÖCHENVEIEN
BYGDØYNESVEIEN
S.H. LUNDHS VEI
CONRAD HEMSENS VEI
GRAAH-BAKKEN
ADMIRAL BORRESENS VEI
HERBERNVEIEN
Sjømanns-kirken
THEODOR LØVSTADS VEI
HARALD RØMCKES VEI
KONSUL SCHJELDERUPS VEI
P.T. MALLINGS VEI
GRANDEVEIEN
BYGDØYLUND
Lille Herbern
DAMMANS VEI
SCHIØTTS VEI
Store Herbern
Oslofjorden
Hukodden
2
3
4
5

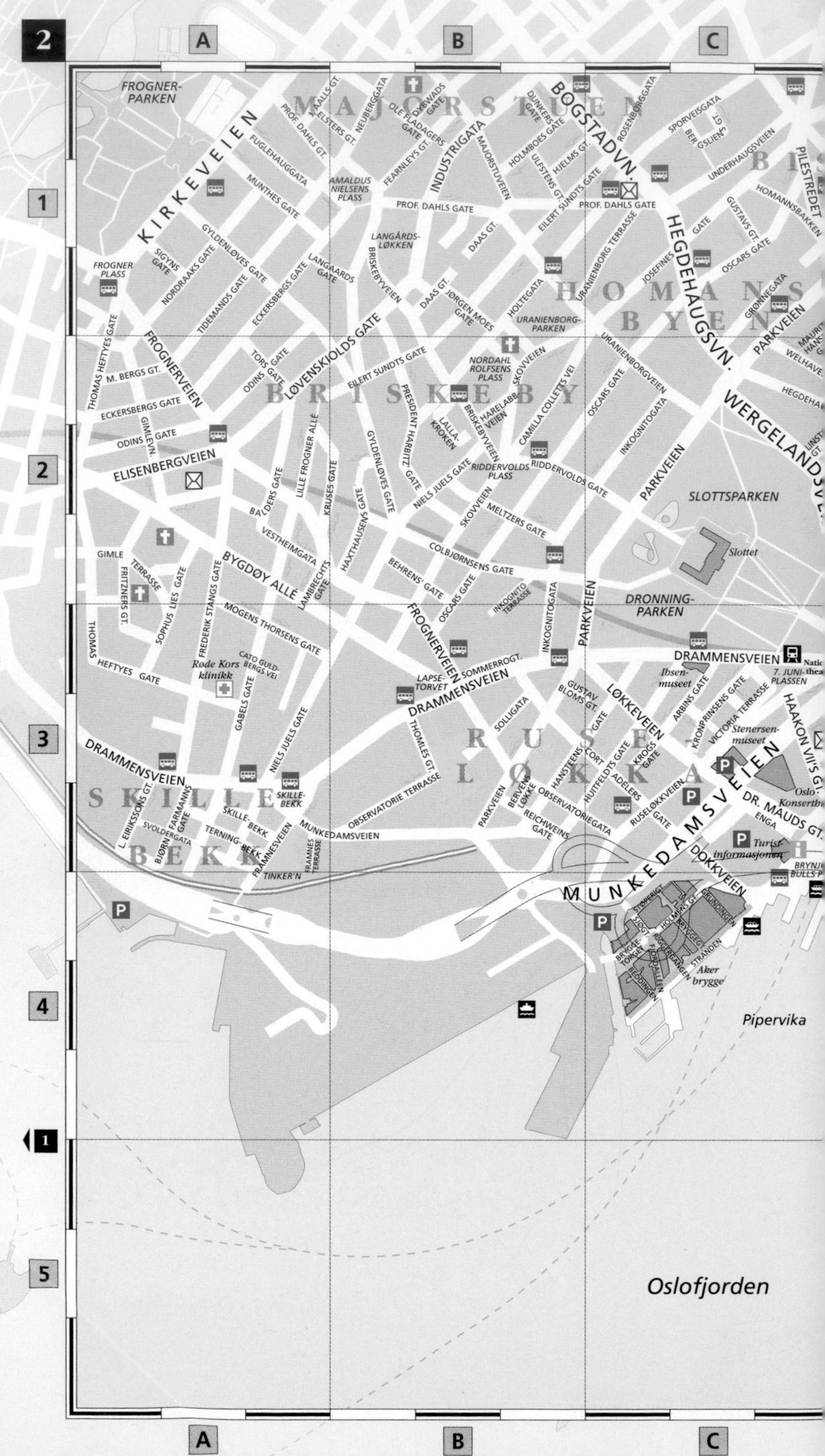
2
A
B
C
1
2
3
4
5
MAJORSTUEN
HOMANSBYEN
BRISKEBY
RUSELØKKA
SKILLEBEKK
FROGNERPARKEN
KIRKEVEIEN
BOGSTADVN.
HEGDEHAUGSVN.
WERGELANDSVEIEN
INDUSTRIGATA
FROGNERVEIEN
LØVENSKIOLDS GATE
ELISENBERGVEIEN
BYGDØY ALLÉ
DRAMMENSVEIEN
MUNKEDAMSVEIEN
PARKVEIEN
LØKKEVEIEN
SLOTTSPARKEN
Slottet
DRONNINGPARKEN
Ibsenmuseet
Stenersenmuseet
Røde Kors klinikk
Aker brygge
Pipervika
Oslofjorden
Turistinformasjonen
7. JUNI-PLASSEN
FROGNER PLASS
AMALDUS NIELSENS PLASS
LANGÅRDSLØKKEN
URANIENBORGPARKEN
NORDAHL ROLFSENS PLASS
RIDDERVOLDS PLASS
LAPSETORVET
PROF. DAHLS GATE
DOKKVEIEN
HAAKON VII'S GATE
DR. MAUDS GT.
1

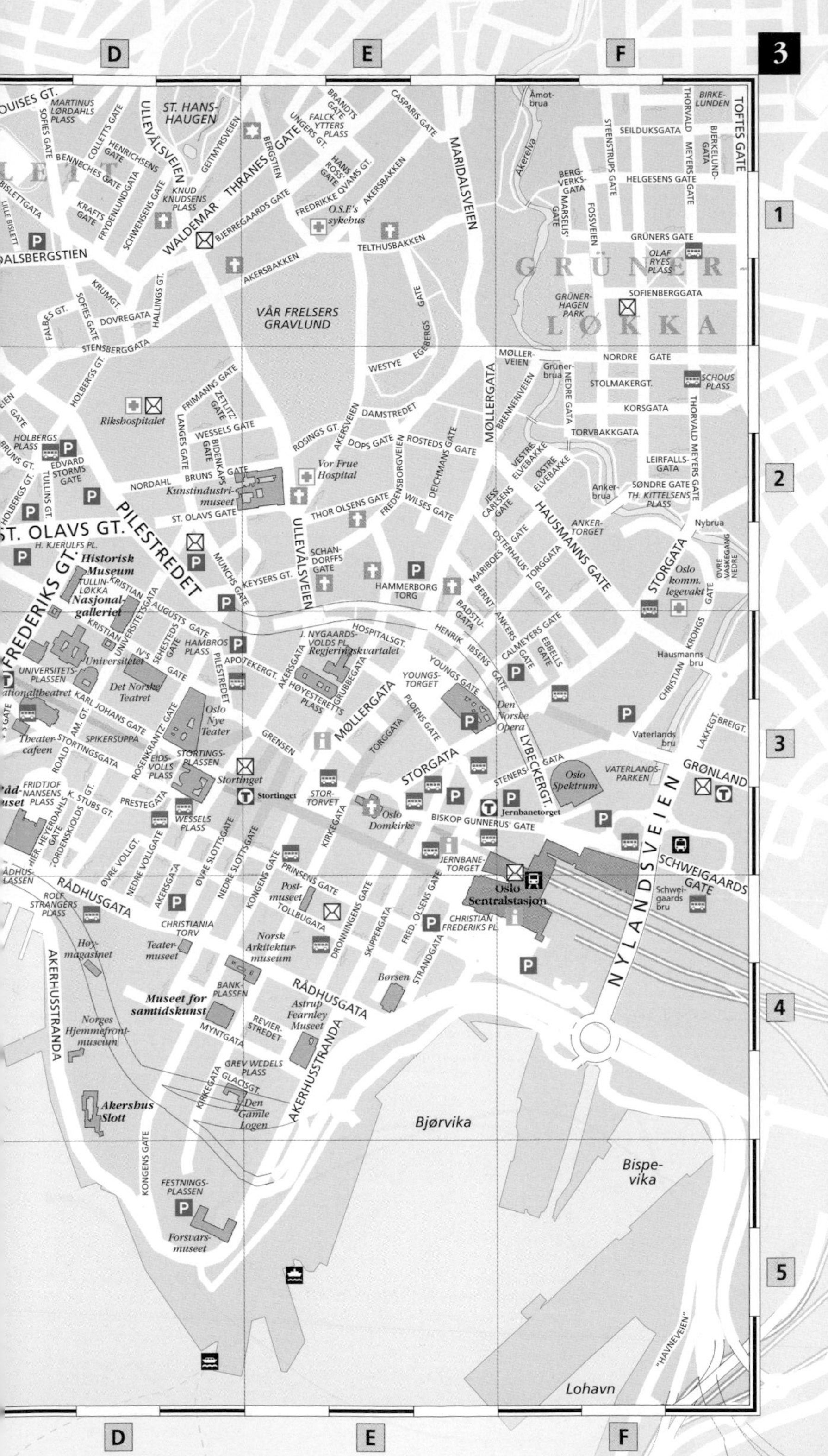
3
D
E
F
1
2
3
4
5
MARTINUS LØRDAHLS PLASS
SOFIES GATE
COLLETTS GATE
ULLEVÅLSVEIEN
ST. HANS-HAUGEN
GEITMYRSVEIEN
BERGSTIEN
BRANDTS GATE
FALCK YTTERS PLASS
UNGERS GT.
CASPARIS GATE
MARIDALSVEIEN
Åmot-brua
Akerelva
BIRKELUNDEN
THORVALD MEYERS GATE
TOFTES GATE
SEILDUKSGATA
STEENSTRUPS GATE
BIRKELUNDGATE
BENNECHES GATE
HENRICHSENS GATE
THRANES GATE
WALDEMAR THRANES GATE
HANS ROSS GATE
FREDRIKKE QVAMS GT.
AKERSBAKKEN
BERG-VERKS-GATA
MARSELIS' GATE
FOSSVEIEN
HELGESENS GATE
BISLETTGATA
LILLE BISLETT
KRAFTS GATE
FRYDENLUNDGATA
SCHWENSENS GATE
KNUD KNUDSENS PLASS
BJERREGAARDS GATE
O.S.F.'s sykehus
TELTHUSBAKKEN
GRÜNERS GATE
OLAF RYES PLASS
GRÜNER
LØKKA
DALSBERGSTIEN
KRUMGT.
HALLINGS GT.
DOVREGATA
FALBES GT.
STENSBERGGATA
VÅR FRELSERS GRAVLUND
EGEBERGS GATE
SOFIENBERGGATA
GRÜNERHAGEN PARK
MØLLERVEIEN
NORDRE GATE
WESTYE EGEBERGS GATE
Grüner-brua
NEDRE GATE
STOLMAKERGT.
SCHOUS PLASS
BRENNERIVEIEN
KORSGATA
HOLBERGS GT.
FRIMANNS GATE
ZETLITZ' GATE
Rikshospitalet
LANGES GATE
AKERSVEIEN
DAMSTREDET
MØLLERGATA
TORVBAKKGATA
HOLBERGS PLASS
EDVARD STORMS GATE
WESSELS GATE
BIDENKAPS GATE
ROSINGS GT.
DOPS GATE
ROSTEDS GATE
DEICHMANS GATE
VESTRE ELVEBAKKE
ØSTRE ELVEBAKKE
LEIRFALLS-GATA
TULLINS GT.
NORDAHL BRUNS GATE
Kunstindustri-museet
Vor Frue Hospital
FREDENSBORGVEIEN
Anker-brua
SØNDRE GATE
TH. KITTELSENS PLASS
PILESTREDET
ST. OLAVS GATE
THOR OLSENS GATE
WILSES GATE
JESS CARLSENS GATE
HAUSMANNS GATE
Nybrua
ST. OLAVS GT.
H. KJERULFS PL.
ULLEVÅLSVEIEN
ANKER-TORGET
ØVRE VASKEGANG
Historisk Museum
SCHANDORFFS GATE
MUNCHS GATE
KEYSERS GT.
HAMMERBORG TORG
MARIBOES GATE
OSTERHAUS' GATE
TORGGATA
STORGATA
Oslo komm. legevakt
FREDERIKS GT.
TULLIN-LØKKA
KRISTIAN AUGUSTS GATE
Nasjonal-galleriet
UNIVERSITETSGATA
BERNT ANKERS GATE
HENRIK IBSENS GATE
HOSPITALSGT.
BADSTU-GATA
CHRISTIAN KROHGS GATE
SEHESTEDS GATE
HAMBROS PLASS
J. NYGAARDS-VOLDS PL.
Regjeringskvartalet
CALMEYERS GATE
EBBELS GATE
Hausmanns bru
UNIVERSITETS-PLASSEN
Universitetet
IV'S GATE
APOTEKERGT.
AKERSGATA
GRUBBEGATA
YOUNGS-TORGET
YOUNGS GATE
Nationaltheatret
KARL JOHANS GATE
Det Norske Teatret
HØYESTERETTS PLASS
PLOENS GATE
Den Norske Opera
ROSENKRANTZ' GATE
Oslo Nye Teater
Vaterlands bru
LAKKEGT.
BREIGT.
Theater-cafeen
STORTINGSGATA
SPIKERSUPPA
GRENSEN
TORGGATA
MØLLERGATA
LYBECKERGT.
ROALD AMUNDSENS GATE
EIDSVOLLS PLASS
STORTINGS-PLASSEN
Stortinget
STORGATA
STENERS GATA
Oslo Spektrum
VATERLANDS-PARKEN
GRØNLAND
FRIDTJOF NANSENS PLASS
K. STUBS GT.
PRESTEGATA
STOR-TORVET
Oslo Domkirke
Jernbanetorget
BISKOP GUNNERUS' GATE
HER. HEYERDAHLS GATE
ORDENSKIOLDS GATE
WESSELS PLASS
ØVRE VOLLGT.
NEDRE VOLLGATE
ØVRE SLOTTSGATE
NEDRE SLOTTSGATE
KONGENS GATE
KIRKEGATA
PRINSENS GATE
JERNBANE-TORGET
Oslo Sentralstasjon
SCHWEIGAARDS GATE
NYLANDSVEIEN
RÅDHUS-PLASSEN
RÅDHUSGATA
ROLF STRANGERS PLASS
Post-museet
TOLLBUGATA
DRONNINGENS GATE
SKIPPERGATA
FRED. OLSENS GATE
CHRISTIAN FREDERIKS PL.
Schweigaards bru
CHRISTIANIA TORV
Høy-magasinet
Teater-museet
Norsk Arkitektur-museum
STRANDGATA
AKERHUSSTRANDA
Børsen
BANK-PLASSEN
RÅDHUSGATA
Museet for samtidskunst
Astrup Fearnley Museet
Norges Hjemmefront-museum
MYNTGATA
REVIER-STREDET
GREV WEDELS PLASS
KIRKEGATA
GLACISGT.
Den Gamle Logen
Akersbus Slott
Bjørvika
KONGENS GATE
Bispe-vika
FESTNINGS-PLASSEN
Forsvars-museet
"HAVNEVEIEN"
Lohavn

Street Finder Index

A

Admiral Børresens Vei 1 B4
Akerhus-stranda 3 D4, 3 E4
Akersbakken 3 E1
Akersgata 3 D4, 3 E3
Akersveien 3 E2
Amaldus Nielsens Plass 2 B1
Ankerbrua 3 F2
Ankertorget 3 F2
Apotekergata 3 E3
Arbins Gate 2 C3

B

Badstugata 3 E3
Balders Gate 2 A2
Bankplassen 3 D4
Beddingen 2 C4
Behrens' Gate 2 B2
Benneches Gate 3 D1
Bergsliens Gate 2 C1
Bergstien 3 E1
Bergverksgata 3 F1
Bernt Ankers Gate 3 F3
Bervens Løkke 2 B3
Bidenkaps Gate 3 D2
Birkelunden 3 F1
Biskop Gunnerus' Gate 3 E3
Bislettgata 3 D1
Bjerkelundgata 3 F1
Bjerregaards Gate 3 E1
Bjørn Farmanns Gate 2 A3
Bogstadveien 2 C1
Brandts Gate 3 E1
Breigata 3 F3
Brenneriveien 3 F2
Briskebyveien 2 B1, 2 B2
Bryggegata 2 C4
Bryggetorget 2 C4
Brynjulf Bulls Plass 2 C3
Bygdøy Allé 1 B1, 2 A2
Bygdøy Kapellvei 1 A3
Bygdøy Terrasse 1 A3
Bygdøylund 1 A4
Bygdøynes 1 C3
Bygdøynesveien 1 B4
Bygdøyveien 1 A1, 1 A2

C

C. A. Pihls Gate 1 C1
Calmeyers Gate 3 F3
Camilla Colletts Vei 2 B2
Casparis Gate 3 E1
Cato Guldbergs Vei 2 A3
Christian Benneches Vei 1 B3
Christian Frederiks Plass 3 E4
Christian Frederiks Vei 1 A2
Christian Krohgs Gate 3 F3
Christiania Torv 3 D4
Colbjørnsens Gate 2 B2
Colletts Gate 3 D1
Conrad Hemsens Vei 1 A4
Cort Adelers Gate 2 C3

D

Daas Gate 2 B1
Dalsbergstien 3 D1
Dammans Vei 1 A5
Damstredet 3 E2
Deichmans Gate 3 E2
Dokkveien 2 C3
Dops Gate 3 E2
Dovregata 3 D1
Drammens-veien 1 C1, 2 A3 2 B3, 2 C3
Dronning Blancas Vei 1 A1
Dronning Mauds Gate 2 C3
Dronningens Gate 3 E4
Dronninghavnveien 1 B3
Dronningparken 2 C2
Dunkers Gate 2 B1
Dybwadsgate 2 B1

E

Ebbellsgate 3 F3
Eckersbergs Gate 2 A1, 2 A2
Edvard Storms Gate 3 D2
Eidsvolls Plass 3 D3
Eilert Sundts Gate 2 B1, 2 B2
Elisenberg-veien 1 C1, 2 A2
Elsters Gate 2 B1
Enga 2 C3
Erling Skjalgssons Gate 1 C1

F

Falbes Gate 3 D1
Falck Ytters Plass 3 E1
Fearnleys Gate 2 B1
Festningsplassen 3 D5
Fjordalléen 2 C4
Fossveien 3 F1
Framnes Terrasse 2 A3
Framnesveien 2 A3
Fred. Olsens Gate 3 E4
Fredensborgveien 3 E2
Frederik Stangs Gate 2 A3
Frederiks Gate 3 D3
Fredrikke Qvams Gate 3 E1
Fredriksborg-veien 1 A4, 1 B3
Fridtjof Nansens Plass 3 D3
Frimanns Gate 3 D2
Fritzners Gate 2 A2
Frognerparken 2 A1
Frogner Plass 2 A1
Frognerstranda 1 C1
Frognerveien 2 A2, 2 B3
Frydenlundgata 3 D1
Frøyas Gate 1 B1
Frøyas Have 1 C1
Fuglehauggata 2 A1

G

Gabels Gate 2 A3
Gange-Rolvs Gate 1 C1
Geitmyrsveien 3 D1
Gimle Terrasse 2 A2
Gimleveien 2 A2
Glacisgata 3 E4
Graahbakken 1 A4
Grandeveien 1 A4
Grev Wedels Plass 3 E4
Grubbegata 3 E3
Grundingen 2 C4
Grünerbrua 3 F2
Grünerhagen Park 3 F1
Grüners Gate 3 F1
Grønland 3 F3
Grønnegata 2 C1
Gustav Bloms Gate 2 B3
Gustavs Gate 2 C1
Gyldenløves Gate 2 A1, 2 B2

H

H. Kjerulfs Plass 3 D2
Hafrsfjordgata 1 C1
Hallings Gate 3 D1
Hambros Plass 3 D3
Hammerborg Torg 3 E2
Hans Ross' Gate 3 E1
Hansteens Gate 2 B3
Harald Rømkes Vei 1 B4
Harelabbveien 2 B2
Hausmanns Bru 3 F3
Hausmanns Gate 3 F2
Havneveien 3 F5
Haxthausens Gate 2 B2
Hegdehaugs-veien 2 C1, 2 C2
Helgesens Gate 3 F1
Hengsengveien 1 A1
Henrichsensgate 3 D1
Henrik Ibsens Gate 3 E3
Herbernveien 1 B4
Hieronymus Heyerdahls Gate 3 D3
Hjalmar Jordans Vei 1 A3
Hjelms Gate 2 B1
Hjørungavåggata 1 C1
Holbergs Gate 3 D2
Holbergs Plass 3 D2
Holmboes Gate 2 B1
Holmens Gate 2 C4
Holtegata 2 B1
Homannsbakken 2 C1
Hospitalsgata 3 E3
Huitfeldts Gate 2 C3
Huk Aveny 1 A4, 1 B3
Huk Terrasse 1 B3
Høyesteretts Plass 3 E3
Haakon VII's Gate 2 C3

I

Industrigata 2 B1
Ingegjerds Vei 1 B1
Inkognito Terrasse 2 B2
Inkognitogata 2 B3, 2 C2

J

J. Aalls Gate 2 A1
J. Nygaardsvolds Plass 3 E3
Jernbanetorget 3 E3
Jess Carlsens Gate 3 F2
Josefines Gate 2 C1
Jørgen Moes Gate 2 B1

K

K. Stubs Gate 3 D3
Karl Johans Gate 3 D3
Keysers Gate 3 E2
Kirkegata 3 D4, 3 E3
Kirkeveien 2 A1
Klingenberggata 3 D3
Knud Knudsens Plass 3 D1
Kongens Gate 3 D5, 3 E4
Konsul Schjelderups Vei 1 A4
Korsgata 3 F2
Krafts Gate 3 D1
Kristian Augusts Gate 3 D2
Kristian IV's Gate 3 D3
Krogsgate 2 C3
Kronprinsens Gate 2 C3
Krumgata 3 D1
Kruses Gate 2 A2

L

Lakkegata 3 F3
Lallakroken 2 B2
Lambrechts Gate 2 A2
Langes Gate 3 D2
Langviksveien 1 B3
Langaards Gate 2 A1
Langårdsløkken 2 B1
Lapsetorvet 2 B3
Leirfallsgata 3 F2
Leiv Eirikssons Gate 2 A3
Lille Bislett 3 D1
Lille Frogner Allé 2 A2
Lille Herbern 1 B4
Linstows Gate 2 C2

Louises Gate **3 D1**
Lybeckergata **3 F3**
Løchenveien **1 B4, 2 C3**
Løvenskiolds Gate **2 A2**

M

Magnus Barfots Gate **1 C1**
Magnus Bergs Gate **2 A2**
Majorstuveien **2 B1**
Mariboes Gate **3 E2**
Maridalsveien **3 E1**
Marselis' Gate **3 F1**
Martinus Lørdahls Plass **3 D1**
Mauritz Hansens Gate **2 C2**
Mellbyedalen **1 B3**
Meltzers Gate **2 B2**
Mogens Thorsens Gate **2 A2**
Munchs Gate **3 D2**
Munkedamsveien **2 B3, 2 C3**
Munthes Gate **2 A1**
Museumsveien **1 A3, 1 B3**
Myntgata **3 D4**
Møllergata **3 E2, 3 E3**
Møllerveien **3 F2**

N

Nedre Gate **3 F2**
Nedre Slottsgate **3 E3**
Nedre Vollgate **3 D3**
Neuberggata **2 B1**
Niels Juels Gate **2 A3, 2 B2**
Nobels Gate **1 C1**
Nordahl Bruns Gate **3 D2**
Nordahl Rolfsens Plass **2 B2**
Nordraaks Gate **2 A1**
Nordre Gate **3 F2**
Nybrua **3 F2**
Nylandsveien **3 F4**

O

Observatoriegata **2 B3**
Observatorie Terrasse **2 B3**
Odins Gate **2 A2**
Olaf Ryes Plass **3 F1**
Olav Kyrres Gate **1 B1**
Olav V's Gate **3 D3**
Ole Fladagers Gate **2 B1**
Oscars Gate **2 B2, 2 C1, 2 C2**
Oscarshallveien **1 B2**
Osterhaus' Gate **3 F2**

P

P. T. Mallings Vei **1 A4**
Parkveien **2 B3, 2 C1, 2 C2**
Pilestredet **2 C1, 3 D2**
Pløens Gate **3 E3**
President Harbitz' Gate **2 B2**
Prestegata **3 D3**
Prinsens Gate **3 E4**
Prof. Dahls Gate **2 A1, 2 B1, 2 C1**

R

Reichweinsgate **2 B3**
Revierstredet **3 E4**
Riddervolds Gate **2 B2**
Riddervolds Plass **2 B2**
Riggergangen **2 C4**
Roald Amundsens Gate **3 D3**
Rolf Strangers Plass **3 D4**
Rosenborggata **2 C1**
Rosenkrantz' Gate **3 D3**
Rosings Gate **3 E2**
Rosteds Gate **3 E2**
Ruseløkkveien **2 C3**
Rådhusgata **3 D4, 3 E4**
Rådhusplassen **3 D3**

S

S. H. Lundhs Vei **1 A4**
Schandorffs Gate **3 E2**
Schiøtts Vei **1 A5**
Schous Plass **3 F2**
Schweigaardsgate **3 F3**
Schweigaards Bru **3 F4**
Schwensens Gate **3 D1**
Sehesteds Gate **3 D3**
Seilduksgata **3 F1**
Sigyns Gate **2 A1**
Sjøgata **2 C4**
Skarpsnoparken **1 C1**
Skillebekk **2 A3**
Skippergata **3 E4**
Skovveien **2 B2**
Slottsparken **2 C2**
Sofienberggata **3 F1**
Sofies Gate **3 D1**
Solligata **2 B3**
Sommerrogata **2 B3**
Sophus Lies Gate **2 A3**
Spikersuppa **3 D3**
Sporveisgata **2 C1**
St Hanshaugen **3 D1**
St Olavs Gate **3 D2**
Steenstrups Gate **3 F1**
Stenersgata **3 F3**
Stensberggata **3 D2**
Stolmakergata **3 F2**
Store Herbern **1 B5**
Storgata **3 E3, 3 F2**
Stortingsgata **3 D3**
Stortingsplassen **3 D3**
Stortorvet **3 E3**
Stranden **2 C4**
Strandgata **3 E4**
Strømsborgveien **1 A3**
Støperigata **2 C4**
Sven Bruns Gate **3 D2**
Svoldergata **2 A3**
7. Juniplassen **2 C3**
Søndre Gate **3 F2**

T

Telthusbakken **3 E1**
Terningbekk **2 A3**
Th. Kittelsens Plass **3 F2**
Theodor Løvstads Vei **1 A4**
Thomas Heftyes Gate **1 C1, 2 A2, 2 A3**
Thomles Gate **2 B3**
Thor Olsens Gate **3 E2**
Thorvald Meyers Gate **3 F1, 3 F2**
Tidemands Gate **2 A1**
Tinker'n **2 A3**
Toftes Gate **3 F1**
Tollbugata **3 E4**
Tordenskiolds Gate **3 D3**
Torggata **3 E3, 3 F2**
Tors Gate **2 A2**
Torvbakkgata **3 F2**
Tostrup Terrasse **1 C1**
Tostrups Gate **1 C1**
Tullinløkka **3 D2**
Tullins Gate **3 D2**

U

Ulfstens Gate **2 B1**
Ullevålsveien **3 D1, 3 E2**
Underhaugsveien **2 C1**
Ungers Gate **3 E1**
Universitetsgata **3 D3**
Universitetsplassen **3 D3**
Uranienborg Terrasse **2 C1**
Uranienborgparken **2 B1**
Uranienborgveien **2 C2**

V W

Vaterlands Bru **3 F3**
Vaterlandsparken **3 F3**
Vestheimgata **2 A2**
Vestre Elvebakke **3 F2**
Victoria Terrasse **2 C3**
Vår Frelsers Gravlund **3 E1**
Waldemar Thranes Gate **3 D1**
Wedels Vei **1 B1**
Welhavensgate **2 C2**
Wergelandsveien **2 C2**
Wessels Gate **3 D2**
Wessels Plass **3 D3**
Westye Egebergs Gate **3 E1**
Wilses Gate **3 E2**

Y

Youngs Gate **3 E3**
Youngstorget **3 E3**

Z

Zetlitz' Gate **3 D2**

Ø

Østre Elvebakke **3 F2**
Øvre Slottsgate **3 D3**
Øvre Vaskegang **3 F2**
Øvre Vollgate **3 D3**

Å

Åmotbrua **3 F1**

Lofoten, with its mountain peaks and rugged coast, one of Norway's many areas of outstanding beauty ▷

NORWAY AREA BY AREA

AROUND OSLOFJORDEN 106-119

EASTERN NORWAY 120-137

SØRLANDET AND TELEMARK 138-153

VESTLANDET 154-181

TRØNDELAG 182-195

NORTHERN NORWAY AND SVALBARD 196-215

Around Oslofjorden

The oldest settlements *in the area surrounding Oslofjorden date from the Stone Age and Bronze Age, and it was here on the eastern and western shores that three of the best preserved Viking ships were unearthed. Although the land around the fjord close to Oslo is built-up, further south it is a haven of serene villages with quaint clapboard houses, quiet islands and boats galore.*

The sight of Oslofjorden on a summer's day teeming with ferries, cruise boats, yachts and leisure craft is breathtaking. The 100-km (60-miles) long fjord extends deep inland from the Skagerrak to the port of Oslo. It narrows around Drøbak before opening out closer to the capital. The counties of Akershus and Østfold lie to the east, and Buskerud and Vestfold to the west.

More than one million people live around the shore in some of the oldest towns and villages in the country. Many of these settlements have a long history of trading and seafaring. The entire region bears evidence of its proximity to the capital. The infrastructure is well developed, road connections are good and Europe's longest road tunnel beneath the sea, 7.2 km (4 miles) long, links Frogn on the east with Hurum on the west. Many people who work in Oslo commute from their homes around the fjord.

The Oslofjorden area offers a combination of an ancient cultural heritage alongside modern industry and commerce. Away from the industrial areas, the coast is peppered with islands large and small, inlets and coves, holiday resorts and marinas, and clusters of painted summer cabins. There are castles and Viking burial mounds to explore, and colourful timber-built villages to relax in with museums and art galleries. Boating, fishing, swimming and walking are among the many pursuits on offer.

Summers are usually warm in this region. Stavern *(see p119)* holds the record for 200 days of sunshine a year. The winters are seldom severe, and the amount of snow varies from place to place according to how high up or how far inland it is situated.

Badeparken at Drøbak, one of the most visited beaches on the eastern side of Oslofjorden

◁ **Figurehead decorating one of the many timber houses in picturesque Drøbak**

Exploring Oslofjorden

OSLOFJORDEN, FROM ITS INNERMOST reaches to the skerries out near Færder Lighthouse, is surrounded by idyllic towns and villages. Bustling harbours are guarded by sturdy fortresses and at Borre National Park the burial mounds of ancient kings have been discovered. One of the most rewarding ways to explore Oslofjorden at close quarters is by sailing boat or motorboat. It is easy to take a trip on a sightseeing boat or simply cross the fjord by ferry. For those travelling by car, it is worth turning off along the minor roads that lead to beaches, quays and waterside hamlets.

Stavern with its many historic buildings from the 18th century when the town was a naval base

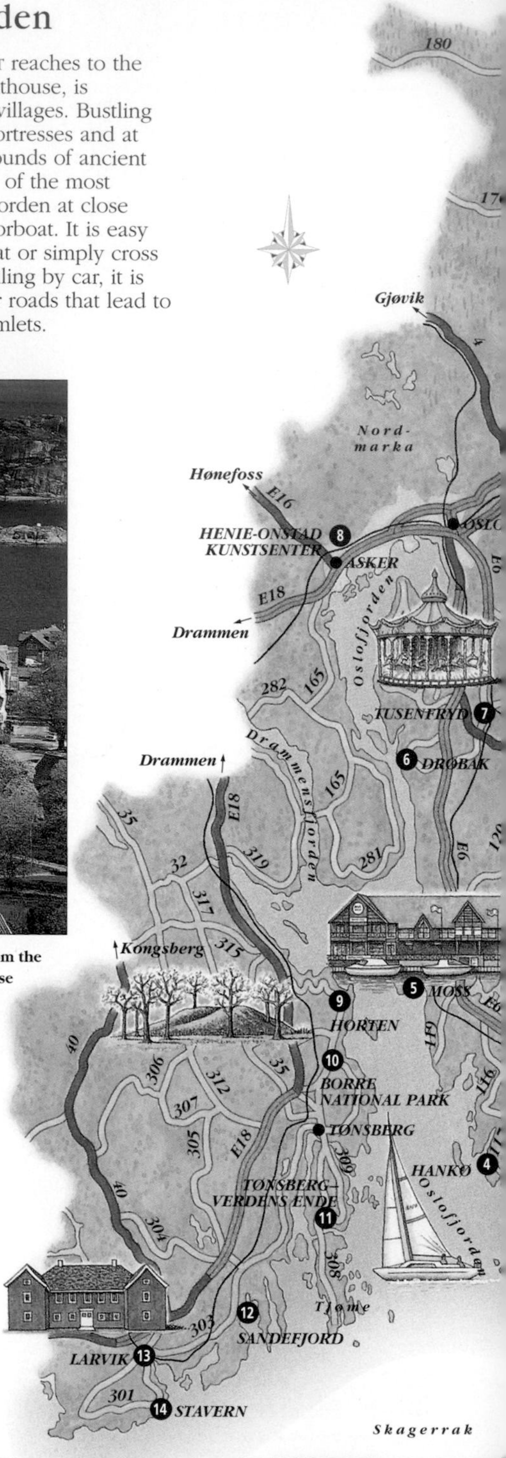

Gjøvik
Nordmarka
Hønefoss
E16
8 HENIE-ONSTAD KUNSTSENTER
ASKER
OSLO
E18
Drammen
Oslofjorden
TUSENFRYD 7
6 DRØBAK
Drammen
Drammensfjorden
E6
Kongsberg
5 MOSS
9 HORTEN
10 BORRE NATIONAL PARK
TØNSBERG
HANKØ 4
TØNSBERG–VERDENS ENDE 11
Tjøme
12 SANDEFJORD
LARVIK 13
14 STAVERN
Skagerrak

KEY

- Motorway
- Major road
- Minor road
- Railway line

SEE ALSO

• ***Where to Stay*** pp220–27

• ***Where to Eat*** pp232–9

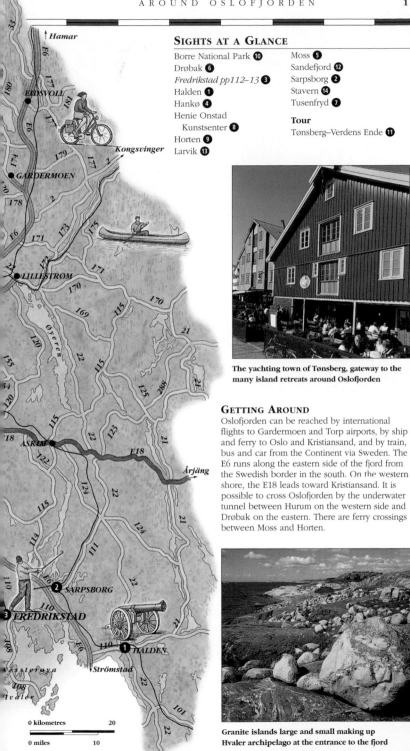

Sights at a Glance

- Borre National Park ⑩
- Drøbak ⑥
- *Fredrikstad pp112–13* ③
- Halden ①
- Hankø ④
- Henie Onstad Kunstsenter ⑧
- Horten ⑨
- Larvik ⑬
- Moss ⑤
- Sandefjord ⑫
- Sarpsborg ②
- Stavern ⑭
- Tusenfryd ⑦

Tour

- Tønsberg–Verdens Ende ⑪

The yachting town of Tønsberg, gateway to the many island retreats around Oslofjorden

Getting Around

Oslofjorden can be reached by international flights to Gardermoen and Torp airports, by ship and ferry to Oslo and Kristiansand, and by train, bus and car from the Continent via Sweden. The E6 runs along the eastern side of the fjord from the Swedish border in the south. On the western shore, the E18 leads toward Kristiansand. It is possible to cross Oslofjorden by the underwater tunnel between Hurum on the western side and Drøbak on the eastern. There are ferry crossings between Moss and Horten.

Granite islands large and small making up Hvaler archipelago at the entrance to the fjord

Halden ❶

County of Østfold. 26,000. Landbrygga 3, 69 19 09 80. Food and Wooden Boat Festival (4th week Jun).

The town of Halden is the gateway to Norway for those arriving from Sweden to the southern regions. It is set back on Iddefjorden between a beautiful archipelago on one side and forests and lakes on the other. The town developed in the 16th and 17th centuries as an outpost on the border with Sweden. It has many well-preserved old buildings, and clusters of Neo-Classical houses.

Halden's crowning glory is **Frederiksten Festning**, an imposing fortress straddling the ridge above the town, complete with ramparts and powder houses and a warren of passageways. The first fortifications were built around 1643–5, and it was here, in 1718, that the Swedish king, Karl XII, was shot during his second attempt to attack the fortress.

The fortress comprises the citadel, beyond which lies Borgerskansen and three outlying forts facing south and east: Gyldenløve, Stortårnet and Overberget. The fortress museums contain extensive collections of war history and civil memorabilia. There is a pharmacy from the 1870s, and the old bakery and brewery in the inner fort.

The canal, Haldenkanalen, is part of Haldenvassdraget, which flows through a series of large lakes. Boats can navigate the 75-km (46-miles) stretch between Tistedal and Skulerud through three groups of locks. The 26.6-m (87-ft) high Brekke Locks, comprising four chambers, are the highest locks in northern Europe.

The M/S *Turisten* operates between Tistedal and Strømsfoss and Strømsfoss and Ørje in summer.

Historic Sarpsborg's busy commercial centre

Fredriksten Festning

1 km (half a mile) S of the centre. 69 17 35 24. **Fortress** *all year.* **Museum** *18 May–31 Aug: daily; Sep: Sun.*

Sarpsborg ❷

County of Østfold. 47,000. Glengsgata, 69 15 65 35. *Gleng Music Festival (May/Jun), Olav's Festival (Jul/Aug).*

King Olav the Holy founded Sarpsborg in 1016, making it Norway's third oldest town. In fact, its history can be traced back 7,000 years through the discovery of burial mounds, primitive fortifications, stone monuments and rock carvings. At nearby Tune, the Viking ship, Tuneskipet, from around AD 900 was unearthed *(see p85)*.

The Glomma river and the waterfall, Sarpsfossen, formed the backbone of the commercial development of the town. The rivers were used for floating timber to the sawmills. The harbour became the country's second largest port for timber in the 19th century and the timber industry is still important to the town today.

Borgarsyssel Museum was opened in 1929 in the area where Olav the Holy had his castle. The ruins can be seen, as can those of a church, Nikolaskirken, from 1115. Medieval stonework from the region is exhibited in Steinhoggerhallen. In the museum's main building, the Østfoldgalleriet contains collections of folk art, arts and crafts and industrial products such as Rococo-style glazed earthenware from Herrebøe. Outside there is a monastic garden with herbs.

The open-air section features a collection of historic houses. Among them is a workmen's dwelling house, St Olavs Vold, from the 1840s. It is made up of 20 apartments each with one room and a kitchen.

Borgarsyssel Museum

Gamlebygaten 8. 69 15 50 11. *May–Aug: daily; Sep–Apr: Tue–Fri.* *public hols.*

Fredriksten Festning providing a dramatic backdrop to Halden

Fredrikstad ❸

See pp112–13.

Hankø ❹

County of Østfold. *302 from Fredrikstad to Vikane.* *Turistinformasjonen, Fredrikstad, 69 30 46 00.*

THE ISLAND OF Hankø lies to the west of Fredrikstad toward the outer part of Oslofjorden. It became especially popular as a holiday resort in the 1950s and 1960s when King Olav had a summer residence, Bloksberg, here.

Although Hankø presents a bare rock face to the fjord, its sheltered eastern side is forested, providing a much favoured harbour and anchorage. The Norwegian Association of Yachting was founded here in 1882, since when the island has been a venue for national regattas, sailing races and world championship events.

Rowing has also had a long tradition on Hankø. The Fredrikstad Rowing Club was established here around 1870.

Galleri 15 occupying the manor house of Alby on Jeløy, near Moss

Moss ❺

County of Østfold. 68,000. *Skogaten 52, 69 24 15 15.* *Momentum Art Festival (May–Aug).*

AN IMPORTANT industrial and trading centre for the County of Østfold, Moss is also known for its art galleries and streets lined with sculptures. Its harbour has long been a junction for boat traffic on Oslofjorden and today car ferries continually ply between Moss and Horten.

The Town and Industry Museum, **Moss by- og Industrimuseum**, charts Moss's industrial development. **Konventionsgården** was built in 1778 and is the main building of Moss Jernverk (Moss Ironworks), which was constructed in the mid-18th century. It was here that the Moss Convention was signed in 1814 to ratify the union between Norway and Sweden rather than Denmark.

Moss is protected to the west by the island of Jeløy, once a peninsula connected to the mainland in the southeast. A canal, dug between Mossesundet and Værlebukta, cut Jeløy from the mainland, but did not deter a rash of house-building here in the 1960s. The manor house on the Alby Gods estate on Jeløy is the location for an art gallery, **Galleri 15**. The elegant Refsnes Gods is now a hotel *(see p223)*.

North of Moss is the idyllic harbour village of **Son**, a popular excursion spot. The buildings in the centre of Son recall a time in the 18th century when the timber trade, shipping and commerce, spinning and the production of spirits were thriving industries. Son has charming little streets, an eco museum, a museum harbour, coastal cultural activities, exhibitions and many cosy places to eat.

Moss by- og Industrimuseum

Fossen 21–23. *69 24 33 00.* *Mon–Fri & Sun.* *public hols.*

Galleri 15

Alby Gård 4 km (2 miles) W of Moss. *69 27 10 33.* *Jun–Aug: Tue–Sun.* *some public hols.*

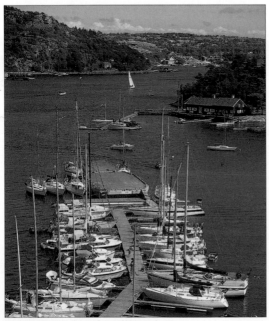

Hankø, a favourite haunt for yachting enthusiasts

Street-by-Street: Fredrikstad ❸

Frederik II, founder of Fredrikstad

When Sarpsborg was burned down in 1567 during the Nordic Seven-Year War, Frederik II gave permission for the inhabitants to move to a spot closer to the mouth of the Glomma river, which would be better placed for trading, shipping and fishing. And so Fredrikstad was established. It became a fortress town in 1663, and Gamlebyen (the Old Town) developed within the bastion walls. Cobbled streets, art galleries, a renowned handicrafts centre, shops and restaurants make Gamlebyen an attractive place. A bridge, built in 1957, leads to the modern industrial and commercial town and the busy town centre.

Old Town Hall
Fredrikstad's first aldermen had their seat in the Old Town Hall (Gamle Rådhus), built in 1784. The lay preacher, Hans Nielsen, was imprisoned here for five weeks in 1797.

★ Provisions House
The sturdy Provisions House (Provianthus), constructed 1674–96, has stone walls 4-m (13-ft) thick. It is the oldest building in Fredrikstad. Two large arched rooms on the ground floor are now used for banquets.

Old Penitentiary
The Old Penitentiary (Gamle Slaveri) was built in 1731 as a detention centre. It contained a room designed to hold 27 inmates. Today it is part of Fredrikstad Museum.

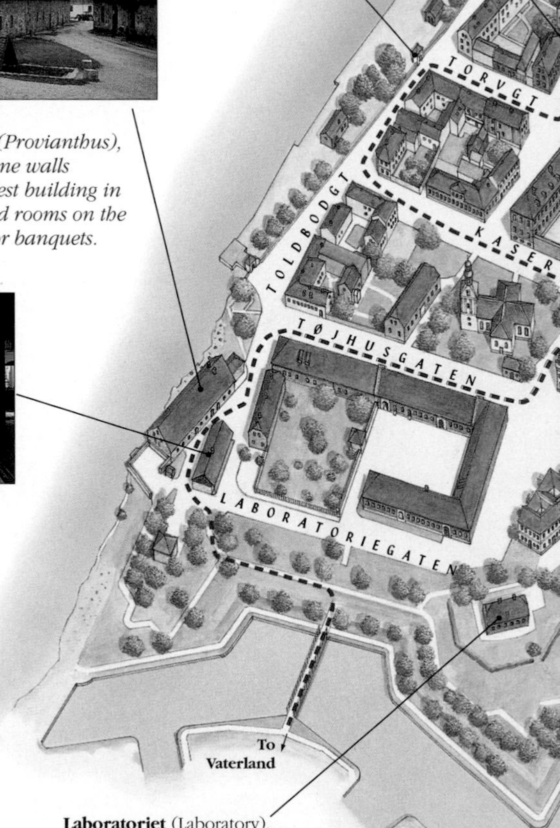

Glomma River

Mellomporten, the Middle Gate, 1727, is adorned with Frederik IV's monogram.

Laboratoriet (Laboratory), was constructed in 1802 as a gunpowder factory.

Star Sights

- ★ Kongens Torv
- ★ Provisions House

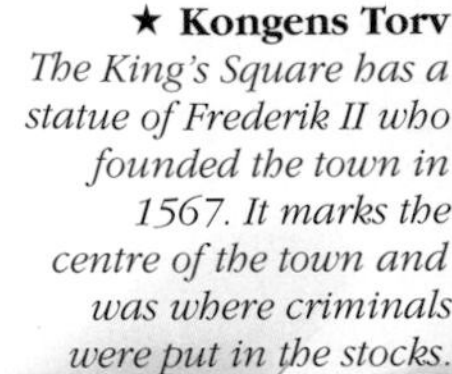

★ Kongens Torv
The King's Square has a statue of Frederik II who founded the town in 1567. It marks the centre of the town and was where criminals were put in the stocks.

VISITORS' CHECKLIST

County of Østfold. 68,000.
St Olavsgate 2. Torvbyen.
Voldportens Vaktstue, Gamlebyen, 69 30 46 00.
Summer market (Sat).
Winter Festival, Old Town (Jan/Feb), Animation Festival (May), Glomma Festival (July), Essens Artistic Music Festival (Sep), Folk and Dance Festival (Oct).

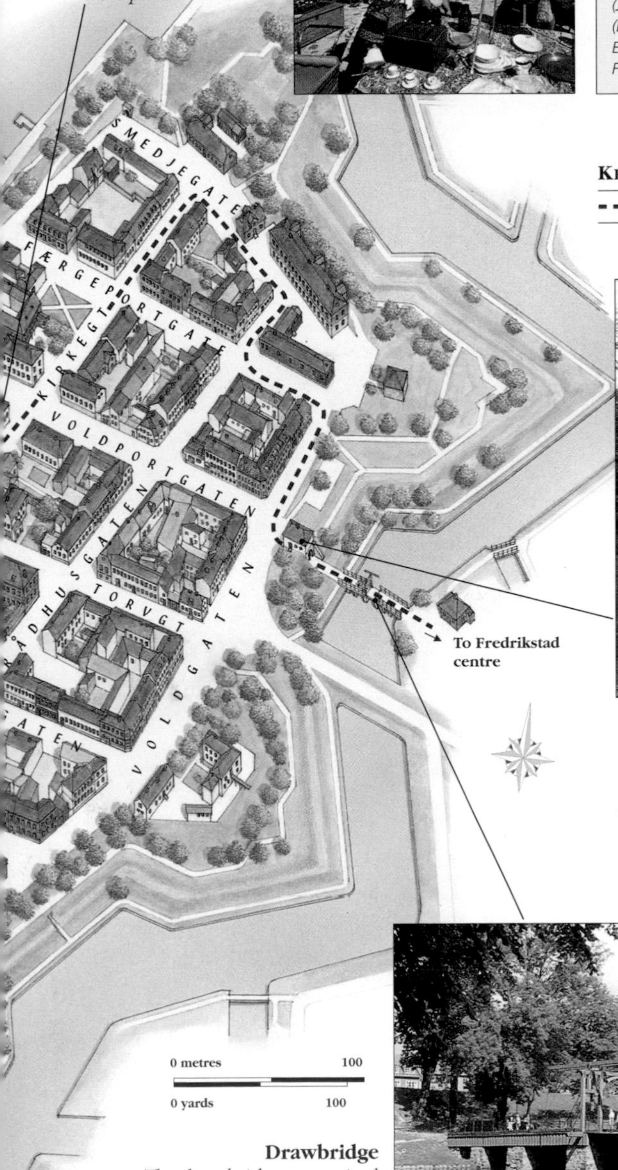

KEY

- - - Suggested route

Rampart Gate
The Rampart Gate (Voldporten) was built in 1695. Above the gateway is Christian V's monogram and his motto, Pietate et justitia *(Piety and Justice).*

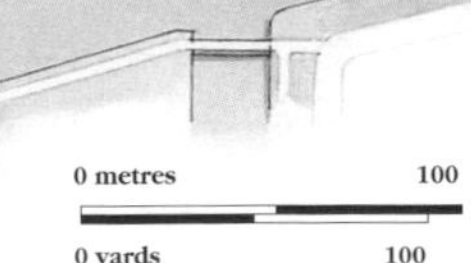

Drawbridge
The drawbridge was raised between last post and reveille. If the mounted postman arrived after it was raised, his sack was sent across the moat on a line.

Drøbak, south of Oslo, at Oslofjorden's narrowest point

Drøbak 6

County of Akershus. 13,000. summer. Havnegaten 4, 64 93 50 87. Oscarsborg plays (Jul).

HALF AN HOUR'S drive south of Oslo on the eastern side of Oslofjorden is the attractive wooden village of Drøbak. Originally it was a pilot station and served as Oslo's winterport when the fjord closer to the capital was ice bound. Today the village, with its narrow 18th- and 19th-century streets, is a popular place to live and a favourite summer holiday spot. From here, the 7.2-km (4.5-mile) Oslofjord Tunnel, opened in 2000, runs deep under the fjord to its western shore.

Drøbak has Norway's largest permanent year-round Christmas exhibition with Julehus (Christmas House) and Julenissens Postkontor (a post office, run by Father Christmas's pixie-like helper). The main square, Torget, and the adjoining streets have shops, art galleries and places to eat. Badeparken, a park area with a beach, is close by.

At the small harbour, the sea-water aquarium, **Saltvannsakvariet**, displays local species of fish and other marine life. Next to it, **Drøbak Båtforenings Maritime Samlinger** (the Maritime Collection), focuses on the area's coastal heritage.

Close to the centre, on Seiersten, is **Follo Museum** with a collection of 200–300-year-old buildings.

On an island just west of Drøbak lies **Oscarsborg Festning**. The fortress is best known for its role in the sinking of the German warship, *Blücher*, on 9 April 1940. Torpedoes fired from here hit the vessel as it made its way toward Oslo with the first occupational forces on board. This delayed the occupation and gave the king time to flee. In summer, plays are staged at the fortress.

Drøbak Båtforenings Maritime Samlinger
Kroketønna 4. 64 93 09 74.
daily.

Follo Museum
Belsjøveien 17. 64 93 99 90.
504. end May–mid-Sep: Tue–Fri. some public hols.

Oscarsborg Festning
Kaholmene. 64 90 42 03.
from Sjøtorget to Drøbak.
Jun–Jul: Tue–Sun.

Tusenfryd 7

County of Akershus. *64 97 64 97. special bus from Oslo Bussterminal every half hour 10am–1pm. May–Sep: daily.*

NORWAY'S LARGEST amusement park, Tusenfryd, is situated in a rural location 20 km (12 miles) south of Oslo at the intersection of the E6 and the E18 motorways.

The park's main attraction is Thundercoaster, the biggest wooden roller-coaster in Northern Europe. Opened in 2001, it thrills visitors with drops of 32 m (105 ft).

There are numerous rides, places to eat, shops and entertainments in addition to an area for water activities. Nearly half a million guests visit Tusenfryd every year.

One of many rides at Tusenfryd amusement park

Henie Onstad Kunstsenter 8

County of Akershus. *67 80 48 80. 151, 152 from Oslo. 10am–9pm Tue–Thu, 11am–6pm Mon, Fri, Sat, Sun.*

THE REMARKABLE centre for modern art, Henie Onstad Kunstsenter, was a gift to the nation from the three-times

Henie Onstad Kunstsenter, a fine collection of modern art

Olympic gold medal-winning skater, Sonja Henie (1928, 1932, 1936), and her husband, Niels Onstad. It houses the couple's art collection, including works by Matisse, Bonnard, Picasso and Miró, as well as Expressionist and abstract painters from the post-war period such as Estève and Soulages.

The trophy collection from Sonja Henie's exceptional sporting career is also on show. Alongside are the medals and cups she received for her outstanding performances in figure skating at the Olympic Games and in no fewer than 10 world championships.

The museum has a library, auditorium, a children's workshop, shop, café and an excellent restaurant.

Model of a three-masted ship at Marinemuseet, Horten

Horten ❾

County of Vestfold. *17,000.* *to Skoppum 10 km (6 miles) W of town.* *Tollbugata 1 A, 33 03 17 08.*

A BRONZE STATUE known as Hortenspiken (the Girl from Horten) welcomes visitors approaching the town from the north. The boat she is holding hints that this is a harbour town popular with pleasure boat owners. Horten developed around the 19th-century naval base of Karljohansvern, with its shipyard and harbour. In the well-preserved garrison buildings is **Marinemuseet**. Established in 1853, it is the oldest naval museum in the world. The museum contains an extensive collection of model ships, artifacts and exhibits relating to naval history. The world's first torpedo boat, *Rap*, 1872, is on display outside. A recent acquisition is the submarine, KNM *Utstein*, 1965, which is open to the public.

Next door is **Norsk Museum for Fotografi** (the Norwegian Museum of Photography). Cameras, photographs and other items are used to illustrate the development of the art.

Horten town centre, with its timber houses, retains much of its 19th-century character. In summer, the streets are decorated with flowers, and speed restrictions force cars to drive slowly. Outdoor cafés add to the charming atmosphere. But the town's main claim to fame is Storgaten, said to be Norway's longest shopping street.

Marinemuseet
Karljohansvern, 1 km (half a mile) E of the centre. *33 03 33 97.*
May–Aug: daily; Sep–Apr: Sun.
public hols.

Norsk Museum for Fotografi
Karljohansvern,1 km (half a mile) E of the centre. *33 03 16 30.*
15 Jun–14 Aug: daily; 15 Aug–14 Jun: Tue–Sun.

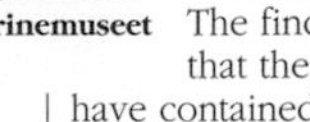

Figurehead, Marinemuseet

Borre National Park with its many burial mounds from the Viking age

Borre National Park ❿

County of Vestfold. *33 07 18 50.* *01 from Horten.* **Park** *all year.* **Midgard Historical Centre** *11am–6pm daily.* *public hols.*

THE SITE OF the most extensive collection of kings' graves in Scandinavia, Borre has seven large and 21 smaller burial mounds. Excavations at the end of the 1980s revealed that the oldest of the mounds dates from AD 600, i.e. before the Viking age, and it is likely that some of the mounds contain kings of the Ynglinge dynasty who had settled in Vestfold after fleeing from Sweden. The burial ground was used for another 300 years. A remarkable selection of craftwork has been unearthed. Given the name Borrestilen, the pieces feature intricate animal and knot ornaments, which were often used to decorate harnesses. The finds also confirm that the mounds might have contained ships similar to the Gokstad and Oseberg ships discovered around Oslofjorden *(see pp84–5)*.

Borre was Norway's first national park. The grassy mounds are set among woodlands in a well-tended area at the water's edge. Each season offers outdoor events with a historic theme, such as Viking Age Markets. The Historical Centre has displays of finds from the area.

Ferry passing through the narrow Drøbaksundet on Oslofjorden ▷

Color Line

A Trip from Tønsberg to Verdens Ende ⑪

THE SHORTEST ROUTE BETWEEN Tønsberg and the southernmost tip of Tjøme, otherwise known as World's End, is just 30 km (19 miles), but plenty of time is needed to explore this stunning archipelago, especially on the eastern side. The tour passes through a string of attractive holiday resorts. There are pretty coves, narrow sounds, old skipper's houses and quaint boathouses. Bridges connect the larger islands and the sea is never far away for a refreshing swim.

One of Tjøme's many waterside holiday homes

Tønsberg ①
Founded in 871, Tønsberg was a prosperous trading centre in the Middle Ages. The 19th-century tower, Slottsfjelltarnet, was built on the ruins of an ancient castle.

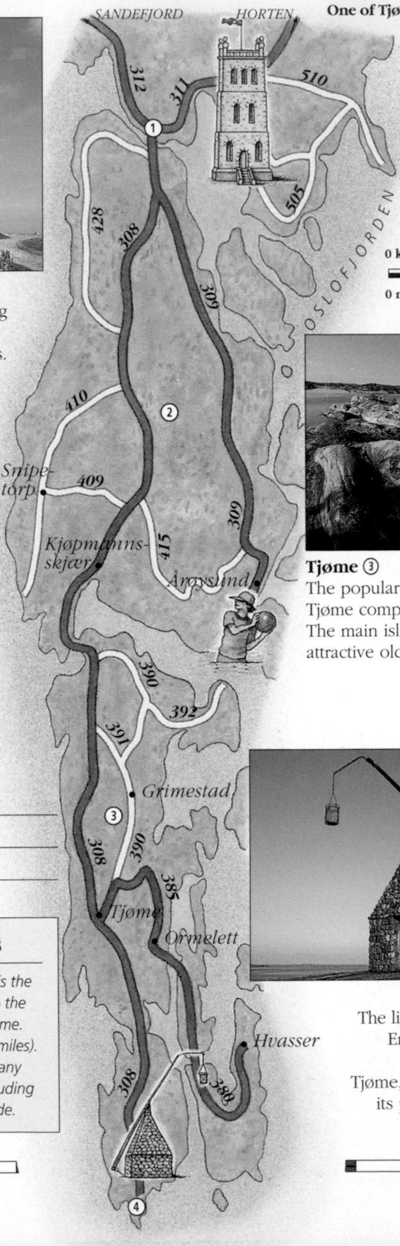

Nøtterøy ②
Between Tønsberg and Tjøme lies the archipelago of Nøtterøy comprising 175 islands. Nøtterøy has a number of ancient monuments, including a 12th-century church.

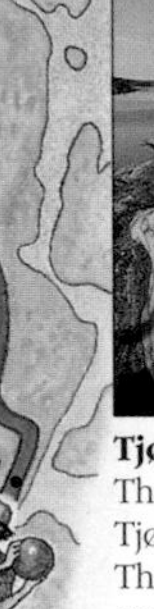

Tjøme ③
The popular holiday area of Tjøme comprises 478 islands. The main island has many attractive old houses.

KEY

Tour route

Other routes

Verdens Ende ④
The lighthouse at Verdens Ende, standing on the southernmost tip of Tjøme, is distinguished by its pivoting fire basket.

TIPS FOR DRIVERS

Starting point: *Tønsberg is the starting point for driving to the islands of Nøtterøy and Tjøme.*
Length: *about 20 km (12 miles).*
Places to eat: *there are many places to eat en route, including a restaurant at Verdens Ende.*

Sandefjord's whaling monument by Knut Steen, 1969

Sandefjord ⓬

County of Vestfold. 40,000. Thor Dahls Gate 1, 33 46 05 90. Midsummer Boat Procession (23 Jun), Summer Show on Rika (Jul), Classical Music on a Summer Night (1st and 2nd week Jul).

THE PRESENT TOWN of Sandefjord is relatively new, but archaeological finds from the Bronze and Viking Ages, such as the Viking ship unearthed at Gokstadhaugen in 1880 *(see pp84–5)*, bear witness to a long history of trading and seafaring. The harbour on the narrow fjord was known around 1200. In 1800, Sandfjord was burned to the ground and rebuilt.

Until the early 20th century, the spa, **Kurbadet** (1837), was renowned for its health-giving mud bath. It has been restored and is now a protected building, although the mud bath is no more.

Whaling was a dominant industry at Sandfjord for many years until it was halted in 1968. **Hvalfangstmuseet** (the Whaling Museum) shows the development of the industry from the primitive methods of catching whales to the introduction of factory ships. There is a special section on Arctic and Antarctic animal life.

The whaling monument on Strandpromenaden was designed by Knut Steen.

Kurbadet
Thor Dahls Gate. 33 46 58 57.
for cultural events and guided tours only. by prior arrangement.

Hvalfangstmuseet
Museumsgate 39. 33 48 46 50.
daily. some public hols.

Larvik ⓭

County of Vestfold. 40,000. Storgata 48, 33 13 91 00. Herregårdsspille plays (mid-Jul), Jazz concerts (Fri in summer).

LARVIK CAME INTO its own in the 17th century during the "Age of the Counts" when Ulrik Frederik Gyldenløve was appointed count of Larvik and the county of Laurvigen. In 1671 the town achieved market town status.

The count's residence, **Herregården**, was built in 1677 and is one of Norway's finest secular Baroque buildings. In 1835 the estate was acquired by the Treschow family who have played a prominent role in Larvik's economic life since then, mostly in the forestry industry alongside the Fritzøes. The **Fritzøe Museum**, in a manor house south of the town, charts their business dealings from 1600 onwards.

Larvik Sjøfartsmuseum (Maritime Museum) focuses on the nautical history of Larvik, particularly the age of sailing ships. Models by the famous boat-builder, Colin Archer, are on display and there is an exhibition on Thor Heyerdahl *(see p23)*. Larvik is also known for being the location of Norway's only mineral water spring.

Herregården
Herregårdssletta 6. 33 17 12 90.
end Jun–mid-Aug: Tue–Sun; mid-Aug–Sep & May–end Jun: Sun. public hols.

Fritzøe Museum
Nedre Fritzøe Gate 2. 33 17 12 90. *end Jun–mid Aug: Tue–Sun; mid-Aug–end Jun: Sun public hols.*

Larvik Sjøfartsmuseum
Kirkestredet 5. 33 17 12 90.
end Jun–mid-Aug: Tue–Sun; mid-Aug–Sep & May–end Jun: Sun. public hols.

Stavern ⓮

County of Vestfold. 2,000. to Larvik. summer: Havnegaten, 33 19 73 00; winter: Larvik. Stavern Festival (Jun/Jul).

A QUAINT MIXTURE of old and new, Stavern is a charming place beloved by holidaymakers. In summer the population more than doubles, due partly to the town's record of more than 200 days of sunshine a year.

From the mid-1750s until 1864, Stavern was Norway's main naval base with a shipyard, Fredriksvern. A gunpowder tower and commandant's house remain on Citadelløya (Citadel Island), today a refuge for artists. The town is made up of wooden buildings, most of them brightly painted in what has become known as "Stavern yellow". The huge monument, Minnehallen, with a plaque containing the names of seamen killed during World Wars I and II, is a fitting memorial to those who lost their lives.

Herregården, Larvik, an example of Norwegian Baroque

EASTERN NORWAY

THE THREE COUNTIES, *Hedmark, Oppland and Buskerud, together make up one-fifth of Norway's total land area. Mountains, valleys and lakes dominate the landscape, except for Buskerud which has a coastal strip to the far south. This is a region that has attracted artists and inspired writers such as Bjørnstjerne Bjørnson and Henrik Ibsen. It has a special appeal for climbers and hikers.*

Stretching through the heart of Eastern Norway like the five fingers on a hand are the long, thin valleys of Østerdalen, Gudbrandsdalen, Valdres, Hallingdal and Numedal. Great rivers such as Norway's longest, the Glomma, cut deep swathes through the landscape. The Glomma is 601 km (374 miles) in length and sweeps through Østerdalen from Riasten in Sør-Trøndelag to Fredrikstad. Lakes such as Mjøsa, measuring 107 km (66 miles) from its northern end near Lillehammer to Vorma in the south, make their mark on the landscape. Mountain villages cling to steep valley sides, topped by highland plateaux.

At the head of the valleys are vast towering mountain chains, which are highest in the north and west. Highland pastures and sparse forests gradually give way to bare rock and plateaux and peaks that are forever snow-covered. Climatically, the valleys have cold winters and warm summers, with a significant disparity between day and night temperatures.

Toward the south of the region, in the rural areas of Solør-Odal, Romerike, Ringerike and Hedemarken, the fertile agricultural land is among the best in the country. Extensive forests cover the landscape at relatively moderate altitudes.

The opportunity for outdoor activities is legion. Hiking trails are well-marked. Cycle routes are signposted and there are facilities for canoeing and other water sports. A network of mountain huts provides comfortable accommodation.

In late summer there is often an abundance of mushrooms and wild berries in the forests. In autumn, the mountains put on a magnificent show of colours before the winter brings snow and the chance to ski.

Cattle grazing in an enclosed pasture at Ringebu, Gudbrandsdalen

◁ **Deep snow creating a heavy burden for a timber cottage in Trysil forest**

Exploring Eastern Norway

THE MOUNTAINS OF EASTERN NORWAY offer exceptional opportunities for mountaineering, from the easy alpine pastures in Alvdal to the demanding peaks of the national parks in the northwest. The best way to experience the peaceful forests which characterize the most easterly parts of Norway is to follow a section of Finnskogleden, a 240-km (150-mile) long trail through Finnskogene (the Finn Forest) on the border with Sweden. However, Eastern Norway is more than just forests and mountains. The valleys and lowlands have a charm of their own, with interesting towns and attractions. Many areas offer good fishing, too.

Peer Gynt memorial stone at Sødorp old cemetery, Vinstra

SIGHTS AT A GLANCE

- Aulestad 8
- Drammen 22
- Dovrefjell 13
- Elverum 2
- Elveseter 16
- Geilo 18
- Hallingdal 19
- Hamar 6
- *Jotunheimen pp134–5* 15
- Kongsberg 21
- Kongsvinger 1
- *Lillehammer pp130–31* 7
- Lom 14
- Mjøsa 5
- Numedal 20
- Otta 11
- Ringebu 9
- Rondane National Park 12
- Trysil 3
- Valdres and Fagernes 17
- Vinstra 10
- Østerdalen and Rendalen 4

KEY

- Motorway
- Major road
- Minor road
- Railway line

The valleys and majestic mountains of Ottadalen, reflected in Lake Vågåvatnet

Ringebu Stavkirke, a 13th-century wooden church in Gudbrandsdalen

SEE ALSO

- *Where to Stay* see pp220–27
- *Where to Eat* see pp232–9

GETTING AROUND

The valleys of eastern Norway are in themselves important arteries. Østerdalen and Gudbrandsdalen have main roads (RV3 and E6) and railway lines running south to north. In Hallingdal the road runs east to west (RV7). Often, it is worth exploring some of the more interesting alternative routes. The mountain passes between the valleys are never far apart. Airports include Gardermoen on the E6 to the south of the region and Røros to the north.

Kongsvinger ❶

County of Hedmark. 17,500. Strandveien 3, 62 81 94 59. Kongsvinger Market (1st week May & Sep).

THE FORTRESS TOWN of Kongsvinger, situated on the Glomma River, was established during the Hannibal Feud in 1644 when a fortification was built here which grew to become a solid fortress. Øvrebyen (the Upper Town) was situated near the castle ramparts.

With the arrival of the railway in the 1860s, Kongsvinger became a market town. New building was concentrated around the train station. Later, the quarter between the station and Øvrebyen developed into the town centre, and a bridge and town hall were built. In 1965 the town was designated as a "Development Centre" which led to industrial expansion.

Kongsvinger Festning (Fortress) is an irregular star-shaped castle with 16 batteries, fine old buildings and a museum of the armed forces. From the castle ramparts there is a splendid view over the town and river toward Sweden.

The forests between Glomma and the Swedish border were settled by Finnish immigrants in the 17th century. **Finnetunet**, a museum of Finnish culture at Svullrya, in Grue Finnskog, is made up of 13 buildings, the oldest dating from the end of the 18th century. It gives a picture of farming culture and the daily life of the people of Finnskogene (Finn Forest). A hiking track, Finnskogleden, heads north through the forests from Finnetunet.

Houses at the Glomdalsmuseet, Elverum, recalling a bygone era

Kongsvinger Festning
1 km (half a mile) N of town centre.
62 88 67 75. **Castle area** *daily.* **Museum** *Jun–Aug: daily.*

Finnetunet
40 km (25 miles) NE of Kongsvinger.
62 94 56 90. *Jul: daily.*

Elverum ❷

County of Hedmark. *18,000.* *Storgata 24, 62 41 31 16.* *Grundsetmart'n (Mar), Culture Festival (Aug), Nordic Hunting and Fishing Days (Aug).*

AT A MEETING ON 9 April 1940, the day of the German invasion, the Norwegian Parliament approved the Elverum Mandate giving the fleeing Norwegian government considerable powers for the remainder of World War II. The following day King Haakon rejected Germany's demand for a new Norwegian government. On 11 April, central Elverum was bombed; 54 people died. At the high school, a monument by Ørnulf Bast commemorates the king's stand.

Elverum quickly rose from the ashes after the war to become an administrative, commercial, educational and military centre.

The quarter on the eastern side of the Glomma River is known as Leiret, and evolved from the buildings below the old fortification, Christiansfjell. Grundsetmart'n, a winter market that between 1740 and 1900 was the most important in Scandinavia, is still held here.

Glomdalsmuseet is a comprehensive collection of 88 buildings from the mountain villages and rural lowland communities and contains some 30,000 exhibits. It is Norway's third largest open-air museum.

Connected by a bridge across the Glomma is **Norsk Skogbruksmuseum** (the Norwegian Forestry Museum), founded in 1954. This is the only museum in the country specializing in forestry, hunting and fishing. The open-air section features different types of buildings, from lumberjack cottages to fishing huts and boathouses.

Kongsvinger Festning and the panoramic view toward Sweden

Glomdalsmuseet
Museumsveien 15. *62 41 91 00.* *Jun–Aug daily.*

Norsk Skogsbruks-museum
Solørveien 151. *62 40 90 00.* *daily.* *some public hols.*

Trysil ❸

County of Hedmark. 7,100. *Storveien 3, 62 45 10 00.* *Trysil Ski Season Finale (end Apr), Swingin' Trysil Blues, Jazz and Rock Festival (end Jun), Sund Market (Sep).*

In the past, the road through the forest from Elverum to Trysil was known as "the seven-mile forest". The trip used to be very slow for drivers with heavy loads, but today the roads are good and the journey quick. Trysil is a typical woodland valley with spruce and pine forests and marshland topped by mountainous terrain.

The valley follows the Trysil River from the lake of Femunden through Engerdal to the Swedish border. Femunden is Norway's third largest lake, stretching 60 km (37 miles) north. Ferries operate in summer. The administrative centre is at Innbygda.

Snowboarder on Trysilfjellet

The mountain of **Trysilfjellet** (1,137 m/3,730 ft) is the site for Norway's biggest alpine skiing centre. Sports fishing is good in the Trysilelva and "little" Ljøra.

In the eastern wilderness is **Femundsmarka National Park**, where the Svukuriset tourist lodge is located, and **Gutulia National Park** with its 300–400 year-old primeval forests.

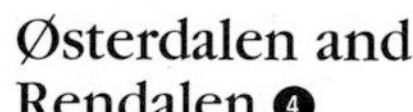

Østerdalen and Rendalen ❹

County of Hedmark. 28,000. *Alvdal Tourist Information, 62 48 89 99.*

The two valleys of Østerdalen and Rendalen run parallel in a south-north direction. The RV3 road through Østerdalen follows the Glomma, Norway's longest river, past several places of interest. **Rena**, the next town north of Elverum, had a ferry crossing already in the Middle Ages, as well as accommodation for pilgrims on their way to the cathedral of Nidarosdomen *(see p125)*. Today, Rena is a skiing centre and the starting point for the Birkebeiner race *(see p130)*.

A further 55 km (34 miles) upriver, **Koppang** has a folk museum with buildings from the region. North of Atna, the road runs through virtually uninhabited forest, passing **Jutulhogget**, a precipitously deep gorge.

Further north, in the small town of **Alvdal**, the Husantunet is a folk museum with 17 houses from around 1600, while **Aukrustsenteret** has paintings and drawings featuring colourful characters from the books of author and illustrator Kjell Aukrust. Alvdal is the starting point for family-friendly mountain walks and also of Norway's second highest *turistvei* (tourist road), which runs to the top of the 1,666-m (5,466-ft) high **Tronfjellet** mountain.

Jutulhogget, a gorge more than 100 m (328 ft) deep

At Tynset, the RV30 leads northeast to the old mining centre of **Tolga** and the village of **Os**, close to the county boundary with Trøndelag.

Rendalen valley can be reached by taking the RV30 south from Tynset through **Tylldalen**, where the harvest-related feast day of *Olsok* (St Olav's Day) is celebrated on 29 July. Alternatively, a road from Hanestad, south of Alvdal, leads to the valley across the mountain passes, ending at the church of **Øvre Rendal** at Bergset, which dates from 1759. Its vicarage has a museum dedicated to Jacob B Bull, who wrote about daily life in the region. From here, there is a mountain road to the fishing village of **Fiskevollen** on Sølensjøen lake, and the 1,755-m (5,758-ft) high mountain of Rendalsølen.

The RV30 runs from Bergset south along the valley toward **Otnes** by **Lomnessjøen** lake, a particularly beautiful part of Rendalen. Rushing south from the lake, the Åkrestrømmen is renowned for its abundance of Common white fish *(Coregonus lavaretus)*. From here the RV217 leads to two other famous fishing spots – **Galten** and **Isterfossen** – 45 km (28 miles) to the northeast.

Åkrestrømmen ends in Storsjøen ("Big Lake") from where the river Rena runs south to join the Glomma at Rena.

An old farm wall providing a sheltered resting place for skiers

Aukrustsenteret

Alvdal centre. 62 48 78 77. *May–Sep: daily, Oct–Apr: by arrangement.*

Mjøsa ❺

Counties of Hedmark & Oppland.
Hamar, 62 51 75 00; Lillehammer, 61 25 92 99.

NORWAY'S LARGEST lake, Mjøsa, is 100 km (62 miles) long and lies at the heart of an agricultural area. Many of the farms in Hedemarken, Helgøya and Totenlandet have been settlements since Viking times. They are bordered by forests and mountains, including Skreiafjellene (700 m/2,296 ft). Three towns, Lillehammer *(see pp130–31)*, Hamar and Gjøvik are spread around the lakeshore.

Before the arrival of cars and trains, Mjøsa was an important communications centre, even in winter when horses and sledges would cross the frozen lake. The completion of the railway to Eidsvoll in 1854 led to the arrival of a paddle steamer, *Skibladner*, known as "The White Swan of Mjøsa". Built in Sweden, it was transported to Mjøsa in pieces and reassembled. Today Norway's oldest ship ferries people between the Mjøsa towns.

Helgøya, "the holy island", situated in the widest part of the lake, was the site of medieval mansions for bishops and the aristocracy, and a seat for the king. Among the farming estates are Hovinsholm and Baldishol, where the Baldishol Tapestry (1200) was found *(see page 59)*. Further north, between Brumunddal and Moelv, lies Rudshøgda, the childhood home of the writer and singer, Alf Prøysen.

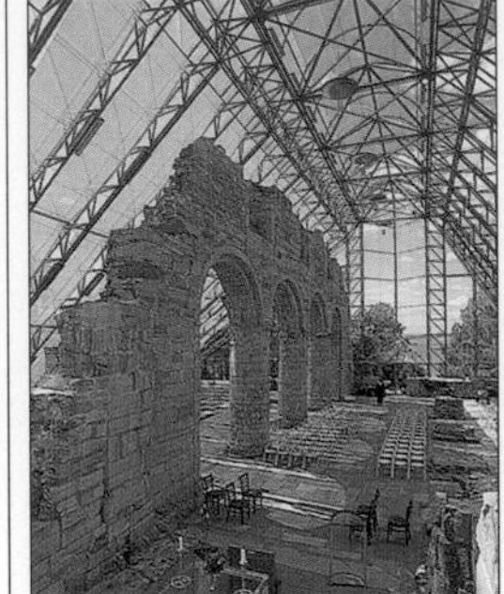

Hamar's ruined 16th-century cathedral encased in a glass dome

Hamar ❻

County of Hedmark. 28,000. summer: Akersvikaveien 3, 62 51 75 00. Hamar Market (Aug/Sep).

THE TOWN OF HAMAR is the largest on Lake Mjøsa. It has had two lives, the first as a Norse market town from 1049 until 1567 when a fire destroyed the cathedral. Then in 1849 Hamar achieved town status and began its second life as a cultural, commercial and industrial centre.

The remains of the cathedral, **Domkirkeruinerna**, are protected by a glass dome. Built in 1100, the cathedral was noted for its triple nave, but after the fire and subsequent pillaging, only crumbling columns and arches give an idea of its original appearance.

Hedmarksmuseet is a folk museum comprising more than 50 traditional buildings and a monastery herb garden. It also has a section devoted to those who emigrated to North America, complete with settlers' houses from North Dakota and Minnesota.

The Railway Museum, **Jernbanemuseet**, features a narrow-gauge railway (the *Tertitbanen*), engines, railway carriages and station buildings.

Hamar Olympic Hall, designed on the lines of an upturned boat, was built as a skating rink for the Winter Olympics in 1994. There is a bird sanctuary at Akersvika, to the south of the town.

Domkirkeruinerna
Strandveien 100. 62 54 27 00.
mid-May–Aug: daily; Sep–mid-May: by arrangement.

Hedmarksmuseet
Strandveien 100. 62 54 27 00.
mid-May–Aug: daily; Sep–mid-May: by appointment.

Jernbanemuseet
Strandveien 132. 62 51 31 60.
May–Aug: daily.

Lillehammer ❼

See pp130–31.

Aulestad, the home of Bjørnstjerne Bjørnson in Østre Gausdal

Aulestad ❽

County of Oppland. 400.
Lillehammer, 61 25 92 99.
Aulestad Festival (May).

THE WRITER Bjørnstjerne Bjørnson (1832–1910) bought the farm of Aulestad, in Østre Gausdal, 18 km (11 miles) northwest of Lillehammer, in 1874. The following year, he moved here with his wife, Karoline.

As well as writing stories, poems and plays, Bjørnson was an outstanding orator and a key politician. He was awarded the Nobel Prize for literature in 1903.

The author's home, known as **Dikterhjemmet på**

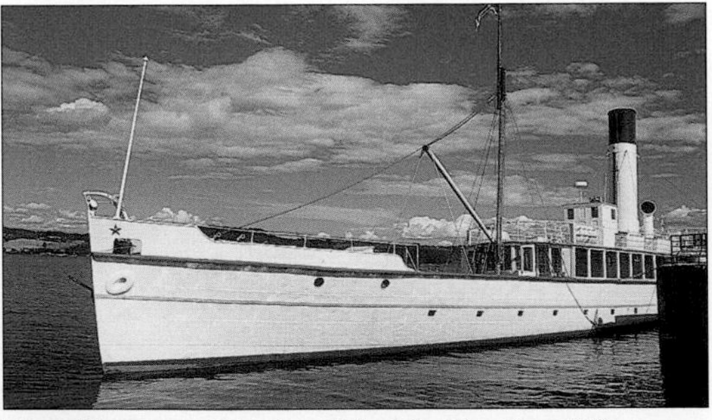

The paddle steamer, *Skibladner*, plying Lake Mjøsa since 1856

The countryside near Ringebu looking toward Lågen river

Aulestad, remains as it was when he lived here. It contains a varied selection of Bjørnson memorabilia and the couple's fine collections of sculptures and paintings, photographs and manuscripts. The property was bought by the state in 1922.

Dikterhjemmet på Aulestad
Follebu, 18 km (11 miles) NW of Lillehammer. 61 22 41 10. *May–Sep: daily.*

Ringebu 9

County of Oppland. *4,700.* *Ringebu Skysstasjon (Train Station), 61 28 47 00.* *Alpine World Cup (Ist week Mar).*

SITUATED ON THE river Gudbrandsdalslågen, the village of Ringebu is known for its stave church. The **Ringebu Stavkirke** dates from the 13th century. It was extended between 1630 and 1631 by the builder Werner Olsen, who rebuilt several stave churches in the Gudbrandsdalen valley. The doorway with dragon motifs is from the original stave church, while the altarpiece and pulpit are Baroque.

ENVIRONS: The long valley of **Gudbrandsdalen**, running from north of Lillehammer up past Dovrefjell *(see p132)*, cuts through a beautiful landscape, with many roads providing access into the mountains. It is at its widest in the district of **Fron**, where it has been compared to Germany's Mosel valley. The octagonal church of Sør-Fron, in Louis XVI style, dates from the 18th century. The area is also known for its distinctive brown, sweet-tasting goat cheese.

Ringebu Stavkirke
1 km (half a mile) S of town centre. 61 28 43 50. *May–Aug: daily; Sep–Apr: by prior arrangement.* *May–Aug.*

Vinstra 10

County of Oppland. *6,000.* *Vinstra Skysstasjon (Train Station), 61 29 47 70.* *Titano Festival (Jul), Peer Gynt-Festival (Aug).*

AT VINSTRA, the **Peer Gynt-samlingen** contains considerable material on both the historical and the literary figure of Peer Gynt.

The 65-km (40-mile) long Peer Gyntveien (Peer Gynt Road) is a mountain toll road running west of the Gudbrandsdalen valley from Tretten to Vinstra. Offering splendid views, it passes a number of hotels and mountain lodges, among them Skeikampen, Gausdal, Gålå, Wadahl and Fefor. The highest point on the road is at 1,053 m (3,455 ft). At Gålå there is the open-air theatre, Gålåvatnet Friluftsteater, which stages a musical interpretation of Ibsen's original *Peer Gynt* every year in early August.

Peer Gynt-samlingen
Vinstra, town centre south. 61 29 47 70. *end-Jun–mid-Aug: daily.*

PEER GYNT

Henrik Ibsen's dramatic poem, *Peer Gynt*, was written in 1867 and is regarded as the most important of all Norwegian literary works. Ibsen had hiked in the area north of Vinstra in 1862 and the farm, Hågå, where his supposed model, the hunter and habitual liar Peder Lauritsen, lived in the 17th century is situated next to the Peer Gynt Road on the northeastern side of the valley – an attraction in itself. Ibsen's play starts with Peer telling his mother, Åse, about the buck ride along Gjendineggen. Åse berates him for running around in the mountains rather than courting the heiress at the farm of Hægstad. So Peer goes there, but instead meets Solveig, who says she will wait for the adventurer "both winter and spring" and who becomes his redeemer.

The "Peer Gynt" farm at Hågå, northeast of Vinstra

Lillehammer 7

THE SKIER IN THE CITY'S COAT OF ARMS signifies that Lillehammer has long been a popular winter sports centre. In 1994 it came to worldwide attention as the venue for the XVII Winter Olympic Games, but its skiing traditions go back to 1206 when the royal infant, Håkon Håkonsson, was carried to safety across the mountains by skiers *(see pp26–7)*. The annual Birkebeiner Race is run on skis from Rena in Østerdalen to Lillehammer in memory of the rescue. Tourists and painters alike have also been attracted to Lillehammer by the beautiful scenery and the quality of the light. The city's other claim to fame, the Maihaugen outdoor museum, is the legacy of Anders Sandvig, a dentist with a passion for antiques and old buildings, who settled here in 1885.

The museum of Maihaugen depicting life in the rural communities

Maihaugen

Maihaugveien 1. *61 28 89 00.* *18 May–30 Sep: daily; 1 Oct–16 May: Tue–Sun.* *public hols.*

In 1887 Anders Sandvig established one of the biggest and most important museums of farming culture in Norway, De Sandvigske Samlinger in Maihaugen.

Sandvig was a dentist who, during his travels in Gudbrandsdalen, started collecting both objects and houses. What began as a hobby grew to include 175 houses reflecting the building techniques and everyday lives of local people. Houses have been rebuilt to create a farming estate, a mountain farm, a crofter's holding and a summer pasture hamlet. The museum aims to show a living environment with animals and people going about their normal activities. One of Norway's oldest stave churches, Garmokirken, can be seen here.

In 1927 a collection of handicrafts and tools from around the country was added.

Lillehammer Kunstmuseum

Stortorget 2. *61 05 44 60.* *Jul–Aug: daily; Sep–Jun: Tue–Sun.* *some public hols.*

It was the 19th-century artist, Fredrik Collett, who first became fascinated by the light and motifs at Lillehammer. Erik Werenskiold, Frits Thaulow and Henrik Sørensen were among the many artists to follow in his footsteps.

Their work forms the basis of the superb collection of Norwegian painting, sculpture and graphic design on show at the museum, which also includes a selection of pieces by Munch, Christian Krohg and Adolf Tidemand.

The building itself is strikingly modern and also features a stone and water garden of stark beauty.

Norsk Kjøretøyhistorisk Museum

Lilletorget 1. *61 25 61 65.* *daily.*

The Norsk Kjøretøyhistorisk Museum (Museum of Historic Vehicles) has around 100 vehicles, including cars,

Historic vehicle in the Norsk Kjøretøyhistorisk Museum

motorcycles, horse-drawn carriages and old pedal cycles such as the velocipede (the so-called "Veltepetter").

For train enthusiasts, there is an electric locomotive from 1909, and a superb large model railway.

Bjerkebæk

Nordseterveien 23. *61 25 22 57.* *closed for refurbishment.*

Lillehammer's most notable resident was the author and Nobel Prize-winner, Sigrid Undset *(see p22)*, who settled here in 1921. She lived with her books in splendid isolation in this house with its magnificent garden protected by a hedge. The house itself had been moved from Gudbrandsdalen and re-erected at Bjerkebæk.

Undset's great work about the medieval heroine, Kristin Lavransdatter, was published at the time she moved to Lillehammer. Her historical oeuvre about Olav Audunssøn in Hestviken was to follow.

Norges Olympiske Museum

Håkonshall, Olympiaparken. *61 25 21 00.* *May–Aug: daily; Sep–May: Tue–Sun.* *some public hols.*

Norges Olympiske Museum (the Olympic Museum) offers an opportunity to experience the atmosphere of the 1994 Winter Olympic Games, when 1,737 participants from 67 countries came to Lillehammer.

Innovative techniques are used to convey the history of the Olympics, going back to the Greek summer and winter games of 776 BC, and to glimpse the societies in which the games took place.

Pierre de Coubertin's re-creation of the games in Athens in 1886 is shown, as are the first Winter Olympics, held in Chamonix in 1924.

◁ **View of Rondane with the peaks of Høgronden, 2,114 m (6,936 ft), and Digerronden, 2,020 m (6,627 ft)**

Olympiaparken

1 km (half a mile) E of town centre.
daily all year round.

The investment for the 1994 Winter Olympics provided Lillehammer with magnificent amenities, including Lysgårdsbakkene Ski Jumping Arena. In winter it is possible to take the chairlift to the top for a fantastic view. Håkons Hall, the ice-hockey arena, has facilities for other sports such as handball and golf. It also has a 20-m (66-ft) climbing wall. Birkebeineren Skistadion is the starting point for a floodlit skiing track and cross-country trails.

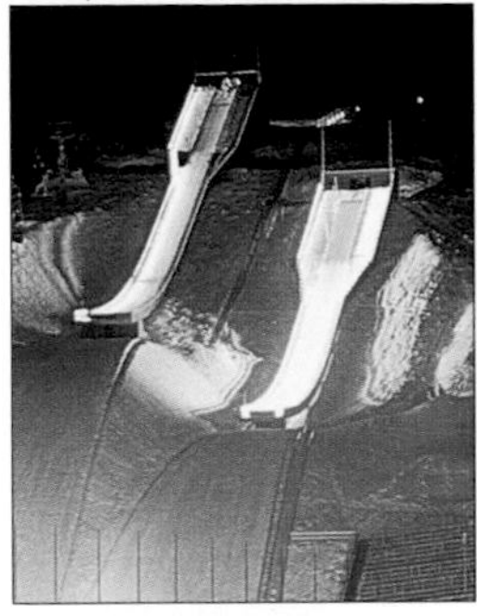

Olympiaparken ski jump complex, 1994 Winter Olympics

Lilleputthammer

14 km (9 miles) N of town centre.
61 28 55 50. *Jun–Aug: daily.*

The pedestrian part of Storgata in Lillehammer is known as "Gå-gata", the model for the miniature town of Lilleputthammer. It is an enjoyable place for children.

Hunderfossen Adventure Park

Fåberg, 13 km N (8 miles) N of town centre. *61 27 72 22. Jun–mid-Aug: daily.*

The world's largest troll and a glittering fairytale palace themed on old Norwegian tales welcome the visitor to Hunderfossen. There are some 40 rides and attractions for both children and adults, including a swimming pool and car circuit.

Nearby, the **Hafjell Alpine Centre**, with 25 km (16 miles) of graded slopes, is the largest skiing complex in the area. There is a 710-m (2,330-ft) long artificially frozen bob-sleigh run with 16 bends, or if ice is in short supply, there is a "wheeled bob" instead.

Visitors' Checklist

County of Oppland. *25,000.* *Elvegaten 19, 61 25 92 99; summer Sliperiveien 2, 61 25 95 05. Winter Festival (Feb), Birkebeiner Race (Mar), Blues Festival (Easter), Literature Festival (May), Lillehammer Festival (Jun), Dølajazz (Oct).*

Water ride at Hunderfossen Adventure Park

Lillehammer Town Centre

Bjerkebæk ④
Lillehammer Kunstmuseum ②
Maihaugen ①
Norges Olympiske Museum ⑤
Norsk Kjøretøyhistorisk Museum ③

0 metres 400
0 yards 400

Hunderfossen Adventure Park
Lilleputthammer
Olympiaparken
Fåberggata
Storgata
Gamlevegen
Nordsetervegen
Sigrid Undsets Gate
Birkebeinervegen
Løkkegata
Tomtegata
Brufoss Gate
Maihaugvegen
Mesnadalsvegen
Jernbanegata
Bankgata
Anders Sandvigs Gate
Langes Gate
Strandpromenaden
Bryggevegen
Mathiesens Gate
Weidemanns Gate
Kirkegata
Mjøsa

Key

- Train station
- Bus terminal
- Parking
- Church
- Tourist information

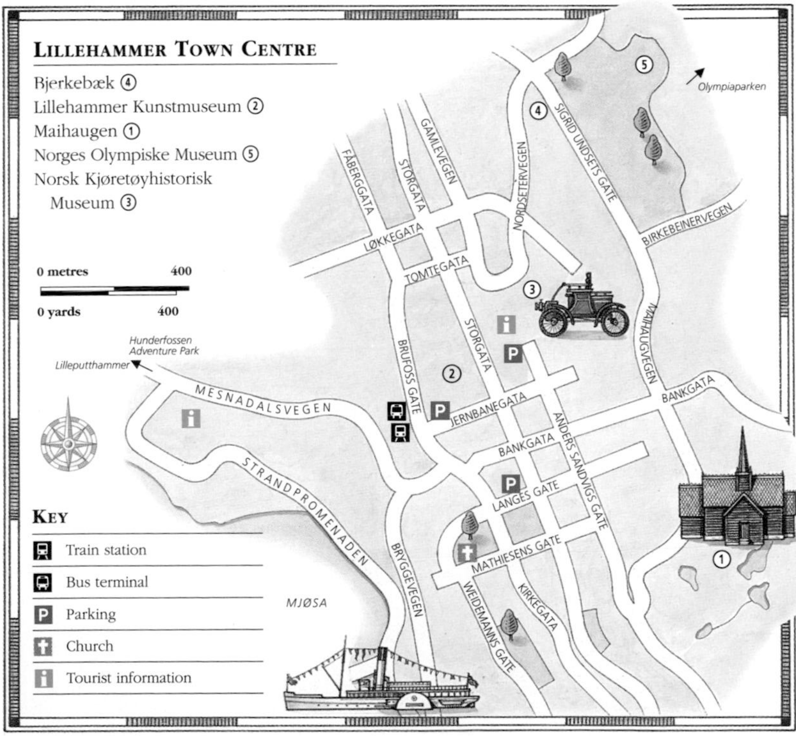

Rondane National Park, a much loved recreational area at all times of the year

Otta ⓫

County of Oppland. 3,500. *Ola Dahl's Gate 1, 61 23 66 50. Dance Festival (mid-Jul), Kristin Festival (1st week Jul), Sjoa Kajak Festival (3rd week Jul), Otta Market (1st week Oct).*

SINCE THE ARRIVAL of the railway in 1896, Otta has been a tourist hub, because of its proximity to the national parks of Rondane, Dovre and Jotunheimen. Otta lies at the junction of the Otta and Lågen rivers. It is the regional centre for North Gudbrandsdalen and a main terminus for buses to and from the adjoining valleys and mountain areas. Historically, Otta is known for the Battle of Kringen in 1612, when an army of local farmers destroyed a Scottish army of mercenaries on their way to fight in the Kalmar War.

At Selsverket there is a summer toll road to Mysuseter and Rondane.

Rondane National Park ⓬

County of Oppland. *Otta Tourist Information, 61 23 66 50.*

ESTABLISHED IN 1962, Rondane was Norway's first national park. It has a well-developed network of routes with several tourist lodges, including Rondvassbu and Bjørnhollia. In the mountains, walkers hike from hut to hut.

The landscape is split by deep gorges: Ilmanndalen runs in an east/west direction; Rondvatnet/Rondvassdalen and Langglupdalen run south to north. There are 10 peaks in excess of 2,000 m (6,562 ft) and even the lowest areas are around 900 m (2,953 ft) above sea level. Rondeslottet ("Ronde Castle") is the highest mountain here, reaching 2,178 m (7,145 ft).

Rondane has both gentle, rounded mountains and wild, practically inaccessible parts with deep, north-facing glacial cirques. Among the geological oddities from the last Ice Age are strange hollows of dead ice (a glacial deposit left behind after the glacier melted). Large numbers of wild reindeer populate the mountains.

The rural centre of **Folldal** grew up around an 18th-century community that mined deposits of copper-rich pyrite. The mines were later moved to Hjerkinn at Dovre. Original houses from Folldal and Dovre have been preserved in a rural museum.

The valley of Einunndalen, extending north from Folldal, is used as a summer pasture.

Dovrefjell ⓭

County of Oppland. *in Dombås, 61 24 14 44.*

THE MOUNTAIN PLATEAU of Dovrefjell marks the conceptual divide between Norway "north of the mountains" and Norway "south of the mountains". In 1814, Dovrefjell was used to signify the unity of the nation when the men at Eidsvoll *(see p38)* sang *Enige og tro til Dovre faller* ("In harmony and faith till Dovre falls").

Kongeveien, the King's Road from the south, crossed the plateau. Mountain huts built nearly 900 years ago

The mighty Snøhetta rising majestically over the Dovrefjell plateau

have saved the lives of many a traveller in these parts. The Dovrebane railway was completed in 1921.

Wild reindeer and musk oxen inhabit the region and rare species of birds, such as short-eared owl, cuckoo and hen harrier, live on the moorlands of Fokstumyrene. **Dovrefjell National Park** was established in 1974. It surrounds Norway's fourth tallest mountain, the 2,286-m (7,500-ft) high Snøhetta ("Snow Cap"). Hjerkinn is the highest point on both the road and the railway. Here, Eysteins Kirke was consecrated in 1969 in memory of King Eystein (c.1100) who built the mountain huts. This is also the starting point of the infamously steep road, *Vårstigen*, to Kongsvoll in the county of Trøndelag *(see p186)*.

Lom Stavkirke constructed in the early Middle Ages

Lom ⓮

County of Oppland. *2,600.* *to Otta.* Norsk Fjellmuseum, *61 21 29 90.* *Flåklypa Veteran Car Rally (May).*

The rural centre of Lom, on the banks of the Otta river, is a gateway to the valley of Bøverdalen, the Jotunheimen mountain range and Sognefjellet mountain. The stave church here, **Lom Stavkirke**, was built in 1000 and retains its original deep foundations. It acquired its cruciform shape around 1600. Details such as the dragon heads on the gables have much in common with the churches seen around Sognefjorden *(see pp174–5)*. **Norsk Fjellmuseum** (the Norwegian

Fossheim Steinsenter, with an 8-m (26-ft) tall model of a rock crystal

Mountain Museum), opened in 1994, is a good source of practical information on the mountain wilderness and it has videos showing mountain routes. This is in addition to its natural history exhibits. The Fossheim Hotel – a piece of cultural history in itself – houses **Fossheim Steinsenter** (the Fossheim Stone Centre) comprising a geological museum and a silversmith workshop.

East from Lom, at a crossing on the Otta river, is Vågå, which is also known for having a stave church (1130). Vågå is the burial site of the reindeer hunter Jo Gjende. Its other claim to fame is Jutulporten, a giant "door" in the mountainside that appears in Norwegian legend.

Lom Stavkirke
Lom. *61 21 73 38.* *mid-May–mid-Sep: daily.*

Norsk Fjellmuseum
Lom. *61 21 16 00.* *May–Sep: daily; Oct–Apr: Mon–Fri*

Fossheim Steinsenter
Lom. *61 21 14 60.* *daily.* *some public hols.*

Jotunheimen ⓯

See pp134–5.

Elveseter ⓰

Bøverdalen, 25 km (16 miles) SW of Lom. *61 21 20 00.* *1 Jun–mid-Sep.*

Lying in the shadow of Galdhøpiggen (2,469 m/ 8,100 ft), Norway's highest mountain, is the farming estate of Elveseter, which has accommodated visitors since 1880. More recently it has been rebuilt as a dedicated tourist hotel *(see p223)* in the architectural style of the valley. The oldest house, Midgard, dates from 1640. Nearby stands Sagasøylen, a 33-m (108-ft) tall monument decorated with motifs from Norwegian history, crowned by Harald Finehair on horseback.

From here, the scenic RV 55, Sognefjellsveien, continues to Skjolden in Sogn. The road was maintained by farmers from Lom and Sogn from around 1400 so that people from northern Gudbrandsdal could reach Bergen to trade their goods. According to a traffic survey from 1878, 16,525 people and 2,658 horses travelled across the mountain in that year.

The current road was built in 1938. Its highest point is 1,440 m (4,724 ft) above sea level. On the way to Skjolden on Sognefjorden it runs past the Sognefjell tourist hut, and Turtagrø hotel, a centre for climbers since 1888.

Elveseter, a farmhouse turned hotel in deepest Jotunheimen

Jotunheimen ⓯

BEFORE 1820 THE JOTUNHEIMEN mountain range was known only to local hunters, fishermen and herdsmen. It was not until the late 19th century that tourists began to discover this wild and mighty mountain region in the heart of the county of Oppland. The National Park was established in 1980. Norway's highest peaks – over 2,300 m (7,546 ft) – are located in Jotunheimen, interspersed between large glaciers, lakes and valleys. A well-developed network of footpaths crosses the mountains, linking 30 mountain huts. Some of these are run by the Norwegian tourist authorities (DNT) and some are privately owned.

Bøverdalen

From Bøverdalen valley a toll road winds up to Juvasshytta (1,841 m/ 6,040 ft). From here there is a relatively easy walk to the top of Galdhøpiggen.

Galdhøpiggen

Even in summer it is possible to ski in the vicinity of Galdhøpiggen, Norway's highest mountain at 2,469 m (8,100 ft). The snow is always good on the glacier.

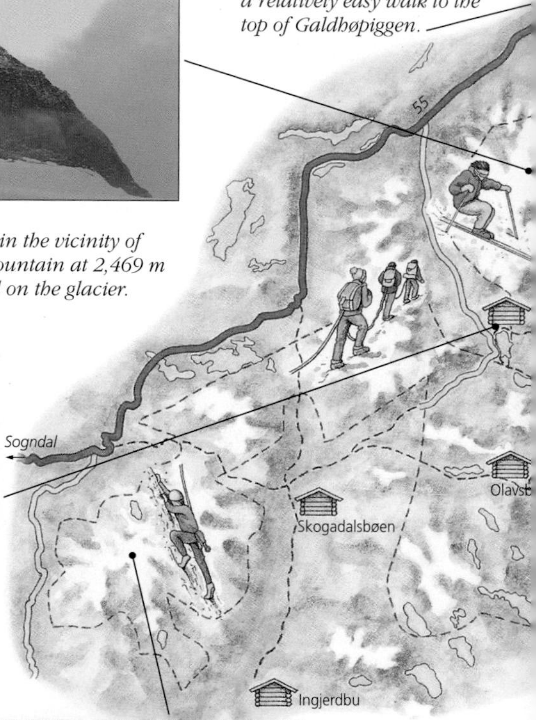

Leirvassbu

The hut is 1,400 m (4,593 ft) above sea level, at the head of Leirdalen, with splendid views of peaks and glaciers.

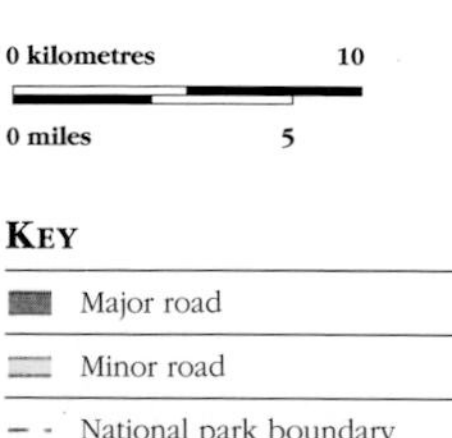

KEY

- Major road
- Minor road
- National park boundary
- Hiking trail
- Mountain hut

Store Skagastølstind

"Storen", 2,403 m (7,884 ft), is Norway's third highest peak and a mountain climbers' dream. It was first scaled by William C Slingsby in 1876.

Fishing
Trout fishing can be good in the rivers and lakes of Jotunheimen. Many walkers take their own fishing equipment with them. Huts and hotels have information about licences, and the chances of a bite.

Visitors' Checklist

County of Oppland. RV 55 from Fossbergom near RV 15.
Jotunheimen Reiseliv, 61 21 29 90. *to Lom, then change on to a local bus (summer only).*
guided walks by arrangement.
www.visitlom.com

Svellnosbreen
The glacier above Spiterstulen has deep crevices, dramatic ice formations and tunnels. Ropes and the services of a glacier guide are essential.

Lom
Røysheim
øverdal
Juvasshytta
Glittertind
2,465 m
(8,088 ft)
Spiterstulen
Glitterheim
Otta
JOTUNHEIMEN NATIONAL PARK
51
Memurubu
Gjendesheim
Gjendebu
Fagernes

Besseggen
The high route across the Besseggen ridge between Gjendesheim and Memurubu is one of the most popular in Jotunheimen. The ridge rises above the green waters of Gjende and the deep blue Lake Bessvatnet.

Gjende
The fabled Lake Gjende, coloured green by glacial water, is considered the soul of Jotunheimen. It is 18 km (11 miles) long, and stretches between two of the most popular lodges, Gjendesheim and Gjendebu.

Valdres and Fagernes ⑰

County of Oppland. 2,000 (Fagernes). Jernbaneveien 7, Fagernes, 61 35 94 10. Valdres Festival (Jul).

NORTH AURDAL IS the biggest community in Valdres, attracting a large number of visitors in both winter and summer. Around 150 years ago it was little more than a farming community, but that changed with the arrival of the railway in 1906. Then long-distance buses made their appearance and in 1987 Leirin airport was built, the highest airport in Norway at 820 m (2,690 ft). Despite the closure of the railway in 1988, the area is easily accessible.

The main valley through Valdres follows the river Begna to Aurdal and Fagernes, where the valley divides into Vestre and Østre Slidre. The mountain resort of **Beitostølen**, with its health and sports centre for disabled people, is at Øystre Slidre.

The Slidre valleys have several stave churches, including Hegge in Øystre Slidre and Lomen, Høre and Øye in Vestre Slidre. Long, narrow lakes and stretches of river characterize the region.

Valdres Folkemuseum is situated on Fagernes, a peninsula in Strandafjorden. It has 70 buildings, some 20,000 artifacts, a separate high mountain section and a regional costume exhibition.

Valdres Folkemuseum
Tyinvegen 27. 61 35 99 00. *Jun–Aug: daily.*

Østre Slidre, looking toward Beitostølen and Jotunheimen

Villandstua, Hallingdal Folkemuseum, featuring traditional rose-painting

Geilo ⑱

County of Buskerud. 3,000. Vesleslåttveien 13, 32 09 59 00. End of skiing season (4th week Apr).

THANKS TO ITS proximity to Hardangervidda *(see pp152–3)* and the mountain of Hallingskarvet (1,933 m/ 6,342ft), Geilo has become one of the most popular tourist destinations in Norway. It is also conveniently located midway between Oslo and Bergen. There is an excellent selection of accommodation, from wooden cabins to elegant mountain hotels, and many places to eat out.

In recent years, Geilo has also gained a reputation as a winter sports centre, with 33 alpine pistes, 17 ski lifts, three snowboard parks and 500 km (311 miles) of prepared tracks up in the mountains. The highest alpine piste is at 1,178 m (3,865 ft) with good snow conditions from November until May.

Hallingdal ⑲

County of Buskerud. 4,200. Sentrumsveien 93, Gol, 32 02 97 00.

THE LONG NARROW valley of Hallingdal, with mountains rising steeply on both sides, widens out beyond Gol to form an agricultural landscape.

Nesbyen, one of the populated areas along the way, is known for its extreme temperatures: the lowest recorded was –38° C, and the highest +35.6° C (a Norwegian record). The **Hallingdal Folkemuseum** in Nesbyen comprises 20 old houses, among them Staveloftet dating from around 1300, and the extravagantly rose-painted Villandstua.

Hallingdal's magnificent mountain regions, including Norefjell and Hallingskarvet, have made it popular with outdoor people. The valley of Hemsedal, on the road to Lærdal, has a ski centre, which is one of Scandinavia's finest.

Hallingdal Folkemuseum
Møllevegen 18, Nesbyen. 32 07 14 85. *Apr–May: Sat; Jun–Aug: daily.* *public hols.*

Numedal ⑳

County of Buskerud. 7,500. Stormogen in Uvdal, 32 74 13 90.

THE LANDSCAPE OF Numedal is dominated by the 18-km (11-miles) long Norefjorden. Rødberg is the site of a massive power station powered by the Numedal river. It flows from its source high on Hardangervidda *(see pp152–3)* to a dam at Tunhovdfjorden. An animal park, **Langedrag Naturpark**, features species adapted to mountain life, such as polar foxes, wolves and Norwegian Fjord Horses.

From Rødberg the valley leads into Uvdal and the pass at **Vasstulan** (1,100 m/3,609 ft). Footpaths from here link into the network of mountain huts on Hardangervidda. The richly decorated **Uvdal Stavkirke** (stave church) dates from 1175.

On the eastern side of Norefjorden the road passes some weather-worn houses and a stave church (1600).

Langedrag Naturpark
30 km (19 miles) NW of Nesbyen.
32 74 25 50. *daily.* *some public hols.* *outside.*

Uvdal Stavkirke
Kirkebygda, Uvdal. *32 74 13 90.*
mid-Jun–Aug: daily.

The 12th-century Uvdal Stavkirke, on the site of an even older church

Kongsberg 21

County of Buskerud. *23,000.* *Karches Gate 3, 32 73 50 00.* *Kongsberg Jazz Festival (1st week Jul), Kongsberg Market (3rd week Feb), Silver Festival (Aug).*

SILVER MINING was for 335 years the main focus of activity at Kongsberg until the Sølvverket (Silverworks) were closed in 1957. It was also the site of the royal mint.

The town was laid out by Christian IV in 1624, and developed rapidly. The large Baroque church, **Kongsberg Kirke**, was opened at the height of the silver rush in

Ore-wagon at Bergverksmuseum (Mining Museum) in Kongsberg

1761. Its lavish interior features wood carvings, *faux* marble work and an altar with biblical motifs. The organ (1760–65), by Gottfried Heinrich Gloger, is considered a masterpiece. The remarkable chandeliers were made at Nøstetangen Glassworks.

Kongsberg is the location for the Norwegian Mining Museum, **Norsk Bergverks-museum**, which contains the Royal Mint Museum and the Sølvverket collections. The former technical school, **Bergseminaret**, is a splendid wooden building dating from 1783. To the west at Saggrenda it is possible to ride on a train deep into **Kongens Gruve** (King's Mine).

Norsk Bergverks-museum
Hyttegata 3. *32 72 32 00.*
daily. *public hols.*
by arrangement.

Kongens Gruve
8 km (5 miles) W of town centre.
32 72 32 00. *18 May–Aug: daily; other times by arrangement.*

Drammen 22

County of Buskerud. *56,000.* *Bragernes Torg 6, 32 80 62 10.* *River Festival (Aug), Working Class Hero Rock Festival (Jun).*

THE RIVER PORT OF Drammen has Norway's largest harbour for the import of cars. Its location on the navigable Drammenselva has been the source of its prosperity. It was mentioned as early as the 13th century as a loading place and port for timber and when the Kongsberg silver mine opened, Drammen became the port for the Silverworks.

In the early days there were two towns, Bragernes and Strømsø, on either side of the river estuary. They were merged into one in 1811.

Drammens Museum, at the manor house of Marienlyst Herregård, has collections of city and farming culture.

The art gallery, **Drammens Kunstforening**, has Norwegian 19th- and 20th-century paintings and a large collection of Italian art from the 17th and 18th centuries.

The Drammenselva river is one of the best in the country for salmon fishing. For panoramic views, take the road via the Spiraltunellen to the summit of Bragernesåsen.

Drammens Museum
Konnerudgaten 7. *32 20 09 30.*
Tue–Sun. *partly.*

Drammens Kunst-forening
Gamle Kirkeplass 7. *32 80 63 99.*
Tue–Sun. *public hols.*

The old manor house of Marienlyst, home to Drammens Museum

1915

SØRLANDET AND TELEMARK

TELEMARK AND THE AREA KNOWN AS SØRLANDET *(the "southern lands") create a gentle transition between the eastern and western parts of southern Norway. High mountain plateaus form a dramatic backdrop to the forests and pastures of the lowlands with their river valleys and lakes. Painted harbour-front houses, sandy beaches and tiny islands draw holiday-makers to the south coast.*

The county of Telemark is dominated by the mountain plateau of Hardangervidda *(see pp152–3)*, topped by the 1,883-m (6,178-ft) high peak of Gaustadtoppen to the northeast. Valleys criss-cross the landscape and a multitude of lakes – many rich in fish – shine like jewels. Rivers such as the Bjoreia plunge from the plateau, providing power for hydro-electricity. The Skienvassdraget underwent a major makeover in the 19th century to create the Telemark Canal *(see p142)*. An important working waterway in its time, it is now popular for boating.

The beautiful and varied scenery has influenced local culture and the temperament of the people. There are few places in the country with such a rich and diverse folklore. Many Norwegian fairytales and folk songs were written, and folk music composed, in the region. Building skills have been preserved and you can literally smell the sunburnt, tarred timber of centuries-old cabins and log barns. The 13th-century Heddal Stavkirke (stave church) is like a cathedral in wood *(see p151)*.

Sørlandet (made up of the counties of Vest-Agder and Aust-Agder) has a coastline 250 km (155 miles) long as the crow flies, from Langesundsfjorden in the east to Flekkefjord in the west. However, the fjords, islands and skerries make the coastline many times longer. This is an area much loved by visitors, with its white-painted villages and towns, bobbing boats and busy quays. The archipelago is a haven for fishing and swimming, and the pleasant, though sometimes old-fashioned towns, make Sørlandet a paradise for holiday-makers. Lindesnes lighthouse casts its beam from Norway's most southerly point *(see p145)*.

Mountain trekking on horseback, a popular way of exploring Hardangervidda

◁ **Lindesnes lighthouse on the Norwegian mainland's most southerly tip, lit for the first time in 1655**

Exploring Sørlandet and Telemark

SØRLANDSKYSTEN (THE SOUTHERN COAST) is known as the sunny side of Norway. It is a summer paradise for holiday-makers. White-painted towns huddle within easy reach of each other; harbours reminiscent of the busy seafaring days of old dot the coast. Boats take visitors around Skjærgårdsparken (meaning, literally, "archipelago park"), which stretches from Risør in the northeast to Lindesnes in the southwest, and the area is great for fishing and beach picnics. Inland in Telemark and Sørlandet there are mountains and hidden valleys with historic stave churches. Indeed, a large part of the mountain plateau of Hardangervidda is in Telemark. To the east of the region boats ply the Telemark Canal toward the mountain passes bordering the west coast, Vestlandet.

Grimstad, one of Sørlandet's many "white towns" attracting holiday-makers throughout the summer season

Getting Around

The main roads through the region from east to west are the E18, E39 and RV42 in the south and the E134 in the north. They are connected to roads running north and south through the valleys, which give access to the rural byways in the south. The railway line, Sørlandsbanen, winds inland, often crossing valleys. The region is well served by bus and express coach routes. The main airport is Kjevik, near Kristiansand. There are airfields at Notodden, Skien and Lista. Kristiansand has ferry connections with Denmark, Sweden and England.

See Also

- ***Where to Stay*** pp220–27
- ***Where to Eat*** pp232–9

Key

- Motorway
- Major road
- Minor road
- Railway line

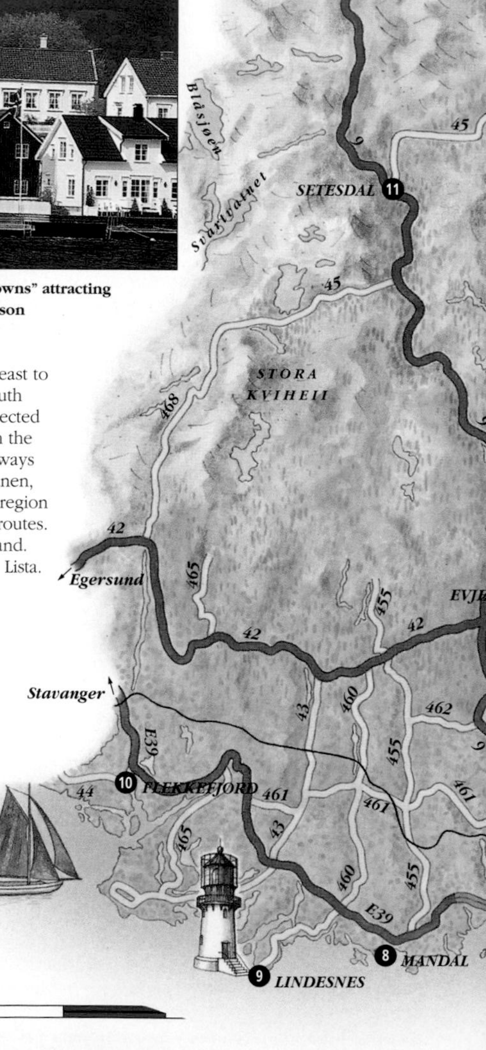

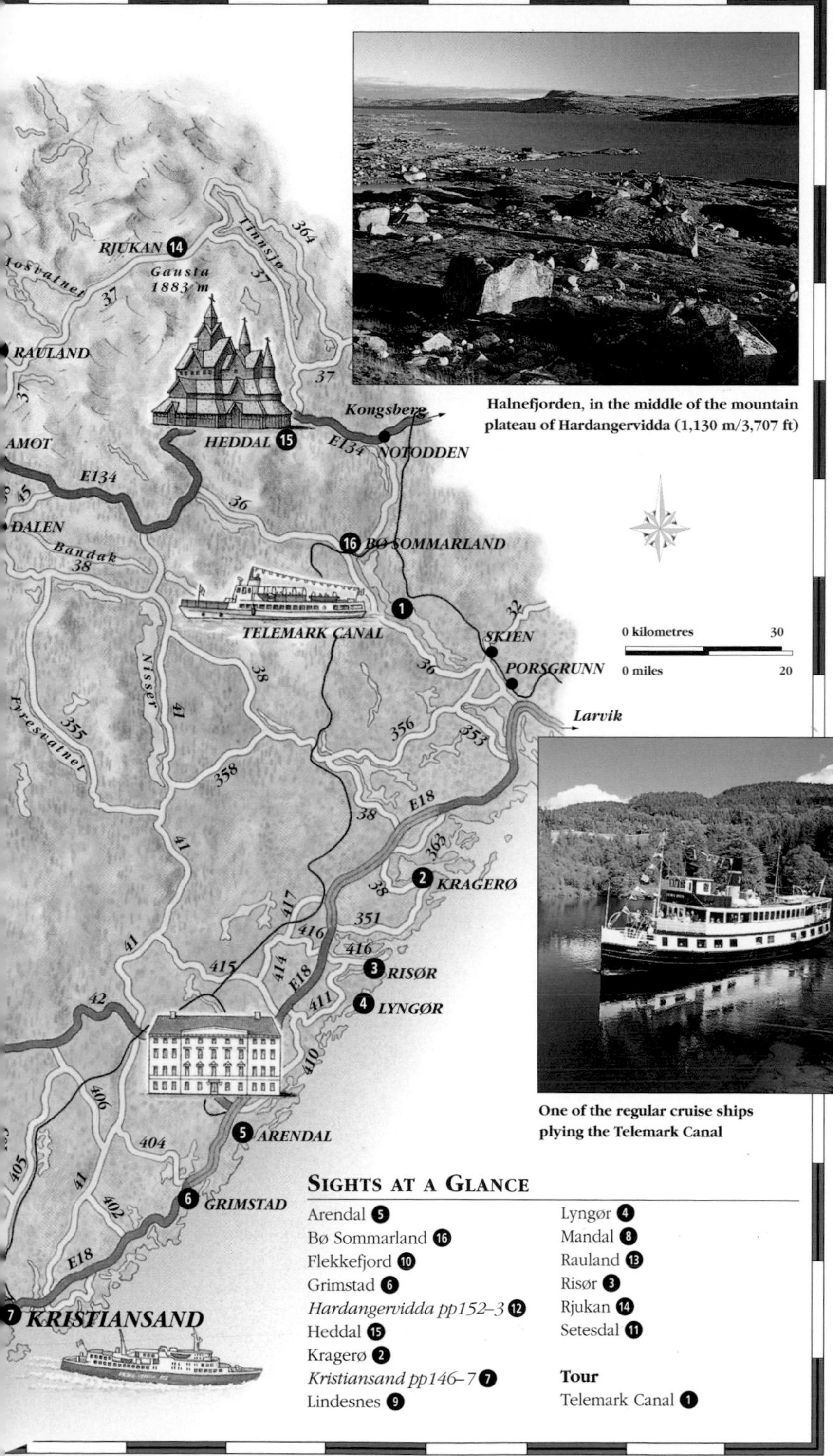

Halnefjorden, in the middle of the mountain plateau of Hardangervidda (1,130 m/3,707 ft)

One of the regular cruise ships plying the Telemark Canal

Sights at a Glance

Arendal 5
Bø Sommarland 16
Flekkefjord 10
Grimstad 6
Hardangervidda pp152–3 12
Heddal 15
Kragerø 2
Kristiansand pp146–7 7
Lindesnes 9
Lyngør 4
Mandal 8
Rauland 13
Risør 3
Rjukan 14
Setesdal 11

Tour

Telemark Canal 1

Tour along the Telemark Canal ❶

In 1861, during the heyday of waterways transport, Telemark's greatest river, Skienvassdraget, was transformed into the Skien-Nordsjø Canal. Thirty years later, the Nordsjø-Bandak Canal to Dalen was completed, creating the 105-km (65-mile) long Telemark Canal. Eight locks were built to lift boats 72 m (236 ft) above sea level. At the time it was hailed as the "eighth wonder of the world". In 1994, the canal received the Europa Nostra Gold Medal for restoration and conservation. Today, it has become one of the biggest attractions in the county.

Cabin-cruiser navigating the Telemark Canal

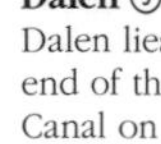

Dalen ⑤
Dalen lies at the end of the Telemark Canal on the magnificent Lake Bandak. The Dalen Hotel *(see p224)* resembles a fairytale castle.

Vrangfoss ④
The once 23-m (75-ft) high waterfall is now a power station, with the canal's largest lock system of six chambers. The lock gate is operated in almost the same way as it was 100 years ago.

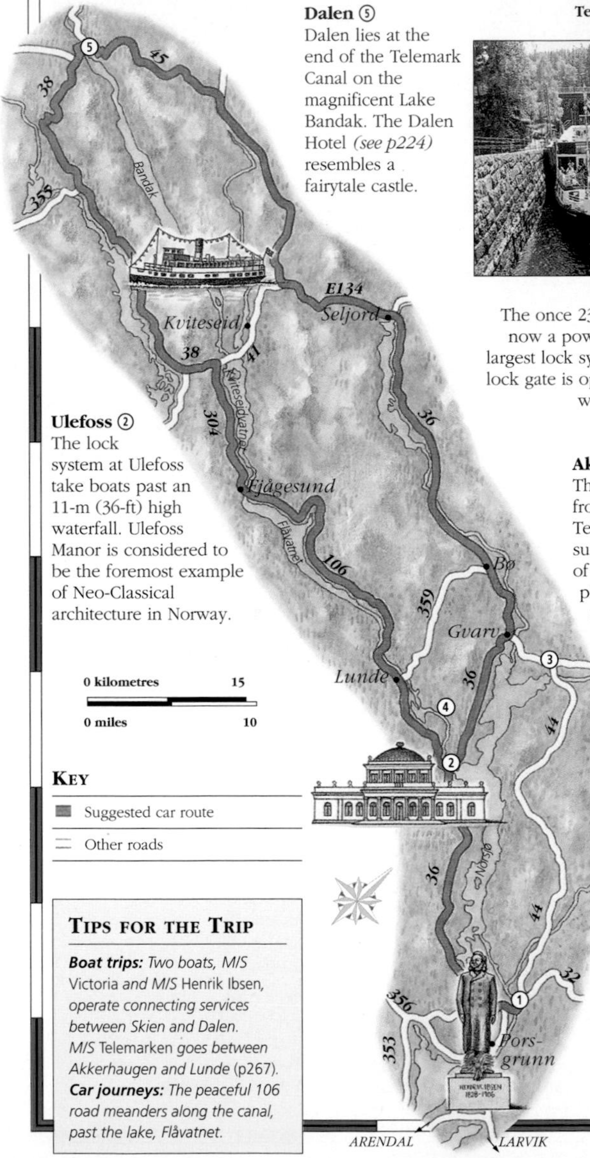

Ulefoss ②
The lock system at Ulefoss take boats past an 11-m (36-ft) high waterfall. Ulefoss Manor is considered to be the foremost example of Neo-Classical architecture in Norway.

Akkerhaugen ③
The M/S *Telemarken* cruises from Akkerhaugen along the Telemark Canal to Lunde. In summer the canal is a hive of activity with canoes and pleasure craft jostling for space in the locks.

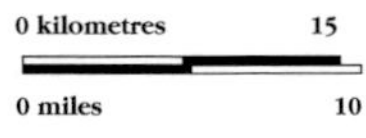

Key

Suggested car route

Other roads

Skien ①
A statue of the dramatist Henrik Ibsen stands in Skien. His childhood home, Venstøp, is 5 km (3 miles) from the town centre and forms part of the Telemark Museum.

Tips for the Trip

Boat trips: *Two boats, M/S* Victoria *and M/S* Henrik Ibsen, *operate connecting services between Skien and Dalen. M/S* Telemarken *goes between Akkerhaugen and Lunde* (p267).
Car journeys: *The peaceful 106 road meanders along the canal, past the lake, Flåvatnet.*

Kragerø ❷

County of Telemark. *11,000.*
to Neslandsvatn.
Torvgata 1, 35 98 23 88.
Summer Ski Festival (4th week Jun), Easter Bathing (Easter Eve), Kragerø Festival (3rd week Jun).

A POPULAR HOLIDAY resort since the 1920s, Kragerø is surrounded by a magnificent archipelago of small islands divided by narrow, twisting waterways. The picturesque little town was the home of the artist Theodor Kittelsen (1857–1914), best known for his fine illustrations of Asbjørnsen & Moe's collection of Norwegian folk tales. Some of these can be seen in his house-museum.

The morainic island of **Jomfruland**, the outermost in the Kragerø archipelago, has a distinctive flora and bird life, an old brick lighthouse from 1839 and a newer one from 1939. It can be reached by local ferry from Kragerø.

Risør ❸

County of Aust-Agder. *7,000.*
to Gjerstad, then bus.
Kragsgate 3, 37 15 22 70.
Festival of Chamber Music (4th week Jun), Arts and Crafts Market (2nd week Jul), Wooden Boat Festival (1st week Aug).

PROTECTED FROM the sea by just a few islets, Risør is known as the "White Town of Skagerrak". It is the row of dazzling white merchants' and ship owners' houses on Solsiden ("the sunny side") by the harbour, as well as the cottages nestling on Innsiden ("the inside") that have given the town its nickname. Despite several fires, the town has preserved much of its 19th-century layout.

Risør had its heyday toward the end of the sailing ship era, from around 1870. The traditions live on, as proved by the Wooden Boat Festival held here every August. Magnificent vessels fill the harbour and boat builders can be seen at their craft.

The wooden church at Risør, **Den Hellige Ånds Kirke**, was built in 1647 with Baroque details and a 17th- to 18th-century interior. The Stangholmen Fyr lighthouse, dating from 1885, has a summer restaurant and bar offering glorious views, as well as temporary exhibitions in its lamp room.

Den Hellige Ånds Kirke
Prestegata 6. *37 15 00 12.* *Jul: daily; other times by arrangement.*
by prior arrangement.

White-painted merchants' houses overlooking Risør harbour

Lyngør, the "Venice of the Norwegian coast" with its narrow waterways

Lyngør ❹

County of Aust-Agder. *100.*
to Vegårshei, then bus. *to Gjerring, then taxi boat.*
Fritz Smiths Gate 1 (Tvedestrand) 37 16 11 01. *Coastal Culture Week (mid-Jul), Tvedestrand Regatta (mid-Jul), Skjærgård's Music and Mission Festival (1st week Jul).*

WINNER OF the "best preserved village in Europe" award in 1991, Lyngør is one of the idyllic islands in Skjaergårdsparken (Archipelago Park) which covers most of the coast of Aust-Agder county. Accessible only by boat taxi from Gjerving on the mainland, the island has no roads for motor vehicles and is a peaceful haven.

Lyngør has fine historic buildings near the old pilot and customs station. Narrow footpaths wind past painted houses with white picket fences and fragrant gardens. The forests that once covered the islands are long gone, but there is an abundance of flowers, initially brought here as seeds in the ballast of sailing ships.

In 1812, Lyngør was the scene of a bloody sea battle when the Danish-Norwegian frigate, *Najaden*, was sunk by the English vessel, *Dictator*. The population sought refuge in Krigerhola, a pothole near the sea. A cultural history museum is connected to the restaurant, *Den Blå Grotte*.

The islands share an early 13th-century church at Dybvåg on the mainland.

Arendal town hall, 1813, Norway's second largest wooden building

Arendal ❺

County of Aust-Agder. 39,000. Kristiansand. Langbrygga 5, 37 00 55 44. Arendal Jazz and Blues Festival (4th week Jul), APL Offshore Race (4th week Jul), International Market (1st week Jul).

Sørlandet's oldest town, Arendal, dates back to 1723. It was built originally on seven islands. The buildings on the peninsula of Tyholmen next to the busy visitors' moorings, Pollen, were saved from fire around 1800. They have since been carefully preserved and were awarded the Europa Nostra conservation medal in 1992.

The town hall, **Rådhuset**, is an architectural gem, built in Neo-Classical style in the early 19th century. At that time, Arendal was the biggest shipping town in the country, with a merchant fleet larger than that of Denmark.

Aust-Agder Museet has archaeological and seafaring exhibits. In the harbour of Merdøy (half-an-hour by boat from Langbrygga) the former captain's home of Merdøgård is open to the public.

From Tvedestrand, there are boat trips on the M/S *Søgne* to the islands beyond.

Rådhuset
Rådhusgaten 10. *37 01 30 00.*
for pre-booked tours only.
by prior arrangement.

Aust-Agder Museet
Parkveien 16. *37 07 35 00.*
Mon–Fri & Sun. public holidays.

Grimstad ❻

County of Aust-Agder. 18,000. Kristiansand. Smith Petersens Gate 3, 37 04 40 41. Short Film Festival (mid–Jun), St Hans Festival (21–24 Jun).

The old centre of Grimstad dates from the days of sailing ships, with narrow streets winding between the hills. **Grimstad Bymuseum**, featuring arts and crafts and a maritime section, is situated in the town centre together with the pharmacy from 1837 where Henrik Ibsen was an apprentice and where he wrote his first plays.

Northeast of the town is **Fjære Kirke**, a church with a memorial stone to Terje Vigen, about whom Ibsen wrote. It was to Grimstad that this brave seaman came rowing from Denmark with two tons of barley in the year of starvation, 1809.

Nørholm, on the south-western outskirts, was the home of Nobel-prize winning novelist Knut Hamsun. The

Grimstad Bymuseum with a bust of Henrik Ibsen in the foreground

coast toward Kristiansand is renowned for its holiday resorts and has often been featured in paintings, poetry and literature.

Lillesand is a charming skerries town, with an elegant town hall and white-washed wooden houses. Sightseeing boats depart from the town for **Blindleia**, a 12-km (7-mile) long series of inlets, which are busy with small craft in summer.

The beauty spots of **Justøy** island and **Gamle Hellesund** in Høvåg are close by. There is a Bronze-Age settlement at **Høvåg**. A coastal ferry calls at one idyllic place after another, including **Brekkstø**, an artists' community on Justøy, a much loved holiday spot.

Grimstad Bymuseum
Henrik Ibsens Gate 14.
37 04 04 90. May–mid-Sep: daily; mid-Sep–Apr: by arrangement.
by arrangement.

Kristiansand ❼

See pp146–7.

Mandal, characterized by narrow streets and wooden houses

Mandal ❽

County of Vest-Agder. 13,500. Kristiansand. to Marnardal or Kristiansand, then bus. Bryggegata 10, 38 27 83 00. Shellfish Festival (2nd week Aug).

Mandal owes its fortunes to the timber trade in the 18th century. But its boom years were shortlived and with the transition from sail to steam, around 1900, one in four inhabitants departed for America. Yet despite emigration, floods and catastrophic fires, the town has retained more of its former characteristics than many others in Sørlandet. **Mandal Bymuseum**, located in an old merchant's house, has a large art collection, a ship gallery and a fishing museum. The town church dates from 1821 and is one of the bigger in the country.

The coastal road to Mandal passes near the harbour of Ny-Hellesund, where the writer Vilhelm Krag (1871–1933) lived. This was also where Amaldus Nielsen painted his famous picture *Morning at Ny-Hellesund* (1885, Nasjonalgalleriet, Oslo).

Norway's finest beach is nearby, the eggshell-white **Sjøsanden**. This is where the salmon river, Mandalselven, flows into the sea.

Mandal Bymuseum
Store Elvegata 5. *38 27 31 25.*
end Jun–mid-Aug: daily; mid-Aug–end-Jun: Sun.

Lindesnes 9

County of Vest-Agder, 35 km (22 miles) W of Mandal. *Lindesnes Informasjonssenter, 38 26 19 02.*
Lighthouse *38 25 88 51.*
May–Sep: daily; Oct–Apr: Sun.

The southernmost point on the mainland of Norway is the Lindesnes peninsula, 2,518 km (1,565 miles) from the North Cape in the far north. Here stands Lindesnes lighthouse, built in 1915 on the site of Norway's first lighthouse, which was lit in 1655.

The peninsula marks a distinctive change in the landscape between the small fjords and gently rounded islands to the east and the longer fjords to the west with more barren islets and wilder looking mountains.

The Skagerrak and North Sea meet at this point, some days with great force. This can be the roughest place on the south coast, but at other times the water can look quite benign and inviting.

Two small harbours on the southeastern side of the peninsula, **Lillehavn** and **Vågehavn**, enable sailors to shelter and weather the worst of the storms.

Traditional boat moored in Flekkefjord's Dutch Town

Lindesnes lighthouse standing at the southernmost point of Norway

Flekkefjord 10

County of Vest-Agder. *8,500.*
to station of Sira, 20 km (12 miles) N of town centre.
Elvegaten 15, 38 32 21 31.
Dutch Festival (3rd week Jun), Salmon Festival (4th week Jul), Gyland Grand Prix (1st week Aug).

The port of Flekkefjord is the biggest fishing and fish farming town on the Skagerrak coast. The Dutch were early trading partners, hence Hollenderbyen (the Dutch Town), dating from 1700. The town museum, **Flekkefjord Bymuseum**, housed in a 1720s patrician building, recreates old shipping scenes.

At the mouth of the fjord is the island of **Hidra**, which can be reached by car ferry from the mainland. It is known for its scenic harbours – Kirkehan, Rasvåg and Eie – and vibrant island community, which has preserved much of its charm from its days as a sailing and fishing centre.

To the west of Flekkefjord is the fishing village of Åna-Sira, which marks the border between Sørlandet and Vestlandet. Nearby, the **Sira-Kvina Kraftselskap** arranges tours of its power station, one of seven on the Sira-Kvina waterway.

Flekkefjord Bymuseum
Dr Krafts Gate 15. *38 32 26 59.*
Jun–Aug: daily; other times by prior arrangement. *partly.*

Sira-Kvina Kraftselskap
60 km (37 miles) N of Flekkefjord.
38 37 80 00. *end Jun–mid-Aug: daily (guided tours only).*

Kristiansand 7

THE CAPITAL OF SØRLANDET, KRISTIANSAND, was founded by Christian IV in 1641. It immediately obtained market town status and certain trading privileges. The layout followed a strict grid pattern and, as a result, the town centre became known as Kvadraturen ("the quad"). Kristiansand expanded in 1922 and again in 1965. Now the fifth largest town in Norway, it is a delightful mixture of old and new. In addition to the town itself, the municipality incorporates the surrounding hills, forests and moors, small quiet lakes and farmland, as well as a stretch of coastline.

Restored house in the popular neighbourhood of Posebyen

Posebyen

NE part of town centre.
Jun–Jul: daily; Aug: Sat.

In Kristiansand's early days as a fortress and garrison town, the soldiers lived in private houses in what has become the best preserved part of the old town. The name Posebyen stems from the French *reposer*, meaning to rest (French was the military language of the time).

The small, pretty houses in this area of town, complete with courtyards, stables and wagon sheds, wash-houses and outbuildings, have survived several fires and the threat of demolition. Nowadays Posebyen is a fashionable place to live, and the historic houses are maintained in good order by the inhabitants.

Christiansholm Festning

Østre Strandgate. *38 07 51 50.*
Jun–Jul: daily; Sep–May: by prior arrangement. *by arrangement.*

One of the main reasons why Christian IV wanted a town on the south coast was to strengthen the Danish-Norwegian union militarily in the frequent wars against neighbouring countries. In 1628 there was a blockhouse at the mouth of the fjord, and around 1640 a permanent fortification was established.

The solid Christiansholm Festning, on Østre Havn (the Eastern Harbour), was erected in the years after 1667. The town became a garrison, and the fortress was long regarded as the most important in the country after Akershus and Bergenhus. The fortress was the scene of a battle in 1807, when it was used to drive off the English warship, *Spencer*. Today, it is a public area.

Domkirken

38 10 77 50. *Jun–Aug: Mon–Fri and during services, Jul also Sat.* *Sun.*

Kristiansand became a diocese in 1682 when the bishopric was moved here from Stavanger. The Neo-Gothic cathedral, Domkirken, is the fourth to be built on the site. It was completed in 1885, after a fire five years earlier, and can hold 2,000 people. The organ in the east gallery dates from 1967 and has 50 pipes. A painting on the altarpiece by Eilif Peterssen shows Jesus in Emmaus.

Gimle Gård

Gimleveien 23. *38 09 02 28.*
20 Jun–20 Aug: daily; 21 Aug–19 Jun: Sun. *public hols.*

The manor house of Gimle Gård was built for the wealthy shipowner Bernt Holm around 1800, in the Neo-Classical style popular at the time. It has a colonnaded loggia, and the interior contains many fine pieces of Empire-style furniture as well as additions from the end of the 19th century.

On the walls are 17th- and 18th-century paintings from Denmark, Germany, Italy and the Netherlands, most of which were part of Holm's private collection.

Turned into a museum in 1985, Gimle Gård provides an excellent glimpse of life of the Norwegian bourgeoisie during the Napoleonic era, from the stately salons to the basement kitchen.

Gimle Gård, a 19th-century manor house with a distinctive colonnade

Vest-Agder Fylkesmuseum

Vigeveien 22. *38 09 02 28.* *20 Jun–20 Aug: daily; 21 Aug–19 Jun: Sun.* *some public hols.*

Established in 1903, the open-air Vest-Agder Fylkemuseum features wooden buildings from around the county, arranged according to origin. The Agdertunet and Setesdalstunet have farmyards, storehouses on stilts and bath houses, while Bygaden consists of 19th-century town houses, shops and workshops from Kristiansand.

In the museum's main building there is an exhibition of traditional folk costumes and examples of the typical rustic decorations known as *rosemalt*, featured on pottery, tools, furniture and walls.

Not far from the museum, **Oddernes Kirke** is one of the oldest churches in the country, dating from 1040.

Animals drawing the crowds at Kristiansand Dyrepark

Kristiansand Dyrepark

10 km (6 miles) E of town centre. *38 04 97 00.* *daily.* *some public hols.*

Wolves, lynx, elk, capercaillies and eagle owls are among the Nordic species that can be seen at the park. From further afield, there are giraffes, apes, alligators and boa constrictors. Other attractions include a bobsleigh track, wave pool and water chutes.

Visitors' Checklist

County of Vest-Agder. *74,000.* *32 Vestre Strandgate, 38 12 13 14.* *International Church Music Festival (mid-Jun), Water Festival (2nd week Jun), Quart Music Festival (1st week Jul).* www.sorlandet.com

Setesdalsbanen Museumsjernbane

Grovane Stasjon, Vennesla, 17 km (11 miles) N of town centre. *38 15 64 82.* *16 Jun–1 Sep: departures 11:30am and 2pm Sun; Jul: departures also at 11:30am, 2pm, 6pm Tue–Fri (and 12 noon Thu).*

Steam trains are running once again on part of the narrow-gauge Setesdalsbanen line between Grovane and Beihølen. The original railway from Kristiansand opened in 1896. It was closed in 1962. There are guided tours of the engine shed and workshops.

Kristiansand Town Centre

Christiansholm Festning ②
Domkirken ③
Gimle Gård ④
Posebyen ①

0 metres 300
0 yards 300

Gimleveien, E18, Egsveien, Torridalsveien, Østerveien, Otra, Kronprinsens Gate, Holbergs Gate, Rådhusgaten, Festningsgata, Dronningens Gate, Tordenskjoldsgate, Kirkegata, Markensgate, Vestre Strandgate, Østre Strandgate

Kristiansand Dyrepark
Vest-Agder Fylkemuseum
Setesdalsbanen Museumsjernbane

Key

- Train station
- Bus terminal
- Ferry terminal
- Parking
- Tourist information

Typical interior from one of the many old mountain farms in Rauland

Setesdal ⓫

County of Aust-Agder, Municipality of Valle. 1,500. Valle Sentrum, 37 93 75 00.

The biggest of the Agder valleys is Setesdal. The steep Setesdalsheiene, 1,000-m (3,280-ft) high spurs of the Hardangervidda plateau, form towering walls on each side of the River Otra, which flows from the Bykleheiene hills.

Setesdal has maintained its distinctive rural culture, which manifests itself particularly in folk music, silversmithing, folk costumes and architecture. The museum, **Setesdalsmuseet**, in Valle, has a medieval open-hearth house and Rygnestadloftet, a small barn from around 1590. Not far from the museum, the fine Hylestad stave church once stood. Objects from the church (demolished in 1668) are sometimes displayed in the museum, although its portal with motifs from the *Volsunga* saga is now in the Historisk Museum in Oslo.

At **Setesdal Mineralpark** in Hornnes, rare minerals such as beryl, aquamarine and amazonite can be seen in large halls hollowed out inside the mountain.

Setesdalsmuseet
Rysstad on RV9. 37 93 63 03. *20 Jun–1 Sep: daily; Sep–19 Jun: Mon–Fri. public hols. by arrangement.*

Setesdal Mineralpark
10 km (6 miles) S of Evje. 37 93 13 10 *May–Sep: daily.*

Hardangervidda ⓬

See pp152–3.

Rauland ⓭

County of Telemark. *1,300.* *Raulandshuset, 35 06 26 30.* *Winter Folk Music Contest (Feb), Arts and Crafts Days (2nd week Jun).*

The mountainous area around the beautiful lake of Totakvatnet is known for its well-preserved buildings and its culture. Many artists had strong ties with the lake-side village of Rauland, and their sculptures, paintings and drawings are on display at **Rauland Kunstmuseum**, including works by Dyre Vaa (1903–80). Just east of here is an abundance of historic buildings, such as the old farmhouses near **Krossen**, and those at **Austbøgrenda**, one of which has wood-carvings from the 1820s. Other collections of wooden buildings, including an 1820s sawmill, are at Lognvik farm by lake Lognvikvatnet.

At the westernmost end of Totakvatnet, in Arabygdi, is the **Myllarheimen** cottage where the fiddler virtuoso Tarjei Agundson (1801–72) lived. In summer, folk music is sometimes performed.

Rauland Kunstmuseum
1 km (half a mile) W of Rauland centre. *35 07 32 66.* *20 Jun–Sep: daily; other times by arrangement.*

Rjukan ⓮

County of Telemark. *4,000.* *Torget 2, 35 09 12 90.* *Rjukan Rock Festival (end May), Women's Mountain Hike (1st week Sep).*

Rjukan's international claim to fame was as the site of the hydrogen factory that was blown up in 1943 in a daring act of heroism by Norwegian Resistance fighters *(see box)*. Before that, however, the small rural community played a key role in Norway's industrial development when a power station was built

The Heroes of Telemark

On the night of 27–28 February 1943, at the height of World War II, there was a powerful explosion in the hydrogen factory at Rjukan. A by-product of the production here was heavy water, which the Allies knew was an important resource for the nuclear research being undertaken by Germany, and the possible production of nuclear bombs.

The sabotage had been meticulously prepared with the help of Allied paratroopers. Nine men from the Norwegian "Kompani Linge" descended from Hardangervidda through deep snow, crossed the precipitous gorge and laid the explosives which destroyed the plant. The heroic operation, code-named "Gunnerside", was one of the most effective acts of resistance during the war.

Kirk Douglas in the film *The Heroes of Telemark*, 1965

◁ **Sheep grazing on a sunny slope in Vest-Agder county**

here in 1911. Fuelled by the 105-m (344-ft) high waterfall, Rjukanfossen, the power station, the hydrogen factory and a chemical plant caused the village to expand into a model industrial community, with everything provided by the company, Norsk Hydro.

A new power station was built in 1971. The old one is now a museum, **Norsk Industriarbeidermuseum**, which tells the story both of the thrilling sabotage and of Norway's industrial past.

On the opposite side of the valley is the cable car, **Krossobanen**, erected by Norsk Hydro in 1928 to enable the residents of the shaded valley to glimpse the sun in winter. It rises to 886 m (2,907 ft) and is an excellent starting point for walking trips on Hardangervidda. Beside Rjukanfossen is the **Krokan Tourist Hut**, opened in 1868 when the untamed waterfall was a popular destination for tourists and painters. Today, because of the power station, the waterfall can be seen at full force only occasionally.

Gaustadtoppen, a peak 1,883 m (6,178 ft) high, can be reached via a well-marked path from the Stavro car park. The walk to the summit takes about two hours.

Norsk Industriarbeidermuseum
7 km (4 miles) W of town centre.
35 09 90 00. Apr: Sat; May–Sep: daily; Oct: Sat; other times by arrangement.

Krossobanen
1 km (half a mile) W of town centre.
35 09 12 90 (bookings).
daily.

The rose-painted Rambergstugo house dating from 1784 at Heddal Bygdetun

Heddal ⓯

County of Telemark, Municipality of Notodden. *12,000 (Notodden).*
Teatergaten 3, 35 01 50 00.
Notodden Blues Festival (1st week Aug).

THE MAIN ATTRACTION in the village of Heddal is **Heddal Stavkirke**, erected in 1242. With its three spires and 64 different roof surfaces, this "wooden cathedral" is the largest of the preserved medieval churches in Norway. It has three naves, a portico and an apse. Notable internal features include the richly carved bishop's chair, the altarpiece and the late 17th-century wall paintings.

Heddal Stavkirke is still the main church in the district. The vicarage barn beside the church houses various exhibitions and a restaurant.

Among the buildings on display at nearby **Heddal Bygdetun** is Rambergstugo, a house decorated in 1784 in the rustic style known as "rose painting", by the well-known painter, Olav Hansson.

The Norsk Hydro company was established in Notodden in 1905. The company museum, **Bedriftshistorisk Samling**, shows its first years of operation, and looks at the life and times of the railway navvies.

Heddal Stavkirke
Heddalsvegen 412. *35 02 04 00. end May–beg Sep: daily; other times by arrangement.*

Heddal Bygdetun
6 km (4 miles) W of Notodden. *35 02 08 40. mid-Jun–mid-Aug: daily.*

Bedriftshistorisk Samling
Notodden town centre.
35 01 71 00. 15 Jun–18 Aug: daily; Jan–14 Jun & 19 Aug–31 Dec: by arrangement.

Bø Sommarland, a paradise for water enthusiasts large and small

Bø Sommarland ⓰

County of Telemark. *35 95 16 99.*
Jun–Aug: daily.

NORWAY'S BIGGEST waterpark, Bø Sommarland, offers more than 100 activities of different kinds and appealing to different ages. There are paddling pools and safe water activities for youngsters. For older children, the range of attractions includes a water carousel, water slides, rafting and an artificial wave pool.

For those seeking bigger thrills, there are diving towers, a water rollercoaster, and the heart-stopping free-fall slide, Magasuget.

Dry land attractions include a fairground and several places to eat. The park lies just north of the small town of Bø.

Rjukan's Vemork power station, scene of a daring sabotage in 1943

Hardangervidda ⓬

Vøringsfossen
The River Bjoreia plunges vertically 145 m (476 ft) down from the plateau into the valley of Måbødalen.

EUROPE'S LARGEST high mountain plateau stands well above the tree line at 1,100–1,400 m (3,608–4,593 ft), punctuated with prominent peaks such as Hårteigen and the glacier of Hardangerjøkulen. A national park covers part of the region. Many rivers have their sources in the mountain lakes, the best known being Numedalslågen and Telemarksvassdraget in the east, and Bjoreia with the waterfall Vøringsfossen *(see p163)* in the west. Ancient tracks and well-trodden paths bear witness to the passage of people across the mountains in times past. Hunters stalked reindeer and fishermen still come to catch trout. Today, though, it is the *hytte-to-hytte* (hut-to-hut) hikers who make up the majority of visitors to Hardangervidda.

Trout Fishing
Hardangervidda is one of Norway's best areas for trout fishing. Information about fishing licences can be obtained in advance from tourist offices and huts.

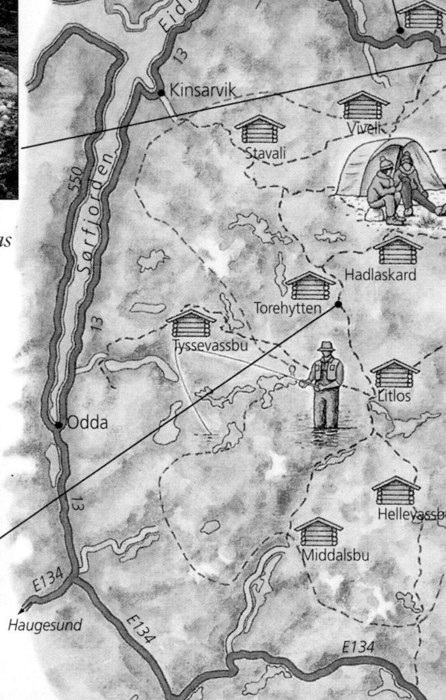

Hårteigen
The strange shape of Hårteigen rises from the plateau. The gneissic outcrop is the remains of an ancient mountain ridge.

0 kilometres 20

0 miles 10

KEY

- Major road
- Minor road
- National park boundaries
- Hiking route
- Mountain hut

Glacier Buttercup
Hardangervidda is the habitat for a rich variety of flowers, including the hardy glacier buttercup, Ranunculus glacialis.

Hardangerjøkulen
The 6th largest glacier in Norway, Hardangerjøkulen is also the most accessible. It attracts visitors all year round, not least in May when many combine a spot of spring skiing with a visit to Hardangerfjord where fruit trees are in blossom.

Visitors' Checklist

Counties of Telemark, Buskerud and Hordaland. *Hardangervidda Natursenter in Eidfjord, 53 66 59 00.* *guided walks by prior arrangement with Eidfjord Turistkontor, 53 67 34 00.*
www.hardangervidda.org

Mountain Huts
Some mountain huts are only a short distance from the road, such as this one near Ustetind, while others can only be reached after a few hours by footpath.

Hiking
The terrain on Hardangervidda is generally easy-going, providing good walking for hikers of all levels.

Wild Reindeer
Hardangervidda's population of around 17,000 wild reindeer is the biggest in Europe. Ancient animal burial sites and other hunting evidence indicate that reindeer have been living on the plateau for many thousands of years.

VESTLANDET

THE LONG, THIN WESTERLY REGION *bordering the North Sea from Stavanger to Kristiansund is known as Vestlandet. This is the land of the fjords, where fingers of deep blue and green water penetrate far inland from the island-studded coast, cutting spectacularly through the awesome mountains. Picturesque villages edge the shoreline, linked by ferries, tunnels and precipitous winding roads.*

Vestlandet comprises four counties which together cover about 15 per cent of Norway: Rogaland, Hordaland, Sogn and Fjordane, and Møre and Romsdal. In the far south in Rogaland are the agricultural plains of Jæren and the towns of Egersund, Sandnes and Stavanger. The Jæren coast features pebbly beaches and broad sandy bays suitable for swimming and other water activities.

Further inland is the rocky heathland of Høg-Jæren, after which the landscape rises steeply to the dramatic Ryfylkefjellene mountains.

North of Stavanger is the fourth longest fjord in Vestlandet, Boknafjorden. One of its arms is the wild Lysefjorden beneath the famous Prekestolen (Pulpit Rock), which can be reached on foot, or seen from a ferry on the fjord below.

Bergen, the second biggest town in Norway is, along with Stavanger and Ålesund, a good starting point for trips to Sunnfjord and Nordfjord. Known as the "enchanting fjords", they are famous for their impressive mountains, waterfalls and glaciers, and idyllic beaches. This region of Hardanger and Sogn is renowned for its stave churches, historical sites and museums. Extending into the sea, the Stad peninsula marks the point where the North Sea meets the Norwegian Sea.

The county of Møre and Romsdal has equally stunning fjords and mountains. Especially noteworthy are Geirangerfjorden and Romsdalsfjorden with its spectacular panorama of towering peaks.

Vestlandet offers excellent opportunities for mountain hiking in both easy and more challenging terrains. For the angler, there is superb sea fishing and salmon and trout fishing in the lakes and rivers. The island of Runde is rich in bird-life.

Historic Bryggen, the wharf area of Bergen, a distinctive feature of the city

◁ **Borgund Stave Church, a jewel of traditional Norwegian timber architecture**

Exploring Vestlandet

VESTLANDET IS RENOWNED FOR ITS FJORDS and each town eagerly extols the virtues of its own particular stretch of deep clear water cutting through the mountain ranges: Bergen has named itself "the gateway to the fjords"; Molde sings the praises of its "Molde panorama" over Romsdalsfjorden and the surrounding peaks; Stavanger boasts "the shortest road to Lysefjorden". The smaller fjords such as Sunnfjord, Nordfjord, Geirangerfjorden and Sunndalsfjorden are equally as beautiful as their larger counterparts and all have villages and towns of interest huddled at the water's edge. Buildings from the past, museums and galleries are to be found in many of the larger towns. Around Sognefjorden are fine examples of Norway's stave churches, including those at Urnes and Borgund.

The Norwegian Fjord horse, typical of the region of Vestlandet

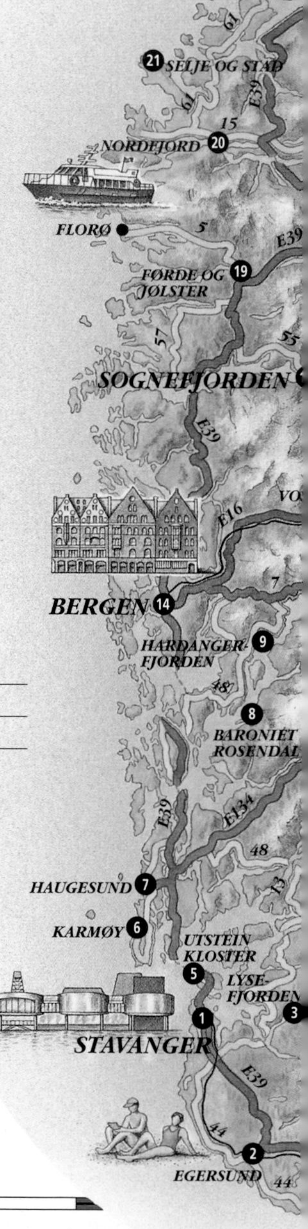

KEY

- Motorway
- Major road
- Minor road
- Railway line

SEE ALSO

- ***Where to Stay*** pp220–27
- ***Where to Eat*** pp232–9

Bergen harbour and the mountain of Fløyfjellet

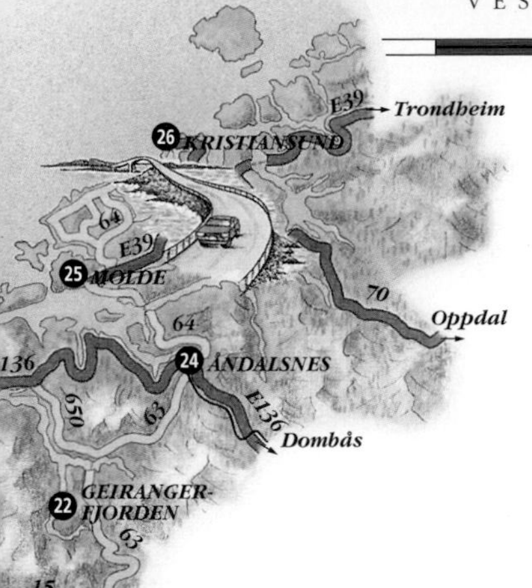

Låtefoss, south of Odda in Hardanger, one of Vestlandet's spectacular waterfalls

Getting Around

It is easy to get to Vestlandet. There are international flights to the large towns, and domestic flights to a number of smaller centres. Car ferries from Great Britain and the Continent have regular services to Bergen and Stavanger. Cruise ships ply the fjords in summer. There is a railway line to Stavanger, Bergen and Åndalsnes from Oslo. For those travelling by car or bus from Eastern Norway, there are several main roads over the mountains. The road network through Vestlandet and out to the islands is well developed with spectacular bridges and tunnels. Where there are no bridges, ferries are usually close at hand. Express boats link many towns and villages, and a large number of car ferries cross the fjords or call in at the islands along the coast. The coastal express, Hurtigruten *(see p205)*, to Northern Norway has its most southerly port-of-call at Bergen.

Stryn on inner Nordfjord, surrounded by mountains and glaciers

Sights at a Glance

Baroniet Rosendal 8
Bergen pp164–171 14
Borgund Stavkirke p177 16
Egersund 2
Eidfjord 11
Førde and Jølster 19
Geirangerfjorden 22
Hardangerfjorden 9
Haugesund 7
Jostedalsbreen 18
Karmøy 6
Kristiansund 26
Lysefjorden 3
Molde 25
Nordfjord 20
Selje and Stad 21
Sognefjorden pp174–6 15
Stavanger pp158–9 1
Suldal 4
Sørfjorden 10
Ulvik 12
Urnes Stavkirke 17
Utstein Kloster 5
Voss 13
Ålesund 23
Åndalsnes 24

Stavanger ❶

SARDINES AND OIL HAVE BEEN THE MAINSTAY of Stavanger's economic development. Before the cathedral was built around 1125, Stavanger was little more than a fishing village. It was not granted status as a market town until 1425. From the 19th century, an influx of herring in the waters offshore gave rise to the town's lucrative fishing and canning industry. Then, in the 1960s, oil was discovered off the coast, boosting the town's prosperity. Today, Stavanger is the third largest town in Norway with 110,000 inhabitants. It is situated between the flat countryside of Jæren to the south and, to the north, Boknafjorden, the southernmost of the west coast fjords.

Gamle Stavanger, with its winding streets of immaculately preserved timber houses

Gamle Stavanger

Stavanger town centre. Jun–Aug, call 51 85 92 00 to book.

Situated to the west and southwest of Vågen harbour is Gamle ("Old") Stavanger, a residential and commercial quarter characterized by its wooden houses and narrow cobbled streets. Between Øvre Strandgate and Nedre Strandgate, there are complete terraces of well-preserved, 19th-century whitewashed timber houses with small front gardens and picket fences. Once the homes of seafarers and local workers, the 156 protected houses are lovingly cared for by their modern-day owners.

Norsk Hermetikkmuseum

Øvre Strandgate 88A. 51 84 27 00. mid-Jun–mid-Aug: daily; mid-Aug–mid-Jun: Sun.

The canning museum, Norsk Hermetikkmuseum, is situated in picturesque Gamle Stavanger. It is housed in an old cannery, and provides an overview of an industry that in its heyday was of greater importance to the town, relatively speaking, than the oil industry is today. In the 1920s there were 70 canneries in Stavanger. Visitors are offered a glimpse of the pioneering time around 1850 when innovations such as "tinned suppers" made their first appearance, followed by developments in technology and the launching of tinned sardines on the world market in the early 20th century.

Stavanger Sjøfartsmuseum

Nedre Strandgate 17–19. 51 84 27 00. Sep–May: Sun; 1 Jun–14 Jun & 16 Aug–31 Aug: Mon–Thu & Sun; 15 Jun–15 Aug: daily. public hols.

The sailing vessel *Anna of Sand* was launched in 1848 and is Norway's oldest sailing ship still in use. Between voyages, it can be seen at the Sjøfartsmuseum (the Maritime Museum), which also owns the pleasure yacht *Wyvern*, built in 1897 by Colin Archer (who built the polar vessel, *Fram*, for the explorer Fridtjof Nansen). The museum is situated in two converted warehouses next to the harbour. It focuses on the maritime history of south-western Norway.

Valbergtårnet

Valberget 2. 51 53 12 19. Mon–Sat: daily. public hols. by arrangement.

The fire lookout tower on the hill of Valberget, designed by C H Grosch, was ready in 1852. Stavanger has suffered many big fires over the years – one, in 1684, was so catastrophic that the possibility of abandoning the town altogether was considered. That didn't happen and today the tower provides a splendid view of the town, the harbour and Boknafjorden.

Norsk Oljemuseum

Kjerringholmen. 51 93 93 00. daily. some public hols. Sun.

Oil production in the North Sea has created an economic boom in Stavanger, with the consequence that the town is the most cosmopolitan in the country. The ultra-modern Norsk Oljemuseum (Petroleum Museum), designed by architects Lunde and Løvseth, was opened in 1999. It provides a graphic account of life at work and play on a drilling platform with a top-to-bottom presentation of an oil rig.

Models of the equipment used are on display, including drilling bits, diving bells and a 28-person survival capsule. Tableaux illustrate the history of the industry with a glimpse into the future.

The Norsk Oljemuseum, featuring the history of Norway's oil industry

Stavanger's historic Domkirken, dating from around 1100

Domkirken

Haakon VII's Gate 7. 51 53 95 80. mid-May–mid-Sep: daily; mid-Sep–mid-May: Wed–Sat.

Reinald, the first bishop of Stavanger, was an Englishman from Winchester, where St Swithun had been a bishop in the 9th century. During the reign of King Sigurd Jorsalfar, Reinald was given the means to construct a cathedral. The imposing Romanesque nave was completed around 1100, and dedicated to St Swithun, who thus became the patron saint of Stavanger.

After a fire in 1272, the cathedral was rebuilt with a magnificent Gothic choir which it still has today. About the same time, the Gothic eastern façade and the Bishop's Chapel were added. The two pyramid-shaped towers on the eastern façade date from 1746. The Baroque pulpit with its biblical motifs was, according to legend, created by the Scottish immigrant Anders (Andrew) Smith in 1658. The stained-glass paintings behind the altar are by Victor Sparre and were installed in 1957.

Along with Nidarosdomen in Trondheim *(see p193)*, Stavanger Domkirke is a remarkable example of a medieval cathedral. Kongsgård School (the Cathedral School) is situated next to the cathedral. Originally it was the home of the bishop.

Stavanger Museum

Muségaten 16. 51 84 27 00. 15 Jun–15 Aug: daily. Other times: Sun. some public hols.

Stavanger Museum was founded in 1877. It contains an extensive collection of prehistoric finds from the county of Rogaland, including items from Viste, where there was a Stone-Age settlement, and two 3,000-year-old, 1.5-m (5-ft) long, bronze lurs. These wind instruments were discovered in Hafrsfjord, site of the Battle of Hafrsfjord in 890 that led to Norway becoming a unified state.

Bronze lur from Hafrsfjord

The museum also has zoological, cultural and ecclesiastical history collections. In 1936 it bought the patrician house, Ledaal. The 200-year-old building now serves both as a museum and a royal residence. The house is thought to be the model for "Sandsgaard" in the novels of Alexander Kielland, who became burgomaster of Stavanger in 1891.

Visitors' Checklist

County of Rogaland. 109,000. 12 km (7 miles) SW of the centre. Jernbaneveien 3. Østre Havn. 1 Rosenkilde-torget, 51 85 92 00. May Jazz (May), Chamber Music Festival (Aug), Glamat Food Festival (end July), Fishing Festival (early Jun). www.stavanger-web.com

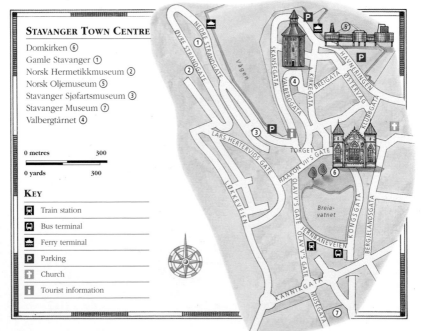

Stavanger Town Centre

Domkirken ⑥
Gamle Stavanger ①
Norsk Hermetikkmuseum ②
Norsk Oljemuseum ⑤
Stavanger Sjøfartsmuseum ③
Stavanger Museum ⑦
Valbergtårnet ④

0 metres 300
0 yards 300

Key

Train station
Bus terminal
Ferry terminal
Parking
Church
Tourist information

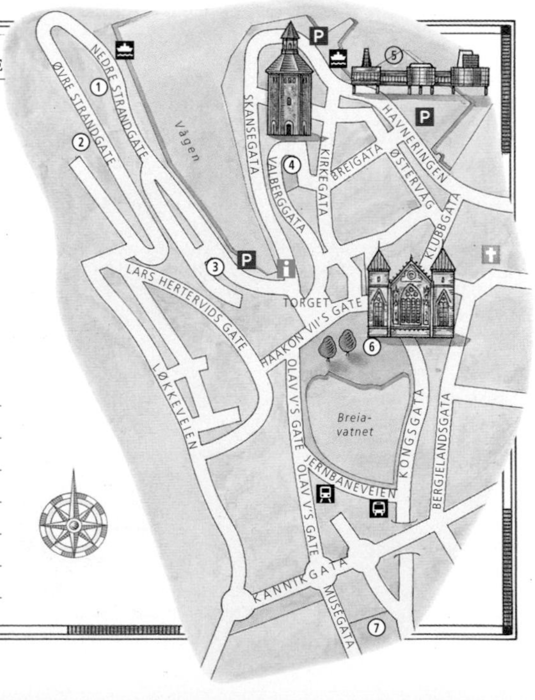

Wide horizons and a small place of worship on the Jæren plains

Egersund ❷

County of Rogaland. 13,000. Jernbaneveien 2, 51 46 82 28. Opening of Summer-Egersund (early Jun), Ballad Festival (Jul), Egersund Festival (1st week Jul).

When the sea is rough, Egersund is the only good natural harbour along the Jæren coast to provide shelter. It is Norway's largest fishing harbour, but picturesque old white wooden houses still perch on the steep rocks around the wharves. The cruciform church dates from 1620.

The cultural history museum, **Dalane Folkemuseum,** is located at Slettebø, once the residence of a high-ranking civil servant. Handicrafts, old farming tools and industrial equipment are on display.

Environs: At Eide, glazed earthenware – once a major local industry – is exhibited in a former faience factory (part of the Dalane Folkemuseum). Northwest of Egersund is a waterfall, **Fotlandsfossen**, with salmon steps.

The agricultural and industrial region of **Jæren** is uncommonly flat for Norway. There are some sandy beaches, but no belt of islands to protect the shore. The towering Eigerøy lighthouse presides over the coast.

Dalane Folkemuseum
2 km (1 mile) N of town centre. *51 49 26 40. mid-Jun–mid-Aug: daily; other times by prior arrangement.*

Lysefjorden ❸

County of Rogaland. car ferry Stavanger–Lysebotn, 4 hrs. Turist-informasjonen, Stavanger, 51 85 92 00.

The breathtaking Lysefjorden cuts through the mountains like the blow of an axe. Only in a few places is the starkness of the mountain sides interrupted by some sparse greenery and a solitary farm. About 12 km (7 miles) from its mouth is the spectacular **Prekestolen** (Pulpit Rock), an overhanging platform. Dropping 597 m (1,959 ft) to the fjord, it is a popular site for base jumping (parachuting from a fixed object). For those less adventurous, the view from the top, reached by footpath, is dizzying enough.

At the inner end of the fjord, the **Lyseveien** road features 27 hairpin bends with views of Kjerag peak, 1,000 m (3,281 ft) above the water. South of Lysefjorden is Frafjorden and the 92-m (302-ft) high waterfall of **Månafossen**.

Dramatic Prekestolen (Pulpit Rock) towering over Lysefjorden

Suldal ❹

County of Rogaland. 4,000. Turistinformasjonen, Sand, 52 79 72 84. Ryfylke Festival (May/Jun), St Olaf Celebration (4th week Jul).

The famous salmon river, Suldalslågen, flows into Sandsfjorden through the town of Sand. Here, beside a waterfall is **Laksestudioet** (the Salmon Studio), where a glass wall enables visitors to watch the salmon and trout as they negotiate the cascade on their journey up river. There is also an exhibition on the history of salmon fishing. The heritage of the English "salmon lords" can be seen throughout Suldal valley in the grand manor houses that they had constructed along the river toward the end of the 19th century. At the **Kolbeinstveit Museum**, further up the river, is a collection of old wooden cottages, smoke houses, mills, storage houses on stilts, and the Guggendal loft and storehouse, dating from 1250. From here, a road inland leads to **Kvilldal Kraftstasjon**, Norway's largest power station.

Laksestudioet in Suldal

At the eastern end of the river, steep mountains on each side of the water form the mighty **Suldalsporten** (Suldal gateway), creating a narrow sound before leading into the lake, Suldalsvattnet, from where the river springs.

Laksestudioet
Sand town centre. *52 79 78 75. 15 Jun–20 Aug: daily; other times by prior arrangement.*

Kolbeinstveit Museum
17 km (11 miles) E of Sand. *52 79 29 50. end Jun–mid-Aug: Thu–Sun.*

Kvilldal Kraftstasjon
Soldalsosen. *52 79 32 00. by prior arrangement. call Suldal Tourist Office, 52 79 72 84.*

Utstein Kloster 5

County of Rogaland. 51 72 47 05. *May–mid-Sep: Tue–Sun (Jul also Mon).* *some public hols.*

On the island of Mosterøy, northwest of Stavanger, is the 12th-century monastery, Utstein Kloster. It stands on what was originally a royal estate from the time of King Harald Hårfagre. Around 1265, it was presented to the Augustinians and remained in their ownership until the Reformation, when it became the property of Norwegian and Danish aristocrats.

The monastery, surrounded by a large estate of 139 farms, has been well preserved despite fires and attacks. In 1935 the buildings were taken over by the state and restored as a national monument.

Haugesund, looking out across Karmsundet

Karmøy 6

County of Rogaland. *Turistinformasjonen, Avaldsnes, 52 83 84 00.* *Viking Festival (Jun), Skude Festival (1st week Jul), Fisheries Festival (4th week Jul).*

The 30-km (19-mile) long island of Karmøy lies like a shield against the sea (the Old Norse word *karmr* means protection). On the inside is the Karmsundet, a shipping channel that was part of the ancient *Nordvegen* (the Northern passage), from which the word *Norge* (Norway) is derived. By the bridge leading to the island, stone megaliths known as the Five Wayward Virgins guard the sound. It is said that they were raised over the five sons of a monarch who fought the king of Avaldsnes, where there was a royal estate (870–1450). The many burial mounds in the area are proof that Avaldsnes was an important centre in prehistoric times.

Olavskirken (St Olav's Church) was built at Avaldsnes by King Håkon around 1250. Next to the church leans the Virgin Mary's Sewing Needle, a 7.5-m (25-ft) high stone pillar. Nearby, on the island of **Bukkøya**, there is a reconstructed Viking estate. Iron Age stone pillars can be seen at Åkrahavn on the western side of Karmøy.

On Karmøy's southern tip lies the whitewashed town of Skudeneshavn with a museum at **Mælandsgården**. Karmøy's main town is Kopervik.

Mælandsgården

Skudeneshavn. 52 84 54 60. *20 May–20 Aug: Mon–Fri & Sun; other times by prior arrangement.*

Skudeneshavn, a pretty coastal settlement on Karmøy

Haugesund 7

County of Rogaland. 30,000. *Karmøy, 13 km (8 miles) S of town centre.* *Hurtigbåtterminalen.* *Kaigaten 1, 52 73 45 24.* *Sildajazz (Aug), Norwegian Film Festival (Aug), Harbour Festival (Aug).*

The three seagulls in the town's coat of arms are a symbol of Haugesund's seaside location, and of herring fishing and shipping which have been integral to the town's development. This is a young town, but the area has important historical connections. To the north is the burial mound of **Haraldshaugen**, where King Harald Hårfagre was buried around 940. Norway's National Monument (Norges Riksmonument) was erected on this site in 1872 to commemorate 1,000 years of a united Norway.

Haugesund has museums, a gallery and a town hall, which is richly adorned with works of art. It is a popular town for congresses and festivals.

Out to sea in the west, and with a good boat connection, is the island of **Utsira**, renowned for its rich bird life.

Haraldshaugen

3 km (2 miles) N of Haugesund town centre.

Utsira

1 hr 20 min W of Haugesund by boat. *Municipality of Utsira, 52 75 01 00.* *230.* *timetable, 52 73 45 24 (Turistinformasjonen, Haugesund).*

The Rosendal estate in Hardanger, Norway's only barony

Baroniet Rosendal 8

County of Hordaland. 53 48 29 60. *from Bergen, Haugesund and Odda.* *guided tours May–Aug: daily; Sep–May: by prior arrangement.*

IN 1658 A BIG WEDDING was celebrated at Kvinherad between Karen Mowatt and the Danish aristocrat Ludvig Rosenkrantz. The groom was the highest ranking administrator in the then fiefdom of Stavanger and war commissioner for Norway. The bride was one of Norway's richest heiresses at the time. Among the many wedding gifts was the estate of Hatteberg, where the couple built a small Renaissance palace, Rosendal, in 1665.

The estate became a barony in 1678. In 1745 it was sold to Edvard Londeman of Rosencrone and remained in the family until it was given to Oslo University in 1927.

The magnificent garden, dating from the 1660s, was extended in the 19th century to include a landscaped park with Gothic towers, fairy-tale houses and walls. At the same time the palace interior was modernized. It contains a number of artworks, among them Meissen porcelain, a French Gobelin (1660) and Norwegian paintings in the National Romantic style.

Nearby is **Kvinherad Kirke**, a fine Gothic church with Baroque interiors (1250).

The library in the baronial palace on the Rosendal estate

Hardanger-fjorden 9

County of Hordaland. *Ulvik Tourist Information, 56 52 63 60.*

HARDANGER FJORD stretches 180 km (112 miles) from the island of Bømlo in the North Sea to Odda. The main fjord extends to Utne, at the tip of the Folgefonn peninsula, where it forks into a number of tributaries. The largest of these are Sørfjorden, Eidfjorden and Ulvikfjorden.

The glacier, **Folgefonna**, lies 1,600 m (5,249 ft) above the fjord with arms extending down to 500 m (1,640 ft). One of these, Bondhusbreen, resembles an almost vertical, frozen waterfall tumbling toward Mauranger, with the Furebergsfossen waterfall nearby. On the western side of the Folgefonn peninsula are Jondal and Utne. Jondal has a ferry quay and museum, **Det Gamle Lensmannshuset** (the Old Sheriff's House). Utne is home to the cultural heritage museum, **Hardanger Folkemuseum**, which gives an idea of how life was lived in the region in the 18th and 19th centuries.

Nordheimsund and **Øystese** are tucked in a bay on the northwestern side of the fjord, near the suspension bridge across Fyksesundet. Both are popular tourist resorts. At Øystese there is a museum featuring the work of the sculptor Ingebrigt Vik.

Det Gamle Lensmannshuset
Viketunet, Jondal. RV550. *53 66 95 00.* *by prior arrangement.*

Hardanger Folkemuseum
Utne. *55 66 69 00.* *daily.*

Captivating scenery around the meandering Hardangerfjorden

Sørfjorden 10

County of Hordaland. *Odda Tourist Information, 53 64 12 97.*

THE LONGEST ARM of Hardangerfjorden is Sørfjorden, which runs along the eastern side of the Folgefonn peninsula. On its western side, below the 1,510-m (4,954-ft) high peak of Aganuten, is the cultural heritage site of **Agatunet**, with 32 medieval timber houses, and **Lagmannsstova**, a court house with a basement prison, dating from 1300.

In the region of **Ullensvang**, where the fjord villages of Lofthus and Kinsarvik are found, Sørfjorden is at its most scenic, especially in spring when more than 200,000 fruit trees bloom on the slopes. Nearly one-fifth of all fruit trees in Norway grow here. The district has always been a centre of prosperity. This is where the monks from the Lysekloster monastery near Bergen grew fruit in the Middle Ages. They educated the farmers, as did the clergyman Niels Hertzberg (d.1841).

The Gothic-style Ullensvang church dates from the early Middle Ages. Its stone walls are 1.4-m (5-ft) thick. In the garden of Hotel Ullensvang is Edvard Grieg's composing hut, where he wrote *Spring* and parts of *Peer Gynt*.

Around the industrial town of **Odda** are a number of beautiful waterfalls, including Låtefoss, with a fall of 165 m (541 ft), and the 612-m (2,008-ft) high Langfoss.

Agatunet
25 km (16 miles) N of Odda.
53 66 22 14. mid-May–mid-Aug: daily; other times by arrangement.

Eidfjord 11

County of Hordaland. *1,000.*
Riksveien 27A, 53 67 34 00.

The scenery around Eidfjord is dramatic. Almost vertical valleys have been scoured out by glaciers and rivers. The Bjoreia river flows through the valley of Måbødalen to **Vøringsfossen**, a dramatic waterfall that plunges 145 m (476 ft) into a formidable gorge extending down toward upper Eidfjord.

The main road through the valley passes through a number of unexciting tunnels, while cyclists and pedestrians can travel on the old road cut into the gorge. Also there is a footpath up **Måbøgaldane** comprising 1,500 steps and 125 bends. A bridleway leads to Vøringsfossen.

Hardangervidda Natursenter, a nature centre containing information about the Hardanger mountain plateau, is at Sæbø.

Hardangervidda Natursenter
7 km (4 miles) E of Eidfjord. *53 66 59 00. Apr–Oct: daily; other times by prior arrangement.*

Hotel in the lush fjord landscape of Ulvik

Ulvik 12

County of Hordaland. *1,200.*
Ulvik town centre, 56 52 63 60.
Poetry Festival (Sep), Norwegian Cultural Traditions (mid-Sep), Accordion Festival (Oct).

The village of Ulvik sits at a softly curving bow at the inner end of a small fjord. It is almost as if the glacier made a special effort to leave a particularly rich type of soil here; terraced farms rise from the fjord with their lush green fields and abundant orchards. A 19th-century church stands on the site of a 13th-century stave church. Its altarpiece dates from the Middle Ages.

The area is ideal for hiking and winter sports and has traditions as a tourist resort since the 19th century. The impressive waterfall of **Røykjafossen** is at Osa, about 10 km (6 miles) from Ulvik.

Voss 13

County of Hordaland. *14,000.*
Hestavangen 10, 56 52 08 00.
Vossajazz (weekend before Easter), Extreme Sport Festival (4th week Jun), Traditional Food Festival (1st week Oct), Osa Festival (mid-Oct).

Isolated until the arrival of the railway in 1883, Voss is today the largest winter sports resort in Western Norway. It has chair lifts, ski lifts and a gondola, **Hangursbanen**, which rises 660 m (2,165 ft) into the mountains. The beautiful landscape attracts visitors all year round.

The cultural heritage museum, **Voss Folkemuseum**, opened in 1928, and focuses on items of historical interest found in Finnesloftet, a building thought to date from around 1250. The museum incorporates the farmstead of Mølstertunet, complete with 16 well-preserved, 400-year-old buildings.

Voss Kirke (1270) is a Gothic-style church with fine interiors.

Voss Folkemuseum
Mølsterveien 143. *56 51 15 11.*
May–Sep: daily; Oct–Apr: Mon–Fri & Sun. public holidays.

Traditional farmhouses in the Voss region

Bergen ⓮

GRANTED TOWN STATUS by King Olav Kyrre in 1070, Bergen was at the time the largest town in the country and the capital of Norgesveldet, a region that included Iceland, Greenland and parts of Scotland. Even after Oslo became capital of Norway in 1299, Bergen continued to grow as a trading centre, especially for the export of dried fish during the era of the Hanseatic League trading company. Following a period of decline in the 15th century the town entered a new era of prosperity as a centre for shipping. In 2000 Bergen was named European City of Culture. Although it is a city it has all the charm and atmosphere of a small town.

Vågen harbour, with the Bryggen area on the right

Exploring Bryggen Area

The area north of Vågen harbour, between the Bryggen quay and Øvregaten, a street lined with Hanseatic buildings, has some of Bergen's most important sights. Old and new architecture provides an exciting backdrop to the hustle and bustle of the streets and the quays busy with ships loading and unloading their goods.

Norges Fiskerimuseum

Bontelabo 2. *55 32 12 49.* *daily.*

Situated on the waterfront, at the furthest end of Vågen harbour's north quayside, Norges Fiskerimuseum (the Norwegian Fishing Museum) provides a comprehensive insight into Norway's long-established fishing industry and its resources.

Fishing boats and equipment through the ages are on show. Other displays cover various types of fishing such as herring and cod fishing, fish farming, whaling and sealing.

Håkonshallen and Rosenkrantztårnet

Bergenhus Festning. *55 31 60 67.* **Håkonshallen** *daily.* **Rosenkrantztårnet** *15 May–Aug: daily; Sep–14 May: Sun.* *public holidays.*

Håkonshallen is a Gothic ceremonial hall built by King Håkon Håkonsson for the coronation and wedding in 1261 of his son, Magnus Lagabøter. It is thought to be the largest secular medieval building remaining in Norway. It was built of local stone with architectural details in soapstone. Originally, the ceremonial hall was situated on the top floor. The middle storey comprised living and working areas and the cellar was used for provisions. In 1683 the hall was redesigned to store corn. The building was later restored and decorated with paintings by Gerhard Munthe, but in World War II it suffered extensive damage. The restoration work that followed created a grand venue for official functions.

Rosenkrantztårnet, a fortified residence built in 1560

The Rosenkrantz Tower is, along with Håkonshallen, part of the old fortifications of Bergenhus (Bergen Castle). The main building dates from the same period as Håkonshallen. The present tower was built in 1560 by the governor of Bergen Castle, Erik Rosenkrantz, as a defence post and residence.

Mariakirken

Dreggen. *55 31 59 60.* *Jun–Aug: Mon–Fri; Sep–May: Tue–Fri.*

Part of the chancel in Mariakirken (St Mary's Church) dates from the 11th century, around the time when Bergen was granted town status by King Olav Kyrre. As such it is the city's oldest surviving church.

In Hanseatic times the German merchants used it as their special church and richly embellished it. There is a splendid Baroque pulpit dating from 1677, decorated with painted constellations and Christian virtues such as Faith, Hope, Love, Chastity, Truth and Temperance.

Bryggens Museum

Dreggsalmenning 3. *55 58 80 10.* *daily.* *some public holidays.* *by arrangement.*

The excavations that were begun after a catastrophic fire on Bryggen in 1955 were the largest of their kind in northern Europe. Bryggens Museum is based on the archaeological findings and provides a picture of everyday life in a medieval town. It features a wealth of well-presented material, both graphic and written, including runic inscriptions from the 14th century.

The old wharf, Bryggen, with the Hanseatiske Museum on the right

Visitors' Checklist

County of Hordaland. *250,000.* *20 km (12 miles) S of town.* *Strømgaten 8.* *Frieleneskaien (Hurtigruten), Strandkaiterminalen (local).* *Vågsallmenningen 1, 55 55 20 00* *Fish Market (Mon–Sat).* *Dragon Boat Festival (May), International Festival (May–Jun), Night Jazz (May–Jun).* www.visitbergen.com

Bryggen

North side of Vågen harbour.
Jun–Aug, 55 55 20 00.

The old timber warehouses on the northern side of the harbour were originally known as Tyskebryggen (the German Quay), because for 400 years, until 1754, they were at the hub of Hanseatic trade in Norway. Long before the German Hansa traders, this part of the town had been a trading centre for fish and fish products. On many occasions over the centuries the medieval gabled houses facing the harbour have been ravaged by fires. The last, in 1955, left only 10 gables standing. Today, Bryggen is a centre for artists and a popular restaurant area. It is included in UNESCO's World Heritage List.

Hanseatiske Museum

Finnegårdsgaten 1A. *55 31 41 89.* *daily.* *24, 25 & 31 Dec, 1 Jan, 17 May.* *summer.*

Established in 1872, the Hanseatisk Museum is located in one of Bryggen's expansive German merchant's houses dating from the end of the Hanseatic era. A number of traders were housed here, next to rooms for drying fish, offices and storerooms. The early 18th-century interiors give a good impression of how they lived and worked.

A separate section of the museum features four assembly rooms used for eating, entertainment, learning, and for keeping warm in winter.

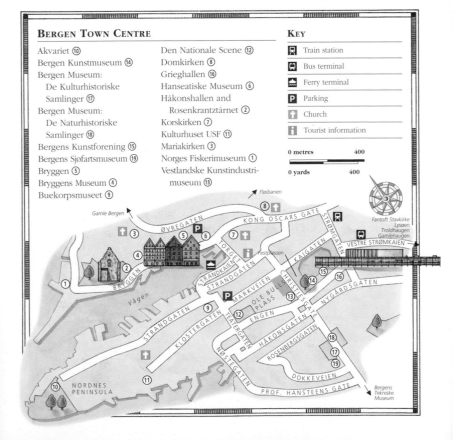

Bergen Town Centre

- Akvariet ⑩
- Bergen Kunstmuseum ⑭
- Bergen Museum: De Kulturhistoriske Samlinger ⑰
- Bergen Museum: De Naturhistoriske Samlinger ⑱
- Bergens Kunstforening ⑮
- Bergens Sjøfartsmuseum ⑲
- Bryggen ⑤
- Bryggens Museum ④
- Buekorpsmuseet ⑨
- Den Nationale Scene ⑫
- Domkirken ⑧
- Grieghallen ⑯
- Hanseatiske Museum ⑥
- Håkonshallen and Rosenkrantztårnet ②
- Korskirken ⑦
- Kulturhuset USF ⑪
- Mariakirken ③
- Norges Fiskerimuseum ①
- Vestlandske Kunstindustrimuseum ⑬

Key

- Train station
- Bus terminal
- Ferry terminal
- Parking
- Church
- Tourist information

0 metres 400

0 yards 400

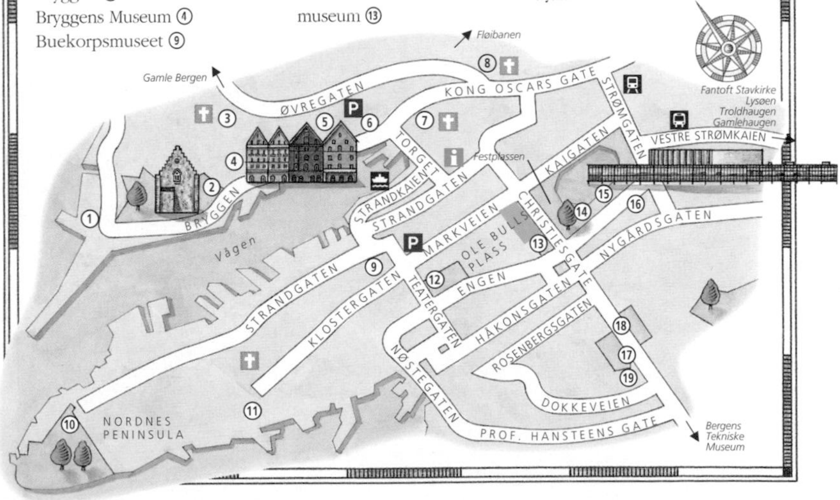

Exploring Bergen Town Centre

Bergen has at its heart the peaceful haven of Lille Lungegårdsvann, a lake surrounded by parkland and trees and, in summer, a colourful show of rhododendrons. On its western side is Festplassen, the city's festival square with its music pavilion. Festplassen opens into the boulevard, Ole Bulls Plass, that leads to Den Nationale Scene (the National Theatre). A few blocks to the north of Festplassen is the famous Fisketorget (the Fish Market). Bergen's most important art galleries are situated on the south side of the lake.

The fish market taking place on Torget, Monday to Saturday

Buekorps boys parading in Bergen town centre

Korskirken

Korskirkealmenningen.
55 31 71 68. Mon–Sat.
7pm Sun; noon Wed.

To the east of Torget and the innermost part of Vågen is Korskirken (the Church of the Cross). It was erected around 1100, originally as a three-aisled Romanesque long church. A south wing was added in 1615 and a north wing in 1623, thus creating its characteristic cruciform plan. A beautiful Renaissance portal with Christian IV's monogram graces the northern end.

Domkirken

Kong Oscars Gate 22. 55 31 23 09.
daily. 11am Sun; Jun–Aug: 9.30am Sun in English.

Bergen's cathedral was originally a parish church, Olavskirken, dating from the latter half of the 12th century. When a Franciscan monastery was established in Bergen around 1250, the church was taken over by the monks. As with so many other buildings in Bergen, Olavskirken was ravaged by fire. On one occasion it was restored by Geble Pederssøn, who in 1537 became Norway's first Lutheran bishop. He built a new tower and installed the clock above the western entrance. The multi-sided Gothic choir with its high windows has remained untouched. The church's large Rieger organ has 61 stops.

The poet Ludvig Holberg, considered the founder of modern Norwegian literature, was a pupil at the nearby Latin School from 1698 to 1702.

Buekorpsmuseet

Murhvelvingen. 55 23 15 20.
mid-Jul–mid-Aug: Sat & Sun.

The 400-year-old Muren (Wall Gate), originally the private home of a high-ranking official Erik Rosenkrantz, houses the Buekorpsmuseet. The Buekorps (literally "Bow Corps") are boys' brigades. They originated in the 1850s in Bergen, and have become a very special part of the town's traditions.

At one time the various Buekorps were rivals, but today their drills and marches are more lighthearted. Their longbows, banners and historic photographs are on display in the museum.

Akvariet

Nordnesbakken 4. 55 55 71 71.
daily. 24, 25 Dec, 17 May.

The aquarium is one of Bergen's most popular attractions. It contains Europe's largest collection of sea and freshwater fish and invertebrates. Inside, there are nine large and 40 smaller tanks. In addition, there are two pools with sea birds, seals and penguins. One section is dedicated to the development of marine life.

Every day 3 million litres (666,000 gals) of seawater are pumped up from the depths of Byfjorden through 8,000 m (26,246 ft) of plastic pipes.

Young spectator at the seal pool in Akvariet (the Aquarium)

Kulturhuset USF

Georgernes Verft 12. 55 31 55 70.
daily.

The former United Sardines Factories (USF) have been renovated to house the USF Cultural Centre, a large contemporary arts complex featuring music, films, theatre,

Den Nationale Scene (the National Theatre), an imposing landmark in the heart of Bergen

dance, visual arts and handicrafts. It is rare in Norway to find such a varied artistic programme under one roof.

Den Nationale Scene

Engen 1. *55 54 97 10.*
Box office *Mon–Sat.*

The first Norwegian National Theatre has its roots in Det Norske Theater in Bergen, founded in 1850 by the violinist Ole Bull. Henrik Ibsen was a director here for six years from 1851, followed by Bjørnstjerne Bjørnson from 1857 to 1859.

Since 1909 the theatre has been housed in a splendid Art Nouveau building. The original theatre building, "the Theatre in Engen", was destroyed by bombs in 1944. Den Nationale Scene has played a significant role in Norwegian theatre history, both with its repertory and its plays.

Vestlandske Kunstindustrimuseum

Nordahl Bruns Gate 9. *55 33 66 33.*
Mon–Sat. *public hols.*

Also known as Permanentum, the West Norway Museum of Decorative Art features a collection of Norwegian and foreign treasures. It includes local goldsmith art and Buddhist/Chinese art from the Sung, Ning and Ching dynasties. Also on show is a violin made by Gaspar de Salo in 1562, which belonged to the musician Ole Bull *(see p171)*. Contemporary arts and crafts are exhibited too. Part of the museum, but situated 5 km (3 miles) and 20 km (12 miles) from Bergen respectively, are the country mansion at Damsgård Hovedgård and the former Alvøen paper factory. The factory has been preserved complete with workers' cottages and the owner's mansion, now a museum.

Bergen Kunstmuseum

Rasmus Meyers Allé 3 & 7, Lars Hilles Gate 10. *55 56 80 00.*
mid-May–mid Sep: daily; mid-Sep–mid-May: Tue–Sun. *public hols.*

The three main collections of Bergen Art Museum are based in two buildings by Lille Lungegårdsvann. Bergen Billedgalleri (the City Art Collection) was established in 1878 and expanded in 2000 with a new building in Lars Hilles Gate. It is known as Vestlandets Nasjonalgalleri (Vestlandet's National Gallery) and has a fine collection of Norwegian and European visual art from the 19th and 20th centuries. Of great historical interest are J F L Dreier's paintings of old Bergen mainly from the 1830s.

In the same building is the Stenersen Collection. It has works by Munch, Picasso, Miró, Klee and Utrillo, among others, donated by Rolf Stenersen *(see p58)*.

The focus of the Rasmus Meyer Collection is on Norwegian and Scandinavian works, 1760–1915, including Edvard Munch, J C Dahl, Adolf Tidemand, Harriet Backer and Christian Krohg. They were donated to Bergen by the art collector Rasmus Meyer, who died in 1916.

Note the decorative Rococo interiors with ceilings painted by Mathias Blumenthal.

***Scene from Bergen's Inner Harbour*, J C Dahl (1834), Bergen Kunstmuseum**

Bergens Kunstforening

Rasmus Meyers Allé 5. 55 32 14 60.
Tue–Sun. *some public hols.*

The Bergen Art Association was established in 1838. It holds nine or ten exhibitions of contemporary art every year at Bergens Kunstforening, of which the prestigious Festspillutstilling (May–August) is the most important. The building was designed by the architect Ole Landmark (1885–1970).

Grieghallen

Edvard Griegs Plass 1. 55 21 61 00.
Box office *Mon–Sat.*

Bergen's modern concert hall, Grieghallen, was opened in 1978. Designed by the Danish architect Knud Munk, it is the country's largest auditorium with 1,500 seats. A smaller hall accommodates 600 people. Grieghallen is also used for opera, ballet, theatrical productions and congresses. It is the central venue for events during the Bergen International Festival (Festspillene). The festival has been held every year in May and June since 1953, attracting artists from all over the world.

Bergen Filharmoniske Orkester (the Bergen Philharmonic Orchestra), also known as Harmonien, holds concerts every Thursday at Grieghallen from September to May. The orchestra was founded in 1765.

Whales skeletons in Bergen Museum's De Naturhistoriske Samlinger

Bergen Museum: De Naturhistoriske Samlinger

Muséplass 3. 55 58 29 20.
Tue–Sat. *public hols.*

Comprehensive botanic, geological and zoological collections as well as a botanical garden and plant house make up Bergen Museum's De Naturhistoriske Samlinger (the Natural History Collection). Both the natural history and the cultural history collections were founded by the president of the Norwegian Parliament, W F K Christie, in 1825. The natural history collection is housed in an imposing hillside building on Nygårdshøyden dating from 1866 and 1898. It was designed by J H Nebelong and H J Sparre.

The zoological section shows stuffed animals, birds and fish from all over the world, including an exhibition titled "Wild Life in Africa".

The geological section features an eye-catching mineral collection with fine samples from the Bergen region and further afield. The life of our early ancestors is exposed in "The Evolution of Man". Other exhibits focus on "Oil Geology" and "The Green Evolution – the Development of the Planet".

The botanical gardens, known as Muséhagen, are a mass of blooms in the

Grieghallen (1978), venue for the annual Bergen International Festival

summer months. In the greenhouses tropical plants can be seen all year round. Muséhagen was established in 1897 and over the years it has amassed 3,000 different species. The selection of plants is particularly large and varied. When the gardens outgrew their original site new gardens and an arboretum were created at Milde about 20 km (12 miles) south of the town centre.

The extensive research carried out by Bergen Museum's natural and cultural history departments paved the way for the establishment of Bergen University, which today has more than 17,000 students, seven faculties and 90 institutes.

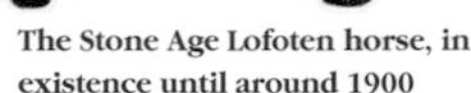

The Stone Age Lofoten horse, in existence until around 1900

Bergen Museum: De Kulturhistoriske Samlinger

Håkon Sheteligs Plass 10.
55 58 31 40. *Tue–Sun.*
public hols.

Situated opposite the Natural History Museum, on the other side of Muséhagen, is the Cultural History Collection of Bergen Museum, De Kulturhistoriske Samlinger. The collection occupies a large building designed by Egill Reimers in 1927.

Innovative displays focus on Norwegian culture and folk art as well as some exhibits from foreign cultures. The unusual archaeological collection is based on finds from the counties of Hordaland, Sogn and Fjordane, and Sunnmøre in Western Norway. Exhibits are shown in themed displays such as "The Stone Age" and "The Viking Age". "Legacy from Europe" depicts the cultural exchange between Norway and the rest of Europe.

The colourful motifs of Norwegian folk art are explored in the "Roses and Heroes" exhibition, while beautiful local folk costumes *(see pp24–5)* are part of the "Rural Textiles" collection.

"Ibsen in Bergen" describes Henrik Ibsen's inspirational work at Det Norske Theatre (the National Theatre) in Bergen from 1851–7.

Anthropological exhibitions include "Between Coral Reef and Rain Forest", "Indians, Inuit and Aleut: the Original Americans" and "Eternal Life: Egyptian Mummies".

The museum is noted for its collection of ecclesiastical art, including Russian icons.

Romanesque bench from Rennebu church, De Kulturhistoriske Samlinger

Bergens Sjøfartsmuseum

Håkon Sheteligs Plass 15.
55 54 96 00. *Jun–Aug: daily; Sep–May: Mon–Fri, Sun.*

The story of Norwegian shipping from early times can be explored in Bergens Sjøfartsmuseum (Maritime Museum), with special emphasis on Vestlandet. The ground floor covers the era up to 1900; the first floor focuses on the 20th century and the age of steam and motor craft, to the present day.

There is an extensive model collection of Viking ships and various working boats, including the deckhouse of the training ship *Statsraad Lemkuhl*. "Coastal and Fjord Boats" describes life aboard for the crew and passengers of the vessels working up and down the coast.

The Maritime Museum was founded in 1921. It is housed in a striking stone building, with an atrium in the centre, designed by Per Grieg and completed in 1962.

In summer children of all ages congregate in the atrium to play with remote-controlled model boats. On the "promenade deck" visitors are invited to relax in deckchairs and look out over one of Bergen's busiest harbours.

Bergens Sjøfartsmuseum, left, and De Kulturhistoriske Samlinger

Bergen Further Afield

WHEN THE OLD TOWN OF BERGEN was combined for administrative purposes with a number of outlying districts in 1972, it increased in size tenfold. The "new" Bergen now includes fjords and mountains, lakes and plateaus, forests and fields, valleys and rivers, and a wealth of architectural treasures.

The funicular railway Fløybanen, with panoramic views of Bergen

Gamle Bergen

Elsesro, 3 km (2 miles) N of town centre. **Museum** 55 39 43 04.
12 May–1 Sep: daily.

An open-air museum, Gamle Bergen was founded in 1949 on the old patrician site of Elsesro in Sandviken. The buildings, furniture, domestic utensils, clothes and everyday items on show provide a graphic illustration of life in Bergen in the 18th and 19th centuries. Workshop interiors and shops give an idea of the living conditions of the different social classes, such as sailors and high-ranking officials, artisans and labourers. Around the houses are streets and paths, squares and alleys designed to imitate the style of the times.

Fløyen

Vestrelidsalmenningen 23.
Kabelbanen 55 33 68 00.
daily.

The mountain of Fløyfjellet, commonly known as Fløyen, is named after the weather-vane at its summit. This has stood here for centuries, showing wind strength and direction for the benefit of sailors entering and leaving the harbour below. It has been blown down, burnt down, even torn down, but each time it has been rebuilt.

A funicular, opened in 1918, carries passengers 320 m (1,050 ft) to the summit from the city centre near Fisketorget. At the top there are wonderful panoramic views and numerous paths for walking.

Fløyen is one of seven peaks around Bergen. Another is Ulrikken (642 m/2,106 ft), celebrated in Bergen's anthem by Johan Nordahl Brun.

Gamle Bergen, an open-air museum depicting life in old Bergen

Fantoft stave church, rebuilt after a serious fire in 1992

Fantoft Stavkirke

Fantoftveien 46, 5 km (3 miles) S of town centre. *55 28 07 10.*
mid-May–mid-Sep: daily.

Fantoft Stavkirke (stave church) was originally built in Fortun in Sogn county around 1150. It was moved to Fantoft in 1882 where it was embellished with dragon finials and high-pitched roofs. In June 1992 the church was destroyed by fire, but was rebuilt within three years.

It was not uncommon for Norway's wooden stave churches to be relocated. Often they were transported by sea as it was more practical than using country roads. Vang Stavkirke in Valdres, for example, was sold to the king of Prussia. In 1842 it was driven across Filefjell mountain to Sogn from where it was shipped to Germany.

Gamlehaugen

Gamlehaugveien 10, 5 km (3 miles) S of town centre. *55 92 51 20.*
Jun–Aug: Mon–Fri. *when King is in residence.*

The King of Norway's official residence in Bergen is Gamlehaugen in Fjøsanger, just south of the city. It was built in 1901 by Professor Jens Zetlitz Kielland for the shipping magnate, Christian Michelsen, and is situated on a hill overlooking the land-locked fjord of Nordåsvannet.

Michelson was Norway's first prime minister after the break up of the union with Sweden in 1905. On his death the property was purchased by the state. It features Swiss chalet-style woodcarvings and contains mostly Norwegian paintings from the late 1800s. English-style landscaped gardens surround the house.

Troldhaugen

Troldhaugveien 65, 8 km (5 miles) S of town centre. 55 92 29 92. *Jan–Apr: Mon–Sat; May–Nov: daily.* Dec.

Troldhaugen, the former home of the composer Edvard Grieg and his wife Nina, is beautifully situated on a promontory on Nordåsvannet. According to local legend, it was a haunt for trolls, hence the name Troldhaugen, meaning "Hill of Trolls".

The couple lived here for 22 years from 1885 until Grieg's death in 1907. Designed by Schak Bull, the interior walls are bare timber in keeping with Norwegian building traditions. The house remains as it was in 1907, complete with Grieg's Steinway piano, a gift on the occasion of the couple's silver wedding anniversary in 1892, and other mementos.

The small Composer's Cabin, where several of Grieg's influential compositions came to fruition, was built in 1892. There is also a museum and a 200-seat concert hall, Troldsalen, which is used for musical recitals. Hidden in a cave facing the lake are the graves of Grieg and his wife.

Edvard and Nina Grieg's home, Troldhaugen, in Fana

Lysøen

25 km (16 miles) S of town centre. 56 30 90 77. *mid-May–Aug: daily; Sep: Sun.*

Ole Bull was one of the greatest violin virtuosos of his time, and in Norway he is regarded as a national hero. He was born in Bergen in 1810 and died at his summer island retreat, Lysøen, in 1880. The extraordinary house, his "little Alhambra", was built in 1872 and extended in 1905.

Interior of Lysøen, violinist Ole Bull's idiosyncratic summer residence

Bull designed his summer residence himself with the help of the architect C F von der Lippe. The house is inspired by a diversity of classical and medieval styles. Built in Norwegian pine, it features a tower with a Russian Orthodox onion dome and a Moorish door, and is exotically decorated both inside and out.

Lysøen is a testament to its capricious creator. In 1973 Bull's great-granddaughter, Sylvia Bull Curtis, donated the property to the Society for the Preservation of Norwegian Ancient Monuments. The island can be explored through its many footpaths.

Bergens Tekniske Museum

Thormøhlens Gate 23. 55 96 11 60. *Sun and, by arrangement, Mon–Fri.*

The old Trikkehallen (tram hall) in Møhlenpris houses Bergens Tekniske Museum (Technical Museum). Its exhibitions on energy, industry, communications and science appeal to all ages.

There are displays of technical appliances ranging from vehicles and washing machines to fire-fighting equipment and military materials. Here it is possible to find vintage cars, motorcycles, buses, a working smithy, a printing-press and an early steam-engine and carriages. The museum also has model boats and a model railway.

EDVARD GRIEG

Edvard Grieg (1843–1907) was Norway's foremost composer, pianist and conductor. He was born in Bergen in 1843. At the age of 15, on the advice of the violinist Ole Bull, he enrolled at the Leipzig Conservatory to study music. Later, in Copenhagen, he came into contact with influential composers of the time, such as Niels Gade. Grieg's aim was to create a Norwegian style of music for which he sought inspiration in folk music. Among his most well-known works is the music for Ibsen's *Peer Gynt*. In 1867 he married his cousin, the soprano singer Nina Hagerup.

Edvard Grieg 1843–1907

Sognefjorden ⓯

THE LONGEST FJORD in Norway, Sognefjorden extends for 206 km (128 miles) from the archipelago in the west to Skjolden below Jotunheimen in the east. It reaches a maximum depth of 1,308 m (4,291 ft). While the outer section maintains a fairly straight line from the west to the small town of Balestrand, the inner section branches in all directions. Five large arms subdivide into long fjord fingers and it is these innermost sections that have the most to offer the visitor. Each one is well-known for its beauty: Fjærlandsfjorden, Sogndalsfjorden and Lustrafjorden to the north, Årdalsfjorden to the east, and Lærdalsfjorden, Aurlandsfjorden and Nærøyfjorden to the south. They encompass some of the finest natural scenery to be found anywhere in the world.

Kvinnefossen
The River Kvinna plunges 120 m (394 ft) down toward Sognefjorden – a beautiful sight when the river is full.

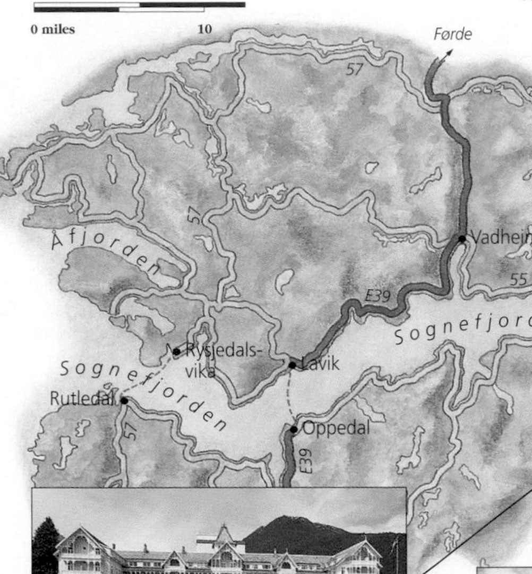

Balestrand
At the scenic resort of Balestrand, surrounded by a landscape changing from benign to harsh, is the Kvikne's Hotel Balholm, a grand timber structure dating from 1877 (see p176).

Vik
There are two churches near the village of Vik: Hopperstad stave church (1130) and a Romanesque stone church from the Middle Ages. At the ferry landing stage stands a 26.5-m (87-ft) high statue of the mythical hero, Fridtjov, a gift from Kaiser Wilhelm II.

KEY

- Major road
- Minor road
- Ferry route
- Tunnel

◁ **Prekestolen (Pulpit Rock), a dramatic viewing point over the spectacular Lysefjorden**

Sogndal
Sogndalsfjorden is surrounded by orchards, which look spectacular in spring. At Sogndalsfjøra, a local trade centre and traffic junction, the main road through the village is appropriately named Gravensteinsgata after an apple (see p176).

Visitors' Checklist

County of Sogn and Fjordane.
Sogndal Tourist Information, 57 67 30 83.
Balejazz (2nd week May), Cheese Festival in Vik (mid-Jun), Jotunheimen Cycle Race (mid-Jul).
www.sognefjorden.no

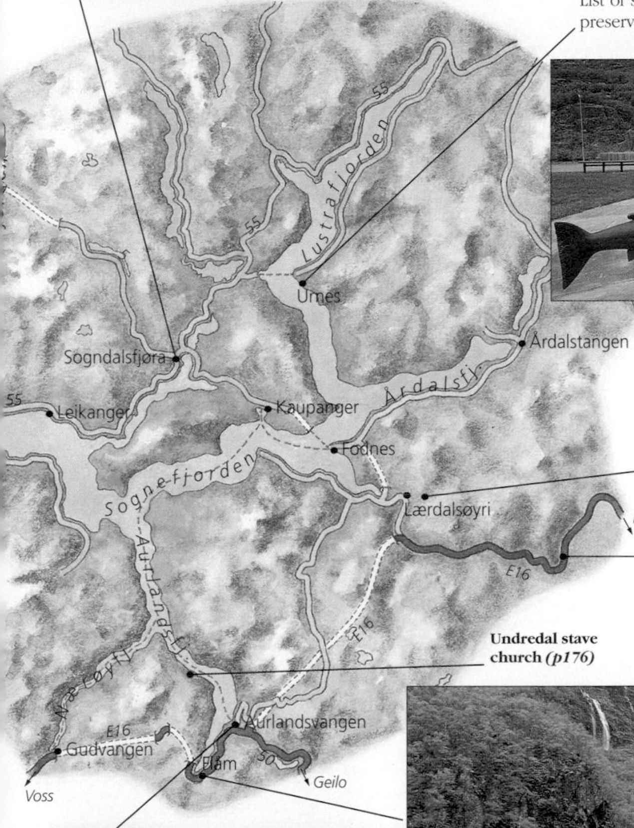

Urnes stave church is on the World Heritage List of sites worthy of preservation *(see p178).*

Lustrafjorden
55
Urnes
Sogndalsfjøra
Leikanger
Kaupanger
Årdalsfj.
Årdalstangen
Fodnes
Sognefjorden
Lærdalsøyri
Fagernes
E16
Aurlandsfj.
Nærøyfj.
Aurlandsvangen
Gudvangen
Flåm
50
Geilo
Voss

Norsk Villakssenter
On the banks of Lærdalselva – a famous salmon river – is the Norwegian Wild Salmon Centre (see p176).

Borgund (1150) is the only stave church to have remained unaltered since the Middle Ages *(see p177).*

Undredal stave church *(p176)*

Aurland and Aurlandsdalen
Aurlandsvangen is the starting point for excursions on the fjord and into the mountains – by car, boat, train, and on foot (see p176).

Flåmsbanen
The spectacular trip on the Flåmsbanen railway line offers stunning views of mountains, waterfalls, picturesque hamlets and curious-looking rock formations on the short but steep route between Flåm and Myrdal (see p176).

Exploring Sognefjorden

THE FIRST TOURISTS CAME TO SOGNEFJORDEN more than 150 years ago. In those days travel was exclusively by cruise ship. Today, a number of ferries, the Hurtigruten cruises *(see p267)*, local buses and the E16 and 55 roads enable an ever-increasing number of visitors to enjoy the area.

Vassbygdvatnet, a picturesque lake in the Aurland valley

Balestrand

It is the scenery above all that makes Balestrand such a popular destination on Sognefjorden. Wide and fertile strips along the shore are set against a backdrop of mighty peaks and glaciers.

The view from Balholm in the centre of town takes in the entire fjord and it is this that has attracted tourists from all over the world, laying the foundations for the early development of hotels and communications. The chalet-style Kvikne's Hotel Balholm *(see p225)*, built in 1877, has a hall with dragon carvings and a large art collection.

There are two Viking burial mounds at Balholm, dating from AD 800. One mound has a statue of Bele, a legendary king in Nordic mythology who was the father of Ingeborg, Fridtjof's beloved.

Sogndal

In the orchard-dotted area of Sogndal, the village of **Kaupanger** features a stave church dating from the 12th century. Nearby is the open-air Sogn Folkemuseum, with 32 historic buildings.

At the innermost tip of the fjord is the fast-flowing River **Årøyelva**, renowned for physically demanding salmon fishing (record catch: a fish weighing 34 kg/75 lb). The path of the salmon is blocked by Helvetesfossen (Hell's waterfall), and the fishing spots below are wryly named "the platforms of despair".

Lærdal

The small centre of **Laerdalsøyri** features a collection of beautiful timber buildings from the 18th and 19th centuries. On the banks of the river Laerdalselva, the **Norsk Villakssenter** (Norwegian Wild Salmon Centre) has an observatory for viewing the salmon. The only way to get from Laerdal to Aurland used to be either by a long detour via ferry, or the so-called Snøveien ("snow road") over the mountains. Open in summer only, it is lined by snow drifts even then. Since November 2000, however, a 24.5-km (15-mile) long tunnel cuts across deep under the mountain, linking the E16 near Laerdalsøyri with Aurlandsvangen and Flåm.

Norsk Villakssenter
Lærdal. 57 66 67 71.
May–Sep: daily.

Aurland

The charming little town of **Aurlandsvangen** retains some of its original buildings, among them the guesthouse Åbelheim (1770). The 13th-century stone church contains stained-glass panels by Emanuel Vigeland. This is a good starting point for the hiking routes in the Aurland valley. Across the Aurland fjord, the 601 road leads to **Undredal**, the smallest stave church in the country.

Further west, on the E16, is **Gudvangen**, from where a ferry plies the dramatically narrow Naerøyfjord before continuing to Kaupanger on the other side of Sognefjord.

Flåmsbanen

One of the world's most breathtaking railway journeys is the Flåmsbanen. It is just over 20-km (12-miles) long, but has an impressive height difference of 864 m (2,835 ft) between Myrdal on the mountain plateau and Flåm by the shore of Aurlandsfjord.

The railway was opened in 1942. There are 20 tunnels on the line and nine stops, each with a different panorama, including the awe-inspiring waterfall of Kjofossen. The 50-minute journey can be taken as part of the "Norway in a Nutshell" tour *(see p266)*.

Lærdalsøyri with its wharfside buildings bordering Sognefjorden

Borgund Stavkirke ⓰

Borgund Stavkirke at Lærdal is the only stave church to have remained unchanged since the Middle Ages. Dedicated to the apostle St Andrew, it dates from around 1150 and is built entirely of wood. The interior is very simple: there are no pews or decorations, and the lighting is limited to a few small openings high up on the walls. The exterior is richly decorated with carvings, dragon-like animals in life and death struggles, dragonheads and runic inscriptions. There is a free-standing belfry with a medieval bell. The pulpit dates from the 16th century.

Visitors' Checklist

County of Sogn and Fjordane, 30 km (19 miles) E of Lærdalsøyri.
from Lærdal. *57 66 81 09.*
2 May–16 Jun: 10am–5pm daily; 17 Jun–12 Aug: 8am–8pm daily; 13 Aug–30 Sep: 10am–5pm daily. *Oct–Apr.*
www.alr.no

Dragonheads
The tower has a three-tiered roof. The first tier is decorated with dragonheads on the gables similar to those on the main roof.

Nave
Twelve posts (staves) around the central part of the nave support the roof. Disappearing into the semi-darkness of the roof, they give an increased sense of height.

The windows were originally simply circular openings in the outer walls.

The roofs are clad in pine shingles.

Crosses decorate the gables above the doorways and apse tower.

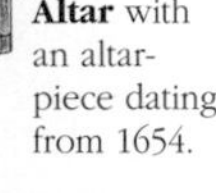

Altar with an altar-piece dating from 1654.

West Door
The exterior of the church is richly adorned. The decorations on the Romanesque west door show vine-like ornamentation and dragon battles.

Crosses of St Andrew border the central nave.

Roof Construction
Seen from below, the roof is composed of an intricate framework using numerous rafters and joists.

Urnes Stavkirke occupying a lofty location above Lustrafjorden

Urnes Stavkirke ⓱

County of Sogn and Fjordane. 17 km (11 miles) NE of Sogndal. *57 68 39 45. 15 min walk from ferry. Jun–Aug: daily.*

THE QUEEN of Norway's stave churches, Urnes is also the oldest. It appears on UNESCO's list of World Heritage sites along with Røros, the Alta rock carvings and Bryggen in Bergen. Built around 1130–50, it contains beams from an 11th-century church that stood on the same site.

The most notable feature of the church is the north portal. This, too, dates from an earlier building and its carvings depict the conflict between good and evil in the form of animals engaged in battle with snakes. Such animal ornamentation is known as the "Urnes Style".

Two candlesticks on the altar in metal and enamel date from the 12th century and were made in Limoges in France.

Also situated in the district of Luster is Sogn's most beautiful stone church, Dale Kirke, built in 1250.

Jostedalsbreen ⓲

County of Sogn and Fjordane. *Jostedalen Tourist Information, 57 68 32 50; Jostedalsbreen National Park Centre, Oppstryn, 57 87 72 00.*

THE LARGEST GLACIAL area in continental Europe, Jostedalsbreen is 100-km (62-miles) long and 15-km (9-miles) wide. Together with Jostefonn, which used to be joined to it, it covers 486 sq km (188 sq miles). Its highest point is Lodalskåpa (2,083 m/ 6,834 ft).

The ice cap sends fingers into the valleys below. In the 18th century a number of these glacial spurs extended so low they destroyed cultivated fields, but since then they have receded.

The starting points for glacier tours include Jostedalen (Nigardsbreen and Bergsethbreen glaciers), Stryn (Briksdalsbreen glacier) and Fjærland (Bøyabreen and Supphellebreen glaciers).

On the innermost reaches of the sparkling green Fjærlandsfjorden is **Norsk Bremuseum** (the Norwegian Glacier Museum), an award-winning "activity museum" devoted to snow, ice, glaciers, glacier hiking and climbing. A panoramic film presentation takes the viewer on a virtual glacier experience.

Norsk Bremuseum

Fjærland. *57 69 32 88. Apr–Oct: daily; other times by prior arrangement.*

Førde and Jølster ⓳

County of Sogn and Fjordane. *10,300. Langebruveien 20, 57 82 22 50. International Folk Music Festival (1st week Jul).*

THE TOWN OF FØRDE lies at the heart of the county of Sogn and Fjordane. It has a cultural centre, **Førdehuset**, housing an arts centre and gallery, library, cinema and theatre. The **Sunnfjord Museum**, comprising 25 buildings from around 1850, is also in Førde.

East of the town, in Vassenden, there is another cultural heritage museum, **Jølstramuseet**, with houses from the 17th century. Nearby is the tranquil rural museum **Astruptunet**, where the painter Nikolai Astrup once lived (1880–1928).

This area is renowned for fishing. The Jølstra river has a salmon ladder dating from 1871. The river flows from Jølstravatnet lake, where trout exceeding 12 kg (26 lb) have been caught. There is good fishing in Gularvassdraget and in the mountain lakes.

Sunnfjord Museum

9 km (6 miles) E of Førde. *57 72 12 20. Jun–Aug: daily; Sep–May: Mon–Fri. public hols.*

Jølstramuseet

20 km (12 miles) E of Førde. *57 72 71 85. 15 Jun–15 Aug: daily.*

Astruptunet

26 km (16 miles) E of Førde. *57 72 67 82. mid-May–mid-Aug: daily.*

Nordfjord ⓴

County of Sogn and Fjordane. *Sandane. Stryn Tourist Information, 57 87 40 51. Summer Skiing Festival in Stryn (Jun); Fish Festival in Stryn (Jul).*

THE NORTHERNMOST fjord in Sogn and Fjordane county is Nordfjord. Measuring 110 km

Astruptunet, home of the painter and graphic artist Nikolai Astrup

The hamlet of Ervik on Stad peninsula

(68 miles) in length, Nordfjord extends from Måløy in the west inland to Stryn near the border with eastern Norway.

The area around Stryn has been a sought-after destination since 1850 when the first English outdoor enthusiasts arrived. Opportunities abound for mountaineering, glacier hiking, skiing and fishing.

There are several glacier spurs from Jostedalsbreen. Briksdalsbreen can be reached by horse and carriage from Briksdal (tickets, Stryn tourist office); the one on Strynfjell is accessible by chairlift from Stryn Summer Ski Centre.

Loen, on Lovatnet lake, was devastated in 1905 when part of the mountain, Ramnefjellet, fell into the lake causing an enormous wave. It killed 63 people, destroyed houses and hurled a steamboat 400 m (1,312 ft) up the mountain.

From Stryn there are two roads around Nordfjorden. The northernmost (RV15) runs along Hornindalsvatnet, Europe's deepest lake, to **Nordfjordeid**, a centre for the breeding and rearing of Norwegian Fjord Horses. The southernmost (RV60, E39) passes through Innvik, Utvik and Byrkjelo to Sandane. The **Nordfjord Folkemuseum** in Sandane comprises 40 18th- and 19th-century houses.

Nordfjord Folkemuseum

Sandane. 57 86 61 22. *15 May–30 Jun: Mon–Fri; 1 Jul–15 Aug: daily; 16 Aug–15 Sep: Mon–Fri; 16 Sep–14 May: by prior arrangement.* *public hols.*

Selje and Stad 21

County of Sogn and Fjordane.
3,100. *Selje Tourist Information, 57 85 66 06.*

From Måløy on the outer reaches of Nordfjorden it is not far to the Stad peninsula and **Vestkapp**, one of Norway's westernmost points. Here stands "Kjerringa", a 460-m (1,509-ft) high rock that plunges steeply into the water. From the top there are panoramic views out to sea. Below, in **Ervik**, a chapel commemorates the loss of the coastal passenger ferry, *St Svithun*, in World War II.

On the island of Selje are the ruins of a monastery built by Benedictine monks in the 12th century. The monastery is dedicated to St Sunniva, daughter of an Irish king, who fled east to escape betrothal to a heathen chieftain. Her party came ashore on Selje and sought refuge in a cave.

Geirangerfjorden 22

County of Møre and Romsdal.
Geiranger, 70 26 30 99.

The inner part of Storfjorden divides to form two of Norway's best-known fjords: Tafjorden to the north and Geirangerfjorden to the south.

The 16-km (10-miles) long Geirangerfjorden is the quintessential fjord. A strip of dazzling green water snakes its way to the village of Geiranger, below precipitous mountains with farms perched on the slopes and cascading waterfalls.

The RV63, Grotli-Geiranger-Åndalsnes, is known as the Golden Route. Driving south from Geiranger, the road passes Flydalsjuvet, an overhanging cliff providing a picture-postcard view of the fjord and surrounding mountains. It continues to the mountain hut of Djupvasshytta, from where it is possible to reach the summit of Dalsnibba (1,476 m/4,843 ft).

North from Geiranger, a dramatic part of the Golden Route leads to Norddalfjorden. This is known as Ørnveien (the Eagle's Road) and offers panoramic vistas. A ferry leads across the fjord to Valldal, where the next section, known as Trollstigveien (the Trolls' Path), leads to Åndalsnes *(see p180)* via some dizzying hairpin bends and great views.

Tafjorden was hit by a tragedy in 1934 when an immense rock from Langhammaren crashed into the fjord, causing a huge wave which killed 40 people in Tafjord.

Geirangerfjorden, known as the pearl of the Norwegian fjords

Ålesund ㉓

Møre and Romsdal. 38,000. Keiser Wilhelms Gate 11, 70 15 76 00. Ålesund Theatre Festival (Mar), Historical Festival (1st week Jul), Norwegian Food Festival (4th week Aug), Dragon Boat Festival (mid-Jun), Ålesund Boat Festival (1st week Jul), Young Jazz (4th week Sep).

THE CENTRE OF Ålesund was destroyed in a catastrophic fire in 1904. Fellow Europeans came quickly to the rescue with help and donations and in just three years the town was rebuilt almost entirely in the Art Nouveau style. For this reason, Ålesund occupies a very special place in the architectural history of Europe. It spans several islands linked by bridges. Today, it is an important fishing port, but Ålesund did not receive town status until 1848.

Art Nouveau detail, Ålesund

The area of Borgund, now part of Ålesund, was a market town and centre of the Sunnmøre region from around 1200. From the mountain lodge, **Fjellstua**, there is a panoramic view over the town.

Ålesund Museum has one section devoted to the town and another to the Arctic. **Sunnmøre Museum** consists of 40 historic houses and boathouses and 30 different types of fishing boats.

The Trolltindane, described in legends as a troll wedding procession

Southwest of Ålesund is the island of **Runde**. It is renowned for its nesting cliffs, which provide a habitat for around one million seabirds. There are 100,000 puffins and 50,000 kittiwake pairs, and the rare northern gannet can also be seen here.

The Dutch East India vessel *Akerendam* went down off the island in 1725 with a valuable cargo. Divers have subsequently recovered a large haul of gold and silver coins from the wreck.

Ålesund Museum
Rønnebergs Gate 16. *70 12 31 70. mid-Mar– mid-Jun & mid-Aug–mid-Nov: Mon–Fri & Sun; mid-Jun–mid-Aug: daily; mid-Nov–mid-March: Mon–Fri. Closed some public hols.*

Sunnmøre Museum
5 km (3 miles) E of town centre. *70 17 40 00. mid-May–23 Jun: Mon–Fri & Sun; 24 Jun–Aug: daily; Sep–mid-May: Mon, Tue, Fri, Sun. summer.*

Runde
30 km (19 miles) SW of town centre. *to Fosnavåg. 70 01 37 90.*

Bird's eye view of Ålesund from Fjellstua

Åndalsnes ㉔

County of Møre and Romsdal. 7,700. Molde. Jernbanegt 1, 71 22 16 22. Norwegian Mountain Festival (mid-Jul), Sinclair Festival (mid-Aug).

WHERE THE RAUMA river enters Romsdalsfjorden lies the resort of Åndalsnes, terminus of the Raumabanen railway. On the eastern side of the valley is Romsdalshorn (1,554 m/5,098 ft). Opposite are the ragged peaks of **Trolltindane** (1,795 m/ 5,889 ft) with a sheer vertical cliff to the valley. This is a popular spot for mountaineering.

Trollstigveien (the Troll's Path) is the thrilling drive to the south between Åndalsnes and Valldalen, with 11 breathtaking hairpin bends. Along the road there are views of the waterfalls, Stigfossen and Tverrdalsfossen. Every summer a ski race, *Trollstigrennet*, is held on the Trollstigheimen pass.

Molde ㉕

County of Møre and Romsdal. 24,000. to Åndalsnes, then bus. Storgata 31, 71 25 71 33. Molde International Jazz Festival (mid-Jul), Bjørnsson Festival (mid-Aug).

KNOWN AS THE "Town of Roses" for its rose gardens and lush vegetation, Molde is an attractive fjord-side place. The term "Molde Panorama" is used to describe the scenery here: from Varden it is possible to see 87 snow-covered peaks on a clear day. In July Molde is the site of a lively jazz festival, attracting top musicians from abroad.

The outdoor museum of timber houses, **Romsdalsmuseet**, also contains a fascinating collection of national costumes.

Fiskerimuseet (the Fisheries Museum), on the island of Hjertøya near Molde, focuses on the cultural history of the coastal population.

While on the Molde peninsula, it is worth visiting both the fishing village of **Bud**, which faces the infamous stretch of sea known as Hustadvika, and the marble cave of **Trollkyrkja** (Troll Church), around 30 km (19 miles) to the north.

On Eresfjorden is a waterfall, **Mardalsfossen**, with the highest unbroken vertical drop in Northern Europe, 297 m (974 ft). It is at its most dramatic from 20 Jun–20 Aug.

Atlanterhavsveien (the Atlantic Road), from Averøy toward Kristiansund, is spectacular. It passes over islets and skerries and across 12 low bridges that have been built right out in the sea.

Romsdalsmuseet
Per Adams Vei 4. *71 20 24 60.*
Jun–mid-Aug: daily.

Fiskerimuseet
Hjertøy (boat from Molde in summer).
71 20 24 60. *end-Jun–mid-Aug: daily.*

Kristiansund 26

County of Møre and Romsdal.
17,000.
Kongens Plass 1, 71 58 54 54.
Opera Festival (Feb), Children's Festival (Apr), Coast Festival (Jun/Jul).

FROM THE CAIRN on the island of Kirkelandet there is a magnificent view over this and the two other islands that comprise Kristiansund.

The sheltered harbour, always busy with boats, gave rise to the coastal settlement of Lille-Fossen, or Fosna. In 1742 when it acquired town status it was renamed Kristiansund. Between 1830 and 1872 the town developed into the country's biggest exporter of *klippfisk* (salted, dried cod). Kristiansund was almost entirely destroyed by bombs in April 1940. The reconstruction created a new image for the town, with modern buildings in many different colours, prime examples of which are the town hall and the church.

The Atlantic Road, winding its way across islands and sounds

Nordmøre Museum contains a special exhibition of archaeological finds from the Fosna culture, and a fisheries exhibition.

North of Kristiansund is the tiny island of **Grip**, inhabited only in summer. All that remains of this former fishing community is a 15th-century stave church in which the population took refuge from the fearsome storms. There is a boat connection in summer.

Long ago Kristiansund could only be reached by boat, but today there is an airport and road connections to the mainland. To the southeast the RV70 passes through a number of tunnels and over bridges as the landscape becomes more mountainous. **Tingvoll Kirke**, otherwise known as Nordmøre Cathedral, dates from around 1200 and has an exquisite altarpiece and runic inscriptions on the chancel wall.

At Tingvollfjorden the road passes Ålvundeid, where there is a side road to the magnificent **Innerdalen** valley with the Dalatårnet peak and the mountains of Trollheimen. At the end of the fjord is **Sunndalsøra**, where the famous salmon and sea trout river Driva has its mouth.

Nordmøre Museum
2 km (1 mile) N of town centre.
71 67 15 78. *Mar–Nov: Tue–Fri & Sun; other times: Tue–Fri.*
partly.

Grip
14 km (9 miles) N of Kristiansund.
from Kristiansund. *Turistinformasjonen, Kristiansund, 71 58 54 54.*

Tingvoll Kirke
55 km (32 miles) SE of Kristiansund.
71 53 03 03. *May–Sep: Tue–Fri (concert 5pm Sat).*

Kristiansund with its colourful houses and imposing church

TRØNDELAG

A JOURNEY OVER DOVREFJELL TO TRØNDELAG *was a challenge in times gone by. The route from southern to northern Norway across the mountains, undertaken by kings and pilgrims of old, was arduous. Travellers would breathe a sigh of relief after negotiating the notorious Vårstigen (Spring Path) and arriving safely on the Trøndelag side of the fells. Today's roads and railway lines make this an easy trip.*

Most of those crossing Dovrefjell, whether royalty, pilgrims or merchants, would have been heading for the city of Trondheim (Nidaros as it was known originally). All roads lead to Trondheim, so it was said. Throughout history Trondheim has been the capital of central Norway, and for a time it was the first capital of the kingdom.

Trondheim was founded by King Olav Tryggvason, who built a house at the mouth of the Nidelv river in 997. However, it was the martyrdom of the future saint, King Olav Haraldsson, at the infamous Battle of Stiklestad in 1030, that led to Kristkirken (the Church of Christ) being built. It became the cathedral, Nidarosdomen, a focal point for pilgrimage in Scandinavia.

South Trøndelag is a mainly agricultural region with coniferous and deciduous forests tailing off into scraggy mountain woodland in the fells. North Trøndelag is dominated by coniferous forests. The style of farm building, especially around Trondheimsfjorden, is unique to the Trøndelag region. The main buildings, *trønderlåner*, are long, narrow, double-storied houses, usually painted white and situated at a high point in the terrain.

The mountainous regions of Børgefjell, Sylene, Rørosvidda, Dovrefjell and the spectacular Trollheimen have much of interest in the way of outdoor activities, hunting and fishing. Many of the rivers offer excellent salmon-fishing from the banks and boats.

The offshore islands, particularly the archipelago of Vikna, are easily accessible. Here, bird-watching and sea fishing are among the attractions.

Sculptures decorating the west front of Nidarosdomen in Trondheim, with Olav the Holy at the centre

◁ **The old bell, *Hyttklokka*, symbol of the copper mining town of Røros in southern Trøndelag**

Exploring Trøndelag

TRØNDELAG IS MADE UP of two counties, Nord-Trøndelag and Sør-Trøndelag, which together comprise 12.7 per cent of Norway. In the west, the mainland and the fjords on the Norwegian Sea coast are mostly protected by a wide band of rocky isles. The landscape around Trondheimsfjorden is generally level, fertile farmland. In the east, near Kjølen and the Swedish border, there are large mountain plateaus with high peaks such as the Sylene range. Great tracts of forest cover the central area. For centuries pilgrims have flocked to the cathedral in Trondheim and to Stiklestad, where Olav the Holy died in battle in 1030.

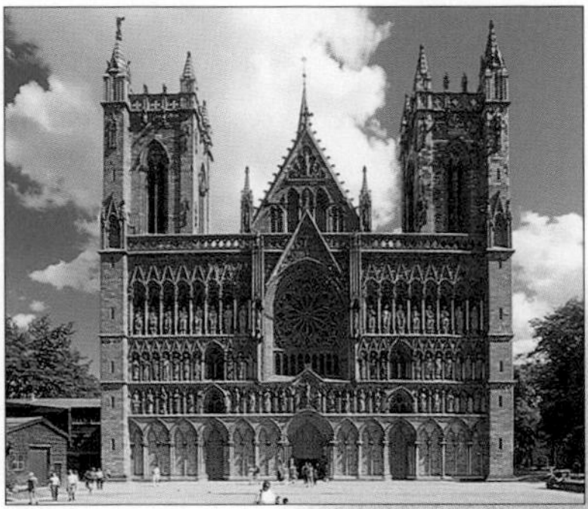

Nidarosdomen in Trondheim, built over the grave of Olav the Holy

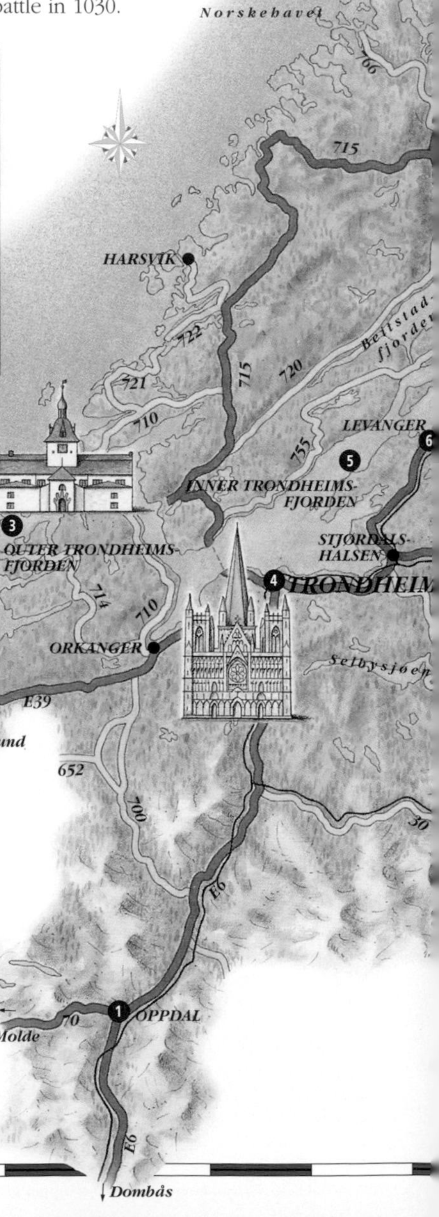

KEY

- Major road
- Minor road
- Railway line
- Ferry route

SIGHTS AT A GLANCE

Inner Trondheimsfjorden 5
Levanger 6
Namsos 9
Oppdal 1
Outer Trondheimsfjorden 3
Røros 2
Rørvik 10
Steinkjer 8
Stiklestad 7
Trondheim pp190–93 4

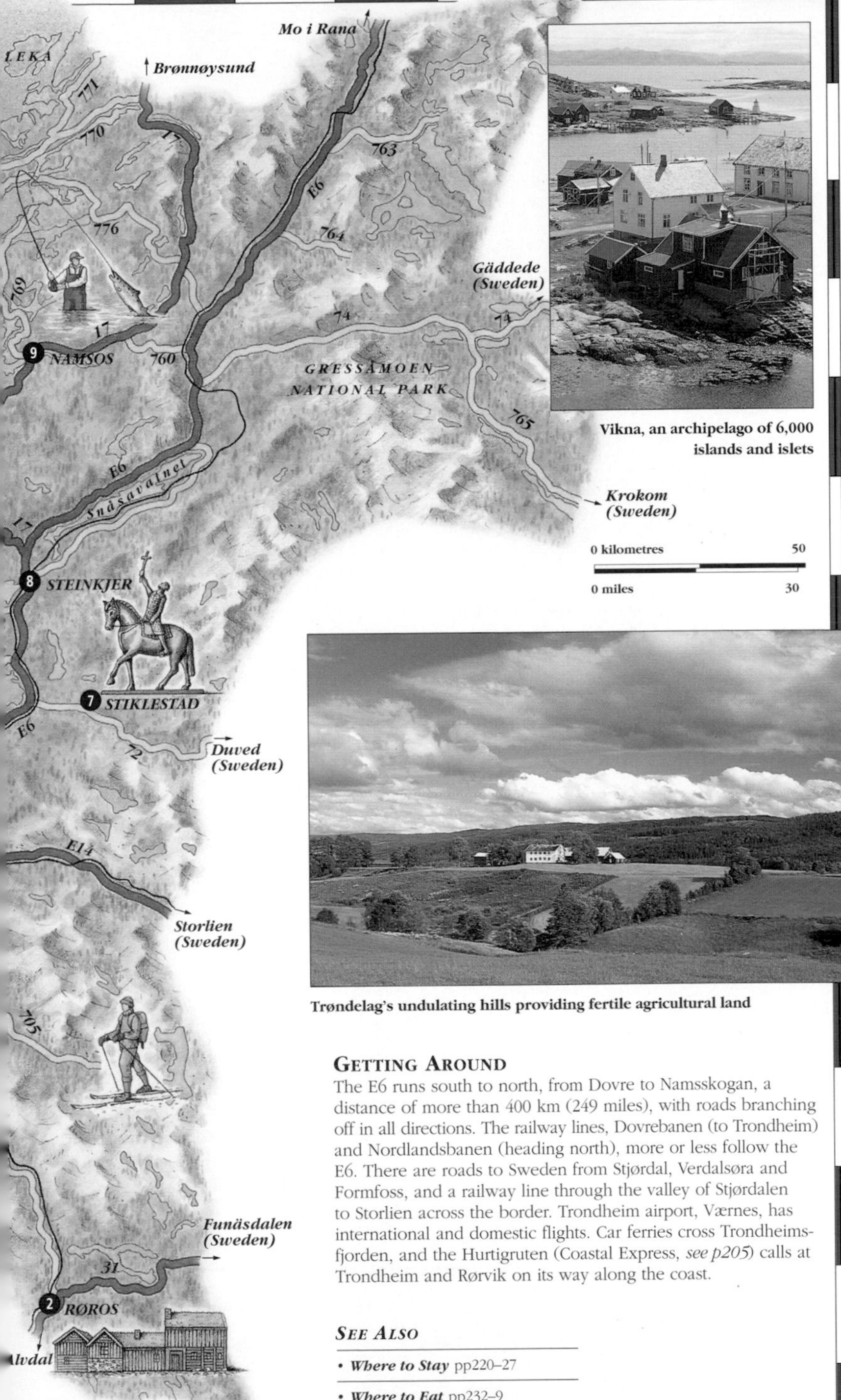

Vikna, an archipelago of 6,000 islands and islets

Trøndelag's undulating hills providing fertile agricultural land

Getting Around

The E6 runs south to north, from Dovre to Namsskogan, a distance of more than 400 km (249 miles), with roads branching off in all directions. The railway lines, Dovrebanen (to Trondheim) and Nordlandsbanen (heading north), more or less follow the E6. There are roads to Sweden from Stjørdal, Verdalsøra and Formfoss, and a railway line through the valley of Stjørdalen to Storlien across the border. Trondheim airport, Værnes, has international and domestic flights. Car ferries cross Trondheimsfjorden, and the Hurtigruten (Coastal Express, *see p205*) calls at Trondheim and Rørvik on its way along the coast.

See Also

- ***Where to Stay*** pp220–27
- ***Where to Eat*** pp232–9

Oppdal ❶

County of Sør-Trøndelag. 6,300. O. Skasliens Vei 15, 72 40 04 70. *Fell Market (Sep), Vintersleppet (1st week Dec), Oppdal Free-ride Challenge (Easter).*

OPPDAL IS A vibrant tourist centre all year round, but particularly in winter. Its excellent winter sports facilities include 200 km (124 miles) of ski slopes, a cable car and ski lifts, ski huts, cafés and restaurants. The skiing season starts with the Vintersleppet festival, while the off-piste Free-ride Challenge race attracts daring skiers around Easter.

The town occupies a beautiful mountain setting. It is an important junction on the Dovrebanen railway and has good road connections.

The open-air **Oppdal Bygdemuseum** has a fine collection of old houses of cultural interest. Outside the town, at **Vang**, there is a large Iron Age burial ground.

Oppdal is the starting point for the journey northward to Vårstigen (the Spring Path), the old pilgrims' route *(see p183)*, through Drivdalen valley and to Dovrefjell National Park *(see pp132–3)*.

From Festa bridge in the west, the toll road heads north to **Gjevilvasshytta**, an elegant tourist lodge incorporating Tingstua, the old courthouse from Meldal.

Oppdal Bygdemuseum
Museumsveien. 72 40 15 60.
end Jun–mid-Aug: daily.

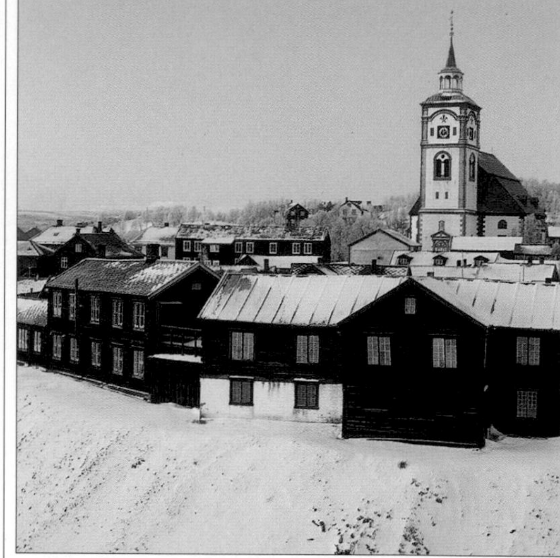

The 17th-century copper-mining town of Røros, preserved for posterity

Røros ❷

County of Sør-Trøndelag. 5,500. *Peder Hiorts Gate 2, 72 41 11 65. Røros Market (3rd week Feb), Winter Festival (mid-Mar), Garpvukku Historical Play (1st week Aug), Festival of Traditional Food (Nov).*

LIFE IN RØROS revolved around the copper mine founded in 1644 on a bleak site 600 m (2,000 ft) above sea level. The mining town, complete with its turf-roofed timber cottages, church and company buildings, has survived, unscathed by fire, to become a UNESCO World Heritage site.

The town's most prominent landmark is the Baroque church of Bergstadens Ziir, built in stone in 1780. Inside there is an imposing Baroque organ, pulpit and altar, and pews where the community were obliged to sit in strict hierarchical order.

Bergskrivergården, the mining company director's house, is situated on Bergmannsgata, the street that was home to those who had wealth and status. The mining museum, **Rørosmuseet**, housed in the reconstructed Smeltehytte (the old smelter), has models of the mines and smelting processes.

About 13 km (8 miles) east of Røros is the disused mine of **Olavsgruva**, featuring Bergmannshallen, a concert hall and theatre built inside the mountain. There are tours of the old mineshafts.

Røros has been immortalized in books by Johann Falkeberget (1879–1967), who lived locally. His story about a peasant girl who transported copper ore was made into a film, *An-Magritt*, starring Liv Ullmann.

Rørosmuseet
Malmplassen. 72 40 61 70.
daily. some public hols.

Olavsgruva
13 km (8 miles) E of town centre.
72 41 44 50. *tours only. Jun–Sep: daily; Oct–May: Sat.*

Oppdal, a region of farmland and mountains renowned for winter sports

Outer Trondheimsfjorden ❸

County of Sør-Trøndelag.
Trondheim Aktivum, 73 80 76 60.

APPROACHING Trondheimsfjorden from the west, the shipping channel passes to the inside of Hitra, the largest island in southern Norway. The fjord itself begins at the promontory of Agdenes.

To the north of the fjord entrance lies the flat and fertile region of Ørlandet, site of the castle of **Austrått**. The estate was owned by the powerful Rømer family. Inger Ottesdatter Rømer, who died in 1555, is the main protagonist in Ibsen's play, *Lady Inger of Østeråt*. The land then passed by marriage to the Bjelke family. The castle was built in Renaissance style between 1654 and 1656 by Chancellor Ove Bjelke, brother to Jørgen Bjelke, who in 1658 recaptured the county of Trondheim from Sweden.

Austrått appears rather stern and unwelcoming from the outside, with its soapstone doorway and coats of arms. Inside, it is quite the opposite. A brightly painted inner courtyard is embellished with carved pillars in the form of female figures – "the wise and foolish virgins".

West of Trondheim, an arm of the fjord leads to Orkanger near the Thamshavnsjenbanen (Thamshavn railway line). Here, the original electric locomotives and three-person carriages from 1908 are on display. Pride of place at **Orkla Industrimuseum** (Orkla Industrial Museum) is given to the lavish train carriage used by the king. The museum also incorporates a mining museum and the old mines of Gammelgruva.

Austrått
Opphaug. *72 52 13 31.*
Jun–mid-Aug: daily.

Orkla Industrimuseum
Løkken Verk (Løkken Mine).
72 49 91 00. Jun–Aug: daily; Sep–May: Mon–Fri. public hols.

Trondheim ❹

See pp190–93.

Inner Trondheimsfjorden ❺

County of Nord-Trøndelag.
Trondheim Aktivum, 73 80 76 60.

ON THE INNER Trondheimsfjorden, the Byneset peninsula west of Trondheim is the site of Gråkallen, one of the city's main areas for sports and recreation. **Munkholm** island, off Fosen Quay in Trondheim, has served as a monastery, fortress and prison. It is now a popular bathing spot.

The fjord is at its widest east of Trondheim. Here, by Vaernes airport, the reputed salmon river of Størdalselva has its mouth. Inland, along the river is **Hegra Festning**. In 1940, General Holtermann and his soldiers – 248 men and one woman – resisted a German attack here for 23 days. Further east at **Reinå**, Engelskstuggu (the English cabin) recalls the early English salmon-fishing pioneers.

On the small island of **Steinvikholm**, off the eastern shore of the fjord, is a castle built by Archbishop Olav Engelbrektsson in 1525. He fled here with the casket of Olav the Holy *(see p194)* during the Reformation. The peninsula of **Frosta** is an old *tingsted* (assembly site). It contains Bronze Age burial mounds and petroglyphs.

Hegra Festning
15 km (9 miles) E of Stjørdal.
Stjørdal Tourist Office, 74 83 45 80. mid-May–Sep: daily; other times by arrangement.

The island of Munkeholmen, in Trondheimsfjorden, once a prison

Levanger ❻

County of Nord-Trøndelag. *17,500. Værnes, 50 km (31 miles) SW. Levanger, 74 05 25 00. Levanger Market (Jul–Aug).*

IN INNER Trondheimsfjorden is Levanger, an administrative centre and site of Iron Age rock carvings, burial mounds and graves. South of here, near Ekne, is the **Falstad Fangeleir**, a former World War II concentration camp.

Out in the fjord is the island of Ytterøy, beyond which the Indreøy peninsula almost blocks the fjord before its end at Steinkjer *(see p194)*. Strauma on **Indreøy** is an idyllic timber-housed hamlet.

Falstad Fangeleir
20 km (12 miles) S of Levanger.
74 01 55 18. mid-May–mid Aug: Wed–Sun; other times by arrangement.

The inner courtyard at Austrått with its "wise and foolish virgins"

Trondheim ❹

Ornament, Stiftsgården

According to the saga writer, Snorre, in 997 King Olav Tryggvason decreed that there should be a town at the mouth of the Nidelva river. The town of Trondheim, then known as Nidaros, quickly became a centre for the Trøndelag region and, for a time, capital of Norway. After King Olav Haraldsson was canonized in 1031, pilgrims flocked to his shrine at the site of Nidaros cathedral. Fire and wars in the 17th century destroyed large parts of the medieval city. The modern town with its grid-like street layout was established after a catastrophic blaze in 1681.

View over Trondheim showing Nidaros cathedral in the background

Exploring Trondheim

Most of Trondheim's sights are within easy walking distance of each other. The town centre, known as Midtbyen, is almost totally surrounded by the fjord and the meandering Nidelva river. The main street, Munkegata, passes right through the heart of the town, from the cathedral of Nidarosdomen in the south to the famous fish market of Ravnkloa in the north.

After the fire in 1681, it was the military engineer Johan Caspar de Cicignon who was mainly responsible for the grid-like layout which exists even today. Yet in the narrow side streets it seems that property owners and chance also had a hand in the layout.

Erkebispegården

Kongsgårdsgaten 1B. *73 53 91 60.*
Jun–Aug: daily; Sep–May: Tue–Sun.
some public hols.
partly.

Erkesbispegården (the Archbishop's Palace) has been a political and spiritual centre of power in Norway since soon after the introduction of Christianity. Part of the north wing of the main house dates from the 12th and 13th centuries, and was built as a fortified bishop's palace. Other parts of the structure were commissioned between 1430 and 1530. After the Reformation, the Archbishop's Palace became the private residence of the feudal overlord. It later served as a military base. In the 19th century it housed the Norwegian crown jewels (now in Nidaros cathedral).

In the museum in the restored south wing there are original sculptures from the cathedral and finds from the palace, among them the archbishop's coin workshop.

There is also an armoury, Rustkammeret, with a large collection of firearms and a section about the Norwegian resistance movement in World War II.

Trondheim Kunstmuseum

Bispegaten 7. *73 53 81 80.*
Jun–Aug: daily; Sep–May: Tue–Sun.

Trondheim Kunstmuseum (Museum of Art) is located close to Nidaros cathedral and the Archbishop's Residence. It contains a fine collection of paintings dating back to its precursor, the Trondheim Art Society, founded in 1845.

The most important works in the gallery are Norwegian paintings from the beginning of the 19th century until today, ranging from the Düsseldorf School to the Modernists. There is also a collection of Danish paintings that would be hard to rival outside Denmark, and an international collection of graphic art.

Nordenfjeldske Kunstindustrimuseum

Munkegaten 5. *73 80 89 50.*
Jun–Aug: daily; Sep–May: Tue–Sun. *some public hols.*

The red-brick buildings of Katedralskolen (the Cathedral School) and Kunstindustrimuseum (the Museum of Applied Art) sit opposite one another next to the cathedral. The museum's collections include furniture, silver and textiles. In a section titled *Three Women, Three Artists,* works by the tapestry artists Hannah Ryggen and Synnøve Anker, and the glass designer Benny Motzfeld, are on show.

Trøndelag Teater

Prinsens Gate 22. *73 80 50 00.*
Box Office *Mon–Sat.*

The splendid Trøndelag Teater complex was completed in 1997. It comprises five separate stages, with seating for between 50 and 500 people in each auditorium, and offers a broad repertoire.

Incorporated into the theatre is the main stage from the original theatre, constructed in 1816. Before this time, the theatre-loving citizens used to perform in their own homes. Another piece of the interior, rescued from the old building, is the Art Nouveau café.

Trøndelag Teater combining five stages in one building

◁ Trondheim's riverfront warehouses mirrored in the water near the mouth of the Nidelva

Vitenskapsmuseet

Erling Skakkes Gate 47. 73 59 21 45. *daily.*

The collections of the Museum of Natural History and Archaeology are housed in three separate buildings, named after the founders of the Royal Society of Norwegian Science (1706).

The Gerhard Schøning building traces Norway's ecclesiastical history and exhibits church interiors and religious art. The Peter Frederik Suhms building focuses on the Middle Ages.

In the Johan Ernst Gunnerus branch there are the departments of zoology and mineralogy. Special displays cover such subjects as "From the Stone Age to the Vikings" and "The Culture of the Southern Sami".

Vår Frue Kirke

Kongens Gate 2. *73 53 84 80.*

Jun–Aug: Wed; other times: Sat.

The words "The holy Mary owns me" are inscribed in Old Norse on the walls of the Vår Frue Kirke (the Church of Our Lady). Built in the late 12th century, it was the only church in Trondheim to survive the Reformation. The church was originally known as Mariakirken (the Church of Mary). It has been extended on several occasions: the tower dates from 1739. The altarpiece came from Nidaros cathedral in 1837.

Vår Frue Kirke, a 12th-century church near the town square

Bryggen

Øvre Elvehavn.

The warehouses and wharves at the mouth of the Nidelva river have been the focus of business and trading since early times. On a number of occasions the buildings were ravaged by fire.

Now restored, the colourful buildings line both sides of the river. On the city centre side in Kjøpmannsgata they are in a terraced area from where it was possible to attack the enemy on the river with cannon fire. On the Bakklandet side, they are situated in the streets of Fjordgata and Sandgata. The oldest remaining wharf dates from around 1700.

Visitors' Checklist

County of Sør-Trøndelag.
150,000. *Vaernes, 50 km (31 miles) E of town centre.* *Brattøra.* *Brattøra.* *Pier 2.*
Munkegata 19, 73 80 76 60.
Festival of St Olav (4th week Jul), Norfishing (2nd week Aug).
www.visit-trondheim.com
www.trondheim.com

Warehouses on the Nidelva river, restored after fire and decay

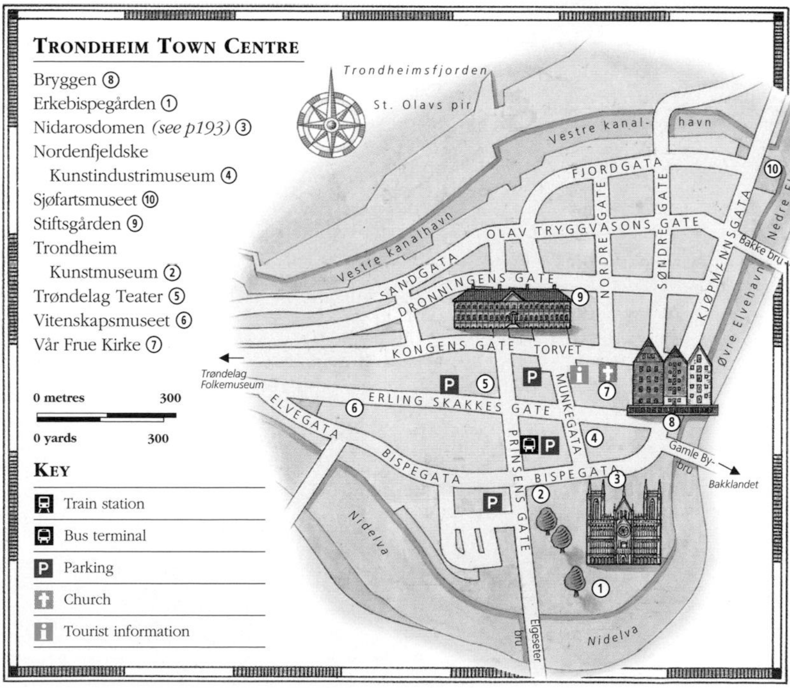

Trondheim Town Centre

Bryggen ⑧
Erkebispegården ①
Nidarosdomen *(see p193)* ③
Nordenfjeldske Kunstindustrimuseum ④
Sjøfartsmuseet ⑩
Stiftsgården ⑨
Trondheim Kunstmuseum ②
Trøndelag Teater ⑤
Vitenskapsmuseet ⑥
Vår Frue Kirke ⑦

0 metres 300
0 yards 300

Key

- Train station
- Bus terminal
- Parking
- Church
- Tourist information

The Queen's Room in Stiftsgården, Scandinavia's largest timber building

Stiftsgården

Munkegaten 23. 73 80 89 50. *Jun–Aug: daily for guided tours only.* *for royal visits.*

This royal residence of Stiftsgården is one of the most imposing old timber mansions in Trondheim. It is an important example of Norwegian wooden architecture, designed by General G F von Krogh and completed in 1778. The style is Rococo, with Baroque details.

The original owner was Cecilie Christine de Schøller, the widow of the privy councillor. Connected to the royal court in Copenhagen, she was influenced by foreign ideas and was keen to build a grand mansion in her attempt to become the "first lady" of Trondheim.

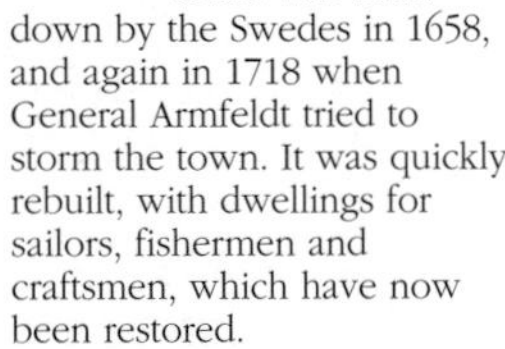
Balustrade detail, Stiftsgården

The building is 58-m (190-ft) long and has 64 rooms. It was given the name of "Stiftsgården" when it was bought by the government in 1800 as a residence for the chief officer of the diocese, the *Stiftsamtmannen*. It became a royal residence in 1906. The dining room, with paintings of London and Venice by J C C Michaelsen, is especially worth a look.

Trondheims Sjøfartsmuseum

Fjordgata 6A. 73 89 01 00. *1 Jun–Aug: 10am–4pm daily; other times by arrangement.*

Trondheim Maritime Museum is housed in a prison building dating from 1725. It has a comprehensive collection of models of sailing ships, figureheads and artifacts relating to maritime life in Trøndelag from the beginning of the 16th century. The exhibits include objects rescued from the frigate *Perlen*, which sank in 1781.

Bakklandet

1 km (half a mile) E of town centre.

East of the Nidelva river lies Bakklandet, a charming quarter with narrow, winding streets dating back to 1650. The area originally belonged to a nunnery. From 1691 it was owned by Jan Wessel, the father of the maritime hero Tordenskiold, who ran a public house here. The Bakke estate was burnt down by the Swedes in 1658, and again in 1718 when General Armfeldt tried to storm the town. It was quickly rebuilt, with dwellings for sailors, fishermen and craftsmen, which have now been restored.

From the town centre, Bakklandet can be reached using the Old Town Bridge, Gamle Bybro, which acquired its carved gates in 1861. High above Bakkland is the fortress of Kristiansten, built by Johan Caspar de Cicignon in 1682.

Ringve Museum

Lade Allé 60, 4 km (2 miles) NE of town centre. 73 92 24 11. *18 May–15 Sep: daily; other times: Sun.*

Ringve is Norway's national museum for music and musical instruments. It was opened in 1952, after Victoria and Christian Anker Bachke had designated in their will their large country estate and collection of musical instruments to become a museum. The instruments had previously been owned by Jan Wessel, father of the maritime hero, Peter Wessel Tordenskiold, after whom the museum café, Tordenskiolds Kro, is named.

The exhibition takes visitors through the stages of musical history, presenting its masters and instruments to the accompaniment of music from each period.

The Botanical Gardens of Ringve, surrounding the mansion, are stocked with 2000 species of plants and trees.

Trøndelag Folkemuseum

Sverresborg Allé, 4 km (2 miles) S of town centre. 73 89 01 11. *daily.* *public hols.* *partly.*

Featuring more than 60 buildings from Trondheim and around, Trøndelag Folkemuseum gives a unique insight into the building traditions and daily life of the region. The museum is located next to the medieval fortress of King Sverre, with a splendid view over the town.

The 18th and 19th-century Gammelbyen (Old Town) has been recreated with a dentist's surgery, a grocery store and a shop selling old-fashioned sweets. Look out for Vikastua, a cottage from Oppdal with an exceptional rose-painted interior. The stave church, originating from Haltdalen, dates from 1170.

Trøndelag Folkemuseum focusing on the traditions of the region

Trondheim: Nidarosdomen

BUILT ON THE SITE OF KRISTKIRKEN, over the grave of Olav the Holy *(see p194)*, the oldest part of Nidaros cathedral dates from around 1320 in Norman, Romanesque and Gothic styles. The cathedral is the largest construction in Norway from the Middle Ages, 102-m (335-ft) long and 50-m (164-ft) wide. Several fires have ravaged it over time and large parts lay in ruins when restoration work began in 1869. A Gothic reconstruction has now been completed. One of the chapels houses the Norwegian crown jewels, including the crowns of the king, queen and prince.

VISITORS' CHECKLIST

Bispegaten 5. *73 53 91 60.* *1 May–19 Jun & 21 Aug–14 Sep: 9am–3pm Mon–Fri, 9am–2pm Sat, 1pm–4pm Sun; 20 Jun–20 Aug: 9am–6pm Mon–Fri, 9am–2pm Sat, 1pm–4pm Sun; 15 Sep–30 Apr: 12 noon–2:30pm Mon–Fri, 11:30am–2pm Sat, 1pm–3pm Sun.* www.nidarosdomen.no

Nave
Inspired by the architecture of Lincoln Cathedral and Westminster Abbey, the nave is 21 m (69 ft) high.

The main tower is 97.8 m (321 ft) high.

Rose Window
Gabriel Kielland created many of the cathedral's beautiful Chartres-inspired stained-glass works, including the magnificent rose window.

Northern transept from the 12th century in Romanesque style.

The altar table is in patinated bronze.

Silver Crucifix
The cross, by W Rasmussen, was donated by Norwegians in the USA for the cathedral's 900th anniversary in 1930.

West Front
The middle row of sculptures on the ornate west wall shows, from left to right, the Norwegian saints Archbishop Øystein, St Hallvard, St Sunniva and St Olav (Olav the Holy), and the heavenly virtue: Love.

The church at Stiklestad, built 100 years after the fatal battle

Stiklestad ❼

County of Nord-Trøndelag, 4 km (2 miles) E of Verdal town centre. to Verdal, then taxi. during Olsok feast.

STIKLESTAD IS ONE of the most famous places in Norwegian history. It was here at a battle in 1030 that King Olav Haraldsson, later St Olav, died. The site is marked by the **Stiklestad Nasjonale Kultursenter** (National Cultural Centre). The St Olav Monument is, according to legend, situated exactly where the body of the king was hidden in a shed the night after the battle. Later his remains were taken to Nidaros (now Trondheim) and buried there *(see p193)*.

Every year, around the time of the St Olav celebrations of *Olsok* (29 July), the play *Spelet om Heilag Olav (The Story of St Olav)*, by Olav Gullvåg and Paul Okkenhaug, is performed in the amphitheatre at Stiklestad, attracting an audience of 20,000. At the top of the amphitheatre is a statue by Dyre Vaa depicting Olav the Holy on his horse *(see below)*.

The altarpiece in **Stiklestad Kirke** is said to have been built above the stone against which Olav the Holy died. A church was built on the site shortly after the battle and replaced 100 years later by the present long church.

The tableaux in the church date from the 17th century and resemble a picture book from the Bible. The frescoes in the choir by Alf Rolfsen, showing scenes from the battle, were commissioned for the church's restoration for the St Olav Jubilee in 1928.

Verdal Museum, near the church, has a typical 19th-century farm from Verdal among its exhibits.

ST OLAV AND THE BATTLE OF STIKLESTAD

Olav Haraldsson was declared king of a united Norway at the assembly of Øretinget in 1016. He went on to convert the entire country to Christianity and in so doing made many enemies, particularly among farmers who feared that the king would become too powerful. Instead, they gave their support to King Canute of Denmark. In 1028, Canute sent 50 ships with an army to invade Norway. Olav was forced to flee. In 1030, Olav returned to re-conquer his realm. In the Verdalen valley he came face to face with his enemy at Stiklestad and died in the ensuing battle, on 29 July 1030. A year after his death, his undecayed body was exhumed and he was declared a saint. Olav was moved from one church to another until, in 1090, he was laid to rest in Kristkirken, on the site of the future Nidaros cathedral. His shrine became a place of pilgrimage. Many churches have been consecrated in his honour.

Statue of Olav the Holy at Stiklestad

Stiklestad Nasjonale Kultursenter
4 km (2 miles) E of Verdal town centre. *74 04 42 00.* *daily.* *some public hols.*

Verdal Museum
4 km (2 miles) E of Verdal town centre. *74 04 42 00.*
10 Jun–10 Aug: daily.

Bølareienen, a 6,000-year-old rock carving of a reindeer

Steinkjer ❽

County of Nord-Trøndelag.
21,000.
Namdalsveien 11, 74 16 36 17.
Steinkjer Market (Aug).

ARCHAEOLOGICAL finds indicate that there has been human settlement in the Steinkjer area for 8,000 years. Burial mounds, stone circles and memorial stones have been discovered at Eggekvammen, Tingvoll and Egge, near the Byafossen waterfall. There are petroglyphs from the Stone Age and Bronze Age near Bardal, and there is also a large area of rock carvings near Hammer, 13 km (8 miles) west of Steinkjer town centre. Other finds indicate that there was an important trade and shipping centre at the head of Beitstadfjorden. Snorre writes in his sagas that Olav Tryggvason established a market town here in 997.

Steinkjer church stands on the hill of Mærehaugen. Before the introduction of Christianity there was a temple to the Norse gods here. This is the third church on the site. The first, from 1150, burnt down, the second was destroyed during a bombing raid in 1940. The new church, designed by Olav Platou (1965), is richly decorated by artists Sivert Donali and Jakob Weidemann.

Steinkjer has good communications: the Nordlandsbanen train line and the E6 pass through the town, and the RV17 leads to the coastal areas of Flatanger and Osen. On the eastern side of Snåsavatnet lake is Bølareienen, a 6,000 year-old life-size rock carving of a reindeer.

Snåsa is the starting point for trips to Gressåmoen National Park, and to the Snåsaheiene hills, noted for their excellent fishing. In the town, **Samien Sitje** is a museum devoted to the southern Sami culture.

Salmon fishing, a popular activity on the Namsen river

Samien Sitje
58 km (36 miles) NE of Steinkjer.
74 15 15 22. 20 Jun–20 Aug: Tue–Fri, Sun; 21 Aug–19 Jun: by prior arrangement.

Namsos 9

County of Nord-Trøndelag. *12,500.*
Stasjonsgata 3, 74 21 73 13. Namsos Market (3rd week Aug).

NAMSOS IS SITUATED at the innermost tip of the 35-km (22-miles) long Namsenfjorden, inside the islands of Otterøy and Jøa, featured in the novels of Olav Duun (1876–1939). The town was established in 1845 as a shipping port, particularly for timber. It was twice destroyed by fire, and was razed to the ground by bombs in World War II, but has since been rebuilt.

The Namsen river, the longest in the county of Trøndelag, enters the sea here. It is one of Norway's best salmon rivers. Popular fishing areas are Sellæg, Grong and Overhalla. Fishing is done from boats known as *harling*, but it is also possible to fish from the bank. The Fiskumfossen waterfall north of Grong has the longest set of salmon steps in northern Europe, at 291 m (955 ft).

The **Namsskogan Familiepark** in Trones features Nordic animals in their natural environment. Further north, a side road leads to Røyrvik, the starting point for a boat connection to the Børgefjell National Park.

Namsskogan Familiepark
70 km (43 miles) N of Namsos.
from Namsos. 74 33 37 00. Jun–Aug: daily; 1 Sep–15 Sep: Sat & Sun. by arrangement.

Rørvik 10

County of Nord-Trøndelag. *3,800.*
Vikna, 74 39 33 00. Rørvik Festival (4th week Jul), Hurtigruten Day (1st week Jul).

NORTH OF NAMSOS is the archipelago of Vikna, comprising nearly 6,000 islands. Rørvik is one of the main centres of population. At the **Nord-Trøndelags Kystmuseum** (Coastal Museum) 19th-century rowing boats used for fishing, typical of Trøndelag, are on display.

A large part of outer Vikna is a conservation area with an abundance of nesting birds, as well as otters, porpoises and several species of seal.

To the north of Vikna, near the county boundary with Nordland, the mountain of Lekamøya rises from the sea. *Leka-møya* (the Leka Virgin) is the principal character in a Nordland folk tale. The main attractions on Leka are cave paintings in Solsemhulen and a burial mound, Herlagshaugen. The museum of cultural history, **Leka Bygdemuseum**, is located nearby.

Nord-Trøndelags Kystmuseum
Museumsgata 2. *74 39 04 41.*
Jun–Aug: daily; Sep–May: Mon–Fri.

Leka Bygdemuseum
1 km (half a mile) N of Leka.
Leka, 74 38 70 00. Jun–Jul: daily.

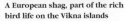

A European shag, part of the rich bird life on the Vikna islands

Northern Norway and Svalbard

THE AUTHOR KNUT HAMSUN DESCRIBED *Northern Norway as "the land hidden behind a hundred miles". Other writers have called it "the land of excitement" or "the land of the high flames". These expressions capture the essence of this northern land – the great distances, the rugged scenery, the dancing Northern Lights of winter and the midnight sun that shines day and night in summer.*

Northern Norway consists of three counties – Nordland, Troms and Finnmark – covering about a third of the country. Busy ports such as Bodø, Narvik, Tromsø, Hammerfest and Kirkenes nestle in sheltered coves or straddle islands along the coast. Inland, the national parks are the habitat of bears and wolves, while out to sea, birds flock to the steep nesting cliffs. Lying 640 km (400 miles) north of the mainland are the Arctic Ocean islands of Svalbard (Spitsbergen), almost 60 per cent covered in glaciers.

Nordland's unspoilt Helgaland coast comprises a multitude of islands, sounds, fjords and snow-clad peaks. The mountains of Lofoten rise like a wall from a sea of islets to the north-west. Here, fishing has been the islanders' life-blood. Further north lies Tromsø, the "Paris of the North" and capital of Northern Norway. Beyond Tromsø the scenery becomes more severe.

Perhaps the ultimate goal of a journey to the top of Norway is to reach Nordkapp (the North Cape). The perpendicular cliffs marking Europe's most northerly point were named by an English sailor, Richard Chancellor, in 1533.

The Finnmark towns of Alta, Kautokeino and Karasjok are rich in Sami culture. Karasjok is home to the Sami Parliament. At Hjemmeluft, magnificent 5,000-year-old rock paintings and carvings have been discovered. There is a distinct Finnish influence in Kirkenes, which is situated close to the borders with Finland and Russia.

Cod hanging up to dry, Lofoten

◁ Tranquil beauty spot near Eggum, in the north of the Lofoten island of Vestvågøya

Exploring Northern Norway and Svalbard

The Lofoten Islands, Nordkapp (the North Cape) and Helgelandskysten in particular have attracted tourists over the years. But it is the magnificent scenery of all of Northern Norway and Svalbard (Spitsbergen), combined with the midnight sun in summer and the wide range of outdoor activities on offer, which make this part of Norway so appealing to travellers. People cross the Arctic Circle to fish in the sea and rivers, to join whale and seal safaris, to go bird watching and cave walking, to take trips into the mountains, or simply to enjoy a holiday in a fisherman's cabin on stilts. Far to the north lies Svalbard, with its distinctive Arctic landscape, flora, animal and bird life.

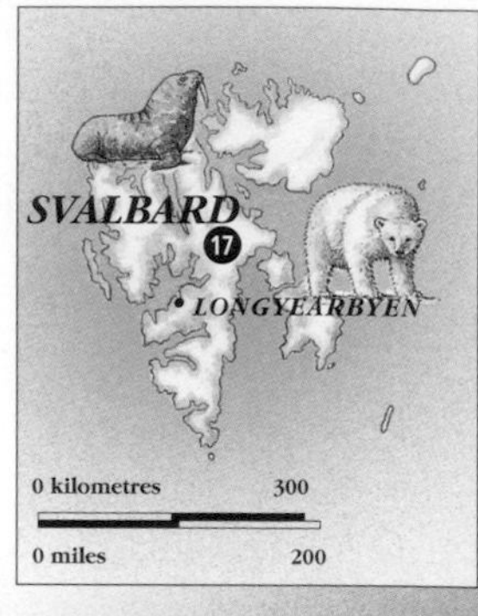

The fishing hamlet of Hamnøy on Vestfjord in the Lofoten Islands

Sperm whale off the island of Andøya in Vesterålen

See Also

- ***Where to Stay*** pp220–27
- ***Where to Eat*** pp232–9

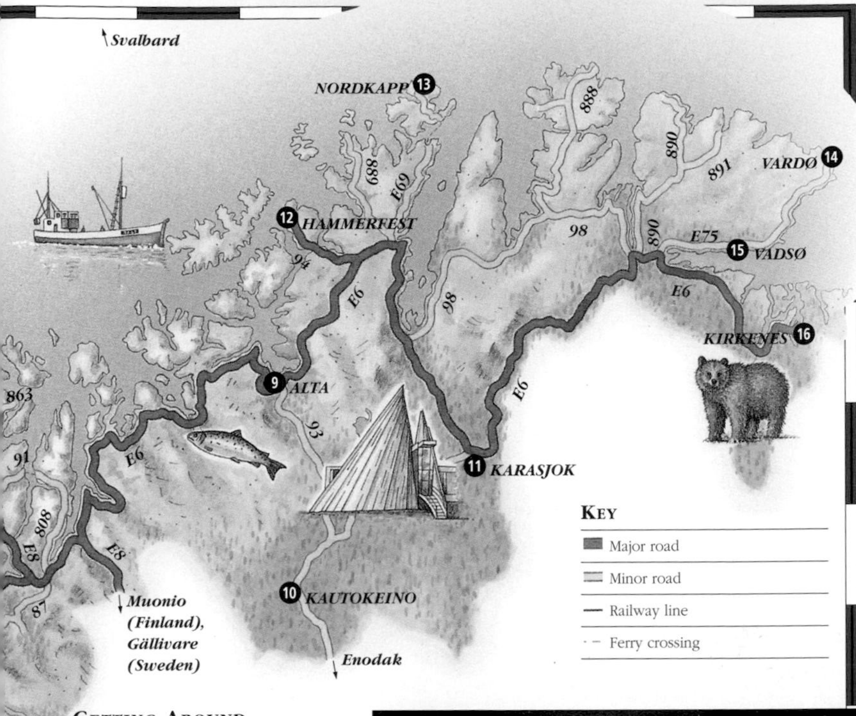

Svalbard
NORDKAPP 13
VARDØ 14
HAMMERFEST 12
VADSØ 15
KIRKENES 16
ALTA 9
KARASJOK 11
KAUTOKEINO 10
Muonio (Finland), Gällivare (Sweden)
Enodak

KEY

- Major road
- Minor road
- Railway line
- Ferry crossing

GETTING AROUND

The most important route through the three counties is the E6, which extends some 1,600 km (994 miles) from southern Nordland to Kirkenes. Four roads go from the E6 to Sweden: from Trofors, Mo i Rana, Storjord and Narvik. Roads lead to Finland from Skibotn, Kautokeino, Karasjok and Neiden, and to Russia from Kirkenes via Storskog. The Nordlandsbanen railway line ends at Bodø. The Hurtigruten coastal express and a number of local boats serve the coast. There are eight main airports, including Svalbard.

The Northern Lights dancing across the sky on a clear winter's night

Sami handicrafts being sold from a *lavvo* (traditional tent)

SIGHTS AT A GLANCE

Alta 9
Bodø 4
Hammerfest 12
Helgelandskysten 1
Karasjok 11
Kautokeino 10
Kirkenes 16
Lofoten and Vesterålen pp202–4 5
Mo i Rana 2
Narvik 6
Nordkapp 13
Saltfjellet-Svartisen National Park 3
Senja 7
Svalbard pp214–15 17
Tromsø 8
Vadsø 15
Vardø 14

The 1,065-m (3,494-ft) long Helgeland Bridge, north of Sandessjøen

Helgelandskysten ❶

County of Nordland.
Helgelandsgaten 1, Sandnessjøen, 75 04 25 80.

THE SHIPPING CHANNEL from Leka northward along the coast of Helgelandskysten passes through a stunning landscape of islands and mountains. Whether seen from aboard the Hurtigruten *(see page 205)*, or from the RV17 as it winds along the coast, this region never fails to delight.

Helgelandskysten is also known as the Realm of the Nessekonge, the wealthy merchants who held power both economically and politically over northern Norway until the early 1900s. They made their fortunes trading with passing cargo ships and fishing vessels.

On the island of **Torget**, near Brønnøysund, is the strange-looking mountain Torghatten, which has a 160-m (525-ft) long passage running right through it, formed when the land was lower than it is now.

On the northern side of Vefsfjorden, on the island of **Alsten**, is the Norse homestead of Tjøtta. The estate has several ruined houses and burial mounds from the Viking Age. The island is dominated by the majestic mountain range, De Syv Søstre (the Seven Sisters), rising to 1,072 m (3,517 ft). The 12th-century stone church, Alstadhaugkirke, was where the writer, Petter Dass (1647–1707, was a clergyman. In the rectory there is a museum devoted to the poet priest. Sandnessjøen is the biggest settlement on the island.

Near the mouth of Ranfjorden is the island of **Dønna**, with the aristocratic estate, Dønnes, and a stone church from 1200. Among the other islands, **Lovunden** is known for its large colony of puffins. **Hestemona**, situated on the Arctic Circle, is dominated by the 568-m (1,863-ft) mountain of Hestmannen, named after a giant troll who, according to an early saga, turned to stone. **Rødøy** island marks the furthest point north on the Helgeland coast.

Mo i Rana ❷

County of Nordland. *25,000.*
O T Olsens Gate 3, 75 13 92 00. *Sjonstock Rock Festival (1st week Aug), Open Air Festival (4th week Aug), Winter Light Festival (Jan).*

LITTLE IS KNOWN about the origins of Mo i Rana, today an industrial town, except that it had a church and a Sami market before 1860. The place was bought by L A Meyer, who started a guesthouse and initiated trade across the border with Sweden. Today central Mo is dominated by Meyergården, a hotel and shopping complex.

The museum, Rana Bygdemuseum, features the collections of Hans A Meyer, with sections on geology, mining and rural culture. Friluftsmuseet, an open-air museum, about 9 km (6 miles) from Mo town centre, is part of Rana Bygdemuseum.

ENVIRONS: From Mo, the E6 runs southward along Ranfjord, eventually reaching **Mosjøen** (75 km/46 miles southwest of Mo) with its beautiful Vefsn Museum, showing works by contemporary Nordland artists. The street Sjøgata is lined with timber buildings and warehouses dating from the early 19th century.

About 20 km (12 miles) north of Mo is **Grønligrotten**, a limestone cave 107-m (351-ft) deep with a gushing stream which re-emerges in nearby Setergrotten. Helmets must be worn in the caves, and a miner's lamp is needed to explore Setergrotten.

The enchanting cave of Grønligrotten with an underground river

Saltfjellet-Svartisen National Park ❸

County of Nordland.
Mo i Rana Tourist Information, 75 13 92 00.

GLORIOUSLY untouched landscapes typify the national park of Saltfjellet and Svartisen. In the east, toward the Nordlandsbanen railway line, E6 and the Swedish border, the undulating terrain is punctuated by peaks rising to 1,700 m (5,577 ft). Further west there are wide mountain plateaus and forested valleys.

Between here and the coast, the Svartisen ice-cap, Norway's second largest glacier, is made up of two glaciers, Østisen and Vestisen. The glacier has several arms running down toward the surrounding valleys. The southeastern one, Østerdalsisen, is strangely contoured. To reach it, take the 32-km (20-miles) long road from Mo, cross Svartisvannet by ferry (in season), and walk 3 km (2 miles) to the glacier toe.

Polarsirkelsenteret (the Arctic Circle Centre) is located in Saltfjellet, just by the Arctic Circle (84 km/52 miles north of Mo i Rana on the E6). It has a tourist information office, slide shows and a restaurant. Nearby there are three Sami sacrificial stones and a memorial to Yugoslav prisoners of war who were killed while working on the railway during World War II.

Polarsirkelsenteret
84 km (52 miles) N of Mo i Rana.
75 12 96 96. May–15 Sep: daily. 17 May.

Marking the Arctic Circle at Polarsirkelsenteret on Saltfjellet

Norsk Luftfartsmuseum, a national aviation centre

Bodø ❹

County of Nordland. 42,000.
Sjøgata 3, 75 54 80 00. Nordland Music Week (4th week Jul).

NORDLAND'S CAPITAL, Bodø, occupies a wonderful setting with Saltfjorden and its islands and nesting cliffs to the west, the mountain ranges of Børvasstindene across the fjord to the south and the island of Landegode to the north. The midnight sun can be seen here from 1 June to 12 July.

Domkirken, Bodø's cathedral, is a modern, three-aisle basilica, designed by G Blakstad and H Munthe-Kaas, and consecrated in 1956. The stained-glass painting above the altar is by Aage Storstein.

Norsk Luftfartsmuseum (the Aviation Museum), illustrating Norwegian civil and military history, is one of Bodø's big attractions. Of particular interest are Catalina seaplanes, Mosquito fighter aircraft, the US spy plane U2 and Junkers 52.

Kjerringøy, 40 km (25 miles) north of Bodø, was Nordland's richest trading post in the 19th century. It is now part of Nordland's county museum and has 15 historic buildings complete with interiors. Nyfjøset (New Barn), which has a tourist information office and a café, is a replica of a barn that was demolished in 1892. The main museum building is located near the cathedral.

A past owner of Kjerringøy was Erasmus Zahl (1826–1900), who helped Knut Hamsun when he wanted to become a writer. In his books, Hamsun *(see p22)* called the place Sirilund.

Saltstraumen is a natural phenomenon taking place 33 km (21 miles) southeast of Bodø. This is one of the world's strongest tidal currents. The water is forced at speeds of up to 20 knots through a 3-km (2-miles) long, 150-m (492-ft) wide strait. It changes direction every six hours. At Opplevelsessentret, a multimedia show explains the current. There is also an aquarium and a seal pool.

Norsk Luftfartsmuseum
Olav V Gata. 75 50 78 50.
daily.

WHALE WATCHING

Killer whales can be seen on organised safaris *(see p253)*, especially in Tysfjord – the deepest fjord in northern Norway – particularly between October and January when they arrive in the fjords to feast on herring. The killer whale is a toothed whale of the dolphin family. The female can be up to 7.5-m (25-ft) long, and a fully-grown male can measure up to 9 m (30 ft). The latter has a particularly powerful, triangular dorsal fin. The killer whale is fast, supple and greedy. It feeds on fish, but is also known to eat other sea animals such as whales and seals.

On the island of Andøya there are safaris to see seals and the enormous sperm whales.

A killer whale patrolling in Tysfjorden

Lofoten and Vesterålen 5

VIEWED FROM VESTFJORDEN, north of Bodø, the mighty mountains of the Lofoten Islands rise up like a wall in the sea. Lofoten comprises five large and many smaller islands. Corries, hollows and sharp peaks create an exciting backdrop to the fjords, moorlands and farms, small towns and fishing villages. The island of Moskenesøya is southernmost of the larger islands. Between Moskenesøya and the remote Skomvær Island lie 60 km (37 miles) of steep nesting cliffs, called *nyker.* Northeast of Lofoten is Vesterålen, which shares the islands of Hinnøya and Vestvågøy with Lofoten, and also includes three other large islands: Langøya, Andøya and Hadseløya.

Kabelvåg
In the 19th century, Kabelvåg was the most important fishing village in Lofoten. The timber-frame church, known as Lofoten's "cathedral", seats 1,200.

Nusfjord
The well-preserved fishing village of Nusfjord on Flakstadøya (see p204), *has many picturesque 19th-century buildings illustrating the development of Lofotfisket (the Lofoten Fisheries).*

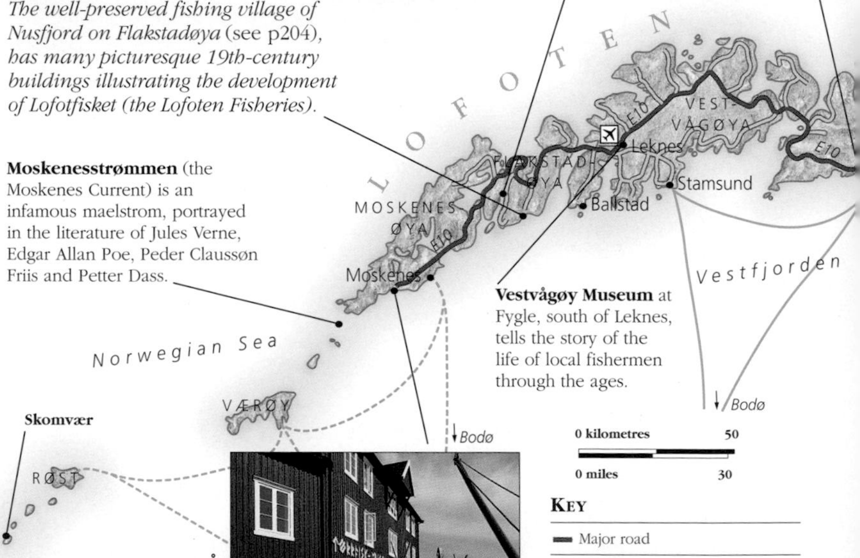

Western Flakstadøya has long, white, sandy beaches and in summer is a good place to swim – even this far north.

Moskenesstrømmen (the Moskenes Current) is an infamous maelstrom, portrayed in the literature of Jules Verne, Edgar Allan Poe, Peder Claussøn Friis and Petter Dass.

Vestvågøy Museum at Fygle, south of Leknes, tells the story of the life of local fishermen through the ages.

Skomvær

Å
The E10 road ends at the southerly village of Å, site of two fishing museums, Lofoten Tørrfisk-museum and Norsk Fiskeværmuseum.

0 kilometres 50

0 miles 30

KEY

- Major road
- Minor road
- Road under construction (2005)
- Hurtigruten route *(see also p205)*
- Other ferry
- Domestic airport

Andenes
Andenes, on the northern tip of Andøya in Vesterålen, has a large fishing quarter, a Polar Museum and the world's most northerly launching pad for rockets and scientific balloons.

VISITORS' CHECKLIST

Counties of Nordland and Troms. *5,000.* *Leknes; Andenes; Svolvær.* *Svolvær, 76 06 98 00.* www.lofoten.info *Cod Fishing World Cup (Apr), Codstock Blues Festival (Whitsun).*

Trondenes
The 40.6-cm calibre Adolf Cannon, a relic from World War II, is one of the attractions at Trondenes (see p204).

GETTING AROUND

There are flights from Bodø to Svolvær and Leknes in Lofoten, and to Andenes in Vesterålen. Helicopters operate to the island of Værøy. Hurtigruten coastal ships call at Stamsund and Svolvær. Road bridges and tunnels, buses, ferries and express boats connect the many islands.

Tjeldsundbrua
The 1,001-m (3,284-ft) long Tjelsund Bridge extends from the mainland across to Hinnøya, Norway's biggest and most populated island. The towers stand 76 m (249 ft) above the waterline.

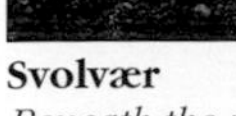

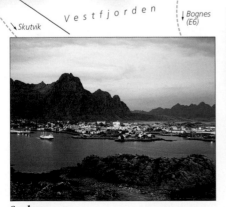

Svolvær
Beneath the mountain of Svolværgeita (Svolvær goat) is Svolvær, the "capital" and transport hub of Lofoten (see p204).

Exploring Lofoten and Vesterålen

THE COASTLINE OF THE LOFOTEN and Vesterålen islands is dominated by sharp peaks such as Tinden and Reka on the island of Langøya, and Møysalen on Hinnøya. Small towns and fishing villages lie at the water's edge. Some of these settlements are deserted, like Nyksund, others, such as Myre, are thriving. At the northernmost tip of the Vesterålen island of Andøya is the port of Andenes. Svolvær is the most important town on Lofoten.

Jagged mountains forming a backdrop to the skerries in Lofoten

Svolvær

Regarded as the "capital" of Lofoten, Svolvær only received town status in 1996. Its location on Austvågsøya and good transport links make it an important gateway for tourism on the islands. The town's economy depends on Lofotfisket (the Lofoten Fisheries). In February and March every year the cod arrive in Vestfjorden to spawn and the fishing boats follow.

Other than fishermen and tourists, artists have long been attracted to Svolvær and a centre for North Norwegian artists has been established in the town, **Nordnorsk Kunstnersentrum**. Vågan town hall is worth a visit. It contains seven paintings by Gunnar Berg showing the battle of Trollfjord in 1880 when fishermen in small boats clashed with the rival new steamships.

The 569-m (1,867-ft) peak, **Svolværgeita** (the Svolvær goat), with its two horns, appears to rise from the town centre and presents a challenge for all climbers.

Nordnorsk Kunstnersentrum
Svolvær. *76 06 67 70.* *mid-Jun–mid Aug: daily; mid-Aug–mid-Jun: Tue–Sun.* *public hols.*

Vestvågøya

From the island of Austvågøya there is a road connection, via Gimsøy and two bridges, to Vestvågøya, where there is an airfield at Leknes and a Hurtigruten coastal express stop at Stamsund. **Stamsund**, like **Ballstad**, is one of the largest and most picturesque fishing villages in west Lofoten. Vestvågøya is also an important agricultural island, which has been farmed since the Stone Age.

Vestvågøy Museum at Fygle has a fine collection, including a fisherman's cabin dating from 1834. The island is rich in Stone and Iron Age monuments and Viking settlements. **Lofotr – Vikingmuseet på Borg** (Viking Museum at Borg), north of Leknes, features a reconstruction of a chieftain homestead from AD 500–900. It is a lively museum, where Viking banquets and crafts demonstrations are arranged.

The old trading post of Sund on Moskenesøya

Vestvågøy Museum
2 km (1 mile) E of Leknes.
76 08 00 43. *Jun–mid-Aug: daily.*

Lofotr – Vikingmuseet på Borg
Prestegårdsveien 59, Borg.
76 08 49 00. *mid-May–Aug: daily; Sep–mid-May: Fri.* *public hols.*

Flakstadøya and Moskenesøya

The island of Flakstadøya is best known for the fishing village of **Nusfjord**. It was chosen in 1975 as part of the European Year of Nature Conservation to be a pilot project for the conservation of building traditions in Norway.

On Moskenesøya there is a string of fishing villages, including Reine, set in a wild mountainous landscape. The charming village of **Å** *(see p202)* lies at the southern end of the Lofoten road. **Sund** has a fishing museum and a smithy for artistic metalwork.

Between Moskenesøya and Værøy whirls the current of **Moskenesstrømmen**, the world's biggest maelstrom. When the wind and the current are in the same direction, the roar can be heard 5 km (3 miles) away.

On **Værøy** and **Røst**, Lofoten's southernmost islands, vast numbers of sea birds nest in the strangely shaped cliffs of Trenykene. The fabled lighthouse of **Skomvær** stands alone at the outermost point.

Vesterålen Islands

Hinnøya is Vesterålen's (and Norway's) largest and most populated island. Its main town is **Harstad**, which developed around 1870 as a result of the abundance of herring. The Northern Norway culture festival, is held here each year, around the summer solstice.

On nearby Trondenes stands an early Gothic church. The northernmost island is Andøya, with the fishing community of **Andenes** *(see p203)*.

Hurtigruten: "The World's Most Beautiful Voyage"

It was Captain Richard With of the shipping company, Vesteraalske Dampskibsselskab, who initiated the coastal express amid much controversy. Few people believed that it would be possible to operate an express route all year round, least of all during the dark days of winter, since only poor maps existed of the treacherous Norwegian coast. However, a contract was signed between With and the government in May 1893. At the beginning there were weekly sailings and nine ports of call between Trondheim and Hammerfest in summer. In winter the boats stopped at Tromsø. The coastal express soon proved to be a lifeline for the communities along the route. Today, two shipping lines operate 11 ships, with daily south and northbound departures *(see p267)*. The cruise from Bergen to Kirkenes, calling at 34 ports, has been called "the world's most beautiful voyage".

Channel beacon

Hurtigruten Ports of Call

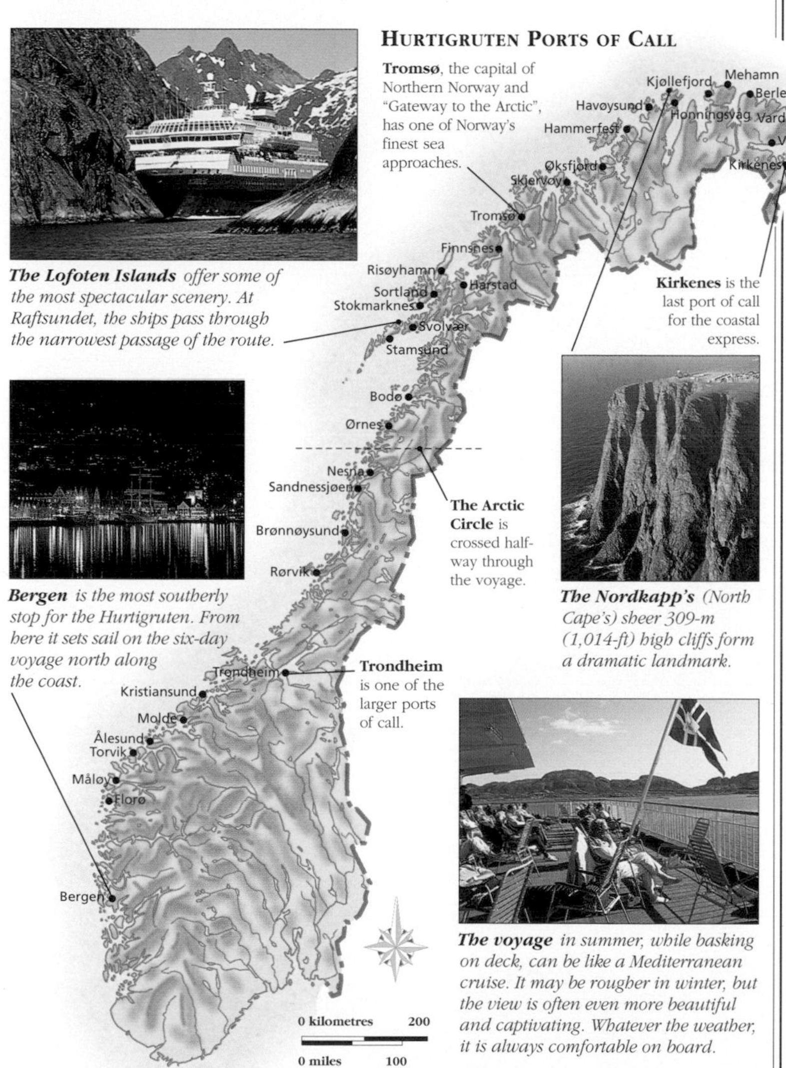

Tromsø, the capital of Northern Norway and "Gateway to the Arctic", has one of Norway's finest sea approaches.

The Lofoten Islands *offer some of the most spectacular scenery. At Raftsundet, the ships pass through the narrowest passage of the route.*

Kirkenes is the last port of call for the coastal express.

The Arctic Circle is crossed halfway through the voyage.

Bergen *is the most southerly stop for the Hurtigruten. From here it sets sail on the six-day voyage north along the coast.*

The Nordkapp's *(North Cape's) sheer 309-m (1,014-ft) high cliffs form a dramatic landmark.*

Trondheim is one of the larger ports of call.

The voyage *in summer, while basking on deck, can be like a Mediterranean cruise. It may be rougher in winter, but the view is often even more beautiful and captivating. Whatever the weather, it is always comfortable on board.*

The busy port of Narvik close to the border with Sweden

Narvik 6

County of Nordland. 18,600. Kongens Gate 26, 76 94 33 09. Winter Festival (2nd week Mar), Black Bear Rally (4th week Jun).

NARVIK DEVELOPED as a shipping port for iron ore from Kiruna in Sweden. The Ofotbanen train line to Kiruna was completed in 1902, after which Narvik was given town status. Heavy bombardment by the Germans in 1940 destroyed most of the town.

After World War II, Narvik rose again to become Norway's second largest shipping town. Activities connected with iron ore still form its economic base. The Ofotbanen passes below the mountains high above Rombaksfjorden, offering stunning views.

From Oscarsborg a cable car, **Fjellheisen**, climbs up to 700 m (2,296 ft). In summer it operates until 2 am (midnight sun: 31 May–14 Jul).

Krigsminnesmuseet (the War Memorial Museum), near the main square, focuses on the military campaigns fought here in 1940. Allied as well as German soldiers are buried near Fredskapellet (the Peace Chapel) in the cemetery.

From Narvik, the E6 runs southward, crossing a number of fjords either by ferry or bridges, including the impressive 525-m (1,722-ft) long bridge spanning the beautiful Skjomenfjorden. On Hamarøy, around 100 km (60 miles) south of Narvik, is the strangely shaped mountain of Hamarøyskaftet and the childhood home of Nobel-prize winning novelist Knut Hamsun (1859–1952).

ENVIRONS: The scenic E10 road, **Bjørnfjellveien**, starts at Rombaksfjorden and ascends to 520 m (1,706 ft) through the wild mountains of Ofoten to the Swedish border.

Krigsminnemuseet

Torvhallen. 76 94 44 26.
Mar–Sep: daily; other times by arrangement. public hols. by arrangement.

Senja 7

County of Troms. 9,000. Storgata 25, Finnsnes, 77 85 07 30. *Finnsnes Festival (4th week Jul), Ocean Fishing Festival (1st week Aug), Tramøy Festival (2nd week Aug), Husøy Festival (Aug).*

NORWAY'S SECOND largest island, Senja, can be reached by road (E6) from Bardufoss, across the bridge at Finnsnes. The landscape is green and welcoming on the mainland side, becoming harsher toward the sea coast. **Ånderdalen Nasjonalpark** has an unspoilt landscape inhabited by elk and eagles.

Family of swans in Ånderdalen Nasjonalpark on Senja island

Back on the mainland, in the south of Troms county large areas of wilderness, including Øvre Dividal national park, are home to bears.

From Skibotn, about 100 km (60 miles) east of Senja, the E8 passes near the point where Finland, Sweden and Norway meet, the Treriksrøysa.

Ånderdalen Nasjonalpark

35 km (22 miles) S of Finnsnes.
Sør-Senja Museum, 77 85 46 77.

Tromsø 8

See pp210–11.

Detail of rock engraving from Hjemmeluft, near Alta

Alta 9

County of Finnmark. 16,000. Sorenskriverveien 13, 78 45 77 77. *Borealis Winter Festival (Mar), Finnmark Race (Mar).*

THE ORIGINAL VILLAGE of Alta, at the mouth of the Alta river, has grown and merged with its neighbours to form the most populated urban area in Finnmark. It includes Bossekop, a commercial market place rich in tradition where Sami and Kvæn people (immigrants of Finnish origin) and Norwegians traded goods. Apart from the church in Bossekop, the entire area was razed to the ground during the German retreat in 1944.

Today, Alta is a growing industrial and educational centre, and an important transport junction on the E6 with its own airport.

The lower part of the Alta Valley is covered in spruce forests and fertile agricultural land. The Gulf Stream and sunny summer nights provide

◁ Scattered development and early winter snow between the sea and the mountains of Northern Norway

Pikefossen, a waterfall on the Kautkeinoelva river in Finnmark

fertile conditions, even at 70ºN. Altaelvar is one of the world's most attractive salmon rivers for fly-fishing. Every year salmon weighing more than 20 kg (44 lb) are caught.

In 1973, rock engravings between 2,000 and 6,000 years old were found near the village of Hjemmeluft. The engravings, now a UNESCO World Heritage Site, show wildlife and hunting scenes.

Alta Museum, winner of the Museum of the Year, 1993, is also located at Hjemmeluft. It features exhibits relating to the Alta River from the Stone Age Komsa culture (7000 BC –2000 BC) through to the latest hydroelectric project.

Alta Museum
Altaveien 19, Hjemmeluft.
78 45 63 30. daily. some public hols.

Kautokeino ⑩

County of Finnmark. *3,000.*
Brebuktnesveien 6, 78 48 65 00.
Easter Festival (Easter), Autumn Festival (Sep).

THE NAME "Kautokeino" is a Norwegianized form of the Sami word, *Guovdageaidnu.* Kautokeino is a mountain town surrounded by barren plateaus where reindeer husbandry is the most important economic activity.

The town has a large Sami community and has become a centre for education with a Sami High School. Reindeer husbandry is one of the courses on the curriculum.

Kulturhuset (the Culture House), opened in 1980, houses the Sámi Instituhtta, a co-ordinating organization for Sami politics and culture. It has a theatre and a library and also mounts exhibitions.

Easter is a time of transition for the Sami, just before they set off with their reindeer for summer pastures on the coast. It is marked by colourful celebrations, with weddings, a *joik* (Sami chanting song) festival and reindeer racing, all attracting large numbers of visitors.

Kulturhuset
1 km (half a mile) N of town centre.
78 48 72 16. Mon–Fri: daily (library) and for cinema or theatre performances. some public hols.

Karasjok ⑪

County of Finnmark. *3,000.*
Porsangerveien 1, 78 46 88 10.
Easter Festival (Easter).

THE SAMI CAPITAL is Karasjok (Karásjohka in Sami). It is the seat of the Sami Parliament, **Sametinget**, opened in 1989. Its new building was inaugurated by King Harald in 2000. The architects, Christian Sundby and Stein Halvorsen, used elements from reindeer husbandry as a base for their design. A long hallway, Vandrehallen, reminiscent of the dividing fences used for the reindeer, winds through the building. The plenary hall is like a *lavvo* (pointed Sami summer tent) and decorated with a magnificent artwork in blue and gold by Hilde Skancke Pedersen.

Around 80 per cent of the population of Karasjok is of Sami origin. Their culture is the subject of **De Samiske Samlinger**, a museum featuring Sami handicrafts and way of life, clothing and building traditions.

The climate in these parts can be extreme. The record low temperature is –51.4° C (–60.5°F), and the highest temperature 32.4° C (90°F).

Sametinget
Kautokeinoveien 50. *78 47 40 00. Mon–Fri.*

De Samiske Samlinger
Museumsgate 17. *78 46 99 50. daily. public hols.*

The striking Sami Parliament building in Karasjok, opened in 2000

Tromsø 8

Roald Amundsen's statue in Tromsø

KNOWN AS THE "Paris of the North", Tromsø is the largest town in the polar region of Scandinavia. It is located 300 km (186 miles) inside the Arctic Circle, on the same latitude as northern Alaska. Central Tromsø covers an island in the busy Tromsøy-sund. There was a farming estate here in early Viking times, and the first church was built around 1250. During the Hanseatic period, trade and commerce boomed; Tromsø officially became a market town in 1794. From the 1820s it developed as a thriving port for sea traffic in the Arctic Ocean. Nansen and Amundsen started their polar expeditions from here. The world's northernmost university opened in Tromsø in 1972.

Tromsøy-sund with Ishavskatedralen and the peak of Tromsdalstind

Polaria

Hjalmar Johansens Gate 12. *77 75 01 00. daily. some public hols.*

Polaria is a national centre for research and information relating to the polar regions, particularly the Arctic. It is also a great place to experience the Arctic landscape. In a fascinating panoramic film from Svalbard *(see pp214–15)*, the viewer becomes a wanderer in a polar landscape beneath the Northern Lights, sensing what it feels like to be in the Arctic wilderness.

An aquarium features Arctic species of fish. Other creatures include the red king crab, *paralithodes camtschaticus*, which can weigh up to 10 kg (22 lb). This Arctic species has migrated from Russia and is spreading steadily southward along the Norwegian coast. Another attraction is the glass-bottomed pool for seals, which can be viewed from below.

Tromsø Kunstforening

Muségata 2. *77 65 58 27. Tue–Sun. some public hols.*

Established in 1877, Tromsø Kunstforening is the oldest art society in Northern Norway. It exhibits Norwegian and international contemporary art, and arranges around 20 exhibitions every year. The society is based in a 19th-century building, which once housed Tromsø Museum.

Façade of Tromsø Kunstforening, built in 1894

Nordnorsk Kunstmuseum

Sjøgata 1. *77 64 70 20. Tue–Sun. some public hols.*

The regional art museum for Northern Norway, Nordnorsk Kunstmuseum, was established in 1985 primarily to show painting and handicrafts from the northern regions, including sculpture and textile art. The museum also arranges temporary exhibitions of work both past and present.

Polarmuseet

Søndre Tollbugata 11. *77 68 43 73. daily.*

Polar hunting and research expeditions are the focal points of Polarmuseet. Displays feature Fridtjof Nansen's journey to the North Pole in his ship *Fram*, the life of Antarctic explorer Roald Amundsen *(see p23)* and Salomon Andrée's attempted balloon flight to the North Pole (1897).

There are exhibitions devoted to the first hunters on Svalbard, the trappers of polar bears, polar foxes and seals, who wintered in the icy wasteland. Everyday articles, utensils and a wealth of other material left by hunters, whalers and sealers around Northern Norway form part of the collection.

The museum is located in the harbour area of old Tromsø, surrounded by sturdy warehouses, fishermen's bunkhouses and wooden buildings from the 1830s.

Ishavskatedralen

2 km (1 mile) E of town centre. *77 75 34 40. mid-Apr–end Sep: daily; other times by prior arrangement and for services.*

Consecrated in 1965, Ishavskatedralen (the Arctic Ocean Cathedral, also known as Tromsdalen Church) was designed by Jan Inge Hovig. It is built of concrete. The shape of its roof symbolizes the way in which the Northern Lights brighten up Tromsø's dark winter months.

A massive 23-m (75-ft) high, triangular stained-glass window by Victor Sparre (1972) fills the east wall. It

The striking east wall of Ishavskatedralen, composed entirely of stained glass

comprises 86 panels of jewel-like glass pieces on the theme of the Second Coming of Christ.

Nordlysplanetariet

3 km (2 miles) N of town centre.
77 61 00 00 (Tourist Information).
until further notice.

Situated on the university campus in Breivika, near Tromsø Botaniske Hage (Botanical Gardens), is Nordlysplanetariet (the Northern Lights Planetarium). It is known for screening the film *Arctic Light*, which provides a realistic experience both of the strange, blue aurora borealis (known as the Northern Lights) – often visible in the Arctic sky during the dark winter months – and of the incredible midnight sun, responsible for the light nights of summer.

The planetarium (unfortunately closed until further notice) should not be confused with the Nordlysobservatoriet (Northern Lights Observatory), a research centre in Skibotn in Lyngen.

Tromsø Museum, Universitetsmuseet

Lars Thøringsvei 10. *77 64 50 00.*
daily.

Now part of the University Museum, Tromsø Museum is the regional museum for Northern Norway. Established in 1872, it holds considerable collections from the Stone Age, Viking era and early Middle Ages, including a reconstructed Viking longhouse. Of particular interest are the late medieval church carvings from the Hanseatic period and those in Baroque style.

From its early days the museum specialized in Arctic landscape and culture. Sami history has a prominent place and there are comprehensive displays devoted to aspects of Sami life.

The museum also has a lot to offer younger visitors with regular film shows and a life-size replica of a dinosaur.

Visitors' Checklist

County of Troms. *60,000.*
4 km (2 miles) NW of centre.
Prostneset. *Prostneset.*
Storgata 61–63, 77 61 00 00.
destinasjontromso.no
Tromsø International Film Festival (2nd week Jan), Northern Lights Festival (3rd week Jan), Midnight Sun Marathon (mid-Jun), Beer Festival (3rd week Aug).

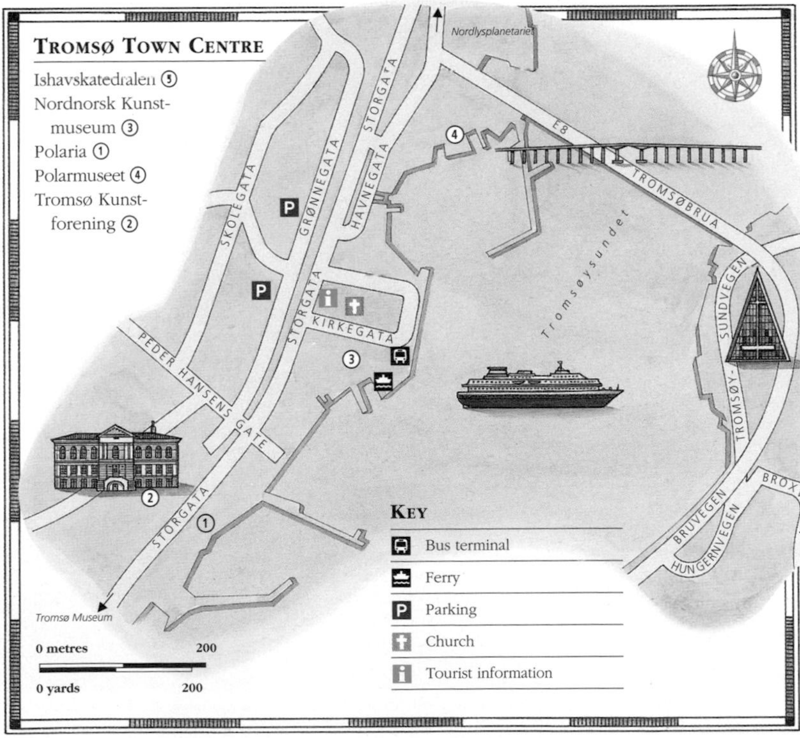

Tromsø Town Centre

Ishavskatedralen ⑤
Nordnorsk Kunstmuseum ③
Polaria ①
Polarmuseet ④
Tromsø Kunstforening ②

Nordlysplanetariet
Storgata
Grønnegata
Havnegata
Skolegata
Kirkegata
Peder Hansens Gate
Tromsøysundet
E8
Tromsøbrua
Sundvegen
Tromsøy-
Bruvegen
Hungervegen
Broxvegen
Tromsø Museum

0 metres 200
0 yards 200

Key

Bus terminal
Ferry
Parking
Church
Tourist information

Verdens Barn (the Children of the World) sculptures at Nordkapp

Hammerfest ⓬

County of Finnmark. 9,200. Havnegaten 3, 78 41 21 85. Hammerfest Days (3rd week Jul), Polar Nights Festival (3rd week Nov).

THE POLAR BEAR featured on Hammerfest's coat of arms recalls the days when this was an important hunting and trapping centre. A settlement already by the 9th century, Hammerfest was given town status in 1789. It is the world's most northerly town at 70° 39' 48"N, as recorded on Meridianstøtten (the Meridian Pillar), which marks the first international measurement of the Earth in the 19th century.

The town has endured many catastrophes over the years, including being destroyed by a hurricane in 1856 and being razed to the ground in World War II. Each time it has been rebuilt in true pioneer spirit. In 1890 it was the first town in Europe to install electric street lighting.

Hammerfest church is unusual in that it has no altar. Instead, the back wall is a monumental abstract painting in glowing colours. The Polar Bear Club, **Isbjørnklubben**, has a museum illustrating the town's Arctic traditions.

The Meridian Pillar at Hammerfest

Isbjørnklubben
Rådhusplassen 1. 78 41 31 00. daily.

Nordkapp ⓭

County of Finnmark. to Honningsvåg, then bus. summer. Honningsvåg Tourist Information, 78 47 25 99.

IT WAS THE ENGLISH sailor, Richard Chancellor, who named Nordkapp (the North Cape) in 1533, during his attempt to find the Northeast Passage to China. Various important people travelled to view the North Cape, including the French king, Louis Philippe of Orleans, in 1795, and Oscar II in 1873. The latter was responsible for encouraging tourist ships to include the North Cape on their itineraries and tourism grew rapidly. An impressive new road – part of it below the sound of Magerøy – links the cape to the mainland.

Every year, more than 200,000 people come to the cliff top. **Nordkapphallen** (the North Cape Hall), inside the mountain, offers a panoramic view of the coast. A videograph showing Finnmark's changing seasons plays on a 225°-wide screen. Visitors also have the chance to become a member of the Royal North Cape Club.

From the top of the North Cape there is a signposted path to the promontory of **Knivskjellodden**, which is Europe's most northerly point, at 71°11'08"N. **Honningsvåg**, 35 km (22 miles) southeast of the cape, is where Hurtigruten *(see p205)* calls. It also has a Nordkapp museum.

Nordkapphallen
35 km (22 miles) N of Honningsvåg. 78 47 68 60. Apr–Sep: daily.

Vardø ⓮

County of Finnmark. 2,700. Kaigata 12, 78 98 82 70. Winter Festival (Apr), Winter Blues (Nov), Pomor Festival (4th week Jul).

TWO EVENTS at the beginning of the 14th century were to enforce Vardø's position as a bastion against incursions from the east: Håkon V built a fortress and Archbishop Jørund consecrated the first church. The fortress, **Vardøhus Festning**, was rebuilt in the 18th century as a star-shaped fortification with parapets of earth and peat, eight cannons and a mortar. There are tours of the commanding officer's residence, the old depots and the barracks. Four kings have written their names on a beam from the original fortress.

Vardø is connected to the mainland by a tunnel below the sound of Bussesundet, constructed in 1982. Fishing and fish processing are the basis of the local economy.

The fishing village of **Kiberg**, to the south, was known as "Little Moscow" because of partisan activity during World War II. To the north, the deserted hamlet of **Hamningberg** lies in a moon-like landscape where the ocean has created strange rock formations.

Vardøhus Festning
Festningsgata. 78 98 85 02. daily. by arrangement.

A sun salute, fired from Vardøhus Festning on the sun's reappearance

Vadsø, on the Barents Sea, owing its development to Finnish immigration

Vadsø ⓯

County of Finnmark. 6,200. Slettengata 21, 78 95 44 90 (summer), 78 94 28 90 (winter).

Originally situated on the island of Vadsøya, the town of Vadsø was moved to the mainland around 1600. Remains of its 15th and 16th-century buildings still exist on the island. Also there is an airship mooring mast on Vadsøya, which was used by Amundsen's expedition to the North Pole in the airship *Norge* in 1926, and to launch Umberto Nobile's airship *Italia* in 1928.

Over the centuries many Finns have settled in Vadsø and the buildings bear the hallmark of Finnish workmanship. **Vadsø Bymuseum** devotes considerable space to the Kvænene (as the Finnish were known). It is located in a Finnish-style farmhouse, Tuomainengården.

Invandrermonumentet (the Immigrant Monument), by the Finnish sculptor Ensio Seppänen, was unveiled in 1977 by King Olav in the presence of the Swedish king and Finnish president.

The so-called Pomor trade with the Russians, by which fish was exchanged for timber, also contributed considerably to the town's development in the 19th and 20th centuries.

Vadsø Bymuseum
Hvistendahlsgate 31. 78 94 28 90. *20 Jun–20 Aug: daily; other times: Mon–Fri. public holidays.*

Kirkenes ⓰

County of Finnmark. 3,500. *Presteveien 1, 78 99 25 44. Barents Ski Race (Mar), Salmon Fishing Festival (1st week Jul), Dark Months Festival (Nov).*

At the head of Bøkfjorden is Kirkenes, the biggest urban centre in eastern Finnmark and the last port of call for Hurtigruten. Iron ore has been the financial cornerstone of the community and when the town was destroyed by the retreating German army in 1944, its 2,000 inhabitants sought refuge in nearby mineshafts.

The mines closed in 1996, but their legacy lives on. Opencast pits at **Bjørnevatn**, south of the town, have created a vast artificial valley with a floor 70 m (230 ft) below sea level.

Kirkenes' proximity to the border with Russia draws tourists to the area. A popular excursion is via Storskog (the official crossing point) to the Grense Jacobselv river on the border, through forests of crooked birch trees overlooking the Barents Sea.

At the mouth of the river there is a chapel built in 1869 as a spiritual watchtower toward the East. It was named after Oscar II who visited the region in 1873. A road leads from Elvenes to Skafferhullet and the Greco-Russian chapel on the Russian side.

The pine forests and moorland of **Øvre Pasvik Nasjonalpark** (National Park), on the Pasvikelva river, extend to the Treriksrøysa monument, where Finland, Russia and Norway meet. The river has been heavily developed for hydroelectricity.

The Midnight Sun

The expression "The Land of the Midnight Sun" is often used to describe Norway and northern Scandinavia. The concept of the "midnight sun" means that the uppermost arc of the sun stays above the horizon for 24 hours. This occurs north of latitude 66.5°N during a few summer months. Correspondingly, there is a period of darkness during the winter, when the sun never rises above the horizon during the day. As if to compensate for this, the Northern Lights may sometimes blaze across the sky. The midnight sun and dark days of winter are caused by the tilt of the earth's axis, and the earth's rotation around the sun. To see the midnight sun in these parts can be a magical experience.

Midnight sun shining over the North Cape

Svalbard ⑰

KNOWN AS THE "LAND OF THE COLD COASTS", Svalbard consists of the Arctic Ocean islands of Spitsbergen (the largest), Nordaustlandet, Edgeøya, Barentsøya, Prins Karls Forland and several smaller ones. The archipelago lies 640 km (400 miles) north of the mainland, about one hour by plane from Tromsø. It was first mentioned in an Icelandic document in 1194. A Dutch explorer, Willem Barents, arrived in 1596. He found a magnificent landscape peppered with ragged peaks, and named it Spitsbergen. To the east the mountains are plateau-like. Glaciers calve noisily into the sea from their huge walls of ice. Svalbard was placed under Norwegian sovereignty in 1925, and in 1935 the Soviet Union became a party to the treaty to share in the local coal mining rights.

Walrus
Since the 1950s the walrus has been a protected species and stocks have increased. It is particularly prevalent on the island of Moffen.

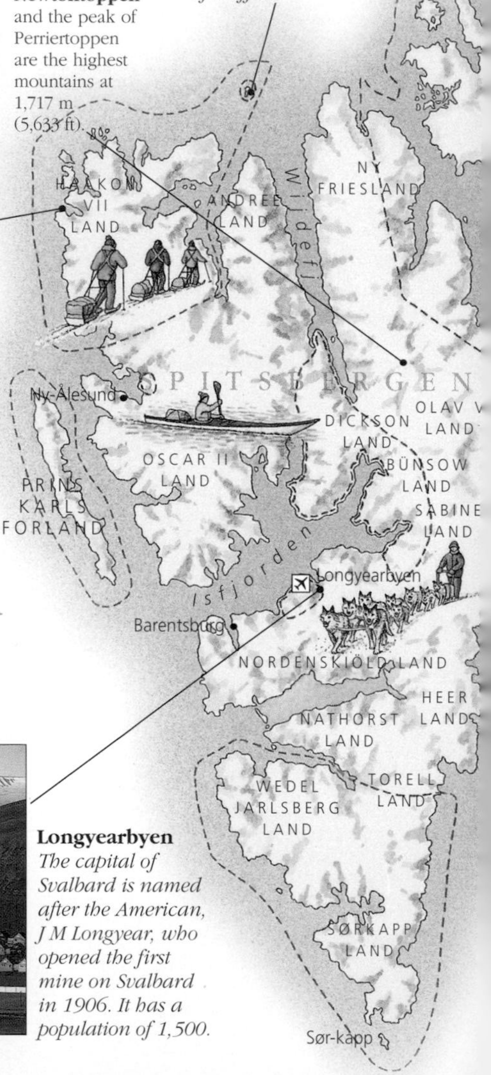

Newtontoppen and the peak of Perriertoppen are the highest mountains at 1,717 m (5,633 ft).

Magdalenefjorden
The scenery around the little fjord of Magdalene on the northwestern coast of Vest-Spitsbergen is awesome. About 60 per cent of Svalbard is covered by glaciers.

HAAKON VII LAND
ANDREE LAND
NY FRIESLAND
Wijdefjorden
SPITSBERGEN
Ny-Ålesund
OLAV V LAND
DICKSON LAND
OSCAR II LAND
BÜNSOW LAND
PRINS KARLS FORLAND
SABINE LAND
Isfjorden
Longyearbyen
Barentsburg
NORDENSKIÖLD LAND
HEER LAND
NATHORST LAND
WEDEL JARLSBERG LAND
TORELL LAND
SØRKAPP LAND
Sør-kapp

KEY

- National park
- Nature reserve
- Plant sanctuary
-  Domestic airport

Longyearbyen
The capital of Svalbard is named after the American, J M Longyear, who opened the first mine on Svalbard in 1906. It has a population of 1,500.

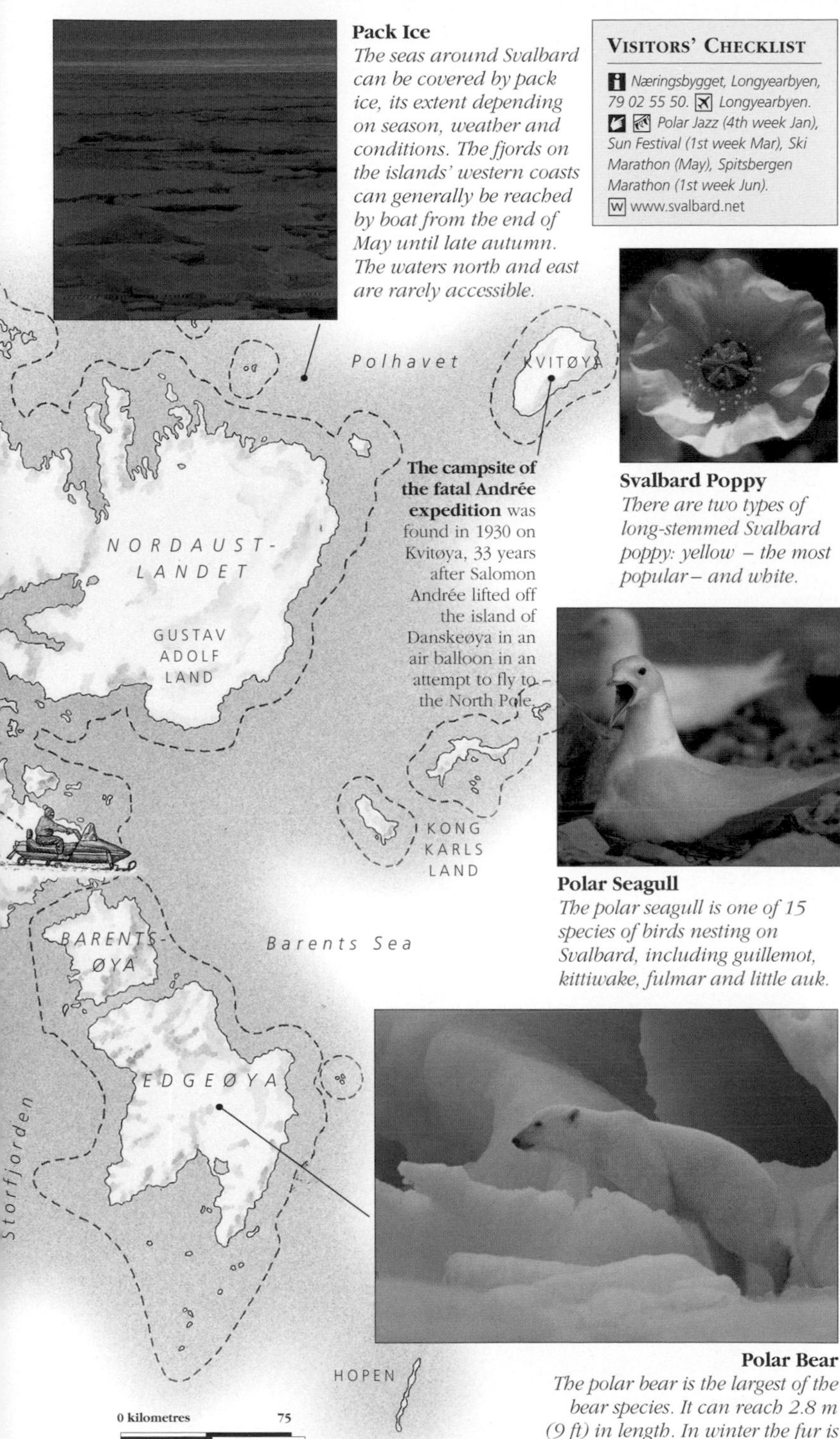

Pack Ice
The seas around Svalbard can be covered by pack ice, its extent depending on season, weather and conditions. The fjords on the islands' western coasts can generally be reached by boat from the end of May until late autumn. The waters north and east are rarely accessible.

The campsite of the fatal Andrée expedition was found in 1930 on Kvitøya, 33 years after Salomon Andrée lifted off the island of Danskeøya in an air balloon in an attempt to fly to the North Pole.

Visitors' Checklist

Næringsbygget, Longyearbyen, 79 02 55 50. Longyearbyen. Polar Jazz (4th week Jan), Sun Festival (1st week Mar), Ski Marathon (May), Spitsbergen Marathon (1st week Jun). www.svalbard.net

Svalbard Poppy
There are two types of long-stemmed Svalbard poppy: yellow – the most popular – and white.

Polar Seagull
The polar seagull is one of 15 species of birds nesting on Svalbard, including guillemot, kittiwake, fulmar and little auk.

Polar Bear
The polar bear is the largest of the bear species. It can reach 2.8 m (9 ft) in length. In winter the fur is snow white, in summer creamier.

Travellers' Needs

Where to Stay 218-227

Where to Eat 228-239

Shopping in Norway 240-245

Entertainment in Norway 246-249

Sports and Outdoor Activities 250-253

Where to Stay

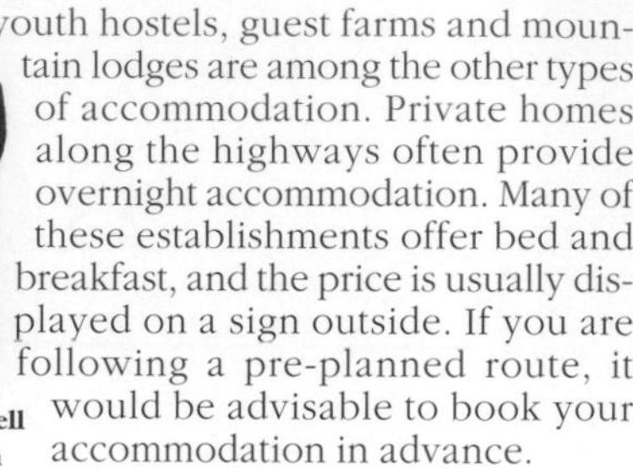

Grand Hotell doorman

Norway has a good selection of hotels covering all corners of the country, with a wide choice in terms of price and quality. Nevertheless, staying in a hotel is not always the best way of getting the most out of your holiday. In Northern Norway, for instance, it has become popular to stay in a *rorbu*, a small cabin once used by fishermen. Mountain huts, youth hostels, guest farms and mountain lodges are among the other types of accommodation. Private homes along the highways often provide overnight accommodation. Many of these establishments offer bed and breakfast, and the price is usually displayed on a sign outside. If you are following a pre-planned route, it would be advisable to book your accommodation in advance.

The distinctive Radisson SAS Plaza hotel in Oslo *(see p221)*

Choosing a Hotel

The choice of places for the visitor to stay in Norway is as diverse as the country's scenery.

There are large, fashionable hotels in the major towns and cities, modest lodges high in the mountains and bed-and-breakfast hotels along the main roads.

In between there is a wide selection of hotels and overnight accommodation in most price categories. The standard of cleanliness is very high in all Norwegian hotels, while room sizes, facilities and service might vary depending on price level.

The large, hotel groups are well represented in the towns and cities. In the outlying districts there are many comfortable *turisthoteller* (tourist hotels) and mountain hotels. The majority of these are situated in spectacular surroundings. In Vestlandet especially, many of the tourist hotels have been run by the same family for generations and maintain a tradition of good service.

Mountain hotels and lodges can be found along many of the passes. They are a good starting point for sporting activities all through the year.

The best option in terms of price is youth hostels.

Booking a Hotel

There is no central booking agency for hotels in Norway. Most of the hotel groups have their own booking centre.

In towns and larger villages the local tourist office can provide help when it comes to booking accommodation for visitors, even if it is outside their district.

Many of the hotels have their own websites and very often it is possible to make bookings on-line.

Rooms can also be booked over the telephone, enabling you to enquire about special rates or negotiate a favourable price reduction.

Elegant suite in the Radisson SAS Royal hotel, Bergen

Hotel Groups

There are a number of large groups with hotels throughout Norway, mainly in the towns and cities. These hotels tend to focus on the business market, but in summer they often offer advantageous rates for tourists.

Best Western is a chain of 27 collaborating private hotels in the mid-price bracket. The hotels are small or medium-sized in a mix of town and country locations.

The Scandinavian group **Choice Hotels** has 70 hotels in Norway. They are divided into three categories: Comfort hotels, catering for business people and providing bed and breakfast; Quality hotels, for tourists and conferences; and Clarion, top-range town and city hotels. The Choice group operates the Nordic Hotel Pass, which gives reduced rates during the summer and at weekends.

The **First Hotels** group comprises business hotels in the upper price range. They are typically medium-sized hotels in towns and cities.

Radisson SAS has 19 hotels in Norway, including the Radisson SAS Plaza in Oslo which, with its 37 floors and 674 rooms, is northern Europe's largest hotel. The group also has a hotel in Svalbard. Radisson SAS has traditionally focused on the business sector, but more recently it has turned its attention to tourism.

Rica Hotels is a Norwegian-Swedish hotel chain with 60 hotels in Norway, ranging from the

◁ **Theatrecafeen in Oslo, an example of the Art Nouveau (Jugend) style of decoration**

Kviknes Hotell *(see p225)* on the shore of Sognefjorden

Rica Dyreparken family hotel in Kristiansand to the Grand Hotell in Oslo. Rica operates a summer holiday pass, which gives discounts on rooms and attractions.

Rainbow Hotels is a Norwegian chain comprising 45 hotels in the medium price range.

Scandic is the leading hotel group in the Nordic region and has 18 hotels in Norway. It is part of Hilton Hotels. The group aims to be environmentally friendly: 97 per cent of the contents of all newly built hotels are of recycled materials.

Prices and Payment

Hotels in Norway vary greatly in price. Those in the cities and towns are generally more expensive than those in the country.

The majority of hotels offer special rates in summer and at weekends. Many hotels operate discount schemes and hotel passes. One two-night stay is all it takes to justify the cost of a hotel pass.

All the usual credit cards are accepted. Larger hotels will also change money, but it is usually cheaper to do this at a bank *(see p260)*.

Youth and Family Hostels

There are 70–75 youth and family hostels in Norway. They are part of **Norske Vandrerhjem** (the Norwegian Hostelling Association).

Hostels are located all over Norway. They are designed to accommodate individuals as well as families. The largest hostel is Haraldsheim in Oslo. Your budget will determine whether you share a dormitory with five or six other people or whether you go for a private room with your family.

Most hostels are of a good standard with favourable prices, and many are situated in attractive areas.

The association does not have a central booking office. Instead you are advised to visit its website to make a reservation. The website also gives details of where the various hostels are located.

DNT's hut on Kobberhaugen in the Oslomarka forest

DNT Huts

Den Norske Turistforening (the Norwegian Mountain Touring Association, or **DNT**) has a network of mountain huts *(hytte)*, in beautiful hiking areas *(see p250)*.

Many huts are staffed and meals can be provided. They are reasonably comfortable with shower and toilet facilities. DNT also has self-service huts with necessities such as sheet sleeping bags and food supplies. Payment is based on the honour principle – you leave your money in the box provided. There are also some unstaffed huts which do not provide any provisions.

Reservations can only be made for the staffed huts, and only for three or more nights, by telephoning the lodge directly. In other cases guests just turn up and are always given a place to sleep.

Directory

Hotel Groups

Best Western
Tel *80 01 16 24 (free).*
FAX *22 55 61 23.*
W www.bestwestern.no

Choice Hotels Scandinavia
Tel *22 33 42 00.*
FAX *22 40 13 10.*
W www.choice.no

First Hotels
Tel *80 01 04 10 (free).*
FAX *+46 84 58 95 20 (Sweden).*
W www.firsthotels.se

Hilton Scandic Hotels
Tel *23 15 50 00.*
FAX *23 15 50 01.*
W www.scandic-hotels.com

Radisson SAS
Tel *00 800 33 33 33 33 (free).*
FAX *+353 1706 0225 (Dublin).*
W www.radissonsas.com

Rainbow Hotels
Tel *23 08 02 00.*
FAX *23 08 02 90.*
W www.rainbow-hotels.no

Rica Hotels
Tel *66 85 45 60.*
FAX *66 85 45 61.*
W www.rica.no

Youth Hostels

Norske Vandrerhjem
Torggata 1, 0181 Oslo.
Map 3 D3. Tel *23 13 93 00.*
W www.vandrerhjem.no

Huts

Den Norske Turistforening (DNT)
Storgata 3, Oslo.
Map 2 E3. Tel *22 82 28 00.*
W www.turistforeningen.no

Choosing a Hotel

The hotels in this guide have been selected across a wide range of price categories for their facilities, location or character. The chart below lists hotels in Oslo by area, followed by a selection of places to stay in the rest of Norway. The prices are in Norwegian kroner. The *Street Finder* for Oslo is on *pp98–101*. A selection of restaurants can be found on *pp232–9*.

Oslo

Hotel	Credit Cards	Facilities for Children	Parking	Restaurant	Bar
Central Oslo West: *Rainbow Hotell Munch* (Kr) Munchs Gate 5, 0165 Oslo. **Map** 3 D2. *23 21 96 00.* FAX *23 21 96 01.* @ munch@rainbow-hotels.no This reasonably priced 1960s hotel, renovated in 2001, is in a central, yet quiet location, near a great choice of eateries. **Rooms:** *183*	AE DC MC V	●	■		
Central Oslo West: *Quality Hotel Savoy* (Kr)(Kr) Universitetsgate 11, 0164 Oslo. **Map** 3 D2. *23 35 42 00.* FAX *23 35 42 01.* An intimate, centrally situated hotel. This is a popular place to stay. It has a welcoming restaurant. **Rooms:** *80*	AE DC MC V	●	■		■
Central Oslo West: *Rainbow Cecil Hotel* (Kr)(Kr) Stortingsgata 8, 0161 Oslo. **Map** 3 D3. *23 31 48 00.* FAX *23 31 48 50.* @ cecil@rainbow-hotels.no A fashionable yet traditional, centrally situated hotel, surrounded by a good range of restaurants and entertainment. **Rooms:** *111*	AE DC MC V	●	■		
Central Oslo West: *Rainbow Hotel Europa* (Kr)(Kr) St Olavs Gate 31, 0166 Oslo. **Map** 3 D2. *23 25 63 00.* FAX *23 25 63 63.* @ europa@rainbow-hotels.no Situated within easy reach of the city centre and its attractions. The ambience is informal. **Rooms:** *167*	AE DC MC V	●	■	●	■
Central Oslo West: *Rainbow Hotel Stefan* (Kr)(Kr) Rosenkrantz' Gate 1, 0159 Oslo. **Map** 3 D3. *23 31 55 00.* FAX *23 31 55 55.* @ stefan@rainbow-hotels.no A newly renovated hotel, well-known for its scrumptious lunch-time buffet which attracts non-residents as well as residents. **Rooms:** *139*	AE DC MC V	●	■	●	■
Central Oslo West: *Hotel Bristol* (Kr)(Kr)(Kr) Kristian IV's Gate 7, 0164 Oslo. **Map** 3 D2. *22 82 60 00.* FAX *22 82 60 01.* @ booking@bristol.no Since 1920 the Bristol has been one of Oslo's top hotels. Modernized in 1999, it has retained its traditional elegance. Bibliotekbaren and the Bristol Grill are popular places to meet for a drink or a meal. **Rooms:** *252*	AE DC MC V	●	■	●	■
Central Oslo West: *Norlandia Karl Johan Hotell* (Kr)(Kr)(Kr) Karl Johans Gate 33, 0162 Oslo. **Map** 3 D2. *23 16 17 00.* FAX *22 42 05 19.* @ service@karljohan.norlandia.no Centrally located hotel with a modern Norwegian atmosphere. Housed in a 19th-century building. **Rooms:** *111*	AE DC MC V	●	■	●	■
Central Oslo West: *Scandic Hotel KNA* (Kr)(Kr)(Kr) Parkveien 68, 0254 Oslo. **Map** 2 B3. *23 15 57 00.* FAX *23 15 57 11.* @ kna@scandic-hotels.com This modernized, tastefully furnished hotel is set in quiet surroundings near Aker Brygge and the harbour, overlooking the fjord. **Rooms:** *189*	AE DC MC V	●	■	●	■
Central Oslo West: *Scandic Hotel St Olav* (Kr)(Kr)(Kr) St Olavs Plass 1, 0165 Oslo. **Map** 3 D2. *23 15 56 00.* FAX *23 15 56 11.* @ stolav@scandic-hotels.com Newly-built hotel on the site of a former theatre. Rooms are named after actors. There are special theatre packages for guests. **Rooms:** *241*	AE DC MC V	●	■	●	■
Central Oslo West: *Hotel Continental* (Kr)(Kr)(Kr)(Kr) Stortingsgate 24–26, 0161 Oslo. **Map** 3 D3. *22 82 40 00.* FAX *22 42 96 89.* @ booking@hotel-continental.no This privately owned, family-run hotel was opened in 1900. It is a member of *The Leading Hotels of the World* and has two award-winning restaurants, Theatercafeen and Annen Etage. **Rooms:** *154*	AE DC MC V	●	■	●	■

Price categories for a standard double room (not per person) per night, including tax, service and breakfast.
- Youth/family hostel
- (Kr) under 1,000 Nkr
- (Kr)(Kr) 1,000–1,400 Nkr
- (Kr)(Kr)(Kr) 1,400–1,800 Nkr
- (Kr)(Kr)(Kr)(Kr) over 1,800 Nkr

Facilities for Children
Cots and high chairs are available. Some hotels also offer a babysitting service.

Parking
The hotel has parking facilities, or there is parking in a nearby multi-storey car park.

Restaurant
The hotel has a restaurant for guests. It is also open to the public – but normally only in the evening.

Bar
The hotel has a bar that is open to guests and the public.

Hotel	Credit Cards	Facilities for Children	Parking	Restaurant	Bar
Central Oslo West: *Radisson SAS Scandinavia Hotel* (Kr)(Kr)(Kr)(Kr) Holbergs Gate 30, 0166 Oslo. **Map** 3 D2. *23 29 30 00.* FAX *23 29 30 01.* www.radisson.com/oslono_scandinavia This soaring hotel built in 1975 is one of the city's best-known establishments. It offers a good and varied selection of rooms and services, including a number of shops. ***Rooms:*** *488*	AE DC MC V	●	■	●	■
Central Oslo East: *City Hotel* (Kr) Skippergaten 19, 0106 Oslo. **Map** 3 E4. *22 41 36 10.* FAX *22 42 24 29.* www.cityhotel.no A simple hotel occupying the upper floors of a city centre building. Intimate and tranquil atmosphere. ***Rooms:*** *52*	AE DC MC V	●			
Central Oslo East: *Best Western Bondeheimen Hotel* (Kr)(Kr) Rosenkrantz' Gate 8, 0159 Oslo. **Map** 3 D3. *23 21 41 00.* FAX *23 21 41 01.* booking@bondeheimen.com A traditional hotel originally built for use by visitors from the countryside. Since modernized, it has retained its simple Norwegian style. The restaurant, Kaffistova, offers Norwegian specialities. ***Rooms:*** *127*	AE DC MC V		■	●	
Central Oslo East: *Comfort Hotel Børsparken* (Kr)(Kr) Tollbugate 4, 0152 Oslo. **Map** 3 E4. *22 47 17 17.* FAX *22 47 17 18.* booking.boersparken@comfort.choicehotels.no Modern hotel opposite the Børs (Oslo Stock Exchange). The emphasis is on providing a homely atmosphere. There is no restaurant, but an evening buffet is available for guests. ***Rooms:*** *198*	AE DC MC V	●	■		■
Central Oslo East: *First Hotel Noble House* (Kr)(Kr) Kongens Gate 5, 0153 Oslo. **Map** 3 D4. *23 10 72 00.* FAX *23 10 72 10.* Modern, new hotel in the oldest area of Oslo near Bankplassen and Akershus Fortress. ***Rooms:*** *69*	AE DC MC V	●	■	●	■
Central Oslo East: *Rainbow Hotel Norrøna* (Kr)(Kr) Grensen 19, 0159 Oslo. **Map** 3 E4. *23 31 80 00.* FAX *23 31 80 01.* hotelln@online.no A quiet, family-friendly hotel. Although part of the Rainbow hotel group, this hotel is run by a Christian organization and no alcohol is served. ***Rooms:*** *93*	AE DC MC V	●	■	●	
Central Oslo East: *Rica Oslo Hotel* (Kr)(Kr) Europarådets Glass 1, 0105 Oslo. **Map** 3 E3. *23 10 42 00.* FAX *23 10 42 10.* www.rica.no Modern hotel near the train station and Jernbanetorget. Norwegian art features strongly with paintings in all the bedrooms. ***Rooms:*** *174*	AE DC MC V	●	■	●	■
Central Oslo East: *Radisson SAS Plaza Hotel Oslo* (Kr)(Kr)(Kr) Sonja Henies Plass 3, 0185 Oslo. **Map** 3 F3. *22 05 80 00.* FAX *22 05 80 10.* www.radissonsas.com This first-class hotel is a prominent sight on the Oslo skyline. The rooms are decorated in different styles, ranging from Oriental to Scandinavian. ***Rooms:*** *674*	AE DC MC V	●	■	●	■
Central Oslo East: *Clarion Hotel Royal Christiania* (Kr)(Kr)(Kr)(Kr) Biskop Gunnerus' Gate 3, 0155 Oslo. **Map** 3 E3. *23 10 80 00.* FAX *23 10 80 69.* christiania@clarion.choicehotels.no A first-class hotel, centrally situated near Jernbanetorvet. The rooms have been decorated with feng shui rules in mind. ***Rooms:*** *503*	AE DC MC V	●	■	●	■
Central Oslo East: *Grand Hotel* (Kr)(Kr)(Kr)(Kr) Karl Johans Gate 31, 0159 Oslo. **Map** 3 D3. *23 21 20 00.* FAX *23 21 21 00.* reservations-grand@rica.no www.grand.no An excellent and fashionable hotel with a good choice of bars and restaurants, and entertainment. It is a favourite with celebrities. ***Rooms:*** *289*	AE DC MC V	●		●	

For key to symbols, see back flap

Price categories for a standard double room (not per person) per night, including tax, service and breakfast.
- Youth/family hostel
- Ⓚ under 1,000 Nkr
- ⓀⓀ 1,000–1,400 Nkr
- ⓀⓀⓀ 1,400–1,800 Nkr
- ⓀⓀⓀⓀ over 1,800 Nkr

Facilities for Children
Cots and high chairs are available. Some hotels also offer a babysitting service.

Parking
The hotel has parking facilities, or there is parking in a nearby multi-storey car park.

Restaurant
The hotel has a restaurant for guests. It is also open to the public – but normally only in the evening.

Bar
The hotel has a bar that is open to guests and the public.

Hotel	Credit Cards	Facilities for Children	Parking	Restaurant	Bar
Further Afield: *Oslo Vandrerhjem Haraldsheim* Haraldsheimveien 4, 0587 Oslo. *22 22 29 65.* FAX *22 22 10 25.* www.haraldsheim.oslo.no Youth/family hostel in a lovely area 4 km (2 miles) from the centre. Views over the city and the fjord. Most rooms have four beds. ***Rooms:** 71*	MC V	●	■		
Further Afield: *Anker Hotel* Ⓚ Storgata 55, 0182 Oslo. **Map** 3 F2. *22 99 75 00.* FAX *22 99 75 20.* www.anker.oslo.no This hotel is situated just outside the inner city, a 10-minute walk to Karl Johans Gate and close to fashionable Grünerløkka. In summer the capacity is increased with the use of the Albert Sommerhotel. TV ***Rooms:** 48*	AE DC MC V		■		■
Further Afield: *Gardermoen Gjestegård* Ⓚ Gardemoveien 2, 060 Gardermoen. *63 94 08 00.* FAX *63 94 08 01.* www.gg-gardermoen.no A timber inn with homely atmosphere in rural surroundings, just a 4-minute drive from Gardermoen airport. TV ***Rooms:** 48*	AE DC MC V		■	●	■
Further Afield: *Best Western Hotel Ambassadeur* ⓀⓀ Camilla Colletts Vei 15, 0258 Oslo. **Map** 2 B2. *23 27 23 00.* FAX *22 44 47 91.* post@hotelambassadeur.no A short walk from the city centre in the exclusive area west of the Royal Palace, this hotel occupies an apartment block dating from the late-19th century. The interior is decorated with art and antiques. TV ***Rooms:** 41*	AE DC MC V				
Further Afield: *Linne Hotel* ⓀⓀ Statsråd Mathiesens Vei 12, 0598 Oslo. *23 17 00 00.* FAX *23 17 00 01.* www.linne.no A homely hotel in rural surroundings in Oslo's eastern suburbs. The city centre is 10 minutes away on the T-bane (metro). TV ***Rooms:** 106*	AE DC MC V	●	■	●	■
Further Afield: *Radisson SAS Park Hotel* ⓀⓀ Fornebuveien 80, 1366 Lysaker. *67 82 30 00.* FAX *67 82 30 01.* www.radissonsas.com The hotel is located on the shores of Oslofjorden, just 100 m (109 yd) from the beach and with its own tennis court. It is 10 minutes by car from the city centre. TV ***Rooms:** 252*	AE DC MC V	●	■	●	■
Further Afield: *Rainbow Gyldenløve Hotel* ⓀⓀ Bogstadveien 20, 0355 Oslo. **Map** 2 B1. *23 33 23 00.* FAX *22 60 33 90.* gyldenloeve@rainbow-hotels.no Situated on one of Oslo's best shopping streets west of the centre. A peaceful place outside shopping hours. TV ***Rooms:** 168*	AE DC MC V	●	■	●	■
Further Afield: *Frogner House Hotel* ⓀⓀⓀ Skovveien 8, 0257 Oslo. **Map** 2 B2. *22 56 00 56.* FAX *22 56 05 00.* www.frognerhouse.com Centrally situated in Frogner. The Victorian style of this exclusive period building has been retained. TV ***Rooms:** 60*	AE DC MC V	●	■		■
Further Afield: *Gabelshus Hotell* ⓀⓀⓀ Gabels Gate 16, 0272 Oslo. **Map** 2 A3. *23 27 65 00.* FAX *23 27 65 60.* www.gabelshus.no Discretely situated in a quiet street on the west side of the city. Period English decor lends an elegant and intimate atmosphere. TV ***Rooms:** 105*	AE DC MC V	●	■		
Further Afield: *Holmenkollen Park Hotel Rica* ⓀⓀⓀ Kongeveien 26, 0787 Oslo. *22 92 20 00.* FAX *22 14 61 92.* www.holmenkollenparkhotel.no A well-appointed hotel with a fairytale castle style wing in tranquil surroundings close to the winter sports arena. TV ***Rooms:** 220*	AE DC MC V		■	●	■
Further Afield: *Radisson SAS Airport Hotel, Gardermoen* ⓀⓀⓀ Hotelveien, 2060 Gardermoen. *63 93 30 00.* FAX *63 93 30 30.* www.radissonsas.com This classy new hotel is just a few minutes' walk from the airport terminal at Gardermoen. TV ***Rooms:** 350*	AE DC MC V	●	■	●	■

AROUND OSLOFJORDEN

Hotel	Price	Cards				
HALDEN: *Grand Hotell* Jernbanetorget 1, 1767 Halden. *69 18 72 00.* FAX *69 18 79 59.* A simple bed and breakfast hotel close to Halden town centre. TV ***Rooms:** 31*	Kr	AE DC MC V				■
HORTEN: *Norlandia Grand Ocean Hotell* Jernbanegate 1, 3187 Horten. *33 04 17 22.* FAX *33 04 45 07.* This modern hotel has the sea as its closest neighbour. It is just a stone's throw from the town centre. TV ***Rooms:** 100*	Kr Kr	AE MC V	●	■	●	■
FREDRIKSTAD: *Victoria Hotel* Turngate 3, 1606 Fredrikstad. *69 38 58 00.* FAX *69 38 58 01.* W www.victoria-fredrikstad.com Intimate hotel, centrally located close to Domkirken (the cathedral). TV ***Rooms:** 65*	Kr Kr	AE DC MC V		■	●	■
LARVIK: *Quality Hotel Grand Farris* Storgata 38, 3256 Larvik. *33 18 78 00.* FAX *33 18 70 45.* W www.grand-hotel-farris.no A cosy hotel offering a variety of rooms, including an exclusive suite named after Larvik's great explorer, Thor Heyerdahl. Lovely location with views over Larvik harbour. TV ***Rooms:** 88*	Kr Kr	AE DC MC V	●	■	●	■
MOSS: *Hotel Refsnes Gods* Godset 5, 1518 Moss. *69 27 83 00.* FAX *69 27 83 01.* W www.refsnesgods.no A former country mansion beautifully situated on the island of Jeløy. Good restaurant and well-stocked wine cellar. TV ***Rooms:** 61*	Kr Kr Kr	AE DC MC V		■	●	
SANDEFJORD: *Rica Park Hotel Sandefjord* Strandpromenaden 9, 3212 Sandefjord. *33 44 74 00.* FAX *33 44 75 00.* W www.rica.no The hotel, built in 1960, is one of the town's landmarks. Comfortable and well appointed, it is close to the centre. TV ***Rooms:** 231*	Kr Kr Kr	AE DC MC V			●	■
STAVERN: *Hotel Wassilioff* Havnegate 1, 3290 Stavern. *33 11 36 00.* FAX *33 11 36 01.* W www.wassilioff.no Intimate, historic hotel from the 1840s in the heart of idyllic Stavern. TV ***Rooms:** 47*	Kr	AE DC MC V			●	■
TØNSBERG: *Hotell Maritim* Storgata 17, 3126 Tønsberg. *33 31 71 00.* FAX *33 31 72 52.* W www.hotellmaritim.no Quiet, comfortable bed and breakfast hotel in the middle of the town. TV ***Rooms:** 33*	Kr	AE DC MC V	●			
TØNSBERG: *Rica Klubben Hotel* Nedre Langgate 49, 3126 Tønsberg. *33 35 97 00.* FAX *33 35 97 97.* W www.rica.no The hotel is as renowned for its popular summer shows in its own theatre as it is for its restaurant and good-quality rooms. TV ***Rooms:** 145*	Kr Kr	AE DC MC V	●	■	●	■

EASTERN NORWAY

Hotel	Price	Cards				
DRAMMEN: *First Hotel Ambassadeur* Strømsø Torg 7, 3044 Drammen. *31 01 21 00.* FAX *31 01 21 11.* W www.firsthotels.com Totally renovated in 2001 in a modern style, this hotel is close to the town centre. TV ***Rooms:** 230*	Kr Kr	AE DC MC V	●	■	●	■
DRAMMEN: *Rica Park Hotel Drammen* Gamle Kirkeplass 3, 3019 Drammen. *32 26 36 00.* FAX *32 26 37 77.* W www.rica.no Reputable full-service hotel with comfortable, recently renovated rooms. Located next to the old Drammen theatre. TV ***Rooms:** 100*	Kr Kr	AE DC MC V	●	■	●	■
ELVESETER: *Elveseter Turisthotell* 2687 Bøverdalen. *61 21 20 00.* FAX *61 21 21 01.* W www.elveseter.no A rustic farm, its oldest building dating from 1640, is now an atmospheric and comfortable hotel, still run by the original family. ***Rooms:** 130*	Kr Kr	AE DC MC V	●	■	●	■
GEILO: *Dr Holms Hotel* Timrehaugveien 2, 3580 Geilo. *32 09 57 00.* FAX *32 09 16 20.* W www.drholms.com Classic building close to the high mountains with excellent opportunities for skiing in the winter season. TV ***Rooms:** 127*	Kr Kr	AE DC MC V	●	■	●	■
HAMAR: *First Hotel Victoria* Strandgaten 21, 2317 Hamar. *62 02 55 00.* FAX *62 53 32 23.* W www.first-hotel-victoria.no Located in the town centre near the park with views toward Lake Mjøsa, this is a good, traditional hotel with a reputable restaurant. TV ***Rooms:** 115*	Kr Kr	AE DC MC V	●	■	●	■

For key to symbols, see back flap

Price categories for a standard double room (not per person) per night, including tax, service and breakfast.
Youth/family hostel
Kr under 1,000 Nkr
KrKr 1,000–1,400 Nkr
KrKrKr 1,400–1,800 Nkr
KrKrKrKr over 1,800 Nkr

Facilities for Children
Cots and high chairs are available. Some hotels also offer a babysitting service.
Parking
The hotel has parking facilities, or there is parking in a nearby multi-storey car park.
Restaurant
The hotel has a restaurant for guests. It is also open to the public – but normally only in the evening.
Bar
The hotel has a bar that is open to guests and the public.

Hotel	Credit Cards	Facilities for Children	Parking	Restaurant	Bar
Hamar: *Quality Hotel Astoria* KrKr Torggata 23, 2317 Hamar. *62 70 70 00.* FAX *62 70 70 01.* W www.choice.no Modern hotel in the centre of the town near Lake Mjøsa. Newly renovated rooms of a good standard. TV ***Rooms:*** *78*	AE DC MC V	●	■	●	■
Lillehammer: *Birkebeineren Hotel/Motel & Apartments* Kr Birkebeinerveien Olympiaparken 24, 2618 Lillehammer. *61 26 47 00.* FAX *61 26 47 50.* W www.birkebeineren.no Scenically situated in Olympia Park, a 10-minute walk from the town centre. Selection of apartments, hotel rooms and motel rooms. TV ***Rooms:*** *120*	AE DC MC V	●	■		
Lillehammer: *Comfort Hotel Hammer* KrKr Storgata 108B, 2615 Lillehammer. *61 26 35 00.* FAX *61 26 37 30.* W www.choice.no The interior reflects the Gudbrandsdal Valley traditions. A good standard, homely hotel with evening meals included in the price. TV ***Rooms:*** *67*	AE DC MC V	●	■		
Lillehammer: *First Hotel Breiseth* KrKr Jernbaneg 1–5, 2609 Lillehammer. *61 24 77 77.* FAX *61 26 95 05.* W www.breiseth.com This pleasant hotel was fully renovated for the 1994 Winter Olympics and offers a high standard of rooms and a quality restaurant. TV ***Rooms:*** *89*	AE DC MC V	●	■	●	■
Lom: *Fossheim Turisthotell* Kr 2686 Lom. *61 21 95 00.* FAX *61 21 95 01.* W www.fossheimhotel.no The same family has run this hotel for generations. It has been extended to offer apartments and huts in traditional style. Reputable restaurant with award-winning chefs. Closed in winter. ***Rooms:*** *50*	AE DC MC V	●	■	●	■
SØRLANDET AND TELEMARK					
Arendal: *Scandic Hotel Arendal* KrKr Friergangen 1, 4836 Arendal. *37 05 21 50.* FAX *37 05 21 51.* W www.scandic-arendal.no Centrally located on Tyholmen, a short distance from the town centre and harbour. Modern rooms, recently renovated. TV ***Rooms*** *84*	AE DC MC V	●	■	●	■
Arendal: *Clarion Hotel Tyholmen* KrKrKr Teaterplassen 2, 4836 Arendal. *37 02 68 00.* FAX *37 02 68 01.* W www.tyholmenhotel.no Full-service hotel with modern facilities in an idyllic, award-winning timber building on the wharfside in the old town. TV ***Rooms:*** *60*	AE DC MC V	●	■	●	■
Dalen: *Dalen Hotel* KrKr 3880 Dalen. *35 07 70 00.* FAX *35 07 70 11.* W www.dalenhotel.no Restored timber building adorned with dragon heads, turrets and spires. Large garden overlooking the lake and mountains. ***Rooms:*** *38*	AE DC MC V	●	■	●	■
Kristiansand: *Clarion Hotel Ernst* KrKr Rådhusgaten 2, 4611 Kristiansand. *38 12 86 00.* FAX *38 02 03 07.* W www.ernst.no Venerable traditions going back to 1858 have been combined with recent upgrading to create a stylish ambience. TV ***Rooms:*** *135*	AE DC MC V	●	■	●	■
Kristiansand: *Comfort Hotel Skagerak* KrKr Henrik Wergelands Gate 4, 4612 Kristiansand S. *38 07 04 00.* FAX *38 07 02 43.* W www.hotel-skagerak.no Modern hotel with a snug atmosphere, situated in the middle of the Kvadraturen quarter, in the heart of Kristiansand. TV ***Rooms:*** *67*	AE DC MC V	●	■		
Kristiansand: *Radisson SAS Caledonien Hotel* KrKr Vestre Strandgate 7, 4610 Kristiansand S. *38 11 05 25.* FAX *38 11 21 01.* W www.radissonsas.com Good full-service hotel situated near the yacht basin and the beach promenade, yet right in the middle of the pretty Kvadraturen quarter. TV ***Rooms:*** *172*	AE DC MC V	●	■	●	■

KRISTIANSAND: *Scandic Hotel Kristiansand* Kr Kr
Markens Gate 39, 4612 Kristiansand S. Tel. *21 61 42 00.* FAX *21 61 42 11.*
@ christianquart@scandic-hotels.com
In the centre of town with a pedestrianized street to one side. The hotel is of a good standard. ***Rooms:*** *112*
AE DC MC V ● ■ ● ■

PORSGRUNN: *Hotell Vic* Kr Kr
Skolegata 1, 3916 Porsgrunn. Tel. *35 55 55 80.* FAX *35 55 72 12.* W www.vichotel.no
The history of the Vic dates back to 1825. The original building is still in use today together with a modern wing. ***Rooms:*** *96*
AE DC MC V ● ■ ● ■

SKIEN: *Rainbow Høyers Hotell* Kr Kr
Kongens Gate 5, 3717 Skien. Tel. *35 90 58 00.* FAX *35 90 58 05.*
@ hoeyers@rainbow-hotels.no
Behind the classic pink façade of Telemark's oldest hotel lies a modern and comfortable building. Situated in the heart of Skien. ***Rooms:*** *77*
AE DC MC V ● ■ ● ■

VESTLANDET

BALESTRAND: *Kvikne's Hotell* Kr Kr
6899 Balestrand. Tel. *57 69 42 00.* FAX *57 69 42 01.* @ booking@kviknes.no
W www.kviknes.com
Historic hotel in a fantastic position on Balholm on the shore of Sognefjorden. The hotel has been expanded and modernized while retaining its olde-worlde atmosphere. ***Rooms:*** *210*
AE DC MC V ● ■ ● ■

BERGEN: *Rainbow Hotell Bryggen Orion* Kr Kr
Bradbenken 3, 5003 Bergen. Tel. *55 30 87 00.* FAX *55 32 94 14.*
@ bryggenorion@rainbow-hotels.no
Situated between Bryggen wharf and Rosenkrantz' tower, close to the city centre. Renowned for its good breakfast. ***Rooms:*** *229*
AE DC MC V ● ■ – ■

BERGEN: *Augustin Hotel* Kr Kr Kr
Sundts Gate 22/24C, 5004 Bergen. Tel. *55 30 40 00.* FAX *55 30 40 10.* W www.augustin.no
Family-run hotel, centrally situated by the harbour and shopping area. Renovated in 1999/2001, it won an award for its design. ***Rooms:*** *109*
AE DC MC V ● ■ ● ■

BERGEN: *Clarion Hotel Admiral* Kr Kr Kr
C Sundts Gate 9, 5004 Bergen. Tel. *55 23 64 00.* FAX *55 23 64 64.* W www.admiral.no
Converted warehouse on Bryggen facing Vågen harbour. Comfortable full-service hotel; very central. ***Rooms:*** *210*
AE DC MC V ● – ● ■

BERGEN: *Neptun Hotell* Kr Kr Kr
Valkendorfs Gate 8, 5012 Bergen. Tel. *55 30 68 00.* FAX *55 30 68 50.*
W www.neptunhotell.no
The hotel's art collection contains more than 700 works. Well-known gourmet restaurant with a fine wine cellar. ***Rooms:*** *124*
AE DC MC V ● ■ ● ■

BERGEN: *Radisson SAS Hotel Norge* Kr Kr Kr Kr
Nedre Ole Bulls Plass 4, 5012 Bergen. Tel. *55 57 30 00.* FAX *55 57 30 01.*
W www.radissonsas.no
Built on a site where a hotel stood already in 1885, this well-appointed, modern hotel has maintained the traditions and quality for which it was renowned. Set in the heart of Bergen. ***Rooms:*** *345*
AE DC MC V ● ■ ● ■

HAUGESUND: *Rica Maritim Hotel* Kr Kr
Åsbygaten 3, 5528 Haugesund. Tel. *52 86 30 00.* FAX *52 86 30 01.* W www.rica.no
Haugesund's largest hotel is situated on the quayside in the centre of town. Rooms vary in size and standard. ***Rooms:*** *312*
AE DC MC V – ■ ● ■

KRISTIANSUND: *Comfort Hotel Fosna* Kr Kr
Hauggata 16, 6509 Kristiansund N. Tel. *71 67 40 11.* FAX *71 67 76 59.* W www.choicehotels.no
A simple homely hotel of a good standard. Views over the harbour and the square. Evening buffet is included in the price. ***Rooms:*** *50*
AE DC MC V ● ■ – ■

MOLDE: *Quality Hotel Alexandra* Kr Kr
Storgata 1–7, 6413 Molde. Tel. *71 20 37 50.* FAX *71 20 37 87.* W www.choicehotels.no
Well-appointed hotel with modern rooms, a restaurant and night-club. Situated in the centre of town. ***Rooms:*** *163*
AE DC MC V ● ■ ● ■

STAVANGER: *Comfort Hotel Grand* Kr Kr
Klubbgate 3, 4013 Stavanger. Tel. *51 20 14 00.* FAX *51 20 14 01.* W www.choicehotels.no
Simple, informal and pleasant hotel in the town centre with rooms of varying sizes. Evening meal is included in the price. ***Rooms:*** *90*
AE DC MC V ● – – ■

For key to symbols, see back flap

Price categories for a standard double room (not per person) per night, including tax, service and breakfast. Youth/family hostel (Kr) under 1,000 Nkr (Kr)(Kr) 1,000–1,400 Nkr (Kr)(Kr)(Kr) 1,400–1,800 Nkr (Kr)(Kr)(Kr)(Kr) over 1,800 Nkr	**Facilities for Children** Cots and high chairs are available. Some hotels also offer a babysitting service. **Parking** The hotel has parking facilities, or there is parking in a nearby multi-storey car park. **Restaurant** The hotel has a restaurant for guests. It is also open to the public – but normally only in the evening. **Bar** The hotel has a bar that is open to guests and the public.	Credit Cards	Facilities for Children	Parking	Restaurant	Bar
Stavanger: *Skagen Brygge Hotell* (Kr)(Kr) Skagenkaien 30, 4006 Stavanger. *51 85 00 00.* FAX *51 85 00 01.* booking@skagenbryggehotell.no Centrally located hotel with cosy rooms. The Vågen harbour façade is in keeping with the old dockside buildings. **Rooms:** *110*		AE DC MC V	●	■		■
Stavanger: *Radisson SAS Atlantic Hotel* (Kr)(Kr)(Kr) Olav V's Gate 3, 4005 Stavanger. *51 76 10 00.* FAX *51 76 10 01.* www.radissonsas.com Large town-centre hotel overlooking Breiavannet lake. Well-appointed with newly renovated rooms. **Rooms:** *350*		AE DC MC V	●	■	●	■
Ålesund: *Comfort Hotel Bryggen* (Kr)(Kr) Apotekergate 1, 6004 Ålesund. *70 12 64 00.* FAX *70 12 11 80.* bryggen@comfort.choicehotels.no Distinctive town centre hotel in a converted warehouse on the water's edge. Evening meal is included in the price. **Rooms:** *85*		AE DC MC V	●	■		■
Ålesund: *Scandic Hotel Ålesund* (Kr)(Kr) Moloveien 6, 6004 Ålesund. *21 61 45 00.* FAX *21 61 45 11.* alesund@scandic-hotels.com Close to the town centre with the sea as its nearest neighbour. Decorated in maritime style. **Rooms:** *118*		AE DC MC V	●	■	●	■
TRØNDELAG						
Røros: *Bergstadens Hotel* (Kr)(Kr) Osloveien 2, 7374 Røros. *72 40 60 80.* FAX *72 40 60 81.* www.bergstaden.no A welcoming hotel in the centre of this old mining town. It has comfortable rooms, two restaurants and four bars. **Rooms:** *88*		AE DC MC V	●	■	●	■
Røros: *Quality Hotel Røros* (Kr)(Kr) An-Magrittveien, 7374 Røros. *72 40 80 00.* FAX *72 40 80 01.* www.roroshotel.no A quiet, friendly hotel in countryside surroundings on the outskirts of the town. Decorated in romantic peasant style using natural materials. The Bergrosa Restaurant offers good food. **Rooms:** *88*		AE DC MC V	●	■	●	■
Steinkjer: *Rainbow Tingvold Park Hotel* (Kr)(Kr) Gamle Kongeveien 47, 7725 Steinkjer. *74 16 11 00.* FAX *74 16 11 17.* www.rainbow-hotels.no/tingvold A mansion has been extended to create a hotel with a mixture of old and new styles and rooms of differing standards. **Rooms:** *51*		AE DC MC V	●	■	●	■
Trondheim: *Munken Hotell* (Kr) Kongens Gate 44, 7012 Trondheim. *73 53 45 40.* FAX *73 53 42 60.* munken.hotell@munken.no Homely, reasonably priced hotel, a few minutes' walk from the centre. The rooms are of a good standard, and some are equipped with a mini-kitchen. **Rooms:** *113*		AE DC MC V	●		●	■
Trondheim: *Quality Hotel Augustin* (Kr)(Kr) Kongens Gate 26, 7011 Trondheim. *73 54 70 00.* FAX *73 54 70 01.* hotel-augustin@hotel-augustin.no A good hotel situated on Trondheim's central square, close to the city's sights and attractions. Evening meal is included in the price. **Rooms:** *113*		AE DC MC V	●			■
Trondheim: *Rainbow Trondheim Hotell* (Kr)(Kr) Kongens Gate 15, 7013 Trondheim. *73 50 50 50.* FAX *73 51 60 58.* www.rainbow-hotels.no/trondheim A pleasant hotel offering a simple bed & breakfast, situated on Trondheim's main square, alongside a large shopping centre. **Rooms:** *131*		AE DC MC V	●	■		■

TRONDHEIM: *Scandic Hotel Residence* (Kr)(Kr)
Munkegata 26, Torvet, 7011 Trondheim. *73 52 83 80.* FAX *73 52 64 60.*
residence@scandic-hotels.com
Good standard business hotel centrally situated on the town square.
Rooms: *66*
AE DC MC V

TRONDHEIM: *Britannia Hotel* (Kr)(Kr)(Kr)
Dronningens Gate 5, 7011 Trondheim. *73 80 08 00.* FAX *73 80 08 01.*
firmapost@britannia.no
Behind the Baroque façade is an elegant hotel offering quality and comfort. Several restaurants, including the Palm Garden. ***Rooms:*** *113*
AE DC MC V

TRONDHEIM: *Radisson SAS Royal Garden Hotel Trondheim* (Kr)(Kr)(Kr)
Kjøpmannsg. 73, 7010 Trondheim. *73 80 30 00.* FAX *73 80 30 50.*
www.radissonsas.com
A well-appointed hotel of high standard. Large exotic gardens in glassed-in courtyards between the wings. Excellent selection of restaurants. ***Rooms:*** *298*
AE DC MC V

NORTHERN NORWAY

BODØ: *Comfort Hotel Grand* (Kr)(Kr)(Kr)
Storgaten 3, 8006 Bodø. *75 54 61 00.* FAX *75 54 61 50.*
booking.grand@comfort.choicehotels.no
Good, welcoming hotel. There has been a hotel on this site for almost two centuries. The current building was renovated in 1998. ***Rooms:*** *97*
AE DC MC V

BODØ: *Radisson SAS Hotel Bodø* (Kr)(Kr)(Kr)
Storgaten 2, 8039 Bodø. *75 51 90 00.* FAX *75 51 90 01.* www.radissonsas.com
Situated in the heart of the town, this is a well-appointed first-class hotel with several popular restaurants. ***Rooms:*** *190*
AE DC MC V

HAMMERFEST: *Quality Hotel Hammerfest* (Kr)(Kr)
Strandgata 2/4, 9600 Hammerfest. *78 42 96 00.* FAX *78 42 96 60.*
www.hammerfesthotel.no
A good, modern hotel next to the harbour and the town square. Many of the rooms are extra large with sea views. ***Rooms:*** *50*
AE DC MC V

HAMMERFEST: *Rica Hotel Hammerfest* (Kr)(Kr)
Sørøygata 15, 9600 Hammerfest. *78 41 13 33.* FAX *78 41 13 11.*
rica.hotel.hammerfest@rica.no www.rica.no
Well-appointed and cosy hotel, situated in the centre of town with sea views.
Rooms: *84*
AE DC MC V

HARSTAD: *Quality Hotel Arcticus* (Kr)(Kr)
Havnegata 3, 9480 Harstad. *77 04 08 00.* FAX *77 04 08 01.*
arcticus@quality.choicehotels.no
Situated next to the quay and the harbour promenade with fjord views. The town's cultural arts centre is in the same building. ***Rooms:*** *75*
AE DC MC V

NARVIK: *Nordstjernen Hotell* (Kr)
Kongens Gate 26, 8514 Narvik. *76 94 41 20.* FAX *76 94 75 06.* nhnarvik@online.no
A simple, homely hotel on the main street. ***Rooms:*** *25*
DC V

NARVIK: *Grand Royal Hotel* (Kr)(Kr)
Kongens Gate 64, 8514 Narvik. *76 97 70 00.* FAX *76 97 70 07.*
grand@grandroyalhotelnarvik.no
Largest hotel in Narvik. Wide selection of facilities. ***Rooms:*** *107*
AE DC MC V

TROMSØ: *Rainbow Polar Hotell* (Kr)
Grønnegata 45, 9008 Tromsø. *77 75 17 00.* FAX *77 75 17 10.* polar@rainbow-hotels.no
Comfortable hotel in the heart of the town. It includes the less expensive Polar Økonomihotell across the road. ***Rooms:*** *113*
AE DC MC V

TROMSØ: *Radisson SAS Hotel Tromsø* (Kr)(Kr)
Sjøgatan 7, 9008 Tromsø. *77 60 00 00.* FAX *77 65 62 21.* www.radissonssas.com
A well-appointed first-class hotel in the centre of the town with rooms of varying sizes. Its Rorbua pub is well-known for its special atmosphere.
Rooms: *195*
AE DC MC V

TROMSØ: *Rica Ishavshotel* (Kr)(Kr)
Fr Langes Gate 2, 9008 Tromsø. *77 66 64 00.* FAX *77 66 64 44.* www.rica.no
Located in the heart of Tromsø overlooking Tromsøsundet and the Arctic Cathedral. Well equipped, with high standard. ***Rooms:*** *180*
AE DC MC V

For key to symbols, see back flap

Where to Eat

New eating places have sprung up in Norway over the last 15 years; 5,000 of them are in Oslo alone. There is something on offer for even the most discerning of palates, including exotic international cuisines. Norwegian specialities such as lamb and cabbage stew, marinated salmon *(gravlaks)*, dumplings *(kumle)* or reindeer medallions are not to be missed. The best selection is to be found in the towns. Look out for seafood dishes. There are daily deliveries of fresh fish from both the Barents Sea and the North Sea. From February to April, spawning cod from the Lofoten islands, *lofotskrei*, is highly recommended. Before Christmas, *lutefisk*, cod marinated in a lye solution, is a speciality. Ethnic cafés and restaurants offer dishes from around the world and the food in less pretentious places is often good and not expensive. The price of alcohol, even beer, is high.

***Smørbrød*, an open sandwich**

Eating Out

The towns offer the greatest choice of places to eat. In Oslo, in particular, an entire spectrum of food is on offer, from truly Norwegian to the more exotic, with a wide variation in standards and prices. There are internationally renowned restaurants presided over by gold medal-winning chefs. Here, the menus will normally feature international cuisine, but will also offer Norwegian specialities with an emphasis on seafood. The best restaurants also have a good selection of game dishes, including reindeer, elk and wild fowl from the Norwegian forests and mountains.

In the mountain and tourist hotels it is standard practice to have dinner in the hotel restaurant, as this is often the only place to eat in the vicinity. The food is normally of a high standard. The same is true of the mountain huts.

Most towns have a selection of ethnic restaurants. Oslo has an especially wide choice of cuisines and the quality is generally of a consistently good standard.

In many of the towns and built-up areas you will also find traditional pubs and bars serving mainly beverages.

Restaurant sign, Bergen

A Great Buffet Lunch

The Norwegian buffet lunch constitutes a varied and very substantial meal. The idea is to help yourself from a buffet table groaning with meat and fish dishes. There is often a separate selection of hot dishes. Norway is the world's largest producer of salmon, and salmon dishes are often well represented. In mountain hotels and tourist lodges the lunch table is one of the highlights of the stay, offering an extravagant choice of delicacies. It is advisable to follow certain unwritten rules about the order in which to eat the food: start with fish and salads, go on to meat and hot dishes and finish with cheese and/or dessert. Feel free to ask the waiters for advice. Drinks are ordered separately at the table.

Local Eating Habits

Norwegian eating habits differ somewhat from those on the Continent, particularly with regard to lunch and dinner. Traditionally, Norwegians only very rarely eat a hot lunch at home. However, in the workplace, canteens are becoming increasingly popular and they serve hot food. If there is no canteen, people often take a packed lunch of wholemeal bread open sandwiches to work. Cafés and restaurants serve hot food at lunchtime.

Lunch is normally served between 11am and 2pm, while dinner is usually eaten around 5pm in the home. When eating out, dinner is usually delayed until 7–8pm. In the evening restaurants open around 5–6pm. It is

Theatercaféen, Oslo, traditionally an artists' haunt ***(see p233)***

The fish market in Bergen, a popular place to buy snacks

rarely necessary to reserve a table for lunch, but a reservation is recommended for dinner, particularly on Wednesday, Friday and Saturday in popular places.

Fast Food

The most common fast food is a hot dog *(pølse)* with a roll or a potato pancake *(lompe)*. This traditional dish is often served from kiosks, food wagons or serving hatches. It is topped with raw onion and various dressings. Some markets, such as the one in Bergen, have stalls selling ready to eat delicacies. Most urban areas have the usual selection of hamburger chains and kebab cafés.

Along the main roads in the more populated areas there are a large number of cafeteria-style places. The food is usually fairly simple and ready-to-eat, and is served so quickly that it almost counts as fast food.

Paying and Tipping

Many eating places offer lunch at reasonable, set prices. In the towns it is possible to have a good meal for around 60–70 Nkr. Drinks add considerably to the price; even mineral water can cost as much as 20–30 Nkr. In a good restaurant, a three-course dinner with wine could cost 600–700 Nkr per person. A number of restaurants have regular, special offers, even for dinner. These are usually advertised on boards or posters outside. In such cases, a good main course can be had for less than 100 Nkr. Most restaurants have menus displayed outside, but this is not mandatory.

Service charge is always included in the bill, but tipping the waiter is still the norm, especially if the service has been good – around 10 per cent is a guideline. Complain if the food does not live up to expectations. The restaurateurs themselves encourage guests to do so.

Children

Children are normally welcome in all cafés and restaurants. Most places have separate children's menus and special chairs for youngsters. If there is no special menu, one can usually be arranged by talking to the waiter. Children's menus will often consist of meatballs, sausages and chips or spaghetti.

It should be noted that it is not the norm to take children to dinner in restaurants. If you do, they will rarely be refused entry, but children are expected to be kept under control and should not leave the table and run around.

What to Wear

There is no need to pack a lot of smart clothes just to wear in restaurants. Norwegians have a relatively informal dress code, and only a few restaurants require a tie to be worn. The rule is much the same in Norway as in other countries – the more expensive a restaurant the better one should dress.

Alcohol

Norway has a restrictive policy on alcohol and the duty levied is among the highest in Europe.

The minimum age for being served wine and beer is 18, and 21 for spirits. Eating places need a licence to serve alcohol, and some establishments often have a licence for beer and wine but not for spirits. Most big restaurants have full licences, and many of them offer a good selection of wine in all price ranges. In bars, people usually pay for their own drinks; buying a round is not the custom.

All wines and spirits are sold in special state monopoly outlets known as *Vinmonopolet*, which are often closed on and around public holidays and on Sundays, too. The state monopoly shops are only found in the larger towns and urban areas. In some smaller municipalities all serving of alcohol used to be prohibited.

Smoking

Norway has very strict smoking laws, and new restrictions have been added in the last few years. Smoking is not permitted indoors in public places, unless there is a separate smoking room. This rule is rarely broken. The restriction also operates on train platforms, arrival and departure halls in airports, private offices and factory buildings. Smoking is not permitted in any restaurants, pubs or cafés, unless there is a separate, screened-off section for smokers.

Engebret Café, dating from 1857, Oslo's oldest restaurant ***(see p233)***

What to Eat in Norway

NORWAY PRODUCES A WIDE VARIETY of fine, fresh ingredients, and over recent years its cuisine has won international acclaim. Fish features largely in Norwegian cooking – salmon, cod and herring are served in a variety of ways. Game is also popular, especially reindeer, elk and woodland fowl. Wild berries are much favoured in Norway, including bilberries, raspberries and cloudberries, which often form the basis of delicious desserts.

Norwegian Cheeses
Jarlsberg is enjoyed even beyond Norway's borders. The sweet, brown goats' cheese, geitost, *is eaten at breakfast.*

SMØRBRØD

Norwegian open sandwiches *(smørbrød)* typically have generous portions of toppings *(pålegg)*. Many of the topping ingredients originate from the sea, but cured meats and roast beef are also among the favourites.

Prawns with mayonnaise, a twist of lemon and lettuce is a meal in itself.

Smoked salmon with scrambled egg and fresh dill is a Norwegian favourite.

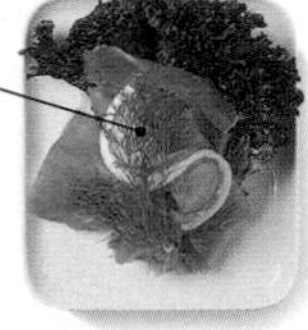

Minced beefsteak is served warm, accompanied by fried onions and a salad garnish.

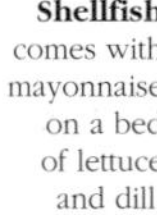

Shellfish comes with mayonnaise on a bed of lettuce and dill.

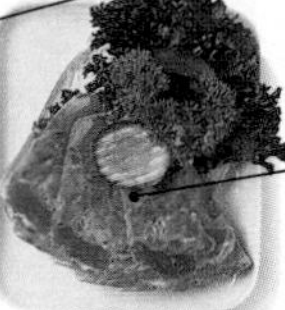

Liver pâté, and lots of it, with finely chopped pickled cucumber and lettuce.

Lamb, boiled and rolled, is served cold with pickled cucumber and lettuce.

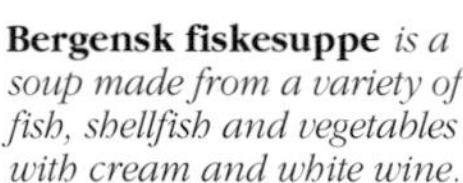

Bergensk fiskesuppe *is a soup made from a variety of fish, shellfish and vegetables with cream and white wine.*

Gul ertesuppe *is made of peas soaked overnight and cooked with a gammon bone, thyme and pepper.*

Friske reker, *large prawns, come with mayonnaise, lemon, butter and French loaf or baguette.*

SPEKESILD

Once considered poor-man's food, marinated herring is a popular dish today, found increasingly on the menu at Christmas. It is served with raw onion, sour cream, lingonberries, butter and flat bread. It goes down well with beer and aquavit.

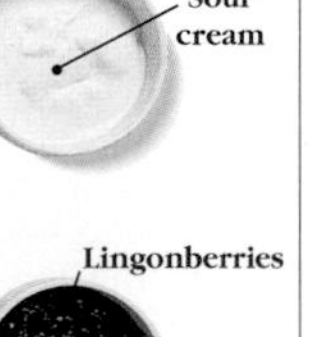

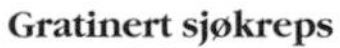

Grillet breiflabb, *grilled monkfish, is served with a herb sauce, julienne vegetables and boiled potatoes. The fillets can also be fried.*

Gratinert sjøkreps *is crayfish topped with grated cheese and grilled. It is served on a bed of lettuce, accompanied by a mustard sauce. Crayfish is just one of many varieties of shellfish from Norwegian waters, such as prawns, crab, lobster, oysters and mussels. Prepared in a variety of ways, they are important in local cooking.*

Kokt torsk, *cod fillets poached gently and served with boiled potatoes, carrots and melted butter, is often accompanied by red wine.*

Får-i-kål *consists of small pieces of lamb layered with finely chopped cabbage and cooked until tender. Served with boiled potatoes.*

Reinsdyrstek, *roast reindeer, is served pink, accompanied by boiled potatoes, a rich full-bodied gravy, broccoli and cowberries.*

Elgstek *is roast elk served in slices and accompanied by potatoes au gratin, broccoli, cowberry jam and a red wine sauce.*

Multekrem med krumkaker, *cloudberries served with whipped cream and wafers, is a nice way to round off a festive meal such as at Christmas Eve.*

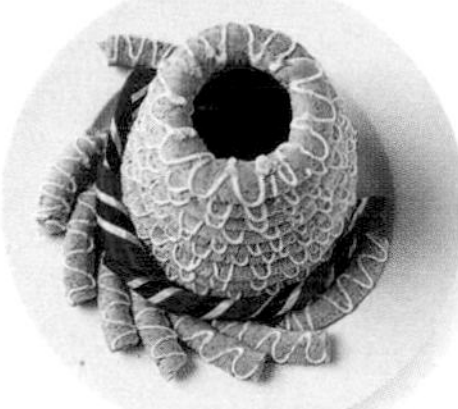

Kransekake, *a traditional cake served on festive occasions, has finely ground almonds and sugar as the main ingredients.*

What to Drink

Norwegian beer *(øl)* is of international standard. Locally produced aquavit *(akevitt)* is a liquor based on a spirit distilled from potatoes to which a number of aromatic agents are added, the most notable being cumin or caraway. *Linje-akevitt* is aged in oak barrels on board ships which have crossed the "line" (the equator). Farris is a mineral water tapped from the Farris spring, free of additives and carbonic acid. St Hallvard is a sweet herb liqueur that goes well with coffee.

Farris mineral water

Ringnes beer

Løitens aquavit

St Hallvard liqueur

Choosing a Restaurant

The restaurants in this guide have been selected across a wide range of price categories for their good value, good food, atmosphere and interesting location. The adjacent chart highlights some of the factors that may influence your choice. Restaurants are listed region by region starting with Oslo. The Street Finder for Oslo can be found on pages 98–101.

Oslo

Restaurant	Credit Cards	Open for Lunch	Open Late	Fixed Price Menu	Good Wine List
Central Oslo West: *Egon Karl Johan* Kr Karl Johans Gate 37, 0162 Oslo. **Map** 3 D3. *22 41 77 90.* Inviting restaurant in Karl Johans Gate in the Paleet shopping complex. Buffet offers a variety of reasonably-priced dishes (no table service) and wine. The menu has been translated into the major languages.	AE DC MC V	●	■		
Central Oslo West: *Mr Hong* Kr Stortingsgata 8, entrance Rosenkrantz' Gate, 0161 Oslo. **Map** 3 D3. *22 42 20 08.* A large restaurant just a few minutes' walk from Stortingsgata with ornate oriental interior. Japanese, Chinese and Mongolian food.	AE DC MC V		■		
Central Oslo West: *Vegeta Vertshus* Kr Munkedamsveien 3B, 0161 Oslo. **Map** 2 C3. *22 83 42 32.* Simple vegetarian restaurant in a side street near Nationaltheatret. Here you can choose from a hearty buffet of salads, soups, warm dishes and desserts. No alcohol served.	AE DC MC V	●	■		
Central Oslo West: *Lorry Restaurant* Kr Kr Parkveien 12, 0350 Oslo. **Map** 2 C2. *22 69 69 04.* Informal, timeless restaurant at the northern corner of Slottsparken with a reputation for its enormous selection of beers. The menu is varied.	AE DC MC V	●	■		■
Central Oslo West: *Babette's Gjestebus* Kr Kr Kr Fridtjof Nansens Plass 2, 0160 Oslo. **Map** 3 D3. *22 41 64 64.* Rustic restaurant in Rådhuspassasjen with a menu that changes to reflect seasonal produce. It has its own café nearby. *Sun.*	AE DC MC V		■		■
Central Oslo West: *Blom* Kr Kr Kr Karl Johans Gate 41B, 0162 Oslo. **Map** 3 D3. *22 40 47 10.* Artists' haunt, set back a little from Karl Johans Gate in the Paleet shopping complex. Old, dignified and comfortable, with paintings, coats-of-arms and mementos of notable people in the field of art. Traditional, good quality food.	AE DC MC V	●	■	●	■
Central Oslo West: *D/S Louise Restaurant & Bar* Kr Kr Kr Stranden 3, 0250 Oslo. **Map** 2 C4. *22 83 00 60.* Large and welcoming restaurant with an international menu. Located on a number of floors in the middle of Aker Brygge, it has a view of the harbour and is decorated with nautical knick-knacks.	AE DC MC V		■	●	■
Central Oslo West: *Dinner Bar & Restaurant* Kr Kr Kr Stortingsgata 22, 0161 Oslo. **Map** 3 D3. *23 10 04 66.* Excellent Chinese restaurant specializing in Szechuan and Cantonese food. Located in modern, stylish premises opposite Nationaltheatret.	AE DC MC V		■		■
Central Oslo West: *Lofoten Fiskerestaurant* Kr Kr Kr Stranden 75, 0250 Oslo. **Map** 2 C4. *22 83 08 08.* Seafood restaurant serving superb dishes with a seasonal twist, located far out on Aker Brygge wharf in modern quayside premises overlooking the fjord and the city. Meat dishes are also available. In summer tables are set outdoors.	AE DC MC V	●	■		■
Central Oslo West: *Mauds – et Norsk Spisested* Kr Kr Kr Brynjulf Bulls Plass 1, 0250 Oslo. **Map** 2 C3. *22 83 72 28.* Norwegian fish and meat dishes dominate the menu, which changes with the seasons. This congenial restaurant has a romantic country-style atmosphere. It is situated in the old train station building, Vestbanebygget. The walls are decorated with photographs of Queen Maud and other famous people.	AE DC MC V		■	●	■

Price categories are for a three-course meal for one person, half a bottle of house wine, and extras such as service charge and cover charge.
(Kr) under 400 Nkr
(Kr)(Kr) 400–500 Nkr
(Kr)(Kr)(Kr) 500–700 Nkr
(Kr)(Kr)(Kr)(Kr) 700 Nkr plus

OPEN FOR LUNCH
Many restaurants are only open in the evening, but restaurants in the large towns and those linked to pubs are often open for lunch, too.

OPEN LATE
The restaurant is open and has full service after 10pm.

FIXED PRICE MENU
Restaurants offering a good menu for lunch or dinner or both at a set price. The menu usually has three courses.

GOOD WINE LIST
Shows that the restaurant has a good selection of wines, or that more exceptional wines are available.

Restaurant	Credit Cards	Open for Lunch	Open Late	Fixed Price Menu	Good Wine List
CENTRAL OSLO WEST: *Theatercafeen* (Kr)(Kr)(Kr)(Kr) **Stortingsgata 24, 0161 Oslo. Map** 3 D3. *22 82 40 50.* Tradition-rich Theatercafeen has a lively atmosphere and attracts guests from all walks of life, ranging from the rich and famous regulars to tourists. The menu is international. This is a place to see and be seen.	AE DC MC V	●	■	●	■
CENTRAL OSLO EAST: *Coco Chalet* (Kr) **Øvre Slottsgate 8, 0157 Oslo. Map** 3 D4. *22 33 32 66.* A pleasant place to eat offering a varied selection of European dishes with an exotic twist in both the café and restaurant.	AE DC MC V	●	■		
CENTRAL OSLO EAST: *Kaffistova* (Kr) **Rosenkrantz' Gate 8, 0159 Oslo. Map** 3 D3. *23 21 42 10.* Buffet with comprehensive choice of traditional dishes. Part of Hotell Bondeheimen, a stone's throw from Karl Johans Gate, the restaurant originally catered for people from the country who missed home cooking, but is now popular with anyone wishing to eat Norwegian specialities. Alcohol is not served. Simple modern furnishings in Norwegian design.	AE DC MC V	●	■	●	
CENTRAL OSLO EAST: *Kafé Celsius* (Kr)(Kr) **Rådhusgata 19, 0158 Oslo. Map** 3 D4. *22 42 45 39.* Oslo's oldest building near to Christiania Torg comprises galleries and a charming place to eat in the courtyard. Pleasant and low-key with Norwegian specialities such as fish and shellfish. *Mon.*	AE DC MC V	●	■		
CENTRAL OSLO EAST: *Stortorvets Gjestgiveri* (Kr)(Kr) **Grensen 1, 0159 Oslo. Map** 3 E3. *23 35 63 60.* The exterior of this 300-year-old building has remained almost unchanged over the centuries, and the restaurant area with its many charming rooms has retained its historic feel. Simple good food.	AE DC MC V	●	■	●	■
CENTRAL OSLO EAST: *Brasserie A Touch of France* (Kr)(Kr)(Kr) **Øvre Slottsgaten 16, 0157 Oslo. Map** 3 D3. *23 10 01 65.* Without doubt a taste of France, this unpretentious and charming brasserie near Egertorget offers a varied menu of classic French food as well as some international dishes.	AE DC MC V		■	●	■
CENTRAL OSLO EAST: *Det Gamle Raadhus Restaurant* (Kr)(Kr)(Kr) **Nedre Slottsgate 1, 0157 Oslo. Map** 3 D4. *22 42 01 07.* Steeped in tradition, this popular restaurant close to Akershus Festning is housed in one of Oslo's oldest buildings, dating from 1641. Norwegian and international fare can be enjoyed in warm, historic surroundings. *Sun.*	AE DC MC V		■	●	■
CENTRAL OSLO EAST: *Engebret Café* (Kr)(Kr)(Kr) **Bankplassen 1, 0151 Oslo. Map** 3 E4. *22 82 25 25.* Little seems to have changed inside this historic building founded in 1857 close to Norges Bank in Bankplassen. The menu attracts a large number of people all year round. In summer there is al fresco dining. *Sun.*	AE DC MC V	●	■		■
CENTRAL OSLO EAST: *Restaurant Mona Lisa* (Kr)(Kr)(Kr) **Grensen 10, entrance on Øvre Slottsgate, 0159 Oslo. Map** 3 E3. *22 42 89 14.* Traditional restaurant located on the first floor, close to Egertorget. The varied menu includes Norwegian, Italian and French cuisine. Inviting interior.	AE DC MC V	●	■	●	■
CENTRAL OSLO EAST: *Solsiden Restaurant* (Kr)(Kr)(Kr) **Søndre Akershus Kai 34, 0150 Oslo. Map** 3 D5. *22 33 36 30.* An old soap warehouse on the quayside below Akershus Festning has been converted into an outstanding fish restaurant. Here you can enjoy the view across the harbour and a menu comprised entirely of fish dishes. *May–Sep.*	AE DC MC V		■	●	■

For key to symbols see back flap

Price categories are for a three-course meal for one person, half a bottle of house wine, and extras such as service charge and cover charge.
(Kr) under 400 Nkr
(Kr)(Kr) 400–500 Nkr
(Kr)(Kr)(Kr) 500–700 Nkr
(Kr)(Kr)(Kr)(Kr) 700 Nkr plus

Open for Lunch
Many restaurants are only open in the evening, but restaurants in the large towns and those linked to pubs are often open for lunch, too.
Open Late
The restaurant is open and has full service after 10pm.
Fixed Price Menu
Restaurants offering a good menu for lunch or dinner or both at a set price. The menu usually has three courses.
Good Wine List
Shows that the restaurant has a good selection of wines, or that more exceptional wines are available.

Restaurant	Credit Cards	Open for Lunch	Open Late	Fixed Price Menu	Good Wine List
Central Oslo East: *Grand Cafe* (Kr)(Kr)(Kr)(Kr) Karl Johans Gate 31, 0159 Oslo. **Map** 3 D3. *24 14 53 00.* Long-established café in the French style overlooking Karl Johans Gate. This popular eaterie dates from the artististic and Bohemian era of the late 19th century when Henrik Ibsen was a regular here. It has a good varied menu.	*AE DC MC V*	●	■	●	■
Central Oslo East: *Statholdergaarden* (Kr)(Kr)(Kr)(Kr) Rådhusgata 11, 0151 Oslo. **Map** 3 E4. *22 41 88 00.* Elegant 350-year-old manor house that was the residence of a high-ranking politician, the *statholder*, in the 17th century. The many small rooms lend an atmosphere of intimacy, while classical paintings on the walls and stucco ceilings bear witness to its history. Gourmet cuisine is prepared under the direction of a former winner of the Bocuse d'Or. ● *Sun.*	*AE DC MC V*		■	●	■
Bygdøy: *Najaden* (Kr)(Kr) Bygdøynesveien 37, 0286 Oslo. **Map** 1 C4. *22 43 81 80.* Situated in Sjøfartsmuseet (the Maritime Museum), this is the place to enjoy a meal on Bygdøy with panoramic views over the fjord and the city. The atmosphere is nautical and the Scandinavian menu offers both fish and meat dishes.	*AE DC MC V*	●		●	■
Further Afield: *Kafe Asylet* (Kr) Grønland 28, 0188 Oslo. *22 17 09 39.* Low ceilings, uneven floors and crooked windows characterize this pleasant, old timber building in the area of Grønland, just northeast of Oslo central station (the entrance is through the back yard). The cooking is simple but good.	*DC MC V*	●	■		
Further Afield: *Big Horn Steak House Majorstua* (Kr)(Kr) Bogstadveien 64, 0366 Oslo. *22 69 03 00.* Themed on the American West, this cellar restaurant specializes in steaks and meat dishes. It is located in lively Majorstua, near Vigelandsparken.	*AE DC MC V*		■		■
Further Afield: *Markveien Mat & Vinhus* (Kr)(Kr) Torvbakkgata 12, entrance in Markveien, 0550 Oslo. **Map** 3 F2. *22 37 22 97.* An attractive venue with art covering the walls, this restaurant serves simple but delectable food with an emphasis on good ingredients. The staff are happy to translate the detailed menu. Good selection of wines. ● *Sun, Mon.*	*AE DC MC V*		■	●	■
Further Afield: *Sult* (Kr)(Kr) Thorvald Meyers Gate 26, 0555 Oslo. *22 87 04 67.* Located in fashionable Grünerløkka, this restaurant offers a Norwegian menu that varies to make the most of good, fresh produce. ● *Mon.*	*AE DC MC V*		■		■
Further Afield: *De Fem Stuer* (Kr)(Kr)(Kr) Kongeveien 26, 0787 Oslo. *22 92 27 34.* Situated in Rica Park Hotell Holmenkollen, the dining rooms offer a warm, romantic, country-style atmosphere with good views of large areas of the city. The international menu is extensive.	*AE DC MC V*	●	■	●	■
Further Afield: *Frognerseteren* (Kr)(Kr)(Kr) Holmenkollveien 200, 0791 Oslo. *22 92 40 40.* Restaurant, café and function rooms offering something to suit every occasion, whether refreshments after a walk in the woods or a large celebratory meal. Truly Norwegian ambience in National Romantic style with panoramic views over the Holmenkollen ski jump.	*DC MC V*	●	■	●	■
Further Afield: *Holmenkollen Restaurant* (Kr)(Kr)(Kr) Holmenkollveien 119, 0787 Oslo. *22 13 92 00.* This historic restaurant overlooking the city from above Holmenkollen has preserved its ancient character. It offers a Norwegian-inspired menu. There is a simple cafeteria next to the restaurant.	*AE DC MC V*	●	■	●	■

FURTHER AFIELD: *Hos Thea* (Kr)(Kr)(Kr) | AE DC MC V
Gabels Gate 11, 0272 Oslo. **Map** 2 A3. *22 44 68 74.*
Stylish eaterie with a homely atmosphere near Drammensveien. The varied menu includes seafood and meat dishes.

FURTHER AFIELD: *Klosteret Restaurant* (Kr)(Kr)(Kr) | AE DC MC V
Fredensborgveien 13, 0177 Oslo. **Map** 3 E2. *23 35 49 00.*
Old brick arches, wrought iron, candlelight and Gregorian music create a romantic atmosphere in this cellar restaurant. The menu features Continental and French cuisine. *Sun.*

FURTHER AFIELD: *Restaurant Kastanjen* (Kr)(Kr)(Kr) | AE DC MC V
Bygdøy Allé 18, 0262 Oslo. **Map** 2 A3. *22 43 44 67.*
Good food and drink is served in rustic, relaxed surroundings with bare oak tables and wrought-iron chairs. The cuisine is French-Italian. *Sun.*

FURTHER AFIELD: *Bagatelle Restaurant* (Kr)(Kr)(Kr)(Kr) | AE DC MC V
Bygdøy Allé 3, 0257 Oslo. *22 12 14 40.*
South of Vigelandsparken, housed behind a discreet façade, is the only restaurant in Norway that currently has two stars in the *Guide Rouge.* It has a superb menu and an extensive wine list. *Sun.*

FURTHER AFIELD: *Feinschmecker Spisested* (Kr)(Kr)(Kr)(Kr) | AE DC MC V
Balchens Gate 5, 0265 Oslo. *22 12 93 80.*
Classic French-inspired gourmet food. With one star in the *Guide Rouge*, this restaurant offers superb cuisine in inviting surroundings. *Sun.*

FURTHER AFIELD: *Restaurant Le Canard* (Kr)(Kr)(Kr)(Kr) | AE DC MC V
President Harbitz Gate 4, 0259 Oslo. **Map** 2 B2. *22 54 34 00.*
Gourmet restaurant that makes the very best of the finest ingredients, with French-inspired cuisine. An unusually extensive selection of wines. *Sun.*

AROUND OSLOFJORDEN

HØVIK: *Bølgen & Moi* (Kr)(Kr)(Kr) | AE DC MC V
Sonja Henies Vei 31, 1363 Høvik. *67 52 10 20.*
Outstanding menu and atmosphere. The interior has clean lines and, in keeping with the fact that the restaurant is located in the Henie-Onstad Kunstsenter, it also has an art exhibition that changes regularly. *Sun, Mon (cafeteria remains open)*

DRAMMEN: *Café Picasso* (Kr) | AE DC MC V
Nedre Storgate 16, 3015 Drammen. *32 89 07 08.*
Café serving meat, fish, pasta and Mexican fare. In summer you can also eat outside in the courtyard at the rear.

DRAMMEN: *Lauritz Restaurant & Bar* (Kr) | AE DC MC V
Bragernes Torg 2A, 3017 Drammen. *32 83 77 22.*
Good, simple food is served at this restaurant in the town's central square. Live music on the last Saturday of each month.

DRAMMEN: *Sofus Vertshus – Kro* (Kr)(Kr) | AE DC MC V
Øvre Torggate 6, 3017 Drammen. *32 83 80 05.*
Steakhouse serving international dishes, housed in a converted stable. Rustic-style brick and timber interiors with equestrian details.

FREDRIKSTAD: *Major-Stuen* (Kr)(Kr) | AE DC MC V
Voldportgaten 73, 1632 Gamle Fredrikstad. *69 32 15 55.*
Folksy restaurant with a wide choice of substantial and light dishes. Situated in the old town of Gamle Fredrikstad.

FREDRIKSTAD: *Balaklava Gjestgiveri* (Kr)(Kr)(Kr) | AE DC MC V
Færgeportgata 78, 1632 Gamle Fredrikstad. *69 32 30 40.*
The focus is on gourmet dishes with an international slant, based on fresh ingredients from the region. The inn comprises five well-preserved buildings situated in the fortress and it also has coffee rooms and hotel rooms. Al fresco dining in the summer.

LARVIK: *Brasserie Vadskjæret* (Kr)(Kr) | DC MC V
Havnegata 12, 3263 Larvik. *33 14 10 90.*
Brasserie set on the north side of the harbour beside a small-boat marina with a view over the fjord. Dishes focus on meat and fish, including whale steak or fillet – a reminder of the area's whaling industry, which played an important role until a few generations ago. Outdoor eating in summer.

Price categories are for a three-course meal for one person, half a bottle of house wine, and extras such as service charge and cover charge.
Ⓚ under 400 Nkr
ⓀⓀ 400–500 Nkr
ⓀⓀⓀ 500–700 Nkr
ⓀⓀⓀⓀ 700 Nkr plus

Open for Lunch
Many restaurants are only open in the evening, but restaurants in the large towns and those linked to pubs are often open for lunch, too.

Open Late
The restaurant is open and has full service after 10pm.

Fixed Price Menu
Restaurants offering a good menu for lunch or dinner or both at a set price. The menu usually has three courses.

Good Wine List
Shows that the restaurant has a good selection of wines, or that more exceptional wines are available.

Restaurant	Credit Cards	Open for Lunch	Open Late	Fixed Price Menu	Good Wine List
Larvik: *Ferdinands Lille Kjøkken* ⓀⓀ Storgata 32, 3256 Larvik. *33 13 05 44.* Recognized for its fish dishes, this welcoming restaurant serves Norwegian food. It is situated in the middle of the town with a view over the harbour from the terrace, where you can sit and eat in summer.	AE DC MC V		■		■
Sandefjord: *Da Vinci Restaurant* ⓀⓀ Klaras Vei 9C, 3244 Sandefjord. *33 46 86 80.* Italian restaurant in the town centre offering diverse fare, including Norwegian dishes.	AE DC MC V	●	■		■
Sandefjord: *Mathuset Solvold* ⓀⓀⓀ Thor Dahlsgate 9, 3210 Sandefjord. *33 46 27 41.* Renowned restaurant which makes a feature of its well-stocked wine cellar. There is an area for light meals, as well as a gourmet restaurant based on French-inspired cooking with flavours from Spain, Italy and Asia. *Sun.*	AE DC MC V		■	●	■
Tønsberg: *Fregatten Restaurant & Bar* Ⓚ Storgata 17, 3126 Tønsberg. *33 31 47 76.* Norwegian and Japanese dishes with fish and shellfish specialities, served in congenial maritime surroundings in Storgaten.	AE DC MC V		■	●	■
Tønsberg: *Brygga Restaurant* ⓀⓀ Nedre Langgate 32, 3126 Tønsberg. *33 31 12 70.* Traditional Norwegian restaurant in a newly-built courtyard on the wharf. Serves a varied menu of meat and fish.	AE DC MC V	●	■		■
Eastern Norway					
Hamar: *Mrs Sippy's Steakhouse* ⓀⓀ Torggata 3, 2317 Hamar. *62 53 52 00.* Extensive American, Creole and Mexican menu. The restaurant is well-known for its spare ribs. Situated near Jernbaneparken, the informal atmosphere is reminiscent of the American South.	AE DC MC V		■		■
Hamar: *Stallgården Restauranthus* ⓀⓀⓀ Torggata 82, 2317 Hamar. *62 54 31 00.* A converted stable yard dating from 1849 comprising a café, bar and nightclub, as well as the atmospheric restaurant, Bykjeller'n, which has a varied Norwegian menu.	AE DC MC V	●	■	●	■
Lillehammer: *Bryggeriet Bar og Biffhus* Ⓚ Elvegaten 19, 2609 Lillehammer. *61 27 06 60.* When the town's brewery was demolished, the cellars dating from 1855 were converted into a pleasant restaurant, one block from Storgaten. Steak dishes are the house speciality, but other fare is also served.	AE DC MC V		■	●	■
Lillehammer: *Nikkers* Ⓚ Elvegaten 18, 2609 Lillehammer. *61 24 74 30.* Norwegian country style is reflected in the restaurant as well as on its menu. There is a bar with several TV screens showing sports on the first floor.	AE DC MC V	●	■		■
Lillehammer: *Blåmann Restaurant & Bar* ⓀⓀ Lilletorget 1, 2615 Lillehammer. *61 26 22 03.* This restaurant is, as the name suggests, decorated in shades of blue. Food ranging from Norwegian to Mexican is served from the open kitchen. There is also a piano bar.	AE DC MC V	●	■		■
Lillehammer: *Paa Bordet Restaurant* ⓀⓀⓀ Bryggerigata 70, 2609 Lillehammer. *61 25 30 00.* A small restaurant in an old timber building one block below the main street. Gourmet menu with a number of select dishes. *Sun.*	AE DC MC V		■	●	■

SØRLANDET AND TELEMARK

ARENDAL: *Madam Reiersen* Kr Kr
Nedre Tyholmsveien 3, 4836 Arendal. *37 02 19 00.*
Friendly restaurant with adjoining bar on the quayside facing the Pollen yacht harbour. It offers a broad spectrum of international dishes.
AE DC MC V | ● ■ ● ■

ARENDAL: *Phileas Fogg* Kr Kr
Nedre Tyholmsveien 2, 4836 Arendal. *37 02 02 02.*
English-inspired restaurant offering a global menu with flavours from around the world. Centrally located next to Pollen.
AE DC MC V | ● ■ ■

KRISTIANSAND: *Brasserie Hvide Hus* Kr Kr
Markens Gate 29, 4611 Kristiansand S. *38 02 18 84.*
Simple Norwegian fare in a warm atmosphere on the first floor overlooking the town's main pedestrianized shopping street. ● *Sun.*
AE DC MC V | ● ■ ● ■

KRISTIANSAND: *Sjøhuset Restaurant* Kr Kr
Østre Strandgate 12A, 4610 Kristiansand S. *38 02 62 60.*
Located in a former salt warehouse dating from 1892 on the waterfront of the town's eastern harbour overlooking the sea, the emphasis here is on fish and shellfish dishes. Outdoor eating during the summer. ● *Sun.*
AE DC MC V | ● ■ ● ■

KRISTIANSAND: *Bakgården Restaurant* Kr Kr Kr
Tollbodgata 5, 4611 Kristiansand S. *38 02 79 55.*
French-inspired cuisine in an unpretentious setting around a courtyard in the town centre. The restaurant is illuminated by paraffin lamps. There are no printed menus, instead the waiters inform guests of the choices. ● *Sun.*
AE DC MC V | ■ ■

KRISTIANSAND: *Luihn Restaurant* Kr Kr Kr
Rådhusgata 15, 4611 Kristiansand S. *38 10 66 50.*
Former patrician house with a welcoming atmosphere, located in a quaint area of Kvadraturen. The high-class menu features French-inspired Norwegian fare. ● *Sun.*
AE DC MC V | ■ ● ■

SKIEN: *Boden Spiseri* Kr Kr Kr
Langbrygga 5, 3724 Skien. *35 52 61 70.*
Located in a wharfside building from the 1850s, there are two dining areas: the one at ground level serves Norwegian and international food in romantic country-style surroundings, while the informal Kulcompagnie in the cellar serves reasonably priced snacks and light meals.
AE DC MC V | ■ ■

VESTLANDET

BERGEN: *Olde Hansa* Kr
Bryggestredet 2, 5003 Bergen. *55 31 40 46.*
Rebuilt after a fire in 1701, this building has been an eating house ever since. The restaurant has the feel of a well-preserved Hansa merchant's house and the serving staff dress in period costumes. The food is inspired by that eaten in Hanseatic times. ● *Sun.*
AE DC MC V | ● ■

BERGEN: *Bryggeloftet & Stuene Restaurant* Kr Kr
Bryggen 11, 5003 Bergen. *55 31 06 30.*
Old and traditional restaurant on the Bergen waterfront. The menu features fish, meat and game.
AE DC MC V | ● ■ ■

BERGEN: *Finnegaardsbrasseriet* Kr Kr
Rosenkrantzgaten 6, 5003 Bergen. *55 55 03 20.*
A 300-year-old building containing a number of dining areas in different rooms. The brasserie is decorated in warm colours and serves a French-Norwegian menu of fish and meat. Finnegaardsstuene is the gourmet restaurant, and there is also a Mexican eaterie. ● *Sun.*
AE DC MC V | ■ ● ■

BERGEN: *Holbergstuen* Kr Kr
Torgalmenningen 6, 5014 Bergen. *55 31 80 15.*
Old and well-known restaurant in the city centre. The menu offers a wide selection of food and drink. The interior is embellished with quotes from the Bergen poet, Holberg, and folk art decor on the walls.
AE DC MC V | ● ■ ■

BERGEN: *Wesselstuen* Kr Kr
Ole Bulls Plass 6, 5012 Bergen. *55 55 49 49.*
One of the most traditional restaurants in Bergen, this is a place where diners from all walks of life, from students to business people, meet to enjoy a varied menu of unpretentious Norwegian food.
AE DC MC V | ● ■ ■

For key to symbols see back flap

Price categories are for a three-course meal for one person, half a bottle of house wine, and extras such as service charge and cover charge.
(Kr) under 400 Nkr
(Kr)(Kr) 400–500 Nkr
(Kr)(Kr)(Kr) 500–700 Nkr
(Kr)(Kr)(Kr)(Kr) 700 Nkr plus

Open for Lunch
Many restaurants are only open in the evening, but restaurants in the large towns and those linked to pubs are often open for lunch, too.

Open Late
The restaurant is open and has full service after 10pm.

Fixed Price Menu
Restaurants offering a good menu for lunch or dinner or both at a set price. The menu usually has three courses.

Good Wine List
Shows that the restaurant has a good selection of wines, or that more exceptional wines are available.

Restaurant	Credit Cards	Open for Lunch	Open Late	Fixed Price Menu	Good Wine List
Bergen: *Smauet Mat & Vinhus* (Kr)(Kr)(Kr) Vaskerelvsmuget 1, 5014 Bergen. *55 21 07 10.* A snug interior resembling a log cabin. The emphasis is on French cuisine, but Italian dishes are also represented. Situated across from Torgalmenningen.	AE DC MC V		■	●	■
Haugesund: *Bestastuå Mat Prat & Vinhus* (Kr) Strandgata 132, 5527 Haugesund. *52 86 55 88.* Large restaurant in an old building in the town centre with select, traditional Norwegian fare. Bar specialising in cognac and cigars. *Sun.*	AE DC MC V	●	■	●	■
Haugesund: *Brovingen Mat & Vin* (Kr)(Kr)(Kr) Åsbygata 3, 5528 Haugesund. *52 86 31 48.* Classical Provençal dishes served in a modern restaurant with views over the sound, Smedasundet. *Sun, Mon.*	AE DC MC V		■	●	■
Stavanger: *Mortepumpen* (Kr)(Kr) Olav V's Gate 3, 4005 Stavanger. *51 76 00 00.* Seafood is the traditional speciality of this restaurant, but a variety of other dishes are offered in addition. The walls are lined with replica façades of historic buildings of Old Stavanger in one-third scale. *Sun.*	AE DC MC V		■	●	■
Stavanger: *Sjøhuset Skagen* (Kr)(Kr) Skagen 16, 4006 Stavanger. *51 89 51 80.* The old restored bunkhouse on the wharf (Skagenkaien) next to the harbour houses inviting restaurants with a maritime atmosphere. Small rooms and niches on different floors create an interesting setting in which to enjoy a menu comprising Norwegian and international dishes.	AE DC MC V	●	■	●	■
Stavanger: *Cartellet Restaurant* (Kr)(Kr)(Kr) Øvre Holmegate 8, 4006 Stavanger. *51 89 60 22.* High-quality restaurant in the centre of the town offering a rich choice of dishes from the sea and land, based on traditional Norwegian cooking, but with an international slant. It is located in a cellar, the walls of which are faced in stone from the old Stavanger quay. *Sun.*	AE DC MC V		■	●	■
Stavanger: *Elisabeth Restaurant* (Kr)(Kr)(Kr) Kongsgata 41, 4005 Stavanger. *51 53 33 00.* Traditional restaurant situated on the bank of Breiavannet Lake in the town centre offering French cuisine with an international touch. The original furnishings have been retained and are complemented with modern elements. *Sun.*	AE DC MC V		■	●	■
Ålesund: *Krambua Ålesund* (Kr) Apotekergata 2, 6004 Ålesund. *70 10 05 80.* Rustic-style restaurant, centrally located, serving a varied selection of international dishes and good Norwegian homely fare, including some local specialities at reasonable prices.	AE DC MC V	●	■		■
Ålesund: *Sjøbua Restaurant* (Kr)(Kr)(Kr) Brunholmgata 1, 6004 Ålesund. *70 12 71 00.* Reputable fish restaurant in a former warehouse built in the Art Nouveau style after the town's catastrophic fire in 1904. Views over Brosundet and the sea. *Sun.*	AE DC MC V		■		■
TRØNDELAG					
Røros: *Vertshuset Røros* (Kr)(Kr) Kjerkgata 34, 7374 Røros. *72 41 24 11.* Typical pub – warm and welcoming. The menu is varied, with an infusion of local dishes.	AE DC MC V		■		

Restaurant	Price	Cards				
TRONDHEIM: *Druen Mat og Vinstue* Munkegata 26, 7011 Trondheim. *73 92 26 00.* A place to relax with a glass of wine, eat a light meal or enjoy a full dinner from a varied, international menu. *Sun.*	(Kr)(Kr)	AE DC MC V	●	■	●	■
TRONDHEIM: *Grenaderen* Kongsgårdsgata 1, 7013 Trondheim. *73 51 66 80.* This 200-year-old building was originally a forge. The menu offers both meat and fish with an emphasis on Norwegian food and ingredients.	(Kr)(Kr)	AE DC MC V		■		■
TRONDHEIM: *Tavern Vertshus* Sverresborg Allé 11, 7020 Trondheim. *73 87 80 70.* Traditional homely fare in an old inn that has remained virtually unchanged since its construction in 1739. Trøndelag Folkemuseum is nearby.	(Kr)(Kr)	AE DC MC V		■		
TRONDHEIM: *Bryggen Restaurant* Øvre Bakklandet 66, 7013 Trondheim. *73 87 42 42.* Gourmet restaurant offering a good selection of meat, fish and wines. Located in a former warehouse with a modern interior and river views. *Sun.*	(Kr)(Kr)(Kr)	AE DC MC V		■	●	■
TRONDHEIM: *Emilies Et Spisested* Erling Skakkes Gate 45, 7012 Trondheim. *73 92 96 41.* A small eaterie a block away from the central square, offering a fixed five-course menu with the option of selecting individual dishes.	(Kr)(Kr)(Kr)	AE DC MC V		■	●	■
TRONDHEIM: *Havfruen* Kjøpmannsgata 7, 7013 Trondheim. *73 87 40 70.* Seafood restaurant with a maritime atmosphere situated in one of the old wharfside warehouses on the Nidelven river right next to the bridge, Gamle Bybro. High-quality fish dishes feature seasonal produce. *Sun.*	(Kr)(Kr)(Kr)	AE DC MC V		■	●	■
TRONDHEIM: *Palmehaven Restaurant* Dronningens Gate 5, 7011 Trondheim. *73 80 08 00.* Since its opening in 1918 this restaurant has been a popular place to meet and enjoy good French cuisine. *Sun, Mon.*	(Kr)(Kr)(Kr)	AE DC MC V	●	■	●	■
NORTHERN NORWAY						
BODØ: *Blix Restaurant* Sjøgata 23, 8006 Bodø. *75 54 70 99.* A number of small rooms make up this charming restaurant overlooking the sea. Varied and traditional menu featuring meat and seafood.	(Kr)(Kr)	AE DC MC V		■		■
BODØ: *Taste Cuisine* Havnegata 1, 8001 Bodø. *75 54 01 80.* International and oriental dishes in a colourful Art Deco interior.	(Kr)(Kr)	AE DC MC V		■		■
HAMMERFEST: *Odd's Mat og Vinhus* Strandgata 24, 9600 Hammerfest. *78 41 37 66.* Small restaurant in the middle of Strandgata next to the harbour. Paintings of nature create a maritime atmosphere. *Sun.*	(Kr)	AE DC MC V		■	●	■
TROMSØ: *Arctandria Sjømat Restaurant* Strandtorget 1, 9008 Tromsø. *77 60 07 20.* Arctic-style menu featuring local seafood specialities as well as reindeer, seal and whale in an atmospheric setting by the harbour. *Sun.*	(Kr)(Kr)	AE DC MC V		■		■
TROMSØ: *Aunegården* Sjøgata 29, 9008 Tromsø. *77 65 12 34.* The restaurant comprises a number of rooms, each with its individual character and history – one of the rooms was once a butcher's shop. It serves snacks and light meals, gourmet food and cakes.	(Kr)(Kr)	AE DC MC V	●	■		■
TROMSØ: *Markens Grøde* Storgata 30, 9008 Tromsø. *77 68 25 50.* Serving fish and game, this restaurant is situated just south of the cathedral. The interior resembles the living room of a local brewing family by the name of Mack. A café doubles as a pub in the evening. *Mon.*	(Kr)(Kr)	DC MC V		■		■
TROMSØ: *Store Norske Fiskekompani* Storgata 73, 9008 Tromsø. *77 68 76 00.* A seafood restaurant serving international cuisine using local fresh ingredients. Centrally situated in an atmospheric old building. *Sun.*	(Kr)(Kr)	AE DC MC V		■		■

For key to symbols see back flap

Shopping in Norway

Norway's larger towns have a wide selection of shopping centres and department stores. Generally, prices are high, but clothes are less expensive. There are often good buys to be had when it comes to gold and silver items, watches, glass and leather articles. VAT on sales is particularly steep in Norway, but foreign visitors can obtain as much as 18.5 per cent off what they spend by taking advantage of the tax-free facility. Among the best buys are hand-knitted sweaters and cardigans in traditional patterns, known as a *lusekofte*. Specialist craft shops in all the towns offer a good selection and the quality is high. These shops also sell beautiful hand-crafted articles made of wood, pewter, silver and linen. Sami crafts and jewellery make exquisite gifts, while Norwegian food specialities and the famous aquavit, available in many varieties, is always appreciated.

Hand-knitted *lusekofte*

Opening Hours

Opening hours vary, but most shops are open between 9am and 5pm on weekdays. Shopping centres and department stores open at 9–10am and close between 6 and 9pm. Shops shut earlier on Saturday, particularly in smaller places where some may close as early as 1pm. In towns it is becoming standard practice to stay open until 2–3pm on Saturday, while shopping centres and department stores open at 9am and close around 6pm. Shops are closed on Sunday, except in the run-up to Christmas when shopping centres and department stores open for business.

Many places have a local petrol station that remains open until midnight, or even around the clock, which can be useful as Norwegian petrol stations resemble small supermarkets. Here you can buy food, gifts, flowers, music and sweets. Some petrol stations also offer fresh coffee and hot dogs. For a snack, you could try a frankfurter with a potato wrap *(lompe)*, topped with mustard and tomato ketchup.

How to Pay

As a rule, department stores and shopping centres accept all internationally recognized credit cards, such as VISA, MasterCard, Diners, Eurocard and American Express. Travellers' cheques are on the decline as a form of payment and not all shops will accept them. If you are using travellers' cheques you must also have identification, such as a passport or driving licence. All shopping centres have cash machines (ATMs) with user instructions in English, German and French.

With the introduction of the Euro in a number of countries, Norwegian shopping centres are considering whether to accept it in the future.

Sales Tax and Tax-free Shopping

Sales tax (moms) levied on goods currently can be up to 18,5 per cent of the purchase price. Since Norway is not a member of the European Union, residents of EU and non-EU states, with the exception of visitors from Sweden, Denmark and Finland, can reclaim the sales tax paid on goods over a specified amount.

More than 3,000 shops in Norway offer tax-free shopping, allowing you to reclaim 11–18.5 per cent of the total price. There are no tax-free concessions in restaurants or for car hire.

Oslo City, one of the busiest shopping centres in the capital

The guidelines to reclaim sales tax are as follows:

1 Use shops offering Global Refund Tax-Free Shopping. Look for the sticker on the door or in the window.

2 Spend more than 310 Nkr.

3 Ask for a Tax Refund cheque when you pay.

4 When leaving Norway you can obtain a refund at one of Global Refund's Cash Refund Desks. These can be found at Oslo Central train station, airports, border crossings and on cruise ships and ferries. You will need to produce the goods and show the Refund Cheque, the receipt and your passport.

5 If you cannot find a Cash Refund Desk on your departure from Norway you can post the Tax

Hand-crafted goods on sale in a market

The exclusive Paleet shopping centre, just a stone's throw from the Royal Palace in Oslo

Refund Cheque to Global Refund. The address is on the back of the cheque. The cheque will first have to be stamped by customs or the police authorities in your home country. The refund can be transferred to your bank or credit card account.

Consumer Rights

Norwegians are very conscientious consumers and even children are aware of their rights according to consumer legislation. This knowledge stems primarily from two popular television programmes that deal with consumer rights.

Shops offer an exchange of goods service that goes far beyond legal requirements. If there is anything wrong with the item you have bought you have the right to have it replaced or the money refunded. If you want to return something just because you regret having bought it, most retailers will take it back – even if they are not obliged to do so by law. The article must not have been used, and should preferably be in its original packaging. Many shops ask for the receipt. Some shops will give you a refund; others will insist that you buy something else instead.

Department Stores and Shopping Centres

Norwegians love shopping. On Saturday, in particular, you could be forgiven for thinking that the country's entire population is on a communal shopping trip. Streets, department stores and shopping centres all bustle with shoppers. Large shopping complexes are a relatively new phenomenon in Norway. They began to take off in the early 1990s and enormous centres were built on the edge of towns. The growth was so rapid that local politicians sounded a warning as smaller retailers in town centres began to suffer economically. Nowadays the development of shopping centres is regulated by local authorities in an attempt to achieve an acceptable balance between the small shops and larger complexes.

Shopping centres in Norway all resemble one another. They each contain between 30 and 80 shops, cafés, restaurants and bakeries. The bigger centres include **Oslo City** in the capital, **Kløverhuset** in Bergen, and **Trondheim Torg**.

Each centre normally comprises exclusive designer shops as well as cheaper chain stores. But one shopping centre that stands out from all the others is **Paleet** in Oslo, which sells only exclusive goods of high quality. Also in the capital, and offering a wide choice of restaurants as well as shops, is the popular **Aker Brygge** *(see p57)*.

Note that the sale of all wine and spirits in Norway takes place in specially designated state monopoly shops called Vinmonopolet. Bottles are normally sold over the counter, and the shop assistants tend to be very knowledgeable and helpful.

Large souvenir shops in Oslo offering a wide selection of goods

Directory

Shopping Centres and Department Stores

Paleet
Karl Johans Gate 37–43, Oslo.
Map 3 D3.
☎ *22 03 38 88.*

Oslo City
Near Oslo Central Station.
Map 3 E3.
☎ *81 54 41 00.*

Aker Brygge
Oslo. **Map** 2 C4.
☎ *22 83 66 70.*

Kløverhuset
Strandgaten 15, Bergen.
☎ *55 31 37 90.*

Trondheim Torg
Kongens Gate 11, Trondheim.
☎ *73 80 77 40.*

Markets

April and May is a popular time for flea markets in Norway when jumble sales are held in practically every sports hall and school playground. They are organized to raise money for sports clubs and school brass bands, and are always advertised in the local paper.

Often jumble sales will have a separate second-hand and antiques section where it is possible to find a bargain. The most valuable antiques are usually auctioned.

Many people think the best thing about a jumble sale is the home-made waffles and coffee. At any rate, they can be a very Norwegian experience, providing you with an opportunity to meet the locals in a positive and entertaining way.

Various market days are also arranged throughout Norway. One of the best-known is the market in Røros *(see p28)*, held at the end of February/ early March. This is a cold, but delightful experience, with everything from clothes to crafts and food on sale. Dress warmly as temperatures in Røros can fall to –20° C (–4° F) at this time of year.

What to Buy in Norway

Trolls from Norwegian legends

If you are planning to take home a memento it is worth looking for something authentically Norwegian. The most popular souvenir is the traditional knitted cardigan, *lusekofte*. There is a wide selection of handcrafted articles such as pewter and glassware to choose from, and if you have a lot of room in your suitcase you could take home a reindeer hide. Sailing and outdoors enthusiasts will find high-quality sports clothes and equipment. Popular gifts for small children include Norwegian trolls, or cuddly toys such as snow-white polar bears and little furry seals.

Polar Bear
A soft little bear from the north is a lovely memento. You can also buy cuddly brown elk toys.

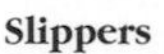

Slippers
Nothing beats felt slippers made from the matted wool of Norwegian sheep for warmth. The soles are leather. Such slippers are available in many mountain huts.

Knitwear
Knitting has a long tradition in Norway. All children, both boys and girls, learn to knit at school, though few acquire the skills required to knit a lusekofte. *Good buys include hats, gloves and cardigans in traditional and modern designs, as well as ear warmers, mittens and scarves.*

Silver and Pewter
Norway has many outstanding goldsmiths and silversmiths whose products can be found in shops such as Husfliden and Heimen in Oslo. Pewter products are particularly popular, especially authentic copies of old beer mugs, dishes and bowls. Queen Sonja sometimes chooses these to present to foreign dignitaries. Some shops offer an exciting range of modern jewellery.

Cheese Slicer
Invented in Norway, the practical cheese slicer comes in many shapes and forms, ranging from traditional to modern. The handle can be made of wood, metal or even reindeer horn.

Linen
Linen tablecloths, napkins and towels, often in traditional patterns, exude quality. Flax cultivation is on the increase in Norway.

Hand-Painted Wood and Porcelain
The painting of floral motifs on all kinds of objects from small boxes to large cupboards is known as "rosemaling" and follows a centuries-old tradition. Porcelain is available from glassware shops, which also stock tableware and ornaments.

Hand-decorated bowl

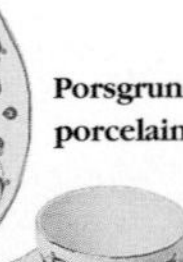

Porsgrunn porcelain

Glass Christmas Figures
Gnomes to decorate the Christmas table are available with either red or blue hats.

Sami Crafts

There are shops all over Norway selling excellent Sami products, but the best buys are probably to be had in Finnmark. Sami shoes (skaller) *have a characteristic curled tip because they were worn for skiing. The Sami would slip the tip under a strap which was fastened to the skis. To keep moisture out of the shoes they packed them with dried grass.*

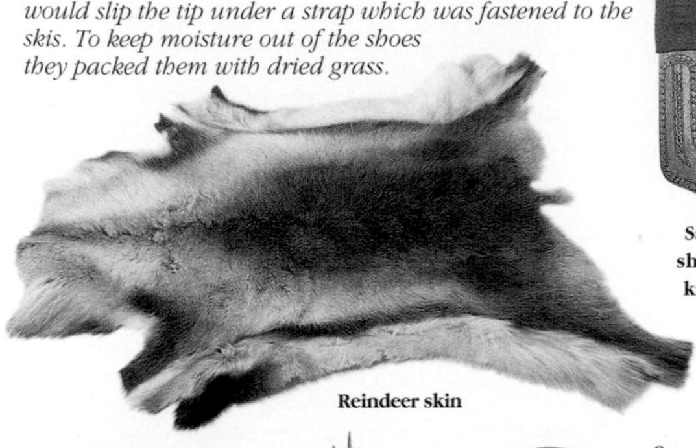

Reindeer skin

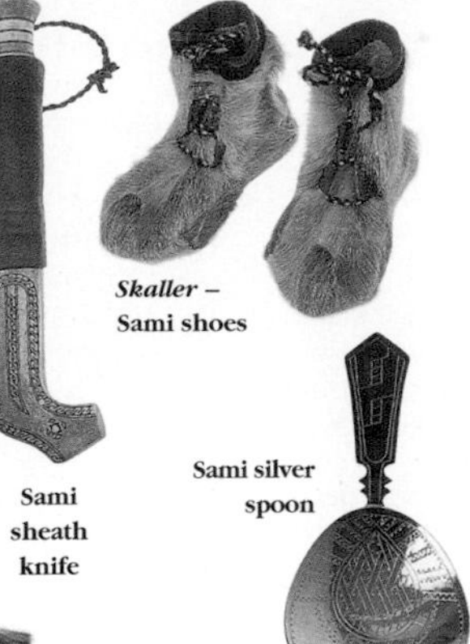

Skaller **– Sami shoes**

Sami sheath knife

Sami silver spoon

Pewter thread bracelet

Silver brooch

Traditional brooch

Sami Jewellery

Beautifully crafted and of excellent quality, traditional bracelets are made of thin pewter thread, plaited in different patterns on a base of soft reindeer skin. Brooches come in ancient and contemporary designs.

Norwegian Specialities

Norwegians cut *geitost*, their brown goats' cheese, into thin slices with a cheese slicer and use it as a sandwich topping. Norwegian smoked salmon is highly regarded by gourmets all over the world, and Norwegian milk chocolate is a perennial favourite.

Sailing Jacket

Helly Hansen is synonymous with quality, whether you want a thick winter fleece, a thin summer jacket or the proper gear for yachting. There is also a large selection of waterproof trousers for sport and leisure.

Geitost cheese

Milk chocolate

Smoked salmon

Life Jacket

In Norway the law requires everyone on board a boat to wear a life jacket. These light life jackets are soft and comfortable to wear and are popular among sailors.

Aquavit in Miniature Bottles

Aquavit (see p231) *can be bought as a set of miniatures, including the richly spiced oak-flavoured Gammel, the strong Taffel (for heavier meals) and the moderately spiced Linie Aquavit.*

Oppland Aquavit

Gammel Aquavit

Taffel Aquavit

Oslo Aquavit

Linie Aquavit

Where to Shop in Norway

Oslo, Bergen, Trondheim, Kristiansand, Tromsø, Stavanger, Ålesund and all the larger towns in Norway have department stores, shopping centres and markets. Even in Hammerfest, in the far north, there are numerous shops. Every self-respecting village or town has a local arts and crafts shop and there are souvenir shops in all the tourist centres. In summer you can visit bustling open-air markets where there are plenty of local items on sale.

Souvenirs

Norwegian souvenirs can be divided into two distinct categories: cheap, mass-produced items and hand-made high-quality articles. The mass-produced souvenirs include mugs, brooches, sew-on badges, fridge magnets, key rings, ashtrays and T-shirts, similar to those found all the world. Popular themes for gift items include the Norwegian flag, rotund trolls, Viking ships and helmets, and typical northern animals such as elk, reindeer, polar bear and seal.

Forest and mountain trolls are available in a multitude of different forms. The cheapest versions are made of rubber, the most expensive are hand-carved from local wood.

Hand-crafted items can be found in all the larger souvenir shops. Popular purchases include the troll figurines in wood, bowls decorated with hand-carved or hand-painted floral motifs in traditional designs, cheese slicers made from various materials, knitted hats, gloves and scarves, porcelain, linen tableware and small silver and pewter objects.

Arts and Crafts

Across rural Norway there are craftsmen and women carving in wood, doing joinery, embroidery, sewing, weaving and painting. Their products are sold at stores such as **Heimen** and **William Schmidt** in Oslo. **Husfliden**, with more than 100 shops in Norway, also sells high-quality handicrafts.

Wooden articles decorated with hand-painted or carved floral motifs, known as *rosemaling*, are popular gifts. The smallest items, such as napkin rings and little bowls and cups, are not expensive. *Rosemaling* is an age-old tradition. In the 17th and 18th centuries painters would travel around to the large farms in Norway offering to decorate cupboards, doors and ceilings. The patterns and colours of this craft have remained the same for hundreds of years.

Antiques

Should you be tempted to invest in an antique hand-decorated beer jug or wooden box you must be prepared to spend a lot of money. Visit **Kaare Berntsen AS** in Oslo or make enquiries about local antique shops.

In summer, shops often display their wares outside. Every year Hammerfest *(see p212)* holds a Sommertorg, a day-long open-air market at which souvenirs can be bought, including traditional knitted sweaters, Sami handicrafts, arts and crafts, reindeer hides, and fresh produce such as sausages and salmon. There are lots of good buys during Hammerfestdagene (the Hammerfest Festival) in July.

Glassware

One of Norway's most popular tourist attractions is **Hadeland Glassverk**, a 70-km (43-mile) drive northeast from Oslo. Here children are allowed to blow their own glass under expert supervision. Hadeland Glassverk is a lovely place to spend the day. The glassworks are set in a rural oasis, with a bakery and a café. The selection of glass for sale is enormous and there are many splendid artifacts to admire.

Another glassworks that is worth visiting is **Magnor Glassverk**, where you can also observe how glass is produced. It is situated a couple of hours' drive east from Oslo, very close to the Swedish border.

Gold and Silver

Gold and silver items are good buys. Norway has many talented goldsmiths who produce jewellery in an assortment of classic and modern designs.

All the larger towns have a number of gold and silversmith shops to choose from. In Oslo, **Thune** and **David-Andersen** in Egertorget have the biggest selection. In Bergen there is **Bryggen Gull og Sølv** in Bryggen; in Trondheim, **Møllers Gullsmedforretning** is the recommended place to visit.

Watches and Clocks

According to the statistics from Global Refund Tax-Free Shopping, wristwatches and clocks are the fourth most popular items purchased by tourists. With a refund for the visitor of up to 18.5 per cent of the purchase price, it can pay to buy watches in Norway, including some of the exclusive Swiss makes.

Urmaker Bjerke has a number of shops in Oslo and Bergen.

Sami Design, Arts and Crafts

The best buys of Sami handicrafts can often be found by the roadside in the Finnmark region, where items are sold from private houses, tents or small outlets.

Popular souvenirs include traditional Sami shoes, jewellery and knives, as well as products made of reindeer hide and horn.

In Kautokeino *(see p209)* it is worth visiting Regine Juhl's **Juhls Silver Gallery**, a large jewellery and design workshop which is open to the public. There are outlets in Oslo and Bergen, too.

Clothing and Fashion

Every town teems with clothes and shoe shops. The widest selection will be found in shopping centres and department stores *(see p241)*, but if you explore the back streets you will find everything from designer boutiques to well-stocked fashion houses.

As Norway is a country with six months of winter, there is an emphasis on functionality and warmth. If you are looking for an overcoat there is an enormous choice. The same applies to outdoor shoes, which are stylish and water resistant. Scandinavia's largest shoe shop, **Grændsens Skotøimagazin**, is in Oslo.

Good and reasonably-priced ladies' clothing is widely available, for example at the **Lindex** stores. If you are planning to buy a sensibly-priced suit or blazer, go to one of the **Dressmann** shops. Childrens' clothing is sold in all the shopping centres – look for **Cubus** or **Hennes & Mauritz**.

Sports Equipment

There are no bad sports shops in Norway. The chain stores all stock similar products. There are frequent offers on sports equipment. Ask whether any of the local sports shops are having a sale.

Gresvig and Intersport are the largest sports stores. Equipment for specialist activities can be found in **Villmarkshuset** in Oslo or **Skandinavisk Høyfjells-utstyr**, which has branches in Lillehammer and elsewhere. There is a low-price sports shop in Oslo, **XXL Sport og Villmark**.

Good Norwegian brands include Helly Hansen, Norrøna, Hjelle (knives) and sportswear collections from the Olympic cross-country skiing champions, Vegard Ulvang and Bjørn Dæhlies.

Fish and Shellfish

The best-known fish market is Bryggen in Bergen, which is renowned for its selection of cod, flounder, catfish, salmon and trout. Lobster is at its best in the winter months. Norwegians eat it with white bread and mayonnaise. Crab is highly recommended. A typical Norwegian activity is to sit on the wharfside eating fresh prawns. All these delicacies are expensive – but it is worth treating yourself and sampling them during your stay.

Fresh fish and shellfish are normally on sale in most coastal towns. If there isn't a market or shops at the harbourside, look for a local fishing boat.

It you are staying in Oslo, it is well worth taking a trip to Aker Brygge. Apart from being one of the best shopping areas in the capital, this is where you will find the luxury delicatessen, **Ica Gourmet**.

Directory

Arts and Crafts

Heimen
Rosenkrantzgate 8, Oslo. **Map** 3 D3.
☎ *23 21 42 00.*

Husfliden
Møllergata 4, Oslo. **Map** 3 E3.
☎ *24 14 12 80.*

William Schmidt
Fridtjof Nansens Plass 9, Oslo. **Map** 3 D3.
☎ *22 42 02 88.*

Antiques

Kaare Berntsen AS
Universitetsgaten 12, Oslo. **Map** 3 D2.
☎ *22 20 34 29.*

Glassware

Hadeland Glassverk
Hadeland, County of Oppland.
☎ *61 31 64 00.*

Magnor Glassverk
Magnor, County of Hedmark. ☎ *62 83 35 00.*

Gold and Silver

Thune
Egertorget, Oslo. **Map** 3 B3.
☎ *23 31 01 00.*

David-Andersen
Egertorget, Oslo. **Map** 3 B3.
☎ *24 14 88 00.*

Bryggen Gull og Sølv
Bryggen, Bergen.
☎ *55 31 56 85.*

Møllers Gullsmed-forretning
Munkegatan 3, Trondheim.
☎ *73 52 04 39.*

Watches and Clocks

Urmaker Bjerke
Karl Johans Gate 31, Oslo. **Map** 3 D3.
☎ *23 01 02 10.*

Urmaker Bjerke
Torgallmenningen, Bergen.
☎ *55 23 03 60.*

Sami Design, Arts and Crafts

Juhls Silver Gallery
Roald Amundsens Gate 6, Oslo. **Map** 3 D3.
☎ *22 42 77 99.*
Bryggen 39, Bergen.
☎ *55 32 47 40.*
Kautokeino.
☎ *78 48 61 89.*

Clothing, Shoes

Cubus
Stenersengata 1, Oslo City. **Map** 3 E3.
☎ *22 36 76 60.*
☎ *66 77 32 00.*

Dressmann
Stortorget 3, Oslo. **Map** 3 E3.
☎ *22 33 71 73.*

Grændsens Skotøimagazin
Near Oslo Central Station. **Map** 3 E4. ☎ *22 82 34 00.*

Hennes & Mauritz
Nedre Slottsgate 10 B, Oslo. **Map** 3 [illegible].
☎ *22 17 13 90.*

Lindex
Karl Johans Gate 27, Oslo. **Map** 3 D3.
☎ *22 47 84 00.*

Sports Equipment

XXL Sport og Villmark
Storgaten 2–6, Oslo. **Map** 3 E3.
☎ *24 08 40 25.*

Skandinavisk Høyfjellsutstyr
Storgt. 81, Lillehammer.
☎ *61 26 71 94.*

Villmarkshuset
Chr. Kroghsgate 14–16, Oslo. ☎ *22 05 05 50.*

Fish, Shellfish

Ica Gourmet
Aker Brygge, Oslo. **Map** 2 C4.
☎ *22 01 78 60.*

Entertainment in Norway

Norwegian cultural life and entertainment are characterized by variety and contrast. There is a wide range on offer between the distinctive and often inherently local traditions of the regions and performances by professional artists of international standing. Stand-up comedians and club musicians add to the vibrant night-life of the cities. Activities are also influenced by the seasons. While the larger theatres in the towns close during the summer (the new season begins either at the end of August or in early September), summer revues and historical plays, both indoor and outdoor, are staged throughout the country. Family parks also offer a variety of popular attractions.

Regional folk dancers

Festivals are an important part of cultural life in Norway, ranging from film, jazz and church music to food, theatre, folklore and the changing seasons. The playwright Henrik Ibsen and the composer Edvard Grieg are the focus of the Ibsen Festival at Nationaltheatret in Oslo and the Bergen International Festival respectively.

Sources of Information

There are 260 authorized tourist information offices in Norway. They have details about local activities and entertainment, and their websites *(see p257)* carry a selection of events listed in English. Oslo has a printed version, *What's On In Oslo*, available in hotels and tourist information offices.

Norges Turistråd (the Norwegian Tourist Board) oversees the tourist information service, which is divided into the following regions: Oslo/Oslo Fjord area, Eastern Norway, Southern Norway, Western Norway and the Fjords, Central Norway and Northern Norway.

Hotels and travel agents can also be of help, and most towns have their own local newspaper with up-to-date information about what's on. If you intend to go to a festival, theatre or concert, contact the organizer direct – most prepare their programme many months in advance.

Booking Tickets

The chances of obtaining tickets depend on the size and popularity of the event. It is advisable to book in advance, either through a travel agent, hotel reception or a ticket office.

Professional ticket agents, such as **Billettservice AS** and **Keith Prowse**, charge a commission for their services, but often have pre-reserved ticket quotas for the use of their customers.

In some places it is possible to buy unclaimed tickets on the evening of the performance for anyone who is prepared to chance it and just turn up. This might be worth investigating, even if all the seats are sold out.

Street musicians in Spikersuppa Square in the heart of Oslo

Orchestral rehearsal with the Oslo Philharmonic in Oslo Konserthus

Large Theatres and Cultural Centres

In addition to the permanent and mostly traditional theatres, many of the larger towns and cities in Norway have, over time, established multi-cultural performing arts centres offering a broad spectrum of events. Some, such as Bergen's **Grieghallen**, **Olavshallen** in Trondheim, **Oslo Konserthus** and **Stavanger Konserthus**, are also the permanent homes of the cities' symphony orchestras and offer a varied programme of classical music. **Chateau Neuf** and **Sentrum Scene** are popular entertainment theatres in Oslo, staging musicals, farces, comedies and cabarets.

The larger cultural arts centres host performances by international stars as well as providing a venue for concerts requiring a large arena.

The programme may include a variety of well-known artists. One such event is the annual gala evening at **Oslo Spektrum**, held in connection with the Nobel Peace Prize ceremony in December. Other productions may feature dance, classical music, a musical, a rock concert or entertainment for the family. There are often performances by foreign stars and ensembles.

The beautiful gold and red Rococo auditorium of Oslo's Nationaltheatret

Traditional Theatre

Henrik Ibsen's plays are the most frequently performed in the world after those of William Shakespeare, making Ibsen the leading ambassador for Norwegian theatre. His dramas are staged at regular intervals in theatres throughout the country, so there are often opportunities to experience Ibsen in his original language, particularly at productions in his "own" theatre, **Nationaltheatret**, in Oslo. Ibsen was himself present at the opening of this theatre in 1899. Today, there is a statue of him in front of the main entrance, alongside that of his fellow writer, Bjørnstjerne Bjørnson.

The theatre organizes a special Ibsen festival in four of its auditoriums every other year. Ibsenmuseet (the Ibsen Museum) is a short walk from the Nationaltheatret, and offers a programme of talks presented by literary experts and theatre professionals.

In addition to the biggest theatres in Oslo – Nationaltheatret, **Det Norske Teatret** and **Oslo Nye** – the Bergen theatre, **Den Nationale Scene**, **Rogaland Teater** in Stavanger and **Trøndelag Teater** in Trondheim also offer broad repertoires featuring Ibsen, Shakespeare and Chekhov, as well as musicals, comedy and more recent Norwegian and foreign drama. All the large theatres also have one or more smaller stages in addition to the main auditorium. During the summer there are often outdoor performances in beautiful surroundings.

Alternative theatre attracting the crowds in Porsgrunn

Theatre festivals include the **Porsgrunn Internasjonale Teaterfestival**, which also has a large street theatre element, and **Figurteater Festivalen** i Kristiansand. This Figure Theatre festival is more than puppet theatre and encourages children to use their imagination.

Several towns have their own intimate comedy theatres, where the audience gets a chance to meet the country's best-known entertainers. **Chat Noir** in Oslo is the oldest revue theatre in the Nordic region.

Classical Music, Ballet, Dance and Opera

Even though a national opera and ballet company was not established in Norway until 1958, with the opera star Kirsten Flagstad as its director, interest in this area is growing fast. A large new opera house is scheduled to open in the centre of Oslo in 2008.

Den Norske Opera (the Norwegian Opera) features many of the world's best-known works in its repertoire, and also presents three or four new works every season. The Norwegian Opera has links with orchestras outside Oslo, and performs in Trondheim, Stavanger, Sandnes and Haugesund.

Nasjonalballetten (the National Ballet) is Norway's only classical ballet company. It also performs modern works by choreographers such as Jiri Kilian, George Balanchine and Mats Ek.

Contemporary dance has a permanent home in Bergen at **Danseteatret**, where the company, Carte Blanche, performs interesting new works by both Norwegian and foreign choreographers.

First-class dance, opera and classical music are presented every year during Bergen's quality international festival, **Festspillene**, when a large number of the world's leading ensembles and soloists visit the country.

Chamber music is increasing in popularity in Norway. Oslo and the picturesque town of Risør on the south coast both organize annual festivals with excellent concert programmes.

In Oslo and Bergen, symphony orchestras such as the Oslo-Filharmonien and the Musikkselskabet Harmonien give regular concerts in **Oslo Konserthus** and the **Grieghallen** respectively. Trondheim, Tromsø, Stavanger and Kristiansand also have permanent orchestras and concert halls. It is worth looking out for chamber and lunchtime concerts, as these can take place in special and often unexpected venues.

Concert at sunrise during the Vestfold Festspillene

Rock, Jazz and Country Music

When the world's pop and rock stars visit Norway, they are most likely to perform in the great hall at **Oslo Spektrum**.

In the summer, the **Quart Festival** in Kristiansand is a must for all rock fans. The town is turned virtually upside down to accommodate concerts day and night, both outdoors and indoors.

International stars make appearances at Norway's other big rock festival, **Norwegian Wood**, in early summer in Oslo.

In Oslo and Bergen the club scene has been revitalized in recent years, especially regarding dance and music venues. Check regional newspapers for information about what's on where.

Jazz enthusiasts also have a large number of festivals to look forward to. In May and June, towns in the west of Norway, including Stavanger, Bergen and Ålesund, stage many excellent jazz events almost around the clock.

The international jazz festivals, **Sildajazz** in Haugesund, **Oslo Jazzfestival** and **Molde International Jazz Festival**, are known for their quality and variety. In Molde in July it is possible to see several of the biggest names in jazz at a time when Western Norway's scenery is at its best. It is advisable to book tickets well in advance. Country music lovers should take a trip through the beautiful landscape of Telemark to Seljord in summer and the biggest country music festival in the Nordic region.

Folk Music and Folk Dancing

Telemark is known for keeping alive traditions in Norwegian folk dancing and music. **Telemark Festival** at Bø is an annual festival of folk music where people from all over the country gather to show off their art.

Norsk Folkemuseum *(see pp82–3)* in Bygdøy, Oslo, also has a long tradition of folk dancing and music, and has its own folk dancing group. Both Crown Prince Haakon and Princess Märtha Louise have participated keenly in folk dancing here.

Many other regional museums, such as Bryggen Museum in Bergen, co-operate with folklore groups or district dance groups that give regular performances during the tourist season.

Traditional dancing at Norsk Folkemuseum, Oslo

Festivals

A great number of festivals, both large and small, are held all over Norway. Most of them take place during the summer. The beauty, romance and drama of Norway in winter can be enjoyed in Tromsø during the **Nordlys-festivalen** (the Northern Lights Festival), a celebration of the return of the sun after weeks of darkness. The world's most northerly sun festival takes place in Svalbard. The town of Røros also celebrates a winter festival with concerts.

Haugesund, in the west of the country, is the venue for **Den Norske Filmfestivalen** (the Norwegian Film Festival). For the past 30 years both professionals and the general public have been invited to seminars and screenings of more than 100 new films, both Norwegian and foreign. Before the final big party, which culminates with the presentation of the Amanda Awards, it is sometimes possible to catch a glimpse of some of the more famous festival participants. A sculpture of Marilyn Monroe adorns the quayside.

A great artistic experience is also on offer every spring in Bergen. **Festspillene** in Bergen is Norway's most important international festival, and the programme for the 10 days offers music, drama and exhibitions of the highest quality. There are also daily concerts at Troldhaugen *(see p171)*, former home of the composer Edvard Grieg.

Oslo **Kirkemusikkfestival** (the Oslo Festival of Church Music) draws thousands of people to the capital's churches in March.

Vestfold Festspillene (the Vestfold Festival) is the venue for all kinds of performing arts, which are often presented in surprising contexts and at unusual times of day. The organizers aim to create an informal summer atmosphere. Around 50 concerts offer audiences the chance to listen to flamenco, blues, musicals and a lot more besides.

Culture Holidays

With a bit of planning, excursions to the many well-preserved historical sights can be an exciting alternative to both city breaks and physically demanding outdoor holidays.

A mining safari is one way to explore the cultural landscape. Guided tours are arranged to the old silver mines in Kongsberg *(see p137)* and to the cobalt mines near **Blaafarveværket** in Modum. Blaafarveværket was established in 1773, and produced cobalt blue for the porcelain and glass industries all over the world. Art exhibitions are also arranged here every summer. In **Vassfaret Bjørne-park** (Vassfaret Bear Park), between the valleys of Hallingdal and Valdres, not only can bears be seen at close quarters, but you can also have the chance to learn traditional needlework techniques. **Tromsø Villmarkssenter** (Tromsø Wilderness Centre) offers insights into traditional Arctic transport. As a participant on a husky safari it is possible to learn to drive a team of dogs across the wild terrain; the day finishes with a gourmet Arctic-style meal of reindeer stew served in a Sami tent.

Visitors at Blaafarveværket in Modum

The **Telemark Canal** *(see p142)* stretches for 100 km (60 miles) inland from the sea to the foot of the mountain plateau, Hardangervidda. At Nøstetangen in Øvre Eiker, where Norway's first glass production was started in the early 1740s, glass is still blown.

To experience Norway's coastal culture, there are several maritime museums and lighthouses to visit. Contact the regional tourist offices for suggestions.

Directory

Information

Norges Turistråd
Stortorget 10, Oslo.
☎ 24 14 46 00.

Booking Tickets

Billettservice AS
Rådhusgate 26, Oslo.
☎ 81 53 31 33.

Keith Prowse
Nedre Slottsgate 21, Oslo.
☎ 22 47 84 70.

Large Theatres & Arts Centres

Chateau Neuf
Slemdalsveien 7, Oslo.
☎ 22 96 15 00.

Grieghallen
Edvard Griegs Pl. 1, Bergen.
☎ 55 21 61 00.

Olavshallen
Kjøpmannsgata 44, Trondheim.
☎ 73 99 40 00.

Oslo Konserthus
Munkedamsveien 14, Oslo.
☎ 23 11 31 00.

Oslo Spektrum
Sonja Henies Pl. 2, Oslo.
☎ 22 05 29 00.

Stavanger Konserthus
Bjergsted, Stavanger.
☎ 51 53 70 00.

Sentrum Scene
Arbeidersamfunnets Pl. 1, Oslo. ☎ 22 98 24 00.

Traditional Theatre

Chat Noir
Klingenberggata 5, Oslo.
☎ 22 99 23 00.

Den Nationale Scene
Engen 1, Bergen.
☎ 55 54 97 00.

Det Norske Teatret
Kristian IV Gate 8, Oslo.
☎ 22 42 43 44.

Figurteater Festivalen
Kongens Gate 2A, Kristiansand.
☎ 38 12 28 88.

Nationaltheatret
Johanne Dybwadsplass 1, Oslo. ☎ 81 50 08 11.

Oslo Nye Teater
Rosenkrantzgate 10, Oslo.
☎ 22 34 86 00.

Porsgrunn Teaterfestival
Sverres Gate 21, Porsgrunn.
☎ 35 55 51 69.

Rogaland Teater
Kannikgate 2, Stavanger.
☎ 51 91 90 00.

Trøndelag Teater
Prinsensgate 18–20, Trondheim.
☎ 73 80 51 00.

Music, Ballet, Dance, Opera

Danseteatret
Sigurdsgate 6, Bergen.
☎ 55 30 86 80.

Den Norske Opera/ Nasjonalballetten
Storgata 23, Oslo.
☎ 23 31 50 00.

Musikkselskabet Harmonien
Grieghallen, Bergen.
☎ 55 21 62 67.

Oslo-Filharmonien
Haakon VIIs Gate 2, Oslo.
☎ 22 01 49 00.

Rock, Jazz and Country Music

Molde International Jazz Festival
Sandveien 1, Molde.
☎ 71 20 31 50.

Norwegian Wood Festivalen
Fjellveien 5, Lysaker.
☎ 67 10 34 50.

Oslo Jazzfestival
Tollbugata 28, Oslo.
☎ 22 42 91 20.

Quart Festival
Bygg 29, Odderøya, Kristiansand. ☎ 38 14 69 69.

Seljord Country Music Festival
Seljord, Telemark.
☎ 35 05 51 64.

Sildajazz
Knut Knutsens Gt 4, Haugesund. ☎ 52 73 44 30.

Festivals

Den Norske Filmfestivalen
Knut Knutsens Gt 4, Haugesund. ☎ 52 73 44 30.

Festpillene i Bergen
Grieghallen, Bergen.
☎ 55 21 06 30.

Nordlysfestivalen
Søndre Tollbodgate 8, Tromsø. ☎ 77 68 90 70.

Oslo Kirkemusikk
Tollbugata 28, Oslo.
☎ 22 41 81 13.

Telemark Festival
Gullbringveien 34, Bø.
☎ 35 95 19 19.

Vestfold Festspillene
Fjordgatan 13, Tønsberg.
☎ 33 30 88 50.

Culture Holidays

Blaafarveværket
3340 Åmot.
☎ 32 78 67 00.

Tromsø Villmarkssenter
Kvaløysletta, Tromsø.
☎ 77 69 60 02.

Vassfaret Bjørnepark
3539 Flå. ☎ 32 05 35 10.

Sports and Outdoor Activities

It is said that Norwegians are born with skis on their feet and rucksacks on their backs. They love the fresh air and engage in outdoor activities all year round, probably more so than any other European nation. But then conditions in every region are ideal for participating in the great outdoors, whether on foot or by boat. There are superb national parks and large tracts of untouched terrain. In many places, including the wild high fells, hiking trails and ski tracks are marked out. In the south of Norway, boating enthusiasts will find numerous visitor harbours providing all the necessary amenities. Norway is also well geared for more demanding pursuits such as hang-gliding and white-water canoeing. Although it is a very long country, there is never far to go to the nearest hiking area or boating haven. Even in the largest towns, the outdoor life is always close at hand.

Signs in Jotunheimen

Hiking

Norway is a paradise for those who love to experience nature on foot, in summer and in winter. The expression, *søndagstur* (Sunday walk), prompts Norwegians to fasten their rucksacks and go out into the woods and fields. Usually they will make their way along narrow forest paths and signposted hiking trails. Many also spend their holidays walking from hut to hut at any time of year.

In the most popular high fell areas you never have far to go between the huts, which provide overnight accommodation *(see p219)*. They are linked by a network of marked trails (and in winter, ski tracks). Most of these tourist huts and cabins are owned by **Den Norske Turistforening** (DNT; the Norwegian Mountain Touring Club) and the 50 or so local branches of DNT situated around the country. There are some 400 huts and cabins in total. The huts vary in terms of standard and service, from the best-equipped, which are similar to a hotel, to the more spartan offering only basic facilities.

If you plan to hike from hut to hut it can pay to take out membership of DNT, which costs 400 Nkr. An overnight stay in a one-to-three-bed hut costs 185 Nkr for members (90 Nkr for children) and 240 Nkr for non-members (120 Nkr for children). Breakfast costs 75 Nkr and supper 175 Nkr for members. Lunch is normally a packed lunch and a drink from a Thermos provided by the hut.

The marked trails and ski tracks in the high mountains are generally positioned where the view is the most spectacular yet where the terrain is not overly challenging. Always enquire at the hut you are leaving about the distance to the next hut and how demanding the walk is likely to be.

Trout fishing in Sysendal in Hardangervidda National Park

The snow lasts for a long time on the high mountain plateaus, and the best time to hike is from May to October. In August and September the mountains are bathed in a pageant of colour.

If you are hiking in the fells at other times of year, always remember to obtain up-to-date information on the snow conditions. In the most popular areas, ski tracks are dug as soon as the first snows fall. They are usually accessible for people of average skiing ability.

DNT and most of the large bookshops stock a good selection of maps. Free maps are also available for planning routes and distances.

Trondsbu hut on the Hardangervidda plateau

Mountain hikers on Besseggen in Jotunheimen National Park

Safety

NATURE CAN BE beautiful and benign, but it can be challenging and dangerous if you overlook simple ground rules. It is important to read and follow the mountain guidelines known as *fjellvettsreglene*, which are a good reminder of how to act in variable conditions in the mountains, particularly in winter. The weather can change rapidly from sunshine to storms. The latest weather report is usually posted on the information board in hotels and huts.

Take clothes that will be suitable should the weather change for the worse *(see p259)*. Good maps are essential and remember to take a compass with you as well. Never go alone unless you are an experienced hiker.

Equipment

WHEN OUT WALKING, it is important to have good equipment and an ample supply of food and drinks. At the same time, try to cut down on weight by selecting what is most appropriate, but take account of likely changes in weather conditions. Sturdy shoes, preferably robust boots, are a necessity. Include a change of clothing, ideally woollen, as well as garments that will insulate you against wind and rain. Pack your gear in a plastic bag before placing it in your rucksack so that it will remain dry.

You should take a standard first-aid kit containing such items as plasters and cream for treating blisters and cuts, as well as mosquito repellent. Sunglasses and sun cream will be needed in the fells in summer as well as winter.

Sufficient energy-rich food and, in particular, adequate fluids are important for day trips. Very often you will come across streams along the way where you can fill your bottles. You can supplement your provisions at the tourist huts.

If you are camping, most of the gear, such as tent, cooking utensils and sleeping bag, needs to be purchased as there are no specialist rental companies for camping equipment in Norway.

Rowing on one of the many lakes in Hardangervidda National Park

Touring the National Parks

NORWAY HAS 18 national parks with a combined area of nearly 14,000 sq km (5,404 sq miles), which is about 4 per cent of Norway's mainland. The national parks have been designated as such because they contain unspoilt, unique or especially beautiful scenery, as well as being the natural habitat of flora and fauna. All activities liable to have an effect on the environment are banned. Information can be obtained from DNT branches, tourist information centres and visitor centres in the parks.

Hardangervidda is the largest national park, covering an area of 3,430 sq km (1,324 sq miles) *(see pp152–3)*. A large part of the park consists of a high mountain plateau. It is easily accessible from Eastern Norway as well as from Vestlandet by car, or by bus or train from Oslo or Bergen. The road and train connections between west and east access starting points for hikes of a moderate degree of difficulty.

A more demanding and spectacular national park is the mountain massive of Jotunheimen in central southern Norway *(see pp134–5)*. Jotunheimen has five peaks exceeding 2,300 m (7,546 ft), and has been an attractive tourist destination since the latter half of the 19th century. It is wild and majestic and can be explored using its network of hiking trails and ski tracks.

Skiers in Rondale taking advantage of the Easter holidays

Skiing

There are good reasons why Norwegian skiers have won more gold medals in the Winter Olympics and World Championships than anyone else. In many parts of the country conditions are ideal for both cross-country and downhill (Alpine) skiing. Distances between ski tows and lifts are never far. Even Oslo is only a short distance away from the ski runs.

The main centres for winter sports are in Eastern Norway. The resorts of Beitostølen, Oppdal, Geilo, Hemsedal, Lillehammer and Trysil are hives of activity all winter.

Cross-country skiing, known as *langren*, is Norway's national sport. The mountains here are less craggy than in Central Europe and are most suited to this form of skiing. The prepared ski tracks comprise two lanes. Always remember to keep to the right to avoid on-coming skiers. The tracks are well marked and circumvent steep hills.

Summer snowboarding and skiing at Stryn Summer Ski-Centre

Many places also have illuminated trails for night-time skiing. These are normally 4–5 km (2–3 miles) long and circular. An evening run on a floodlit track is particularly atmospheric. Some skiers use headlamps to ski on unlit tracks.

There are facilities for downhill skiing all over Norway and the runs are graded in terms of difficulty. You can also try to master the Telemark technique – downhill skiing on cross-country skis. The larger ski centres have cross-country, downhill, Telemark and snowboarding equipment for hire. Do not be tempted to ski off-piste in unprepared areas, especially in unfamiliar terrain. It is possible to trigger an avalanche by off-piste skiing.

DNT provides information on cross-country conditions. **Skiforeningen** (Norwegian Ski Association) maintains the 2,600-km (1,616-miles) long network of ski-tracks in Oslo and its environs and provides daily updates on trail conditions on its website.

Mountaineering

With its mountainous terrain, Norway offers climbing for every ability from the less experienced to the serious mountaineer. Although the mountains are not as high as the Alps, they can be equally dramatic. The sharp peaks of Jotunheimen in the south of Norway are particularly appealing to climbers. Further north, popular climbing areas include Lofoten *(see p204)* and Lyngsalpene (Lyngen Alps) in Troms. Romsdalen's precipitous rock faces, which include Trollveggen (the Troll Wall), are among the most challenging.

The season for summer climbing is relatively short. Be prepared for harsh conditions, including snow and wind, at any time in the most exposed areas. Larger towns have training areas for climbers, such as at Kolsås, 15 km (9 miles) west of Oslo.

A number of books are available describing Norway's peaks and climbing routes. **Norges Klatreforbund** (the Norwegian Climbing Federation) has an informative website with details of mountaineering opportunities throughout the country.

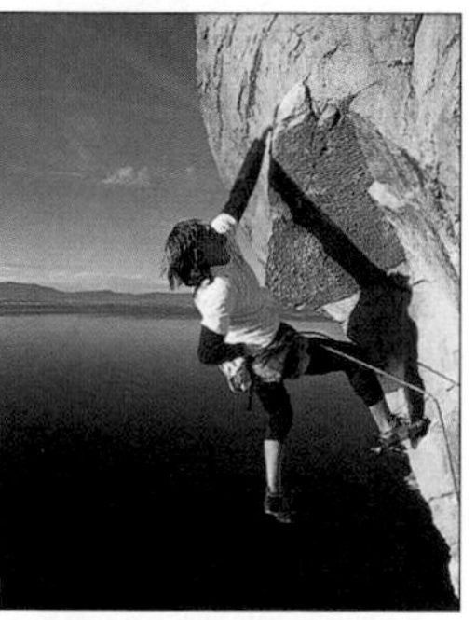

A challenging climb high above a shimmering fjord

Boating, Rafting and White-water Canoeing

Norway has an enormously long coastline interspersed with fjords and islands, making it a boating paradise. Marinas hire out boats, including canoes, kayaks, yachts and motor boats. There are no special requirements to operate smaller craft, although you have to have basic seafaring skills.

The national centre for river sports is located in Heidal in

Gudbrandsdalen. For people without their own vessel (kayak or raft), guided tours can be arranged.

A number of rivers throughout Norway are great for white-water canoeing. **Norges Padleforbund** (the Norwegian Canoe Association) provides information on the best places to go.

Fishing

More than 50 per cent of Norwegians go fishing one or more times a year, a larger proportion than in any other country. But then the country has rich opportunities for both sea and freshwater fishing. The most common types of fish for sports anglers are cod and trout. There are 230 other salt-water species and 40 freshwater species.

Sports fishing is practised with a rod, hand reel and a single line with a hook. Along the coast, good catches can be made by fishing from the shore. If you have access to a boat it is possible to make excellent catches of cod, coley and mackerel. Norway also has a number of outstanding salmon rivers.

Be careful to observe the fishing regulations. Sea angling is free for recreational fishermen. Freshwater fishing is regulated; here, either state or private property rights need to be observed. Always check whether fishing is permitted in a particular watercourse. Rules and regulations vary from place to place. All anglers over 16 years must buy a fishing card, sold in shops, hotels, tourist offices and post offices. The cards are valid for specific areas by the day or for longer periods. Fishing with live bait is forbidden.

Information is available from **Norges Jeger-og Fiskerforbund** (Norwegian Hunting and Fishing Association) or Fylkesmannens Miljøvernavdeling (County Environmental Departments).

Whale Safaris

Every summer male sperm whales leave their families in the southern latitudes and migrate north to the coastal areas off Northern Norway. They visit the coast off the islands of Vesterålen to feed on fish and squid.

Whale-watching cruises operate from Andenes and Tysfjord, weather permitting. A whale safari lasts for six to eight hours.

The tours will almost certainly bring you close to these giants, which can measure up to 20 m (66 ft) long. Sometimes they will lounge on the surface of the water close to the boat while they take in air before descending to the depths of the ocean *(see p201)*. You may be lucky and also spot humpback, minke, fin and killer whales in addition to dolphins.

Seal and seabird safaris are also available.

Hunting

Game hunting takes place all over Norway. It is regarded as having great utilitarian value and hunters value the experience of being with nature. Animals hunted include elk, roe-deer, stags, small game, forest birds and grouse. Regardless of whether you hunt on private land or common land, you will need to pay for the right to hunt.

The hunting season is strictly regulated. Generally it runs from Aug–Dec, but local regulations may permit the hunting of some species until May. Note that a number of species are protected throughout the year.

Directory

Useful Organizations

Den Norske Turistforening DNT
Visitors' address: Storgata 3, Oslo. **Map** 2 E3.
22 82 28 00.
www.turistforeningen.no

Norges Jeger-og Fiskerforbund
66 79 22 00.
www.njff.no

Norges Klatreforbund
21 02 98 30.
www.klatring.no

Norges Padleforbund
21 02 98 35.
www.padling.no

Skiforeningen
22 92 32 00.
www.skiforeningen.no

Whale Safaris

Hvalsafari
Fyrvika, Andenes.
76 11 56 00.

Tysfjord Turistcenter AS
Storfjord, Tysfjord.
75 77 53 70.

Enthusiastic tourists on a whale safari in Tysfjorden, Nordland, spotting a killer whale

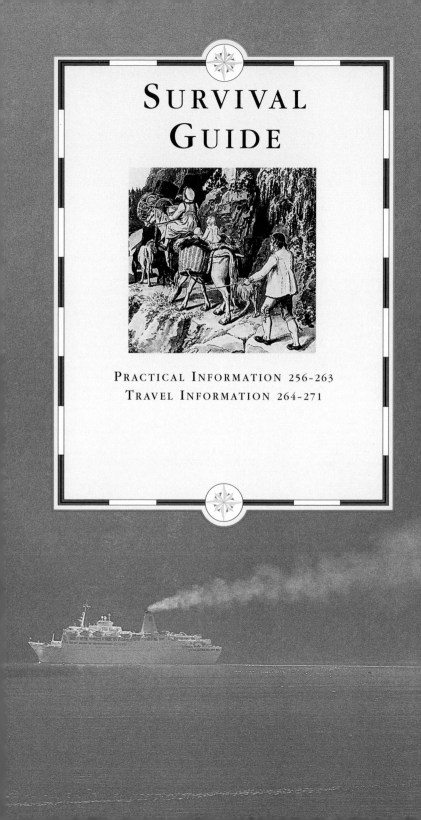

SURVIVAL GUIDE

PRACTICAL INFORMATION 256-263
TRAVEL INFORMATION 264-271

PRACTICAL INFORMATION

NORWAY IS A VAST country. The distance from Oslo to the North Cape is the same as from Oslo to Rome. It is therefore advisable to spend a little time planning your trip.

Tourist office sign

Most reasonably-sized towns in Norway have a tourist information centre. The country can be explored by car, plane, ferry and train. The road system is well developed and train connections extend as far as Bodø, north of the Arctic Circle. The coastline is indented with fjords, but a comprehensive ferry and tunnel network makes it easy to reach the islands and cross the fjords. The towns all have modern facilities for the traveller.

Many of the natural attractions such as national parks, skiing, hiking, fishing and mountaineering areas are situated off the beaten track, so good maps are a necessity.

TOURIST INFORMATION

NORWAY HAS A number of tourist information offices abroad. **Norges Turistråd** (Norwegian Tourist Board) provides practical information on holidays on its website. It also lists the addresses and telephone numbers of the many local tourist offices.

Oslo has two main information centres, **Turistinformasjonen på Vestbanen** and Turistinformasjonen at Oslo Central Station. These offices have a joint website and you can obtain answers here to specific queries by e-mail. Brochures and travel tips may also be requested via e-mail or can be picked up from the tourist offices abroad or from local tourist offices in Norway. Every town has its own tourist office providing information on where to stay, where to eat and sightseeing in the area.

Tourist information office at Vestbanen, Oslo

WHEN TO VISIT

THE BEST TIME to visit Norway is in the summer between May and September. Eastern Norway along with the Oslo area has the most stable weather. Nevertheless, it is advisable to pack some lightweight waterproofs.

If you plan to experience the midnight sun, you will need to travel north of the Arctic Circle. At Bodø the sun is visible at midnight from 20 May–20 July, in Tromsø from 16 May–27 July, at the North Cape from 13 May–29 July. In the rest of the country at this time the nights are very short and light.

Besides having good summers, Norway is a winter wonderland with lots of opportunities for sport and outdoor pursuits. The severity of the winter between November and April varies from region to region. Cold and snow prevail for long periods in the north of the country, in the mountains and in the inland parts of southern Norway. The climate is often milder along the coast.

Norway has the most snow in January and February. This is a popular time to visit the hotels and tourist huts in the mountains, especially when combined with a skiing holiday.

PASSPORTS AND CUSTOMS REGULATIONS

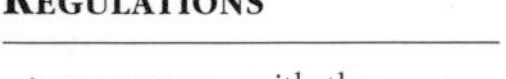

ALL VISITORS, with the exception of those from the Nordic countries, require a valid passport. Citizens of some countries also require a visa. Contact the Norwegian Embassy or consulate in your home country for details.

Norway is one of the few European countries which is free of rabies, and every precaution is taken to maintain this status. You are advised against bringing a pet with you. If you do, it will have to be kept in quarantine for four months before being admitted.

Duty-free allowances on entering the country are 2 litres of beer, 1 litre of spirits, 1 litre wine and 200 cigarettes. The minimum age for bringing spirits into the country is 20; for wine and tobacco the age is 18. You are only permitted to bring medicines for personal use and you should have a letter from your doctor certifying your need for them.

OPENING HOURS AND ADMISSION FEES

IN NORWAY YOU will need to pay an admission fee to visit most museums and art galleries. There is usually a discount for families, students, adolescents, pensioners and groups. Children are often admitted free of charge. In Oslo admission is free to Nasjonalgalleriet *(see pp52–3)* and to Frognerparken with Gustav Vigeland's sculpture

◁ **Cruise ship approaching the stunning Geirangerfjorden**

garden *(see pp90–91)*. The opening hours of museums vary; they usually open sometime between 9 and 11am and close between 4 and 7pm. From September to May the opening hours can be shorter. Most attractions open daily; some close on Monday.

Norway's protestant churches are normally closed outside services. Churches of special importance, such as cathedrals and stave churches, have longer hours to accommodate visitors, especially during the summer.

If you are planning to visit a number of sights in the capital, it is worth buying an *Oslo Kortet* (Oslo Card) which, for a fixed price, gives admission to most museums and galleries and unlimited travel on public transport (except night buses and trams). Cardholders are also entitled to discounts on other attractions. Available at tourist offices, most hotels, and Narvesen newsagents *(see p263)*, the card can be bought as a single or family card, for one or more days. A variation on the Oslo Card is the Oslo Package, which includes hotels. Towns such as Bergen and Trondheim have similar arrangements.

The Bergen Card

Disabled Travellers

It has become increasingly common for hotels to cater to the needs of disabled guests with improved access and specially adapted rooms.

NSB, the Norwegian State Railways, has special carriages to meet the needs of those with impaired mobility. The new Coastal Express ships are equipped to accommodate disabled passengers. **Norges Handikapforbund** (the Norwegian Association for the Disabled) can supply details.

Etiquette

Norwegians are easy-going and informal. Following an initial introduction, people are generally on first-name terms, and this applies to men and women. When meeting someone for the first time it is customary to shake hands.

However, there are two special rules of etiquette. After a meal it is the practice to thank the host/hostess by saying *"takk"*.

In a slightly more formal context, at the beginning of the meal the host will propose a toast, *"skål"*. It is polite not to touch your drink before this toast is made.

After having spent a pleasant day or evening together with good friends, it is customary to ring the hosts a day or two later to thank them *("takk for sist")*.

Driving, Alcohol and Tobacco

In Norway it is illegal to drive a car if your blood alcohol level is more than 0.2 per mil. For most people this is equivalent to less than a glass of wine. This rule virtually equates to a complete ban on drinking and driving.

Norway also has relatively strict laws regarding the use of tobacco in communal rooms. In restaurants and bars smokers are directed to separate screened-off areas. Smoking is prohibited in all public buildings.

The sale of all alcoholic drinks is subject to special restrictions. Beer with an alcoholic content on a par with pilsner (lager) can be purchased in grocery shops and supermarkets. Wines and spirits, however, are only sold in the specially designated, state-owned Vinmonopolet *(see p229)*.

The state-owned Vinmonopolet selling wines and spirits

Directory

Tourist Information in Norway

Norges Turistråd
Stortorvet 10, Postboks 722 Sentrum, 0105 Oslo.
Map 3 E3.
☎ *24 14 46 00.*
FAX *24 14 46 01.*
W www.visitnorway.com
@ norway@ntr.no

Oslo Turistinformasjon Vestbanen
Brynjulf Bulls Plass 1, 0250 Oslo.
Map 2 C3.
☎ *23 11 78 80.*
FAX *22 83 81 50.*
W www.oslopro.no
@ touristinfo@oslopro.no

Lillehammer Turistinformasjon
Elvegata 19, 2609 Lillehammer.
☎ *61 25 92 99.*
FAX *61 25 65 85.*
W www.lillehammerturist.no

Kristiansand Turistinformasjon
Vestre Strandgate 32, 4612 Kristiansand.
☎ *38 12 13 14.*
FAX *38 02 52 55.*
W www.sorlandet.com

Bergen Turistinformasjon
Vågsallmenningen 1, 5014 Bergen.
☎ *55 55 20 00.*
FAX *55 55 20 01.*
W www.visitbergen.com

Trondheim Turistinformasjon
Munkegata 1, 7013 Trondheim.
☎ *73 80 76 60.*
FAX *73 80 76 70.*
W www.visit-trondheim.com

Tromsø Turistinformasjon
Storgata 61/63, 9053 Tromsø.
☎ *77 61 00 00.*
FAX *77 61 00 10.*
W www.destinasjontromso.no

Disabled Travellers

Norges Handikapforbund
(information for disabled people)
Schweigaards Gate 12, 0185 Oslo.
Map 3 F3. ☎ *24 10 24 00.*
FAX *24 10 24 99.*
W www.nhf.no

Personal Security and Health

Police insignia

NORWAY IS A SAFE tourist destination, even in the cities and towns, with one of the lowest crime rates in Europe. But just as anywhere else, it is always sensible to take basic safety precautions. In all built-up areas there are places which are more exposed to crime than others and Oslo is no exception. According to statistics, however, the few violent episodes that do occur usually involve the criminal fraternity and rarely affect tourists. Nevertheless, it is always advisable to lock your car and avoid leaving valuables visible to passers-by, regardless of where you are in the country.

Policeman Policewoman

Police car

Personal Security

PICKPOCKETING CAN be a problem in Oslo. The capital is visited periodically by well-organized international gangs. They operate in crowded places, particularly in busy shops and airport terminals. Do not carry your wallet in your back pocket. Valuables should be kept close to your body so they are difficult to steal. In restaurants and cafés be careful not to hang your handbag over the back of a chair. Put it on the floor beside your chair and place a foot on the strap, or keep it on your lap.

Always keep your passport and tickets separate from your wallet, and keep your credit card and PIN number separate from each other.

Most hotels have safes that you can use to avoid carrying large amounts of money around. Even though theft from hotel rooms is unusual, avoid placing valuables where they are visible.

In Norway it is now common practice to withdraw money from cashpoint machines. Should you encounter technical problems when making a withdrawal, be on your guard for anyone standing behind you in the queue offering to "help" you. You should politely decline and look for another cashpoint or go into a bank.

Police and Sheriffs

NORWAY IS DIVIDED into 27 police districts each with its own police chief *(politimester)*. Some police districts have a number of smaller sheriff offices *(lensmannskontorer)*, which also have police jurisdiction. The Directorate of Police is the body responsible for police administration.

Norwegian police are generally unarmed. They are helpful and polite. Feel free to ask police officers on patrol for directions or advice. Remember that it is strictly against the law to drive when you have been drinking. Even a relatively moderate amount of alcohol in the blood can result in an unconditional prison sentence and a hefty fine. It can be expensive to infringe traffic regulations, especially speed limits.

Standard sign displayed outside Norwegian police stations

Lost Property

INFORM THE police immediately if anything of value is lost or stolen. In order to make a claim with your insurance company you will need a document from the police to confirm that the item has been stolen.

It is possible that missing items will be found and handed in at a public lost property office. Bus stations, airport terminals and train stations usually have their own lost property offices.

If you lose your passport you are advised to contact your nearest embassy or consulate immediately.

Medical Treatment

THE NORWEGIAN health service is well developed across the whole spectrum, from private doctors to large public hospitals. In towns there are both public and private out-of-hours clinics for emergencies known as *legevakt*. Waiting times for private rather than public medical treatment are generally shorter, but private is more expensive. Emergency medical treatment is free in Norway for EU and EEA citizens. Treatment only covers urgent help, with the exception of renal dialysis and refilling visitors' own oxygen cylinders.

You are strongly advised to obtain form E111 from your local social security office or post office before you travel as treatment of citizens from EU and EEA countries is conditional on their being entitled to social security benefits at home. Citizens of non-EU and non-EEA countries must meet the cost of medical treatment themselves if they do not have travel insurance.

PHARMACIES

IN NORWAY only pharmacies are permitted to sell medicines. Some remedies can be bought without a prescription, but most require a doctor's written instruction. If you are dependent on a prescription-only drug it is advisable to bring enough supplies to cover your entire stay. However, you are entitled to visit a doctor's surgery and request any medicines if necessary.

Pharmacy sign

Pharmacies have similar opening hours to other shops. Larger cities have a 24-hour opening rota system – all pharmacies display a list.

Mountain rescue patrol equipped with stretchers and sleighs

FORCES OF NATURE

NORWAY IS A VAST country with wide variations in geographical and climatic conditions. Both at sea and in the mountains the wind and weather can change rapidly, and there is good reason to respect the forces of nature.

Unfortunately drowning accidents claim many lives. Those affected include tourists who have ventured out to sea in unseaworthy vessels or in bad weather. It is advisable to consult local people with a knowledge of the area and conditions before setting forth into unknown waters.

The mountains are renowned for sudden bad turns in the weather. Sunny, still conditions can change in just a few hours to heavy mist, snow or howling wind. Again, follow the ground rules and take advice from people familiar with the terrain and weather before setting off. Staff at your accommodation will be able to recommend signposted paths and how long it should take from one point to the next.

In summer mosquitoes are a problem in some areas and you will need to cover up. Mosquito sticks and sprays are available from pharmacies and grocery stores.

Although bears and wolves roam freely in certain areas, there is no need to be alarmed. They are timid and avoid contact with people. There have been no serious confrontations between humans and these animals in recent times.

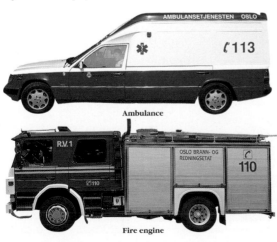

Ambulance

Fire engine

DIRECTORY

EMERGENCY NUMBERS

Fire *110.*

Police *112.*

Ambulance *113.*

EMBASSIES

Australia
Jernbanetorget 2, Oslo.
Map 3 E3. 22 47 91 70.

Canada
Wergelandsveien 7, Oslo.
Map 2 C2. 22 99 53 00.

Ireland
Haakon VIIs Gate 1, Oslo.
Map 2 C3. 22 20 43 70.

United Kingdom
Thomas Heftyes Gate 8, Oslo.
Map 2 A2. 23 13 27 00.

USA
Drammensveien 18, Oslo.
Map 2 C3. 22 44 85 50.

Banking and Local Currency

Travellers to Norway may bring in and take out unlimited amounts of cash. However, Norges Bank must be notified of amounts exceeding 25,000 Nkr. The use of credit cards is widespread. It is easy to use your credit card to obtain local currency, although travellers' cheques are a safer option. There are exchange bureaux at all the international airports. Many hotels will also change money, but for the best exchange rates and the lowest commission charges go to a bank. Note that Norway is not a member of the EU.

A minibank, one of the commercial banks' automated teller machines

Banks and Foreign Exchange Bureaux

The majority of banks have foreign exchange bureaux and there is little variation in the exchange rates they offer. Most banks also have ATMs, known as Minibanks, which accept major bank and credit cards, such as MasterCard, Bank Accept and Visa, to withdraw Norwegian currency. These cash machines usually have multilingual instructions. The amount of commission charged for withdrawals depends on the type of card you have. Normally, you can withdraw up to 9,900 Nkr over four days with a maximum of seven withdrawals. Alternatively, you can withdraw cash at the counter using Visa. These withdrawals can take time because the bank must first obtain authorisation.

There are exchange bureaux on arrival at most airports, at the busiest border crossings and at the *flytog* terminal (for the express train between Oslo's Gardermoen airport and the city centre).

Banking Hours

Banks in Norway stay open from 9am to 3.30pm, although in summer they close a bit earlier, at 3pm.

All banks are closed on Saturday and Sunday, but some have extended opening hours on Thursday, usually to around 5 or 6pm.

On days before a public holiday, such as New Year's Day, most banks close earlier than the usual time of 3.30pm.

The head office of Den Norske Bank at Aker Brygge in Oslo

Foreign exchange bureau at Oslo Central Station

Credit Cards

The use of credit cards is widespread in Norway. They are accepted in hotels, restaurants, service stations and most shops. MasterCard and Visa are the most widely used cards. Some places do

Directory

Banks

Den Norske Bank (DnB)
Kongens Gate 18, 0021 Oslo.
Map 3 E3. ☎ *22 48 10 50.*

Gjensidige NOR Sparebank
Kirkegata 18, 0153 Oslo.
Map 3 E3. ☎ *22 31 90 50.*

Nordea
Stortorvet 7, 0155 Oslo.
Map 3 E3. ☎ *22 48 50 00.*

Postbanken
Post offices in most urban areas.

Foreign Exchange Bureaux

Nordea Oslo Lufthavn
Gardermoen Flyplass.
☎ *63 94 88 00.*

Nordea Flytogterminalen
Sentralbanestasjonen, Oslo.
☎ *22 48 50 00.*

American Express
Fridtjof Nansens Plass 6, Oslo.
Map 3 D3. ☎ *22 98 37 35.*

Lost Credit Cards

American Express
☎ *22 96 08 00.*

Diners Club
☎ *23 00 10 00.*

MasterCard
☎ *80 01 26 97.*

Visa
☎ *80 01 28 02.*

not accept American Express because of the high transaction fees charged to retailers.

It is possible to withdraw cash on a credit card in most banks. It is also possible to get cash back when making purchases in most shops.

Travellers' Cheques

Travellers' cheques can be purchased from your local bank at home. They are accepted almost everywhere. Remember to sign your travellers' cheques. If you do not they can be misused if they are lost or stolen, and you will be liable for the loss.

Travellers' cheques are steadily losing ground to credit cards. In terms of security, however, travellers' cheques are generally more secure than cards.

Telegraphic Transfers

Norwegian banks are helpful when it comes to receiving money transferred telegraphically from abroad. But this type of transaction can be slow and costly. The sender's bank abroad forwards money to its banking partner in Norway, which transfers it to a bank for the receiver to collect. Quicker transfers can be made via MoneyGram to American Express in Oslo.

Currency

Norway's currency is the Norwegian *krone* (kr, Nkr or NOK). One *krone* equals 100 *øre*. The smallest coin is 50 *øre*, the largest is 20 *kroner*. Notes are issued in denominations from 50 Nkr to 1,000 Nkr.

Using the 1,000 Nkr note should not be a problem, but it is most practical to carry notes no larger than 500 Nkr.

In view of the fact that Norway is not a member of the European Monetary Union, the Euro is not legal tender, except in certain places such as at airports and tax-free shops. However, it is up to individual retailers how they stand with regard to the Euro. Time will tell if it becomes accepted in an increasing number of outlets.

50 kr

Bank Notes
Norwegian notes are issued in five denominations – 1,000, 500, 200, 100 and 50 kroner. *They each carry a portrait of a well-known cultural figure.*

100 Nkr

200 Nkr

500 Nkr

1000 Nkr

Coins
Norwegian coins are issued in denominations of 20, 10, 5 and 1 kroner, *and in 50* øre. *On the front is a traditional Norwegian design. The new 1 Nkr and 5 Nkr coins have a hole in the centre.*

50 *øre*

1 Nkr

5 Nkr

10 Nkr

20 Nkr

Communications

Post Office logo

Telecommunications services in Norway are generally of a high standard. Norwegians are among the world's largest users of mobile telephone services; out of a population of 4.5 million, there are 3.5 million mobile phone users. The use of the Internet is also common and households as well as companies regularly access the Internet and send e-mails. The leading telecommunications company is the former state-owned enterprise, Telenor. It offers a wide range of specialist services. Payphones accept cash, Norwegian phone cards and most credit cards.

Public Telephones

There are two types of payphones in Norway, both operated by Telenor. The red telephone boxes found in most large towns accept phone cards *(telekort)*, a range of credit cards and Norwegian coins. Phone cards can be purchased in the Narvesen kiosks located throughout the country. The green telephone kiosks only accept phone cards and credit cards, not cash.

It is possible to be called back by the person you are talking to. Ask the person to ring the number given in the telephone box.

Telephone kiosk

Mobile Telephones

The demand for public telephones has decreased considerably in the wake of the mobile phone, the use of which is particularly widespread in Norway. Generally, visitors from Europe can use their mobile phones in Norway. If you have pre-paid cards, contact your local dealer for information on operating in Norway. Mobile telephones from the USA and Japan cannot usually be used in Norway.

It is worth noting that it is the receiver of a telephone call who pays most of the cost when calls are received from abroad. The person phoning pays only the local rate; the difference in the cost is paid by the receiver.

The GSM network covers 97 per cent of the population and 70 per cent of the country. NMT is a system used in Norway, Sweden and Finland. The system is also known as "the wilderness network" *(villmarkstelefonen)*, as its coverage is wider than that of GSM. But it is advisable not to rely on GSM and NMT to provide a comprehensive nationwide service.

Mobile telephones are useful to have when travelling in wilderness areas, but remember that the coverage is not total, and you should not rely on a mobile phone as a guarantee that you will always be able to call for help.

Fax, Telegram and E-mail

The majority of places offering overnight accommodation will be helpful when it comes to sending faxes, telegrams and e-mails.

Large hotels often have some rooms with ISDN or broadband connections enabling you to plug in your laptop. Request these services – and ask the price – before

Using a Card-Only Telephone

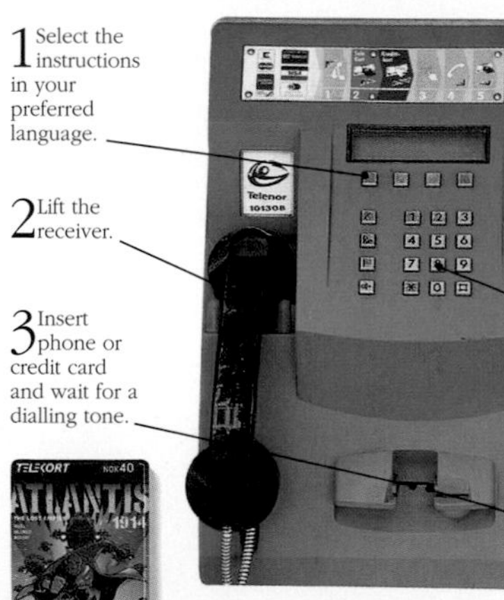

1 Select the instructions in your preferred language.

2 Lift the receiver.

3 Insert phone or credit card and wait for a dialling tone.

4 Dial the number and wait to be connected. If you require assistance or information about charges, ring 80 08 20 65.

5 Remove the card. You will hear a signal if you forget to remove the card.

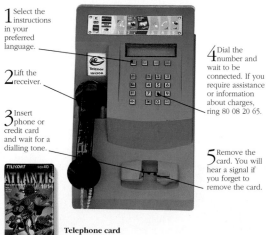

Telephone card worth 40 Nkr

Making a Telephone Call

- Norwegian telephone numbers have 8 digits; there are no area codes.
- To phone abroad from Norway dial 00, then the country code, area code (minus the initial 0), then the number.
- The country code for Norway is 47.
- International operator assistance: 115.
- Domestic directory enquiries: 1881; international directory enquiries: 1882.
- For a wake-up call, dial **55, the time (4 digits) #.
- Telenor customer services: 05000.

Norwegian postage stamps (5.50 Nkr, 7 Nkr and 10 Nkr)

checking into your room. If you are travelling without your own computer and need access to the Internet, an increasing number of hotels have terminals for the use of guests.

Public libraries and Internet cafés also have facilities for Internet access.

Sending Letters

There are post offices in all towns and nearly all villages. In addition, some shops have postal services.

Post offices are usually open from 9am–5pm on weekdays and 10am–1pm on Saturday. Opening hours for postal services in shops are the same as the retailers' opening hours and vary from shop to shop.

You can buy stamps at post offices, in shops, kiosks and bookstores. The cost to send a normal letter or postcard weighing less than 20 g to a European country is 9 Nkr. Heavier letters, up to 50 g, cost 13.50 Nkr. Postage to the rest of the world is 10 Nkr and 20 Nkr respectively. To send a letter within Norway costs 5.50 Nkr or 8.50 Nkr. The cost to other Nordic countries is 7 Nkr and 11 Nkr.

Red boxes for national and international post, yellow for local mail

There are postboxes everywhere. They are red and occasionally yellow. When a red postbox is on its own, letters to all addresses can be posted in it. When a red and yellow postbox stand next to each other, the red box is for national and international letters; the yellow box is for local mail and you need to check that the postal code on your letter corresponds to that on the box. Collection times are given on the postboxes.

Norwegian postal codes have four digits and the code precedes the place name. In addresses, the street number comes after the street name.

It is possible to receive mail via Poste Restante. Addresses should contain the name of the addressee, and the name and postal code of the post office where the letter will be collected. Courier services are provided by a number of international companies.

TV and Radio

Almost all hotel rooms in Norway are equipped with colour TV, and can receive both Norwegian and international programmes. The Norwegian channels are NRK1, which is state owned and non-commercial, and NRK2, an auxiliary channel to NRK1. TV2 is Norway's leading commercial television channel. TV2 transmits weather forecasts periodically in the morning. The other Norwegian commercial channels are TV3 and TV Norge. All channels show foreign films and series in their original language (mostly English).

Hotels often have international channels such as Eurosport, MTV and CNN. The larger hotels also offer pay-TV with a choice of films. Many hotels have their own channel broadcasting information for guests.

The most popular radio stations are P1 and P2, which broadcast news and weather on the hour. There are a number of other Norwegian stations which broadcast music, classical and modern, 24-hours a day.

Newspapers

Norway has an impressive number of newspapers for its population and size. Most towns have one or more local or regional newspapers while the three national ones are *Aftenposten*, *Verdens Gang* and *Dagbladet*. Two newspapers have English versions on the Internet: www.aftenposten.no/english and www.norwaypost.no. International newspapers are available from **Narvesen** kiosks in larger towns.

Directory

Main Post Offices

Posten Norge BA
Dronningens Gate 15. **Map** 3 E4.
23 14 90 00.

Bergen Postkontor
Småstrandgaten 3, Bergen.
55 54 15 00.

Courier Companies

DHL
81 00 13 45.

Federal Express
63 94 03 00.

TNT
81 00 08 10.

Internet Cafes

Studenten
Karl Johans Gate 45, Oslo.
Map 3 D3. *22 42 56 80.*

Accezzo Internettcafé
Galleriet, Torgallmenningen 8, Bergen. *55 31 11 60.*

Foreign Newspapers

Narvesen
Stortingsgata 24–26, 0161 Oslo.
Map 3 D3. *22 42 95 64.*

Bystasjonen (bus station), 5015 Bergen.
55 32 59 06.

Trondheim Central Station, 7491 Trondheim.
73 88 30 30.

Travel Information

The majority of visitors coming to Norway by plane arrive at Oslo's Gardermoen airport. Torp in Vestfold and some of the larger towns and cities in western Norway, such as Bergen, Stavanger and Trondheim, also have international airports. There are good car ferry connections to southern Norway and Bergen from Great Britain, Denmark and northern Germany. Many visitors also travel to Norway by bus, car, train and cruise ship. It is worth noting that you are entitled to shop duty-free when travelling to and from Norway, as it is not a member of the European Union *(see p240)*. Despite the many natural obstacles such as fjords and mountain chains, travelling around Norway is easy thanks to the many car ferries, tunnels and bridges, and a good road network. Train and bus links are also well developed.

Scandinavian Airlines (SAS) aeroplane

Interior of the new terminal at Oslo's Gardermoen airport

Arriving by Air

Many European cities and some in the USA have flight connections to Norway. Gardermoen, the country's main international airport, has excellent road and train connections into Oslo. The journey by bus takes 45 minutes. Flytoget, the express shuttle train to the city centre, departs every 45 minutes, and takes 21 minutes. Taxis are expensive and take longer than Flytoget.

SAS (Scandinavian Airlines) is the leading airline in the region, with flights to and from Great Britain and other European countries. The services are either direct or routed via Copenhagen. SAS also has daily flights from the USA and the Far East. **Braathens** is a subsidiary of SAS, with flights from London Gatwick, Newcastle and Aberdeen to Oslo, Bergen, Stavanger and Trondheim. **Widerøe**, with its Dash 8 planes, operates from Aberdeen and Newcastle to Stavanger with connections to a large number of smaller destinations throughout Norway. **Coast Air** operates a service between Aberdeen and Haugesund.

International airlines with flights to Oslo include **British Airways**, **bmi british midland**, Lufthansa, Finnair and Icelandair. The low-cost airline, **Ryanair**, operates between London Stansted and Torp near Sandefjord, about 130 km (81 miles) south of Oslo. Ryanair offers discounted tickets for the two-hour bus journey to Oslo.

Timetables are subject to constant change so it is advisable to contact the airline or a travel agent for up-to-date information.

Flytoget, the fastest connection between Oslo and Gardermoen airport

Flight Prices

Ticket prices to and from Norway vary greatly. In addition to the cut-price deals offered by most airlines, there are large price variations for children, students, families and for booking well in advance.

SAS logo

A rule of thumb is that the nearer the date of departure a booking is made the more difficult it becomes to obtain a discount. Booking just prior to departure often means that only full-price tickets are available.

APEX tickets, which need to be booked well in advance, are reasonably priced, but be aware that they cannot be changed or refunded.

There is stiff competition between the airlines and it can often pay to look into what offers are available; check airline websites for special deals. Charter flights can sometimes be more favourable than individual flights.

Ask your local travel agent about the various package deals to Norway.

Car ferry docking in Kristiansand harbour in southern Norway

Arriving by Ferry

Norway's coastline is the longest in Europe and ferries have always been an important means of travel to and around Norway.

DFDS Seaways operates between Newcastle and Kristiansand, as well as to Gothenburg (Sweden), and from Harwich to Esbjerg (Denmark). It also has a service between Copenhagen and Oslo. **Fjord Line** operates between Newcastle and Stavanger, Haugesund and Bergen.

From Denmark, **Stena Line** sails between Frederikshavn and Oslo; **Color Line** runs services between Hirtshals and Oslo, Hirtshals and Kristiansand, Frederikshavn and Larvik and Kiel (Germany) and Oslo. There are crossings from Hanstsholm to Bergen, and Strømstad to Sandefjord.

All crossings are by means of large and comfortable car ferries with various categories of cabins. They usually have a good selection of restaurants and tax-free shops.

Arriving by Train and Coach

Oslo is served by good daily train connections from Copenhagen and Stockholm. Trains from Copenhagen follow the route along Sweden's west coast.

From London, **Eurolines** operates a coach service to Copenhagen from where **NOR-Way Bussekspress** runs to Oslo. Nor-Way Bus Express also operates from Gothenburg and Stockholm to Oslo. In Northern Norway there are bus connections between Skellefteå in Sweden and Bodø, and Umeå in Sweden and Mo I Rana; and from Rovaniemi in Finland to Tromsø, Tana Bru, Lakselv, Karasjok and Kautokeino.

Main entrance, Oslo Central Station

Arriving by Car

Norway borders three countries and has a large number of border crossings from Svinesund in the south to Grense Jakobselv on the border with Russia in the far north.

All crossings are open to private vehicles. Most travellers by car enter from Sweden via the busiest border crossing at Svinesund.

It is not advisable to drive into Norway from Sweden on a Saturday or Sunday afternoon when traffic is often at its busiest with long queues on both sides of the border crossing. This is because Norwegians regularly travel to Sweden to shop, as the price of many items is lower across the border.

There are customs posts at the border, but if you have nothing to declare you can simply drive through. There are occasions when you may be waved over for a customs check. You should note that this can also happen a considerable distance from the border crossing.

Directory

Airlines

bmi british midland
T *0870 607 0555 (UK).*
W www.flybmi.com

Braathens
T *0191 214 0991 (UK).*
W www.braathens.no

British Airways
T *0845 773 3377 (UK).*
W www.britishairways.com

Coast Air
T *020 8283 9745 (UK).*
W www.coastair.no

Ryanair
T *08701 569569 (UK).*
T *0818 303030 (Eire).*
W www.ryanair.com

SAS
T *0845 607 2772 (UK).*
T *800 221 2350 (US).*
W www.scandinavian.net

Widerøe
T *0047 81 00 12 00 (Nor).*
T *0845 607 2772 (UK).*
W www.wideroe.no

Ferry Companies

Color Line
T *0047 81 00 08 11 (Nor).*
W www.colorline.no

DFDS Seaways
T *0870 533 3000 (UK).*
W www.dfdsseaways.co.uk

Fjord Line
T *0191 296 1313 (UK).*
W www.fjordline.co.uk

Stena Line
T *0870 570 7070 (UK).*

Train and Coach Companies

Eurolines
T *0870 514 3219 (UK).*
W www.eurolines.co.uk

NOR-Way Bussekspress
T *0047 815 44 444 (Nor).*
W www.nor-way.no

Rail Europe
T *0870 584 8848 (UK).*
W www.raileurope.co.uk

Travelling by Air, Train, Bus and Boat

DISTANCES ARE SO GREAT IN NORWAY that nearly all travel between the north and south of the country takes place by plane. There are comprehensive air services between the major towns with connections to outlying districts. To get the most out of your visit to Norway, it is often a good idea to combine flying with the train and ferry. In Northern Norway in particular, combining air travel with the Hurtigruten ferries *(see p205)* offers the chance to visit the more remote communities that lie outside the airline network. Bus travel is another option.

Widerøe flight calling at Svolvær in the Lofoten Islands

Domestic Flights

NEARLY ALL the provincial towns have airports with daily domestic flight connections. There is also a good network of smaller airports so you are rarely far from an air strip. Travelling times are relatively short unless you are flying between the north and the south. The flights from Oslo to Bergen, Oslo to Stavanger and Oslo to Trondheim take 50 to 60 minutes. The Oslo-Tromsø route takes about one and a half hours. The longest flight is from Oslo to Kirkenes in the far north, a journey that takes 3 hours 20 minutes, including a stop-over.

SAS is the leading airline and has taken over **Braathens** and **Widerøe**. However, all three operate as independent companies. Also there are several small companies with limited scheduled flights.

SAS serves 14 domestic airports and Braathens operates to nearly as many. Widerøe, the third airline company, has 35 mostly smaller destinations. Between them, the three airlines maintain a comprehensive network of flights. Airline tickets can be purchased at travel agents or directly from the airlines. Domestic travel in Norway is not cheap, but if you are flexible with respect to flight times, it is possible to get good discounts. Widerøe's Explore Norway Ticket offers unlimited air travel for 14 days.

Up-to-date flight times and information about delays is continually posted on NRK's *tekst-TV, page 600*. SAS also offers a text messaging service for checking arrival and departure times. Be aware that the timetables vary between summer and winter.

Travelling by Train

FROM HALDEN IN the south to Bodø in the north there is an excellent train network. Services to the west of the country, such as to Stavanger and Bergen, are also good.

The trains in Norway are operated by Norwegian State Railways, **NSB** (Norges Statsbaner). Both the trains and the railway stations are of a generally high standard. Compartments are always clean and comfortable. There are special facilities for the disabled. Skis and bicycles can be carried as luggage, but on long-distance trains you need to make a reservation for your bike as well as for yourself. Luggage can also be sent in advance. The NSB website has detailed information.

Norwegian trains are divided into three categories. Local trains in the Oslo area, Bergen, Stavanger and Trondheim serve the immediate vicinity. Agenda and InterCity trains operate on medium-distance routes between towns in Eastern Norway. Long-distance trains include NSB Signatur, Ekspress (express train) and Nattog (night train). For long-distance trains it is necessary to book tickets in advance, with a seat reservation. On regional trains, no seat reservation is required, and unless you wish to book in advance, you can buy your ticket at the station or on board the train (many smaller stations are unmanned).

The most spectacular train journey is that on the steeply

Flåmsbanen, one of Norway's most dramatic stretches of railway line

M/S *Telemarken* at Akkerhaugen wharf on the Telemark Canal

winding Flåmsbanen *(see p176)*. This can be taken as part of the "Norway in a Nutshell" tour, a round trip from Bergen via train and bus, which also includes a fjord cruise. To book, contact Bergen tourist information *(see p257)*.

Travelling by Bus

Most towns and regions have their own local bus companies, with frequent services in urban areas and less frequent services in rural districts. Oslo airport is served by *flybusser* (airport shuttles) from the towns around the capital.

NOR-Way Bussekspress operates the largest network of buses in the country with domestic and international routes. The company offers a seat guarantee scheme. This makes it unnecessary to reserve tickets in advance. If the bus is full, another bus will be put into service.

Buses offer a range of discounts, such as for children and pensioners, and for return journeys. There are frequent departures; between Oslo and Bergen there are three buses per day in each direction. Coffee and tea are served on board. On night buses the seats can be reclined. Blankets and pillows are available on some services.

Many of the bus companies arrange round trips in Norway and abroad. Ask your travel agent for information.

Boarding a fleet of sightseeing buses in Eidfjord

Travelling by Ferry

Car ferries and express boats link the islands and fjords along Norway's coast. Not only do they provide a vital means of communication for these areas, but they are also a splendid way of seeing the country.

The famous coastal express, **Hurtigruten**, offers daily cruises between Bergen and Kirkenes in both a northerly and southerly direction *(see p205)*. The boats make 34 stops along the way. The return journey takes 11 days and the route is planned so that the stretches which are covered during the day in one direction are passed at night on the return trip. The ships vary in terms of age and size, but all are of a high standard.

Some of the counties along the coast have their own ferry companies with car ferries *(see p269)* and express boats, providing the opportunity to experience the spectacular scenery of the fjords. On the majority of these, you pay once aboard the ferry. It is often possible to take a day trip, for instance on Sognefjorden, from Bergen to Flåm, or between Svolvær in the Lofoten Islands and Narvik. Tickets for the Telemark Canal, from Skien to Dalen and Akkerhaugen *(see p142)*, can be purchased through **Telemarkreiser**.

Directory

Domestic Airline Reservations

Braathens
☎ *815 20 000.*
W www.braathens.no

SAS
☎ *815 20 400.*
W www.sas.no

Widerøe
☎ *810 01 200.*
W www.wideroe.no

Train Operator

NSB
☎ *815 00 888.*
W www.nsb.no

Ferry Travel

Hurtigruten (NNDS)
☎ *810 30 000 (Nor).*
☎ *020 8846 2666 (UK).*
W www.hurtigruten.com
W www.norwegiancoastalvoyage.com

Telemarkreiser
☎ *35 90 00 30.*
W www.telemarkreiser.no

Bus Travel

NOR-Way Bussekspress
☎ *815 44 444.*
W www.nor-way.no/nbeweb

Travelling by Car

"Scenic road" sign

NORWAY HAS AN EXTENSIVE road network. Most of the roads are of a high standard. The majority are tarred, but gravel roads may be found in more remote areas. A large number of highways are toll roads. With some planning it is possible to avoid the tolls in most cases. The journey may take a little longer, but almost certainly there will be more to see along the way especially if there is a sign for "Turistveg", indicating a scenic route. Below are details on how to pay the motorway tolls and information regarding the rules and regulations for driving and parking, as well as how to cope with road conditions in winter.

Traffic Regulations

TRAFFIC IS well-regulated, and Norwegian motorists are law-abiding, possibly because there are stiff fines for breaking the rules.

Be particularly aware of the speed limits. Driving 20 km/h (12 mph) over the speed limit may cost you 1,500–3,000 Nkr. If you exceed the speed limit by any more you risk having your licence confiscated on the spot, in addition to a hefty fine. Most main roads have cameras to catch speeding motorists.

The speed limit on highways is normally 80 km/h (50 mph). On motorways it is between 80 and 90 km/h (50–56 mph) and on certain stretches 100 km/h (60 mph).

You should also be aware of the strict regulations for drink-driving. The maximum legal blood alcohol concentration is 0.2 per mil, which means that you virtually cannot drink any alcohol before driving. Concentrations of 0.2–0.5 per mil will result in a very large fine. Driving with a blood alcohol level in excess of 0.5 per mil warrants an unconditional custodial sentence of a minimum of 21 days, confiscation of driving licence and a big fine.

The use of seatbelts is compulsory, and applies to back-seat passengers, too. Young children are required to sit in special child seats.

Dipped headlights have to be used at all times.

It is advisable to ensure your car is in good order before arriving as there are spot checks, albeit infrequently.

Be aware of the many roundabouts. Drivers entering the junction must always give way.

Traffic lights must always be observed. Under no circumstances should you be tempted to drive through a red light even if the road is clear.

One of Norway's spectacular bridges connecting islands and skerries

Automatic toll road station with sign displaying fees

Road Tolls

SEVERAL OF THE larger conurbations are surrounded by toll stations and you are required to pay to enter the town. Make sure you have some Norwegian coins to hand.

Most toll stations are automatic and you simply throw the coins into a special receptacle. There are manned booths, too, for which you also need Norwegian money. Tolls vary between 20 Nkr and 30 Nkr per entry.

Tolls are also payable on a number of main roads and at some tunnels and bridges. A toll is levied in both directions. Most toll stations have both manual and automatic collection.

Certain private roads also charge tolls, particularly over mountain passes or in areas with holiday cabins. This is, however, more the exception than the rule.

Private road tolls are paid by putting a coin in an envelope marked with the registration number of the car, then placing the envelope in a special box. Envelopes are available at the barrier. There are controls to check that the fee for passing the barrier has been paid. The cost of the toll varies from 10 Nkr to 100 Nkr.

Parking

IN MOST TOWNS and urban areas there are parking meters or multi-storey car parks. In Oslo, if you exceed the allocated time on your meter, you will be fined 500 Nkr – the parking wardens are known for their efficiency. In car parks you pay on departure, so there is no risk of exceeding the time limit. Parking charges vary considerably; in the capital parking can cost 20–30 Nkr per hour.

Road Standards

Norwegian roads are divided into so-called Europe roads *(europaveier)*, national roads *(riksveier)* and smaller roads. The standard of the *europaveier* is often very high, especially in southern Norway. The *riksveier* are also good. Smaller roads vary in quality. In western Norway there are numerous tight bends, so adjust your speed.

Hiring a Car

There are a number of local Norwegian car hire companies, as well as the international chains, **Avis**, **Budget** and **Hertz**. Car hire firms can be found at the main airports and in the towns. Bookings can be made either through the international network of the big companies, or directly.

The minimum age for hiring a car is 20. For the hire of more exclusive cars and for paying by credit card the minimum age is 25. The hire conditions are more or less the same as in other countries.

Prices, however, may vary significantly compared to other countries. The cost of car hire will often be higher in Norway, but there are a variety of special offers which are worth enquiring about.

Car Ferries

The Norwegian coastline is broken up by numerous fjords penetrating deep inland. In places car ferries are an indispensable means of transport. There is an extensive network of ferries, with frequent sailing times.

Usually tickets are bought either just before boarding, or from a ticket collector on board. During the summer months, however, it is best to book in advance for larger ferries to popular destinations, such as Lofoten. Reservations can be made by calling the ferry company OVDS. The cost of ferry tickets is heavily subsidised, and therefore low. Most car ferries have cafeterias serving simple food.

Petrol Stations

As a rule, it is never far from one petrol station to another in Norway. Many towns have manned 24-hour petrol stations and most have automatic credit card payment facilities. If you are driving at night, however, start out with at least half a tank of petrol.

Even though Norway is an oil producing nation, neither petrol nor diesel is cheap.

NAF (Norges Automobilforbund), **Falken** and **Viking** are the main vehicle recovery organisations. Members of the AA and RAC are able to obtain help from NAF in case of a breakdown or accident.

Petrol station run by Norway's state-owned oil company

Road Signs

International road signs prevail in Norway. There are a few exceptions: a white M on a blue background denotes a passing place.

Don't be tempted to take an elk warning sign home as a souvenir. Elks are common in Norway and the signs serve an important purpose, indicating the risk of an elk crossing the road just ahead of you. You should adjust your speed accordingly. Collisions between elks and cars can result in serious damage and have even been known to cause death.

Beware, elk on the road

Winter Driving and Safety

Driving conditions during the winter vary considerably from one part of the country to another. In Oslo and the coastal areas of eastern Norway and Vestlandet the roads are normally free of ice and snow all year round. However, they may be slippery, and special winter tyres or studded tyres are strongly recommended for use between November and April. In the mountains and in the north of the country there is a risk of snow and ice for five or six months of the year. Appropriate tyres and sometimes a set of chains may be necessary.

The most exposed roads are fitted with barriers. In case of difficult or impossible driving conditions, these roads are closed. Some mountain passes are shut for most of the winter season. Road closures are usually signed up well ahead.

On those mountain passes which are normally kept open throughout the winter, snowfalls may make driving difficult. At such times, a snowplough will drive through at set intervals with cars following in convoy.

It is always advisable to check on conditions before setting out. Take warm clothes and extra food with you when driving in the mountains during the winter.

Directory

Car Hire

Avis
☎ *81 53 30 44.*
W www.avis.no

Budget
☎ *80 03 02 10.*
W www.budget.no

Hertz
☎ *67 16 80 00.*
W www.hertz.no

Vehicle Recovery

Falken ☎ *02222.*
NAF ☎ *810 00 505.*
Viking ☎ *800 32 900.*

Car Ferries

OVDS ☎ *769 67 600.*

Getting Around Oslo

It is easy being a tourist in Oslo. Most places of interest are centrally situated, and the various museums, attractions and restaurants are close at hand. The best way to experience Oslo is on foot or by bicycle. From the principal thoroughfare, Karl Johans Gate, it is only a few minutes' walk or cycle ride to the main sights. The capital also has an extensive public transport network that branches out from the city centre. Frequent services mean that even the outskirts of the city are easily accessible. It is advisable to avoid using private cars during the morning and afternoon rush-hour when the roads can become very congested.

Pedestrian crossing on Oslo's Karl Johans Gate

Walking in Oslo

There is no better way to enjoy Oslo than on foot. This way you can experience the city from close quarters. Traffic is not a hindrance to pedestrians and in the centre there are several pedestrianized streets.

Note that you are not allowed to cross the road if the light is red, even if there are no cars nearby. In some places you need to press a button to get a green light. When the "green man" appears, you can cross. When crossing at a pedestrian crossing without traffic lights, cars must give way to pedestrians, but do take care.

The streets in Oslo are generally well signposted, and with the Oslo Street Finder *(see pp98–101)* it is easy to find your way around.

Karl Johans Gate *(see p50)* is Norway's street for parades and an attraction in itself. It leads from the Central Station past the Parliament building and the National Theatre to the royal palace. The area around it is pedestrianized.

A 10-minute walk from here brings you to the harbour and the commercial centre of Aker Brygge. The harbour teems with life, with small boats and ferries coming and going. The best view of Akershus Festning, the historic fortress facing Oslofjorden, is from the harbour. Walk up to Akershus for an even more splendid view of the fjord.

Driving in Oslo

If you are used to driving in cities then driving in Oslo should not pose a problem. The traffic density in the capital is no greater than any other city. As in many other urban areas, however, there is an extensive one-way system in the centre, which might be difficult to negotiate unless you have a map on which it is marked.

Rush-hour traffic causing long queues on the approach into Oslo

As long as you avoid the rush hour (7am–10am and 3pm–6pm) getting around Oslo is straightforward. The speed limit in the centre varies between 30 and 50 km/h (18–31 mph). Near schools and on some residential roads the limit is 30 km/h (19 mph).

Be aware of speed bumps. On smaller roads they are very close together, and if taken at speed the shock can be fierce enough to damage the car.

Tunnels make it easy to drive through the city. The largest tunnels are Rådhus-tunnel (along the fjord under Rådhuset) and Vålereng-tunnelen (from the east going in a northerly direction).

Oslo has numerous large multi-storey car parks, including those at Østbanen, Grønland, Ibsen and Aker Brygge. If you park on a controlled parking bay in the city centre between 8am and 5pm you will need to obtain a ticket from a pay-and-display machine. At other times and on Sunday parking is free. Parking becomes increasingly expensive the nearer the city centre you are. Do not forget to pay during the specified parking times. The fine for failing to pay is high. Private parking places and multi-storey car parks charge at all times.

Always lock your car and keep valuables out of sight, preferably by locking them in the boot.

Taxi Services

Getting a taxi in Oslo is easy, except at the height of the rush hour. Taxis have a sign on the roof. When the light is on, the taxi is for hire. Official taxis can be hailed on the street or at special taxi ranks. They can also be booked in advance, up to 20 minutes before the required time. Most taxis can take four passengers, but it is also possible to request a larger vehicle for more people.

Oslo has a number of cab companies – **Oslo Taxi**, the yellow taxis driven by **NorgesTaxi**, and **Taxi 2**.

A market has also grown for so-called pirate taxis in the city, where private people offer to drive for an agreed price. However, they are not to be recommended.

Yellow taxi operated by NorgesTaxi

Public Transport

Oslo has an efficient public transport system with trams, buses, trains and the Tunnelbane (metro), also known as T-bane, with frequent services between the city centre and the outskirts. There are also routes connecting outlying areas without crossing the city centre. Tunnelbane lines radiate from the city centre *(see map, inside back cover)*. Call **Trafikanten** for information on routes, timetables and connections.

Sign for a bicycle route

Tickets can be purchased from machines and from staffed Tunnelbane stations, or on buses and trams. If there is no conductor then you must stamp your ticket in the automatic machine. Penalties are high for travelling without a valid ticket.

A single ticket is valid for an hour after it has been stamped, on all forms of public transport within the city. It also allows an unlimited number of changes during this time slot.

You can also buy a ticket that is valid for several trips, a 24-hour ticket, known as a *dagskort*, or a weekly card which gives you unlimited travel for seven days.

The Oslo Card *(see p257)* entitles the holder to free public transport (except on night buses and trams).

Ferry connecting Bygdøy with Oslo city centre

Ferry Services

A boat service operated by **Nesoddbåtene** runs between Aker Brygge and the peninsula, Nesoddtangen, on the east of Oslofjorden, every hour. In rush-hour the service is more frequent.

From the end of April to early October you can take the **Bygdøyfergene** (Bygdøy Ferry) for a scenic trip across the water to the museums on Bygdøynes *(see pp78–9)*, or to Dronningen Pier for a walk to the outdoor museum, Norsk Folkemuseum.

Cycling

It is easy, enjoyable and practical to cycle around Oslo, especially if you choose routes that pass through parks and quiet streets. Norwegian drivers are not particularly well-disciplined with regard to cyclists, so you will need to be cautious and not assume that drivers will stop automatically for you.

You may walk with your bike on the pavement and you may cycle on the pavement if conditions require and you are not causing a nuisance to pedestrians.

Bicycles can be rented by the day at **Vestbaneplassen Sykkelutleie**.

Sightseeing Tours

An alternative to touring the city on your own is to take a guided tour. A typical itinerary for a three-hour guided tour by coach arranged by **Båtservice Sightseeing** or **HMK**, for example, would include the centre of Oslo, Vigelandparken, the Holmenkollen Ski Jump and Museum and the museums in Bygdøy. Tailor-made tours with a personal guide can be arranged by companies such as **Oslo Guideservice** or **Oslo Guidebureau**. They offer traditional itineraries as well as walking, cycling and themed excursions.

There are also cruises on Oslofjorden between May and September. **Båtservice Sightseeing** operates a 50-minute mini-cruise of the harbour every hour, and a 2-hour sightseeing trip around inner Oslofjorden departing every 3–4 hours. The boats depart from Bryggen in front of Rådhuset (City Hall) *(see pp56–7)*.

Directory

Public Transport Information

Trafikanten
177.
www.trafikanten.no

Taxi Services

NorgesTaxi
08000.

Oslo Taxi
02323.

Taxi 2
02202.

Ferry Services

Bygdøyfergene
23 35 68 90.

Nesoddbåtene
22 42 68 01.

Sightseeing Tours

Båtservice Sightseeing
23 35 68 90.

HMK
23 15 73 00.

Oslo Guideservice
22 42 70 20.

Oslo Guidebureau
22 42 28 18.

Bicycle Hire

Vestbaneplassen Sykkelutleie
22 83 52 08.

Index

The Norwegian letters **Æ**, **Ø** and **Å** (also spelt **AA**) come at the end of the alphabet, after Z. This index follows Norwegian alphabetical order.

Page numbers in **bold** type refer to main entries

A

Aall, Hans 82
Accezzo Internettcafé 263
Admission fees 256–7
Adventure parks see Amusement parks
Agatunet 162, 163
Agundson, Tarjei 150
Air travel **264**, 265
  domestic flights **266**
Aker Brygge (Oslo) 44, 47, **57**, 59
Aker Brygge shopping centre (Oslo) 241
Akershus Slott (Croning) 69
Akershus Slott (Oslo) 45, 63, **68–9**
  Street-by-Street map 65
Akkerhaugen
  Telemark Canal tour 142
Akvariet (Bergen) **166**
Alcohol
  driving regulations 257, 258, 268
  shopping 16, 229, 241, 257
  What to Drink 229
Alfred the Great, King of England 33
Alsten 200
Alta 197, **208–9**
Alvdal 125
Ambulances 259
American Embassy 259
American Express 260
Amundsen, Roald 23, 40
  Frammuseet (Oslo) 79, 81
  skiing 26
  Tromsø 210
  Vadsø 213
Amusement parks
  Bø Sommarland **151**
  Hunderfossen Adventure Park (Lillehammer) **131**
  Tusenfryd **114**
Andenes 203, 204
Andrée, Salomon 210, 215
Andøya 198, 202, 204
Animals, customs regulations 256
Anker, Bernt 92
Anker, Peder 97
Anker, Synnøve 190
Antiques shops **244**, 245
Aquariums
  Akvariet (Bergen) **166**
  Polaria (Tromsø) 210
Archer, Colin 81, 119, 158
Arctic Circle 13
  Hurtigruten 205
  map 198–9
  midnight sun **213**, 256
  Polarsirkelsentret 201
  Tromsø 210
  wildlife 21
  see also Northern Norway and Svalbard
Arctic Ocean 197, 214
Arendal **144**
  hotels 224
  restaurants 237
Armfeldt, General 192
Arneberg, Arnstein 56, 84, 86
Arnesen, Liv 26
Artists **22**
Arts and crafts shops **244**, 245
Arøyelva, river 176
Asbjørnsen & Moe 143
Astrup, Hans Rasmus 72
Astrup, Nikolai 22, 178
Astrup Fearnley Museet (Oslo) **72**
Atlantic coast, wildlife 20
Atlantic Road 181
Aukrust, Kjell 125
Aulestad **126–7**
Aurland 175, **176**
Aurlandsdalen 175
Aurlandsvangen 176
Aurora borealis
  see Northern Lights
Aust-Agder, *bunad* 24
Austbøgrenda 150
Australian Embassy 259
Austrått 187
Autumn in Norway 30
Avaldsnes 161
Avis (car rental) 269

B

Bachke, Victoria and Christian Anker 192
Backer, Harriet 22, 167
Bacon, Francis 72
Badeparken (Drøbak) 107
Bakklandet (Trondheim) **192**
Balestrand 174, **176**
  hotels 225
Balke, Peder
  Stetind in the Fog 53
Ballet **247**, 249
Ballstad 204
Bank notes 261
Banking **260–61**
Barents, Willem 214
Barents Sea 14
Barentsøya 214
Baroniet Rosendal **162**
The Battle in the Marketplace 38
Beaches
  Hukodden (Oslo) **86**
Beer 231, 257
Beitostølen 136
Berg, Gunnar 204
Bergen 14, 155, 156, **164–71**
  festivals 28, 31
  hotels 225
  Hurtigruten 205
  map 165
  restaurants 237–8
  weather 30
Bergen Blues and Roots Festival 28
Bergen Kunstmuseum **167**
Bergen Museum: De Kulturhistoriske Samlinger **169**
Bergen Museum: De Naturhistoriske Samlinger **168–9**
Bergen Postkontor 263
Bergen Turistinformasjon 257
Bergens Kunstforening **168**
Bergens Sjøfartsmuseum **169**
Bergens Tekniske Museum **171**
Bergslien, Brynjulf 48
Bergslien, K.
  The Birkebeiner rescue of young Prince Håkon 26
Bernadotte, Jean Baptiste
  see Karl Johan, King
Besseggen 135
Best Western 218, 219
Bicycles, in Oslo 271
Billettservice AS 246, 249
Birds **20–21**
  Lofoten Islands 204
  Runde 180
  Vikna 195
  see also Wildlife
Birkebeiner race 27, 28
The Birkebeiner rescue of young Prince Håkon (Bergslien) 26
Bjelke, Jørgen 187
Bjelke, Ove 187
Bjerkebæk (Lillehammer) **130**
Bjoreia river 152, 163
Bjørlo, Per Inge
  Inner Room V 70
Bjørnfjellveien 208
Bjørnson, Bjørnstjerne 16, 22, 40, 121
  Aulestad **126–7**
  Bjørnstjerne Bjørnson Festival (Molde) 29
  Christiania Theatre 67
  Den Nationale Scene (Bergen) 167
  Nationaltheatret (Oslo) 51
  statue of 49

Bjørnson, Karoline 126
Blaafarveværket 249
Black Death 36
Blakstad, G 201
Blindleia 144
Blumenthal, Mathias 167
bmi British Midland 264, 265
Boats
  Bergens Sjøfartsmuseum (Bergen) **169**
  boating **252–3**
  Christian Radich (Oslo) 64
  ferries 19, **265**, **267**, 269, 271
  Hurtigruten 205, 267
  Kon-Tiki Museum (Oslo) 79, 80
  Norges Fiskerimuseum (Bergen) **164**
  Norsk Sjøfartsmuseum (Oslo) 79, 81
  Sjøfartsmuseet (Stavanger) **158**
  Viking ships 34
  Vikingskipshuset (Oslo) 44, 77, 78, **84–5**
Bodø 197, **201**
  hotels 227
  restaurants 239
Bogstad Herregård **97**
Boknafjorden 155
Bonnard, Pierre 115
Borgund Stavkirke 155, **177**, 175
Borre National Park **115**
Botanisk Hage and Museum (Oslo) **94**
Braathens 264, 265, 266, 267
Brekkstø 144
The Bridal Procession in Hardanger (Tidemand and Gude) 10, 22
British Airways 264, 265
Brun, Johan Nordahl 170
Brundtland, Gro Harlem 15, 23, 41
Bryggen (Bergen) 155, 164, **165**
Bryggen (Trondheim) **191**
Bryggen Gull og Sølv (Bergen) 245
Bryggens Museum (Bergen) **164**
Bud 181
Budget (car hire) 269
Buekorpsmuseet (Bergen) **166**
Buffet lunches 228
Bukkøya 161
Bull, Georg A 57
Bull, Henrik
  Historisk Museum (Oslo) 54
  Nationaltheatret (Oslo) 49, 51
Bull, Jacob B 125
Bull, Ole 16, 22, 59
  Lysøen (Bergen) **171**
  Den Nationale Scene (Bergen) 167
  Vestlandske Kunstindustrimuseum (Bergen) 167
Bull, Schak 171
Bunad (national dress) 15, **24–5**
Buses **267**
  in Oslo 271
Buskerud 121
Bygdøy (Oslo) 44, **77–87**
  area map 77
  Bygdøynes: Street-by-Street map 78–9
  Norsk Folkemuseum (Oslo) **82–3**
  restaurants 234
  Vikingskipshuset (Oslo) **84–5**
Bygdøy Kongsgård (Oslo) **86–7**
Bygdøyfergene 271
Bygdøynes (Oslo)
  Street-by-Street map 78–9
Bø Sommarland **151**
Børgefjell 183
Børsen (Oslo) 72–3
Bøverdalen 134
Båtservice Sightseeing 271

C

Canadian Embassy 259
Canal, Telemark 139, 141, 142
Canoeing **252–3**
Canute, King of Denmark 194
Carlsen, Bjørn 72
Cars **268–9**
  alcohol regulations 257, 258, 268
  arriving by car **265**
  driving in Oslo 270
  ferries 19, 269
  hiring 269
  Norsk Kjøretøyhistorisk Museum (Lillehammer) **130**
  parking 268–9
  petrol stations 269
  road standards 269
  road tolls 268
  traffic regulations 268
  winter driving and safety 269
  see also Tours by car
Cash machines 240, 258, **260**
Cathedrals
  Domkirken (Kristiansand) **146**
  Domkirken (Stavanger) **159**
  Ishavskatedralen (Tromsø) **210–11**
Cathedrals (cont.)
  Nidarosdomen (Trondheim) 14, 183, 184, **193**
Central Oslo East **63–75**
  Akershus Slott **68–9**
  area map 63
  hotels 221
  Kvadraturen: Street-by-Street map 64–5
  Museet for Samtidskunst **70–71**
  restaurants 233–4
Central Oslo West **47–59**
  area map 47
  Historisk Museum **54–5**
  hotels 220–21
  Karl Johans Gate: Street-by-Street map 48–9
  Nasjongalleriet **52–3**
  Rådhuset **56–7**
  restaurants 232–3
Centralteateret (Oslo) 74
Chancellor, Richard 197, 212
Chat Noir (Oslo) 249
Chateau Neuf (Oslo) 249
Children
  Det Internasjonale Barnekunstmuseet (Oslo) **95**
  in restaurants 229
Choice Hotels Scandinavia 218, 219
Christian III, King 36
Christian IV, King **36**, 37
  Akershus Slott (Oslo) 69
  Kongsberg 137
  Korskirken (Bergen) 166
  Kristiansand 146
  Oslo 64, 66
Christian IV's Glove (Gulbransen) 64, 67
Christian V, King 113
Christian Frederik, King 38, 86
Christian Radich (Oslo)
  Street-by-Street map 64
Christianholm Festning (Kristiansand) **146**
Christiania *see* Oslo
Christiania Theatre (Oslo) 67
Christiania Torv (Oslo) **67**
  Street-by-Street map 64
Christie, W F K 168
Christmas 31
  Christmas markets 31
  Drøbak **114**
Churches
  opening hours 257
  Borgund Stavkirke 155, **177**, 175
  Domkirken (Bergen) **166**
  Fantoft Stavkirke (Bergen) **170**
  Heddal Stavkirke 139, 151
  Korskirken (Bergen) **166**
  Mariakirken (Bergen) **164**

Churches (cont.)
Oslo Domkirke (Oslo) **73**
Ringebu Stavkirke 123, **127**
Urnes Stavkirke 175, **178**
Uvdal Stavkirke 137
Vår Frue Kirke (Trondheim) **191**
Cicignon, Johan Caspar de 190, 192
Cinema 29
City Hall (Oslo) *see* Rådhuset
The Clan (Vigeland) 91
Climate 14, **30**, 256
safety 259
Clock shops **244**, 245
Clothes
bunad (national dress) 14, **24–5**
hiking 251
in restaurants 229
shops **245**
traditional Sami costumes 25
Coach travel **265**
Coast Air 264, 265
Coins 261
Collet, Fredrik 130
Color Line 265
Communications **262–3**
Composers **22–3**
Consumer rights 241
Coubertin, Pierre de 130
Country music **248**, 249
Courier companies 263
Crafts 244
Sami 243, **244–5**
Credit cards **260–61**
in hotels 219
in shops 240
Crime 258
Croning, Jacob
Akershus Slott 69
Cubus (Oslo) 245
Cultural centres **246–7**, 249
Cultural Festival in Northern Norway 29
Culture holidays **249**
Currency **261**
Curtis, Sylvia Bull 171
Customs
border posts 265
regulations 256
Cycling, in Oslo 271

D

Dahl, J C 22, 53
Bergen Kunstmuseum 167
From Stalheim 49
Scene from Bergen's Inner Harbour 167
Dalen
hotels 224
Telemark Canal tour 142
Dance **247**, 249
folk dancing **248**
Danseteatret (Bergen) 249
Dass, Petter 200, 202
David-Andersen (Oslo) 245
Day of Dance 28
Day of Music (Oslo) 29
Department stores 241
DFDS Seaways 265
DHL 263
Dialling codes 262
Digerronden 130
Diners Club 260
Disabled travellers 257
Discounts, admission fees 256, 257
DNT huts 219
Doctors 258–9
Domkirken (Bergen) **166**
Domkirken (Kristiansand) **146**
Domkirken (Stavanger) **159**
Donali, Sivert 195
Douglas, Kirk 150
Dovrefjell **132–3**, 183
Drammen **137**
hotels 223
restaurants 235
Drawbridge (Fredrikstad)
Street-by-Street map 113
Dreier, J F L 167
Dressmann (Oslo) 245
Drinks 229, 231
Driving *see* Cars
Dronningen (Oslo) **80**
Street-by-Street map 79
Dronningparken (Oslo)
Street-by-Street map 48
Drowning accidents 259
Drøbak 107, **114**
Drøbaksundet 115
Dukketeateret (Oslo) 74
Duty-free allowances 256
Duun, Olav 195
Dybwad, Johanne 55
Døhlen, Anne Sofie 86
Dønna 200

E

E-mail 262–3
Easter 28
Eastern Norway **121–37**
hotels 223–4
Jotunheimen **134–5**
Lillehammer **130–31**
map 122–3
restaurants 236
Edgeøya 214
EFTA 41
Egersund 155, **160**
Eggum 197
Egner, Thorbjørn 22
Eide 160
Eidfjord **163**
Ekofisk oil field 14
Elverum **124**
festivals 29
Elveseter **133**
hotels 223
Emanuel Vigeland Museum (Oslo) **96**
Embassies 259
Emergencies 259
Eng, Turid 58
Engebret Café (Oslo)
Street-by-Street map 65
Engelbrektsson, Archbishop Olav 36, 187
Entertainment **246–9**
Equipment, hiking 251
Erik of Pomerania 36
Erik the Red 33, 35
Erkebispegården (Trondheim) **190**
Estève 115
Ervik 179
Etiquette 257
Etnografisk Museum (Oslo) 54
Eufemia, Queen 86
Eurolines 265
European Union (EU) 17, 41, 240
Euros 261
Explorers **23**
Expressionism 52, 93
Extreme Sports Week (Voss) 29
Eystein, King 133

F

Fagernes **136**
Falkeberget, Johann 186
Falken 269
Falstad Fangeleir 187
Family hostels 219
Famous Norwegians **22–3**
Fantoft Stavkirke (Bergen) **170**
Fartein Valen Days (Haugesund) 30
Fast food 229
Fax services 262
Fearnley, Thomas 72
Federal Express 263
Femunden, Lake 125
Femundsmarka National Park 125
Ferries
arriving in Norway **265**
coastal ferries 19, **267**, 269
Hurtigruten (NNDS) **205**, 267
in Oslo 271
Festival of Northern Lights (Tromsø) 31
Festivals **28–31**, **248**, 249
bunad (national dress) **24–5**
Festspillene i Bergen (Bergen) 249

Figurteater Festivalen (Kristiansand) 249
Film festivals 29
Finnmark 15, 197
Finnmarksvidda 14
Fire services 259
First Hotels 218, 219
Fishing 14, **253**
Akvariet (Bergen) **166**
Hardangervidda 152
Jotunheimen 135
Laksestudiet (Suldal) 160
Lofoten Islands 204
Namsos 195
Norges Fiskerimuseum (Bergen) **164**
Norsk Villakssenter (Lærdal) 175, 176
shopping **245**
Fiskevollen 125
Fiskumfossen 195
Fjell, Kai
Nationaltheatret (Oslo) 51
Regjeringskvartalet (Oslo) 75
Stenersenmuseet (Oslo) 58
Fjord Line 265
Fjordane 155
Fjords 13, **18–19**
Vestlandet 155
wildlife 21
Fjæreheia Grimstad 29
Flagstad, Kirsten 23, 75, 247
Flakstad, Nils 74
Flakstadsøya **204**
Flekkefjord **145**
Flintoe, Johannes 51
Fløyen (Bergen) **170**
Fløyfjellet 156
Flåmsbanen 175, **176**
Folgefonna 162
Folk music and dancing 16, **248**
Folldal 132
Food and drink
What to Eat in Norway 230–31
see also Restaurants
Football 17
Foreign exchange bureaux 260
Forests, wildlife 20
Forsvarmuseet (Oslo) **72**
Fotlandsfossen 160
Fougner, Gunnar 93
Fountain (Vigeland) 91
Frammuseet (Oslo) **81**
Street-by-Street map 79
Frederik II, King 112, 113
Frederik III, King 36–7
Frederik IV, King 37
Frederik VI, King 37, 50
Fredrikstad
hotels 223
restaurants 235
Street-by-Street map 112–13
Freud, Lucian 72
Friis, Peder Claussøn 202
Frognerseteren **97**
From Stalheim (Dahl) 49
Fron 127
Frosta 187
Førde **178**

G

Gaarder, Jostein 16, 22
Gade, Niels 171
Galdhøpiggen 133, 134
Galleries *see* Museums and galleries
Game hunting **253**
Gamle Bergen (Bergen) **170**
Gamle Hellesund 144
Den Gamle Logen (Oslo) **67**
Gamle Stavanger (Stavanger) **158**
Gamlebyen (Oslo) 83, **92–3**
Street-by-Street map 78
Gamlehaugen (Bergen) **170**
Garbarek, Jan 23
Garborg, Arne 22
Gardens *see* Parks and gardens
Gaustadtoppen 139, 151
Geilo **136**
hotels 223
Geirangerfjorden 155, **179**
Geologisk Museum (Oslo) **94**
Gerhardsen, Einar 41, 75
Gimle Gård (Kristiansand) **146**
Gingerbread houses (Bergen) 31
Gjende, Jo 133
Gjende, Lake 135
Gjensidige NOR Sparebank 260
Gjøa 79, 81
Glaciers
fjords 18, 19
Folgefonna 162
Hardangerjøkulen 153
Jostedalsbreen **178**
Norsk Bremuseum (Jostedalsbreen) 178
Saltfjellet-Svartisen National Park 201
Glassware shops **244**, 245
Gloger, Gottfried Heinrich 137
Glomma river 110, 112, 121, 125
Gold and silver, shopping **244**, 245
Golden Route 179
Grauer, Johan 97
Greater Oslo **89–97**
area map 89
hotels 222
map 11, 89
restaurants 234–5
Greater Oslo (cont.)
Vigelandsparken (Oslo) **90–91**
El Greco
The Repentant Peter 53
Grensen Skotøymagasin (Oslo) 245
Grieg, Edvard 16, 22–3, 59, **171**, 246
Hotel Ullensvang 163
Peer Gynt 163
statue of 67
Summer Concerts at Troldhaugen 29
Troldhaugen (Bergen) **171**
Grieg, Per 169
Grieghallen (Bergen) **168**, 249
Grimstad 140, **144**
Grip 181
Grosch, Christian H 72–3, 158
Grünerløkka (Oslo) **95**
Grøndahl, Agathe Backer 23
Grønligrotten 200
Gudbrandsdalen 121, 127
Gude, Hans 16, 22
The Bridal Procession in Hardanger 10, 22
Gudvangen 176
Guideservice 271
Gulbransen, Wenche
Christian IV's Glove 64, 67
Gulf Stream 14
Gullvåg, Olav 194
Gundersen, Gunnar S
Winter Sun 70
Gunnerus, Johan Ernst 191
Gustav Vasa, King of Sweden 36
Guttormsgaard, Guttorm 75
Gutulia National Park 125
Gyldenløve, Ulrik Frederik 119
Gålåvann Gudbrandsdalen 29

H

Hadeland Glassverk 245
Hadseløya 202
Hafjell Alpine Centre (Lillehammer) 131
Hafrsfjord, Battle of (890 AD) 33
Hagen, Else 74
Hagerup, Nina 171
Halden **110**
hotels 223
Hallingdal 82, 121, **136**
bunad 24
Hallvard, St 193
Halnefjorden 141
Halvard, St 56
Halvorsen, Stein 209
Hamar **126**
hotels 223–4
restaurants 236

Hammerfest 197, **212**
hotels 227
restaurants 239
Hamningberg 212
Hamnøy 198
Hamsun, Knut 22, 197
Grimstad 144
Kjerringøy 201
Narvik 208
Theatercafeen (Oslo) 55
Handball 17
Hankø **111**
Hanseatic League 36, 164, 165
Hanseatisk Museum (Bergen) **165**
Hansson, Olav 151
Harald V, King 15, 41, 209
Harald Fine-Hair (Harald Hårfagre), King
Battle of Hafrsfjord 33
Elveseter 133
Haraldshaugen (Haugesund) 161
Utstein Kloster 161
Hardanger 82, 155
Hardangerfjorden **162**
Hardangerjøkulen 153
Hardangervidda 14, 139, **152–3**
Harold II, King of England 35
Harstad 204
festivals 29
hotels 227
Haugesund **161**
festivals 29, 30
hotels 225
restaurants 238
Haukland, Lars 75
Health **258–9**
Heddal **151**
Heddal Stavkirke 139, 151
Hedmark 121
Hegra Festning 187
Heimen (Oslo) 245
Helgaland 197
Helgelandskysten 198, **200**
Helgøya 126
Henie, Sonja 115
Henie Onstad Kunstsenter **114–15**
Hennes & Mauritz (Oslo) 245
Heroes of Telemark **150**
Hertz (car rental) 269
Hertzberg, Niels 163
Hestemona 200
Heyerdahl, Thor 16, 23, 40
Kon-Tiki Museum (Oslo) 79, 80
Larvik Sjøfartsmuseum (Larvik) 119
Hidra 145
Hiking **250–51**
equipment 251
Hardangervidda 153
Hiking (cont.)
in national parks 251
safety 251
Hilton Scandic Hotels 219
Hinnøya 202, 204
Hiring cars 269
Hirst, Damien 72
Historisk Museum (Oslo) **54–5**
Street-by-Street map 49
History **33–41**
Hitra 187
Hjemmefrontmuseet (Oslo) *see* Norges Hjemmefrontmuseum
Hjemmeluft 197
HMK 271
Holberg, Ludvig 22, 166
Holidays, public 31
Holm, Bernt 146
Holmenkollen 89, **96**
Holmenkollen Ski Festival 17, 26–7, 28
Holtermann, General 187
Holtsmark, Karen 74
Honningsvåg 212
Hordaland 155
Horten **115**
hotels 223
Hospitals 258–9
Hostels 219
Hotels **218–27**
Eastern Norway 223–4
Northern Norway 227
Oslo 220–22
Oslofjorden 223
Sørlandet and Telemark 224–5
Trøndelag 226–7
Vestlandet 225–6
Hovedscenen (Oslo) 74
Hovig, Jan Inge 210
Hukodden (Oslo) **86**
Hunderfossen Adventure Park (Lillehammer) **131**
Hunting **253**
Hurtigruten (NNDS) **205**, 267
Husfliden (Oslo) 245
Hvaler archipelago 109
Hvalsafari 253
Høg-Jæren 155
Høgronden 130
Høstens promenade (Ravensberg) 58
Høvik, restaurants 235
Høvåg 144
Høymagasinet (Oslo) **66**
Street-by-Street map 64
Haakon Magnus, Crown Prince 15, 73
Håkon V Magnusson, King 33
Akershus Slott (Oslo) 68
Bygdøy Kongsgård (Oslo) 86
Vardø 212
Håkon VI Magnusson, King 33, 36
Haakon VII, King 40, 41
Slottet (Oslo) 51
tomb of 69
World War II 124
Håkon the Good 33, 35
Håkon Håkonsson, King 33
Håkonshallen (Bergen) 164
Karmøy 161
Lillehammer 130
Håkonshallen (Bergen) **164**
Haaland, Tore 75
Hårteigen 152

I

Ibsen, Henrik 16, 22, **59**, 121, 246, 247
Bergen Museum: De Kulturhistoriske Samlinger 169
Christiania Theatre (Oslo) 67
A Doll's House 39
Grimstad 144
Ibsenmuseet (Oslo) **58–9**
Lady Inger of Østeråt 187
Nasjonalgalleriet (Oslo) 52
Den Nationale Scene (Bergen) 167
Nationaltheatret (Oslo) 51
Peer Gynt 127, 171
Skien 142
Ice Gourmet (Oslo) 245
Impressionism 52
Indreøy 187
Ingstad, Anne Stine 23
Ingstad, Helge 23
Inner Room V (Bjørlo) 70
Innerdalen 181
Insect repellant 259
Det Internasjonale Barnekunstmuseet (Oslo) **95**
International Court at The Hague 40
Internet 262–3
Internet cafés 263
Ishavskatedralen (Tromsø) **210–11**

J

Jarlsberg, Baron Herman Wedel 97
Jazz **248**, 249
festivals 28, 29
Jenssen, Olav Christopher 72
Jomfruland 143
Jondal 162
Jordaiens, J 69
Jostedalsbreen 19, **178**
Jotunheimen **134–5**

Juhls Silver Gallery (Oslo) 245
Justøy 144
Jutulhogget 125
Jæren 155, 160
Jølster **178**
Jørund, Archbishop 212

K

Kaare Berntsen AS (Oslo) 245
Kabakov, Ilya
 The Rubbish Man 71
Kabelvåg 202
Kalmar Union 36
Karasjok 197, **209**
Karl XII, King 37
 Akershus Slott (Oslo) 68
 Halden 110
Karl XIII, King 38
Karl Johan, King 37, 38, 45
 Bygdøy Kongsgård (Oslo) 86
 Slottet (Oslo) 51
 statue of 48, 51
Karl Johans Gate (Oslo) 45, **50**
 Street-by-Street map 48–9
Karmøy **161**
Kaupanger 176
Kautokeino 15, 197, **209**
Keith Prowse 246, 249
Kiberg 212
Kiefer, Anselm 72
Kielland, Alexander 159
Kielland, Gabriel 193
Kielland, Jens Zetlitz 170
Kirkenes 197, 213
 Hurtigruten 205
Kitaj, R B 72
Kittelsen, Theodor 143
Kjerringøy 201
Kjerulf, Halfdan 22
Klee, Paul 167
Kløverhuset (Bergen) 241
Knivskjellodden 212
Kolbeinstveit Museum (Suldal) 160
Kon-Tiki Museum (Oslo) **80**
 Street-by-Street map 79
Kongelig Norsk Seilforning 79
Kongens Torv (Fredrikstad)
 Street-by-Street map 113
Kongsberg **137**
Kongsberg Jazz Festival 29
Kongsvinger **124**
Koppang 125
Korskirken (Bergen) **166**
Krag, Vilhelm 145
Kragerø **143**
Kristiansand **146–7**
 festivals 29
 hotels 224–5
 map 147
 restaurants 237
Kristiansand Dyrepark **147**
Kristiansand Turistinformasjon 257
Kristiansund **181**
 festivals 31
 hotels 225
Krogh, General G F von 192
Krohg, Christian
 Bergen Kunstmuseum 167
 Leiv Eiriksson discovers America 34–5
 A Little a-Port 52
 Nationaltheatret (Oslo) 51
 Norsk Sjøfartsmuseum (Oslo) 81
 Rådhuset (Oslo) 57
Krohg, Per 58
Krossen 150
Krøyer, P S 51
Kulturhuset USF (Bergen) **166–7**
Kunstindustrimuseet (Oslo) **59**
Kvadraturen (Oslo)
 Street-by-Street map 64–5
Kvaen people 208
Kvilldal Kraftstasjon 160
Kvinnefossen 174

L

Labour Party 15, 41, 75
Lagmannsstova 162
Laksestudiet (Suldal) 160
Landmark, Ole 168
Landscape
 Fjords **18–19**
 Landscape and Wildlife **20–21**
Langedrag Dyrepark 137
Langfoss 163
Langlet, Emil Victor 74
Langøya 202, 204
Language 16
Lapps *see* Sami
Larsen, Terje Rød 23
Larvik **119**
 hotels 223
 restaurants 235–6
Lauritsen, Peder 127
Lauritzen, Morten 97
League of Nations 40
Leirvassbu 134
Leiv Eiriksson 33, 34–5
LeWitt, Sol
 Tilted Form No. 3 71
Levanger **187**
Leyniers, E 69
Lie, Trygve 23, 40
Lighthouses
 Lindesnes 139, **145**
 Skomvær 204
 Verdens Ende 118
Lighting the Christmas Tree 31
Lillehammer **130–31**
 hotels 224
 map 131
 restaurants 236
 weather 30
Lillehammer Kunstmuseum (Lillehammer) **130**
Lillehammer Turistinformasjon 257
Lillehavn 145
Lilleputthammer (Lillehammer) **131**
Lillesand 144
Lindesnes 13, **145**
Lindesnes lighthouse 139, **145**
Lindex (Oslo) 245
Lindisfarne 34
Linstow, H D F 48, 50, 51
Literature 22
A Little a-Port (Krohg) 52
Lodalskåpa 178
Loen 179
Lofoten and Vesterålen 13, 197, 198, **202–4**
 Hurtigruten 205
 map 202–3
Lofotr – Vikingmuseet på Borg 204
Lom **133**
 hotels 224
Lomnessjøen 125
Londeman, Edvard 162
Longyear, J M 214
Longyearbyen 214
Lost property 258
 credit cards 260
Louis Philippe of Orleans 212
Lovunden 200
Lunch 228–9
Lunde and Løvseth 158
Lyngør **143**
Lysefjorden 155, **160**, 174
Lyseveien 160
Lysøen (Bergen) **171**
Lærdal 19, **176**
Lærdalsøyri 176
Låtefoss 157, 163

M

Madssen, Ada 48
Maelstrom 202
Magdalenefjorden 214
Magnor Glassverk 245
Magnus Lagabøter 164
Maihaugen (Lillehammer) **130**
Malling, Christian H 67
Mandal **144–5**
Maning, Per 71
Maps
 Bergen 165
 Eastern Norway 122–3
 Fredrikstad 112–13
 Hardangervidda 152–3

Maps (cont.)
Hurtigruten 205
Jotunheimen 134–5
Kristiansand 147
Lillehammer 131
Lofoten and Vesterålen 202–3
Northern Europe 11
Northern Norway and Svalbard 198–9
Norway 10–11
Oslo 44–5
Oslo: Around Bygdøynes 78–9
Oslo: Bygdøy 77
Oslo: Central Oslo East 63
Oslo: Central Oslo West 47
Oslo: further afield 89
Oslo: Greater Oslo 11
Oslo: Karl Johans Gate 48–9
Oslo: Kvadraturen 64–5
Oslofjorden 108–9
Sognefjorden 174–5
Stavanger 159
Svalbard 10, 198, 214–15
Sørlandet and Telemark 140–41
Tromsø 211
Trondheim 191
Trøndelag 184–5
Tønsberg to Verdens Ende tour 118
Vestlandet 156–7
The World of the Vikings 35
Mardalsfossen 181
Margrete, Queen 36
Mariakirken (Bergen) **164**
Marka 27
Markets 241
Martha, Queen 69
Märtha Louise, Princess 15
MasterCard 260
Matisse, Henri 115
Maud, Queen 40
Slottet (Oslo) 51
statue of 48
tomb of 69
May Jazz (Stavanger) 28
Medical treatment 258–9
Mette-Marit, Crown Princess 15, 73
Meyer, Hans A 200
Meyer, L A 200
Meyer, Rasmus 167
Michaelsen, J C C 192
Michelsen, Christian 39, 40, 170
Midnight sun 14, **213**, 256
Midsummer 29
Minerbi, Arrigo 73
Miró, Joan 115, 167
Mjøsa, Lake 121, **126**
Mo i Rana **200**
Mobile telephones **262**
Modigliani, Amadeo
Portrait of Mme Zborowska 53
Mohr, Hugo Louis 73
Molde **180–81**
festivals 29
Molde International Jazz Festival 29, 249
Monasteries
Utstein Kloster 161
Money **260–61**
Monolith (Vigeland) 90
Moore, Henry 86
Morgedal 26
Mosjøen 200
Moskenesstrømmen 202, 204
Moskenesøya 202, **204**
Mosquitoes 259
Moss **111**
hotels 223
Mosterøy 161
Motzfeld, Benny 190
Mountains
mountaineering **252**
safety 251, 259, 269
wildlife 21
winter driving 269
Mowatt, Karen 162
Munch, Edvard 16, 22, **93**
Aula (Oslo) 50
Bergen Kunstmuseum 167
Lillehammer Kunstmuseum (Lillehammer) 130
Munch-museet (Oslo) **93**
Nasjonalgalleriet (Oslo) 52
The Night Wanderer 93
The Scream 52, 93
Stenersenmuseet (Oslo) 58
Theatercafeen (Oslo) 55
Munk, Knud 168
Munkholm 187
Munthe, Gerhard 73, 164
Munthe-Kaas, H 201
Museums and galleries 16
admission fees 256–7
opening hours 257
Astrup Fearnley Museet (Oslo) **72**
Bergen Kunstmuseum **167**
Bergen Museum: De Kulturhistoriske Samlinger **169**
Bergen Museum: De Naturhistoriske Samlinger **168–9**
Bergens Kunstforening **168**
Bergens Sjøfartsmuseum **169**
Bergens Tekniske Museum **171**
Bjerkebæk (Lillehammer) **130**
Bogstad Herregård **97**
Bryggens Museum (Bergen) **164**
Museums and galleries (cont.)
Buekorpsmuseet (Bergen) **166**
Emanuel Vigeland Museum (Oslo) **96**
Erkebispegården (Trondheim) **190**
Forsvarmuseet (Oslo) **72**
Frammuseet (Oslo) 79, **81**
Gamle Bergen (Bergen) **170**
Geologisk Museum (Oslo) **94**
Gimle Gård (Kristiansand) **146**
Hanseatiske Museum (Bergen) **165**
Henie Onstad Kunstsenter **114–15**
Historisk Museum (Oslo) 49, **54–5**
Høymagasinet (Oslo) 64, **66**
Ibsenmuseet (Oslo) **58–9**
Det Internasjonale Barnekunstmuseet (Oslo) 31, **95**
Kon-Tiki Museum (Oslo) 79, **80**
Kunstindustrimuseet (Oslo) **59**
Lillehammer Kunstmuseum **130**
Lysøen (Bergen) **171**
Maihaugen (Lillehammer) **130**
Munch-museet (Oslo) **93**
Museet for Samtidskunst (Oslo) 65, **70–71**
Nasjonalgalleriet (Oslo) 49, **52–3**
Nordenfjeldske Kunstindustrimuseum (Trondheim) **190**
Nordnorsk Kunstmuseum (Tromsø) **210**
Norges Fiskerimuseum (Bergen) **164**
Norges Hjemmefront-museum (Oslo) 64, **66**
Norges Olympiske Museum (Lillehammer) **130**
Norsk Arkitekturmuseum (Oslo) 65, **66**
Norsk Folkemuseum (Oslo) 29, 44, 78, **82–3**
Norsk Hermetikkmuseum (Stavanger) **158**
Norsk Kjøretøyhistorisk Museum (Lillehammer) **130**
Norsk Oljemuseum (Stavanger) **158**
Norsk Sjøfartsmuseum (Oslo) 79, **81**
Oslo Bymuseum **92**
Polaria (Tromsø) **210**

Museums and galleries (cont.)
Polarmuseet (Tromsø) **210**
Postmuseet (Oslo) **73**
Ringve Museum (Trondheim) **192**
Setesdalsbanen Museumsjernbane (Kristiansand) **147**
Skimuseet (Oslo) **96**
Stavanger Museum (Stavanger) **159**
Stavanger Sjøfartsmuseum (Stavanger) **158**
Stenersenmuseet (Oslo) **58**
Teatermuseet (Oslo) 64, **67**
Teknisk Museum (Oslo) **95**
Troldhaugen (Bergen) **171**
Tromsø Kunstforening **210**
Tromsø Museum, Universitetsmuseet **211**
Trondheim Kunstmuseum **190**
Trondhjems Sjøfartsmuseum (Trondheim) **192**
Trøndelag Folkemuseum (Trondheim) **192**
Vest-Agder Fylkesmuseum (Kristiansand) **147**
Vestlandske Kunstindustrimuseum (Bergen) **167**
Vigelandsmuseet (Oslo) 90, **92**
Vikingskipshuset (Oslo) 44, 77, 78, **84–5**
Vitenskapsmuseet (Trondheim) **191**
Zoologisk Museum (Oslo) **94–5**
Music **22–3**
classical music, ballet, dance and opera **247**, 249
festivals 28, 29, 30, 31
folk music 16, **248**
rock, jazz and country music **248**, 249
Musikkselskabet Harmonien (Bergen) 249
Myklebust, Einar 93
Myllarheimen 150
Myntkabinettet (Oslo) 54
Mælandsgården 161
Møllers Gullsmedforretning (Trondheim) 245
Møre 155
Møsvann
festivals 31
Måbøgaldane 163
Månafossen 160

N

NAF 269
Namsen river 195
Namsos **195**
Nansen, Fridtjof 23
Frammuseet (Oslo) 79, 81
League of Nations 40
skiing 26
Tromsø 210
Napoleon I, Emperor 37
Narvesen 263
Narvik 197, **208**
hotels 227
Nasjonalballetten (Oslo) 249
Nasjonalgalleriet (Oslo) **52–3**
Street-by-Street map 49
The National Assembly at Eidsvoll (Wergeland) 38, 74
National Day 15, 24, 28, 38, 44, 50
National parks
Borre **115**
Dovrefjell 133
Femundsmarka 125
Gutulia 125
Jotunheimen **134–5**
Rondane 17, 130, **132**
Saltfjellet-Svartisen **201**
touring **251**
Øvre Pasvik 213
Ånderdalen 208
National Romanticism 16, 22, 52, 53
National Theatre (Oslo) 30
Den Nationale Scene (Bergen) **167**, 249
Nationaltheatret (Oslo) **51**, 249
Street-by-Street map 49
NATO 17, 40, 41
Nebelong, J H
Bergen Museum: De Naturhistoriske Samlinger 168
Oscarshall Slott (Oslo) 87
Slottet (Oslo) 51
Neo-Romanticism 53
Nerdrum, Odd 72
Nesbyen 136
Nesch, Rolf 75
Nesjar, Carl 75
Nesoddbåtene 271
Nessekonge 200
Newspapers 16, **263**
Newtontoppen 214
Nidarosdomen (Trondheim) 14, 183, 184, **193**
Nidelva river 191
Nielsen, Amaldus 58, 145
Nielsen, Hans 112
Night Jazz Bergen 28
The Night Wanderer (Munch) 93
Nobel Peace Prize 13, 17
Nobile, Umberto 213
NOR-Way Bussekspress 265, 267
Nordaustlandet 214
Nordea 260
Nordea Flytogterminalen (Oslo) 260
Nordea Oslo Lufthavn 260
Nordenfjeldske Kunstindustrimuseum (Trondheim) **190**
Nordfjord 155, 157, **178–9**
Nordheim, Arne 23
Nordheimsund 162
Nordic Hunting and Fishing Days (Elverum) 29
Nordkapp (North Cape) 13, 14, 197, 198, **212**
Hurtigruten 205
Nordland 197, 201
bunad 25
Nordlysfestivalen (Tromsø) 31, 249
Nordlysplanetariet (Tromsø) **211**
Nordnorsk Kunstmuseum (Tromsø) **210**
Nordraak, Rikard 22
Nordsjkø-Bandak Canal 142
Norges Bank 38, 39
Norges Fiskerimuseum (Bergen) **164**
Norges Handikapforbund 257
Norges Hjemmefrontmuseet (Oslo) **66**
Street-by-Street map 64
Norges Jeger-og Fiskerforbund 253
Norges Klatreforbund 253
Norges Olympiske Museum (Lillehammer) **130**
Norges Padleforbund 253
Norges Taxi 271
Norges Turistråd 246, 249, 257
Norheim, Sondre 26
Norland Festival 29
Norsk Arkitekturmuseum (Oslo) **66**
Street-by-Street map 65
Norsk Bremuseum (Jostedalsbreen) 178
Norsk Folkemuseum (Oslo) 29, 44, **82–3**
Street-by-Street map 78
Norsk Hermetikkmuseum (Stavanger) **158**
Norsk Kjøretøyhistorisk Museum (Lillehammer) **130**
Norsk Oljemuseum (Stavanger) **158**
Norsk Sjøfartsmuseum (Oslo) **81**
Street-by-Street map 79
Norsk Villakssenter (Lærdal) 175, 176
Den Norske Bank (DnB) 260

Den Norske Filmfestivalen (Haugesund) 249
Den Norske Opera (Oslo) **75**, 249
Det Norske Selskab 37
Det Norske Teatret (Oslo) **55**, 249
Den Norske Turistforening (DNT) 219, 253
Norske Vandrerhjem 219
North Aurdal 136
North Cape *see* Nordkapp
North Pole 23, 213, 215
North Sea Festival (Haugesund) 29
Northern Lights 14, 199, 213
  festival 31
  Nordlysplanetariet (Tromsø) **211**
  Polaria (Tromsø) 210
Northern Norway and Svalbard **197–215**
  hotels 227
  Hurtigruten **205**
  Lofoten and Vesterålen **202–4**
  map 198–9
  restaurants 239
  Svalbard **214–15**
  Tromsø **210–11**
Norwegian Employers' Confederation (NAF) 39
Norwegian Federation of Trade Unions (LO) 39
Norwegian Film Festival (Haugesund) 29
Norwegian Mountain Marathon 29
Norwegian Trades Union Federation 75
Norwegian Wood (Oslo) 29
Norwegian Wood Festivalen (Lysaker) 249
Notodden International Blues Festival 29
Novgorod School 52
NSB 266, 267
Numedal 121, **136–7**
Nusfjord 202, 204
Nygaardsvold, Johan 40
Nøtterøy
  Tønsberg to Verdens Ende tour 118

O

Odda 163
Oil 14
  Norsk Oljemuseum (Stavanger) **158**
Okkenhaug, Paul 194
Olav IV, King 36
Olav V, King 40, 41
  Akershus Slott (Oslo) 68
Olav V, King (cont.)
  Bygdøy Kongsgård (Oslo) 86
  Hankø 111
  Holmenkollen 96
  tomb of 69
  Vadsø 213
Olav the Holy (Olav Haraldsson), King 14, 33
  Battle of Stiklestad 184, **194**
  Nidarosdomen (Trondheim) 184, 193
  Sarpsborg 110
  Steinvikholm 187
  Trondheim 183, 190
Olav Kyrre, King 164
Olav Tryggvason, King 33, 35
  Steinkjer 194–5
  Trondheim 183, 190
Olavsgruva 186
Olavshallen (Trondheim) 249
Old Penitentiary (Fredrikstad)
  Street-by-Street map 112
Old Town Hall (Fredrikstad)
  Street-by-Street map 112
Olsaksamlingen (Oslo) 54
Olsen, Werner 127
Olympiaparken (Lillehammer) **131**
Onstad, Niels 115
Opening hours 257
  banks 260
  restaurants 228–9
  shops 240
Opera **247**, 249
  Den Norske Opera (Oslo) **75**
  Opera Week (Kristiansund) 31
Oppdal **186**
  bunad 25
Oppland 121
Orkla Industrimuseum 187
Os 125
Oscar I, King 38
  Oscarshall Slott (Oslo) 87
  Slottet (Oslo) 45, 51
Oscar II, King 39
  Bygdøy Kongsgård (Oslo) 86–7
  Frognerseteren 97
  Kirkenes 213
  Nordkapp 212
  Norsk Folkemuseum (Oslo) 82
Oscarsborg Festning (Drøbak) 114
Oscarshall Slott (Oslo) **87**
Oslo 13, **43–103**
  Bygdøy **77–87**
  Central Oslo East **63–75**
  Central Oslo West **47–59**
  festivals 29, 30
  further afield **89–97**
Oslo (cont.)
  hotels 220–22
  map 44–5
  restaurants 232–5
  Street Finder **98–103**
  travel **270–71**
  weather 14, 30
Oslo Bymuseum **92**
Oslo Chamber Music Festival 29
Oslo City shopping centre 241
Oslo Domkirke **73**
Oslo Festival of Church Music 28
Oslo-Filharmonien 249
Oslo Guidebureau 271
Oslo Horse Show 30
Oslo Jazzfestival 249
Oslo Kirkemusikk 249
Oslo Konserthus **58**, 249
Oslo Nye Teater **74**, 249
Oslo Spektrum **75**, 249
Oslo Taxi 271
Oslo Turistinformasjon Vestbanen 257
Oslofjorden 13, **107–19**
  Fredrikstad: Street-by-Street map 112–13
  hotels 223
  map 108–9
  restaurants 235–6
  A Trip from Tønsberg to Verdens Ende 118
Otnes 125
Otra, river 150
Otta **132**
Ottadalen 123
Ottar 33
OVDS 269

P

Painting **22**
Palaces
  Oscarshall Slott (Oslo) **87**
Paleet (Oslo) 241
Parking 268–9
  in Oslo 270
Parks and gardens
  Bergen Museum: De Naturhistoriske Samlinger 168–9
  Bogstad Herregård 97
  Botanical Gardens of Ringve (Trondheim) 192
  Botanisk Hage and Museum (Oslo) **94**
  Dronningparken (Oslo) 48
  Vigelandsparken (Oslo) **90–91**
Parliament (Oslo) *see* Stortinget
Passports 256
Pedersen, Hilde Skancke 209
Pederssøn, Geble 166

Peer Gynt **127**
Peer Gyntsamlingen (Vinstra) 127
Perriertoppen 214
Personal security **258**
Peterssen, Eilif 37, 146
Petrol stations 269
Pharmacies 259
Picasso, Pablo 75, 115, 167
Pickpocketing 258
Pikefossen 209
Planetarium
Nordlysplanetariet (Tromsø) **211**
Platou, Olav 195
Poe, Edgar Allan 202
Polar Jazz Svalbard 31
Polaria (Tromsø) **210**
Polarmuseet (Tromsø) **210**
Polarsirkelsentret 201
Police **258**, 259
Politicians **23**
Porsgrunn, hotels 225
Porsgrunn Teaterfestival 249
Portrait of Mme Zborowska (Modigliani) 53
Posebyen (Kristiansand) **146**
Postal services **263**
Postbanken 260
Posten Norge BA (Oslo) 263
Postmuseet (Oslo) **73**
Poulsson, Magnus 56
Prekestolen (Pulpit Rock) 155, 160, 174
Prins Karl Forland 214
Provisions House (Fredrikstad)
Street-by-Street map 112
Prøysen, Alf 126
Public holidays 31

Q

Quart Festival (Kristiansand) 29, 249
Quisling, Vidkun 41, 67

R

Radio **263**
Radisson SAS 218, 219
Rafting **252–3**
Raftsundet 205
Rail Europe 265
Railways *see* Trains
Rainbow Hotels 219
Rainfall 30
Rakfisk Festival (Valdres) 31
Ramberg, Torstein 74
Rampart Gate (Fredrikstad)
Street-by-Street map 113
Rasmussen, W 193
Rauland **150**
festivals 31
Rauland National Folk Music Contest 29
Ravensberg, Ludvig O
Høstens promenade 58
Reformation 16, 36
Regjeringskvartalet (Oslo) **74–5**
Reimers, Egill 169
Reinald, Bishop of Stavanger 159
Reinå 187
Rena 125
Rendalen **125**
The Repentant Peter (El Greco) 53
Restaurants 228–39
Eastern Norway 236
Northern Norway 239
Oslo 232–5
Oslofjorden 235–6
Sørlandet and Telemark 237
Trøndelag 238–9
Vestlandet 237–8
What to Eat in Norway 230–31
Revoldt, Axel 56
Rica Hotels 218–19
Richter, Gerhard 72
Ringebu 121, **127**
Ringebu Stavkirke 123, **127**
Ringve Museum (Trondheim) **192**
Risør **143**
festivals 29
Rjukan **150–51**
Road signs 269
Road tolls 268
Road travel **268–9**
Road tunnels 19
Rock carvings
Alta 209
Hjemmeluft 197
Steinkjer 194, 195
Rock music **248**, 249
Rogaland 155
Rogaland Teater (Stavanger) 249
Rolfsen, Alf 194
Rollo 35
Romsdal 155
Romsdalsfjorden 155
Romsdalshorn 180
Rondane National Park 17, 130, **132**
Rose, Knut 72
Rosenkrantz, Erik 164, 166
Rosenkrantz, Ludvig 162
Rosenkrantztårnet (Bergen) **164**
Royal Mausoleum (Oslo) 69
Royal Palace (Oslo) *see* Slottet
The Rubbish Man (Kabakov) 71
Runde 180
Ryanair 264, 265
Ryfylkefjellene mountains 155
Ryggen, Hannah 190
Rødøy 200
Rømer, Inger Ottesdatter 187
Røros 183, **186**
festivals 28
hotels 226
restaurants 238
Rørosvidda 183
Rørvik **195**
Røst 204
Røykjafossen 163
Rådhuset (Oslo) **56–7**

S

Safety
in mountains 251, 259, 269
winter driving 269
St Hallvard 56
St Hans 29
St Olav 194
Sales tax 240–41
Salmon Fishing Season 29
Salo, Gaspar de 167
Saltfjellet-Svartisen National Park **201**
Saltstraumen 201
Sami 197, 199
Alta 208
crafts 243, **244–5**
Easter celebrations and weddings 28
Karasjok **209**
Kautokeino 209
language 16
Samien Sitje (Steinkjer) 195
Sami parliament 41, 209
traditional costumes 25
Tromsø Museum, Universitetsmuseet 211
Sandefjord **119**
hotels 223
restaurants 236
Sandel, Cora 22
Sandnes 155
Sandvig, Anders 130
Sarpsborg **110**
SAS (Scandinavian Airlines) 264, 265, 266, 267
Scene from Bergen's Inner Harbour (Dahl) 167
Schirmer, Adolf 52
Schirmer, H E 51, 52
Schøller, Cecilie Christine 192
Schøning, Gerhard 191
Scott, Robert 23
The Scream (Munch) 52, 93
Sculpture **22**
see also Vigeland, Gustav
Sea mammals 21
see also Whales
Seafood for All (Bergen) 30

Security **258**
Seidelin, Jens S 67
Selje **179**
Seljord Country Music Festival (Telemark) 249
Senja **208**
Sentrum Scene (Oslo) 249
Seppänen, Ensio 213
Serra, Richard
  Shaft 70
Setesdal 83, **150**
Setesdalen Jernvegsmuseum (Kristiansand) **147**
Shaft (Serra) 70
Sheriffs 258
Sherman, Cindy 72
Shetland Islands 35
Ships *see* Boats
Shoe shops 245
Shopping **240–45**
  What to Buy in Norway **242–3**
Shopping centres 241
Sightseeing tours, Oslo 271
Sigurd Jorsalfar, King 69, 159
Sildajazz (Haugesund) 29, 249
Silver, shopping **244**, 245
Sira-Kvina Kraftselskap 145
Sitter, Inger 75
Sjøfartsmuseet (Stavanger) **158**
Sjømannskirken (Oslo) **86**
Sjøsanden 145
Skagerrak 145
Skandinavisk Høyfjellsutstyr (Lillehammer) 245
Ski-Kite (Møsvann) 31
Skien
  hotels 225
  restaurants 237
  Telemark Canal tour 142
Skien-Nordsjø Canal 142
Skienvassdraget 139, 142
Skiforeningen 253
Skiing 17, **26–7**, **252**
  Holmenkollen 96
Skomvær Island 202, 204
Skudeneshavn 161
Slingsby, William C 134
Slottet (Oslo) 45, **51**
  Street-by-Street map 48
Smith, Anders 159
Smoking 229, 257
Smørbrød 230
Snorre Sturlason 22, 190, 194–5
Snow 256
  winter driving and safety 269
  Snow Sculpture Festival (Vinje) 31
  see also Skiing
Snøhetta 132, 133
Sogn 155
Sogndal 175, **176**
Sognefjorden 19, **174–6**
  map 174–5
Sohlberg, Harald 22
  Winter Night in the Mountains 53
Son 111
SOS Children's Villages 95
Soulages, Pierre 115
Souvenirs **242–3**, 244
Sparre, H J 168
Sparre, Victor 159, 210–11
Speed limits 268
Spitsbergen 214
Sports 17, **250–53**
Sports equipment, shopping **245**
Spring in Norway 28
Stad peninsula 155, **179**
Stamsund 204
Stavanger 14, 155, **158–9**
  festivals 28, 29
  hotels 225–6
  map 159
  restaurants 238
Stavanger Konserthus 249
Stavanger Museum **159**
Stave churches
  Borgund Stavkirke 155, 175, **177**
  Fantoft Stavkirke 171
  Heddal Stavkirke 139, 151
  Ringebu Stavkirke 123, **127**
  Urnes Stavkirke 175, **178**
  Uvdal Stavkirke 137
Stavern 108, **119**
  hotels 223
Steinkjer **194–5**
  hotels 226
Steinvikholm 187
Stena Line 265
Stenersen, Rolf **58**, 167
Stenersenmuseet (Oslo) **58**
Stetind in the Fog (Balke) 53
Stiftsgården (Trondheim) **192**
Stiklestad **194**
Stock Exchange (Oslo) *see* Børsen
Stoltenberg, Thorvald 23
Store Skagastølstind 134
Storm, Per Palle 51
Storstein, Aage 201
Stortinget (Oslo) 15, 45, **74**
Stryn 157, 179
Stryn Summer Ski Festival 29
Studenten (Oslo) 263
Suhms, Peter Fredrik 191
Suldal **160**
Suldalsporten (Suldal) 160
Summer Concerts at Troldhaugen 29
Summer in Norway 29
Sun, midnight 14, **213**, 256
Sun Party at Svalbard 28
Sund 13, 204
Sundby, Christian 209
Sunndalsøra 181
Sunnfjord 155
Sunniva, St 179, 193
Sunshine 30
Svalbard **214–15**
  festivals 28, 31
  maps 10, 198, 214–15
  see also Northern Norway and Svalbard
Svellnosbreen 135
Sverdrup, Otto 81
Sverre Sigurdsson, King 33, 192
Svolvær 203, **204**
Swithun, St 159
Sylene 183
Sæverud, Harald 23
Sørensen, Henrik 56, 130
Sørfjorden **162–3**
Sørlandet and Telemark **139–53**
  Hardangervidda **152–3**
  Heroes of Telemark 150
  hotels 224–5
  Kristiansand **146–7**
  map 140–41
  restaurants 237
  A Tour along the Telemark Canal **142**

T

Tafjorden 179
Tandberg, Odd 75
Tax-free shopping 240–41
Taxi 2 (Oslo) 271
Taxis, in Oslo 270–71
Teatermuseet (Oslo) **67**
  Street-by-Street map 64
Teknisk Museum (Oslo) **95**
Telegrams 262
Telegraphic transfers, money 261
Telemark *see* Sørlandet and Telemark
Telemark Canal 139, 141
  A Tour along the Telemark Canal **142**
Telemark Festival 29, 249
Telemarkreiser 267
Telephones **262**
Television **263**
Tellefsen, Arve 23
Temperatures 30
Thaulow, Frits 130
Theatercafeen (Oslo) **55**
Theatre 246, **247**, 249
Theft 258
Thrane, Marcus 38, 39
Thune (Oslo) 245
Tickets
  for entertainments 246, 249
  travel in Oslo 271

Tidemand, Adolf 10, 16, 22
Bergen Kunstmuseum 167
The Bridal Procession in Hardanger 10, 22
Lillehammer Kunstmuseum (Lillehammer) 130
Oscarshall Slott (Oslo) 87
Tilted Form No. 3 (LeWitt) 71
Tipping 229
Tjeldsundbrua 203
Tjøme
Tønsberg to Verdens Ende tour 118
TNT 263
Tolga 125
Toll roads 268
Tordenskiold, Peter Wessel 37, 192
Torget 200
Torghatten 200
Torriset, Kjell 72
Tourist information offices 246, **256**, 257
Oslo **57**, 256, 257
Tours by car
A Tour along the Telemark Canal **142**
Tønsberg to Verdens Ende **118**
Traffic regulations 268
Trafikanten 271
Trains **265**, **266–7**
Flåmsbanen 175, **176**
Trams, in Oslo 271
Travel **264–71**
air **264**, 265, **266**
buses **267**, 271
Bygdøy (Oslo) 77
cars **265**
coaches **265**
cycling 271
Eastern Norway 123
ferries **265**, **267**, 271
Lofoten and Vesterålen 203
Northern Norway and Svalbard 199
Oslo **270–71**
Oslofjorden 109
Sørlandet and Telemark 140
taxis 270–71
trains **265**, **266–7**
trams 271
Trøndelag 185
Vestlandet 157
Travellers' cheques 240, **261**
Treschow family 119
Triangle (Vigeland) 90
Troldhaugen (Bergen) **171**
festivals 29
Trollheimen 183
Trollkyrkja 181
Trolltindane 180
Troms 197
bunad 25
Tromsø 197, **210–11**
festivals 31
hotels 227
Hurtigruten 205
map 211
restaurants 239
weather 30
Tromsø Kunstforening **210**
Tromsø Museum, Universitetsmuseet **211**
Tromsø Turistinformasjon 257
Tromsø Villmarksenter 249
Trondenes 203, 204
Trondheim 183, **190–93**
hotels 226–7
Hurtigruten 205
map 191
Nidarosdomen 14, 183, 184, **193**
restaurants 239
weather 30
Trondheim Kunstmuseum **190**
Trondheim Torg 241
Trondheim Turistinformasjon 257
Trondheimsfjorden 183, **187**
Trondhjems Sjøfartsmuseum **192**
Trysil 121, **125**
Trysilfjellet 125
Trøndelag **183–95**
hotels 226–7
map 184–5
restaurants 238–9
Trondheim **190–93**
Trøndelag Folkemuseum (Trondheim) **192**
Trøndelag Teater (Trondheim) **190**, 249
Tunnels, under fjords 19
Turtveit, Gunnar 73
Tusenfryd **114**
Tylldalen 125
Tysfjord Turistcenter AS 253
Tysfjorden 201
Tønsberg
hotels 223
restaurants 236
Tønsberg to Verdens Ende tour **118**

U

Ulefoss
Telemark Canal tour 142
Ullensvang 162
Ullman, Liv 186
Ultima Contemporary Music Festival (Oslo) 30
Ulvik **163**
Undredal 176
Undset, Sigrid 22
Bjerkebæk (Lillehammer) **130**
UNESCO World Heritage Sites
Alta 209
Bryggen (Bergen) 165
Røros 186
Urnes Stavkirke 175, **178**
United Kingdom Embassy 259
United Nations 17, 40
Universitetet (Oslo) **50**
Street-by-Street map 49
Urmaker Bjerke (Bergen) 245
Urmaker Bjerke (Oslo) 245
Urne, Christopher 68
Urnes Stavkirke 175, **178**
Utne 162
Utrillo, Maurice 167
Utsira 161
Utstein Kloster **161**
Uvdal Stavkirke 137

V

Vaa, Dyre 150, 194
Vadsø **213**
Valbergstårnet (Stavanger) **158**
Valdres 121, **136**
festivals 31
Valen, Fartein
Fartein Valen Days (Haugesund) 30
Vang 186
Vardø **212**
Vassfaret Bjørnepark 249
Vasstulan 137
Verdens Ende
Tønsberg to Verdens Ende tour 118
Verne, Jules 202
Vesaas, Tarjei 22
Vest-Agder Fylkesmuseum (Kristiansand) **147**
Vestbaneplassen Sykkelutleie 271
Vesterålen Islands 198, **204**
see also Lofoten and Vesterålen
Vestfjord 198
Vestfold
bunad 24
Vestfold Festspillene (Tønsberg) 29, 249
Vestkapp 179
Vestlandet 14, 16, **155–81**
Bergen **164–71**
Borgund Stavkirke **177**
hotels 225–6
map 156–7
restaurants 237–8
Sognefjorden **174–6**
Stavanger **158–9**
Vestlandske Kunstindustrimuseum (Bergen) **167**
Vestvågøy Museum (Fygle) 202, 204

Vestvågøya 197, 202, **204**
Vigeland, Emanuel
Aurlandsvangen 176
Emanuel Vigeland Museum (Oslo) **96**
Oslo Domkirke (Oslo) 73
Vigeland, Gustav 22
The Clan 91
Fountain 91
head of Ibsen 52
Monolith 90
Nationaltheatret (Oslo) 51
Triangle 90
Vigelandsmuseet (Oslo) 90, **92**
Vigelandsparken (Oslo) **90–91**
Wheel of Life 90
Vigen, Terje 144
Vik 174
Vik, Ingebrigt 162
Viking (vehicle recovery) 269
Vikings 13–14, 33, **34–5**
Vikingskipshuset (Oslo) 44, 77, 78, **84–5**
Street-by-Street map 78
Vikna 183, 185, 195
Viksjø, Erling 74, 75
Villmarkshuset (Oslo) 245
Vinje
festivals 31
Vinmonopolet 16, 229, 241, 257
Vinstra 122, **127**
VISA (card) 260
Visas 256
Vitenskapsmuseet (Trondheim) **191**
Von der Lippe, C F 171
Voss **163**
bunad 25
festivals 29
Vozzajazz Hordaland 28
Vrangfoss
Telemark Canal tour 142
Værøy 204
Vøringsfossen 152, 163
Vågehavn 145
Vågå 133
Vågåvatnet, Lake 123
Vår Frue Kirke (Trondheim) **191**

W

Walking
in Oslo 270
see also Hiking
Wassmo, Herbjørg 16
Watches, shopping **244**, 245
Waterfalls 18
Fiskumfossen 195
Fotlandsfossen 160
Kvinnefossen 174
Waterfalls (Cont.)
Låtefoss 157
Mardalsfossen 181
Månafossen 160
Odda 163
Pikefossen 209
Røykjafossen 163
Ulefoss 142
Vrangfoss 142
Vøringsfossen 152, 163
Waterparks
Bø Sommarland **151**
Weather 14, **30**, 256
safety 259
Weidemann, Jakob 58, 195
Werenskiold, Dagfin 73
Werenskiold, Erik 22, 51, 130
Wergeland, Henrik 22, 38
statue of 49
Wergeland, Oscar
The National Assembly at Eidsvoll 38, 74
Wergmann, Peter Frederik 51
Wessel, Jan 192
Western Flakstadøya 202
Whales 21
whale safaris **253**
whale watching **201**
Wheel of Life (Vigeland) 90
Wheelchair access *see* Disabled travellers
White-water canoeing **252–3**
Widerøe 264, 265, 266, 267
Wiklund, Marit 67
Wildenvey, Herman 55
Wildlife
Akvariet (Bergen) **166**
Dovrefjell 133
Hardangervidda 152–3
Kristiansand Dyrepark **147**
Landscape and Wildlife **20–21**
Lofoten Islands 204
Runde 180
safety 259
Svalbard **214–15**
Utsira 161
Vikna 195
whale safaris **253**
whale watching **201**
Wilhelm II, Kaiser 97, 174
William Schmidt (Oslo) 245
Wine shops 16, 229, 241, 257
Winter Festival (Røros) 28
Winter in Norway 31
driving and safety 269
Winter Market (Rauland) 31
Winter Night in the Mountains (Sohlberg) 53
Winter Olympic Games 17, 26, 130–31
Winter Sun (Gundersen) 70
With, Captain Richard 205
Wooden Boat Festival (Risør) 29
World War I 40
World War II 40–41
Heroes of Telemark **150**
Norges Hjemmefrontmuseet (Oslo) 64, **66**
Writers **22**

X

XXL Sport og Villmark (Oslo) 245

Y

Ynglinge dynasty 115
Young, Jørgen 75
Young Jazz Ålesund 30
Youngstorget (Oslo) **75**
Youth hostels 219

Z

Zahl, Erasmus 201
Zoologisk Museum (Oslo) **94–5**

Ø

Ørlandet 187
Østerdalen 121, **125**
Øvre Pasvik Nasjonalpark 213
Øystein, Archbishop 193
Øystese 162

Å

Å 202, 204
Åberg, Gösta 58
Ålesund **180**
festivals 30
hotels 226
restaurants 238
Åmli *bunad* 24
Åndalsnes **180**
Ånderdalen Nasjonalpark 208

Acknowledgments

STREIFFERT FÖRLAG would like to thank the following staff at Dorling Kindersley:

SENIOR MAP CO-ORDINATOR
Casper Morris

SENIOR DTP MANAGER
Jason Little.

MANAGING ART EDITOR
Jane Ewart.

PUBLISHING MANAGER
Anna Streiffert.

PUBLISHER
Douglas Amrine.

DORLING KINDERSLEY would like to thank all those whose contributions and assistance have made the preparation of this book possible.

MAIN CONTRIBUTOR
Snorre Evensberget, former chief editor at Gyldendal Norsk Forlag and author of *Thor Heyerdahl, Oppdageren (Thor Heyerdahl: The Explorer),* Norwegian and English Editions 1994, the reference works *Bevingede Ord,* 1967, and *Litterært Leksikon,* 2000. Evensberget has also edited works on Norway, including *Bygd og By i Norge, 1-19, Norge, Vårt Land, 1-9,* and many books on Norwegian nature, hunting and fishing.

EDITOR, UK EDITION
Jane Hutchings.

EDITORIAL ASSISTENCE, UK EDITION
Karen Villabona

PROOF READER
Stewart J Wild.

INDEX
Hilary Bird.

PHOTOGRAPHY PERMISSIONS
DORLING KINDERSLEY would like to thank all the churches, museums, restaurants, hotels, shops, galleries and other sights too numerous to thank individually, for their permission to photograph their establishments.

PICTURE CREDITS
Key: t = top; tl = top left; tlc = top left centre; tc = top centre; tr = top right; cla = centre left above; ca = centre above; cra = centre right above; cl = centre left; c = centre; cr = centre right; clb = centre left below; cb = centre below; crb = centre right below; bl = bottom left; b = bottom; bc = bottom centre; bcl = bottom centre left; bcr = bottom centre right; br = bottom right; d = detail.

Every effort has been made to trace the copyright holders. Dorling Kindersley apologizes for any unintentional omissions. We would be pleased to insert the appropriate acknowledgments in any subsequent edition of this publication. The publishers are also grateful to the following individuals, companies and picture libraries for their kind permission to reproduce their photographs and artwork:

All Over Press: 22br, 23tr, 23cl, 23br, 40c, 41br, 150br.

Amarok AB: Magnus Elander, 21bl, 214tr, 215tl 215cra, 215cr, 215br, 253b.

Tom Arnbom: 201br.

Liv Arnessen: 26bc.

Barnekunstmuseet: 95b.

Bergen Kunstmuseum: *Bergens Våg, 1834,* by J. C. Dahl 167bl.

Bergen Museum: De Naturhistoriske Samlinger: 169cl.

Studio Lasse Berre AS: 5clb, 24tl, 24cla, 24ca, 24cra, 24clb, 24cb, 24crb, 24bl, 24bc, 24br, 25tl, 25tc, 25tr, 25cla, 25ca, 25cr, 25cb, 25crb.

© **Bono:** Frits Solvang *Shaft* by Richard Serra 70b, *Einar Gerhardsen* by Nils Aas 75cl, *Monolitten* by Gustav Vigeland 89t, *Sinataggen* by Gustav Vigeland 90tl, *Livshjulet* by Gustav Vigeland 90ca, *Monolittplatået* by Gustav Vigeland 90cb, *Triangel* by Gustav Vigeland 90b, *Fontenen* by Gustav Vigeland 91cr, *Slekten* by Gustav Vigeland 91t.

British Museum: Peter Anderson 34bc, 35cb.

C. M. Dixon: 34tr.

English Heritage: 34cl.

Fjellanger-Wideroe: 10cl.

Jiri Havran: 51b, 171tr.

Det Kgl. Bibliotek, København: 36t.

Knudsens Fotosenter: 14t, 14b, 15t, 15b, 17b 25bl, 28cl, 29cl, 29b, 31tr, 31b, 111b, 135cra, 137cl, 166cl, 175bl, 178tl, 188–189, 193cla, 193cra, 193bl, 199cr, 209tl, 212tl, 212c, 213t, 213b, 214bl, 249tr, 252cr, 259t, 266t.

Kunstindustrimuseet i Oslo: *Baldisholteppet* 59t, 59crb.

Kviknes Hotell: 219t.

Håkon Li: 177cl, 177cr, 177bl, 177br.

Lunds Historiska Museum: 33t.

Munch-Museet: *Nattvandreren,* Edvard Munch ©Bono 93b.

Museet for Samtidskunst: *Vintersol* by Gunnar S. Gundersen © Bono 70tr, *Indre Rom* by Per Inge Bjørlo © Bono 70cl, *Søppelmannen* by Ilja Kabakov © Bono 71tl, *Form No 3* by Sol Le Witt © Bono 71cra, *Uten titel* by Per Maning © Bono 71b.

Nasjonalbiblioteket: 39br.

Nasjonalgalleriet: *Brudeferd i Hardanger* by A. Tidemand & H. Gude 8–9, *Leiv Eirikson Oppdager Amerika* by Christian Krohg 34c,

Fra Hjula Veveri by Wilhelm Peters 39cl, *Fra Stalheim* by J. C. Dahl 49cra, *Babord Litt* by Christian Krohg 52c, *Portrett av Mme Zborowska* by Amadeo Modigliani 53tc, *Den Angrende St Peter* by El Greco 53cra, *Vinternatt i Rondane* by Harald Sohlberg 53cr, *Stetind i Tåke* by Peder Balke 53b, *Skrik* by Edvard Munch © Bono 52clb, *Ibsen* by Gustav Vigeland © Bono 52b.

Norsk Folkemuseum: 3, 12, 82ca.

Norsk Hjemmefront Museum: 41clb, 66bl.

Oslo Bymuseum: *Det Konglige Slott 1845* av O. F. Knudsen 9, *Prøvetur på Eidsvollsbanen* 39tl.

Oslo Spektrum: 75b.

Sametinget: 209br.

Samfoto: Kim Hart 26c.

Scanpix: 022cl, 027cra, 27br.

Mick Sharp: 35cr.

Tiu Similä: 21tr.

Skimuseet: 26tr, 26cl.

Statens Historiska Museum, Stockholm: Peter Anderson 34tl, 35tl, 35crb.

Statens Vegvesen: 19br.

Stenersenmuseet © Bono *Høstens Promenade* by Ludvig O. Ravensberg 58br.

Tofoto: 205t, 205cla, 205cr, 205cl, 205b.

Danny Twang: 247bl.

Universitetets Kulturhistoriske Museer: Ove Holst 34br.

Universitetets Oldsakssamling: 33b; Peter Anderson 4br, 034bl, 54cl, 84b, 85bl; Ann Christine Eek 54tr, *Livets Hjul* 55tl, 55b; Ove Holst 84tl; Eirik Irgens Johnsen 49tl, 54ca, 54b, 76, 84cl, 85tl, 85tc.

O. Væring: *Birkebeinerferden* by K. Bergslien 26clb, *Håkon Håkonsson Krones* by Gerhard Munthe 32, *Bærums Verk* by C. A. Lorentzen 36br, *Sjøhelten Peter Wessel Tordenskiold* by Balthasar Denners 37c, *En Aften i det Norske Selskap* by Eilif Petersen 37t, *Torvslaget i Christiiania 17.5 1829* by H. E. Reimers 38br, *Nasjonalforsamlingen på Eidsvoll 1814* by O. Wergeland 38tl, *Christian Michelsen og Kongefamilien 7/6 1905* by H. Ström 40tl, *Akershus Slott* by Jacob Croning 69tl.

Vestfold Festspillene: 248tl.

Linda Whitwam: 104–105, 196, 197b, 210tl, 210cl, 210bc.

Staffan Widstrand: 013c, 21bcl, 21br, 214cl.

Vigelandsmuseet: 22tr.

JACKET
Front - CORBIS, Paul A. Souders main image; DK PICTURE LIBRARY, Linda Whitwam bl; KUNSTINDUSTRIMUSEET , OSLO bc; STAFFAN WIDSTRAND crb. Back - DK PICTURE LIBRARY, Rolf Sørensen and Jørn Bøhmer Olsen b; GETTY IMAGES, Paul Souders t. Spine - CORBIS, Paul A. Souders.

Phrase Book

When reading the imitated pronunciation, stress that part which is underlined. Pronounce each syllable as if it formed part of an English word and you will be understood sufficiently well. A few sounds, particular to Norwegian, are represented by small capitals in the pronunciation guide. Below is an explanation of these.

EW: try to say 'ee' with your lips rounded (or the French 'u')
H: the 'h' sound as in 'huge'
I: the 'i' sound as in 'high'
UR: the 'u' sound as in 'fur'

Norwegian Alphabetical Order
In the list below we have followed Norwegian alphabetical order. The following letters are listed after z: **æ, ø, å**.

'You'
There are two words for 'you': du (addressing one person) and dere (addressing two or more people). The polite form, de, is seldom used.

In an Emergency

Help!	**Hjelp!**	yelp
Stop!	**Stopp!**	stop
Call a doctor!	**Ring etter lege!**	Ring etter lege
Call an ambulance!	**Ring etter ambulanse!**	Ring etter amboolangsseh
Call the police!	**Ring til politiet!**	Ring til pohliteeat
Call the fire brigade!	**Ring til brannvesenet!**	Ring til brannvesenet
Where is the nearest telephone?	**Hvor er nærmeste telefon?**	vohr er nairmeste telefawn?
Where is the nearest hospital?	**Hvor er nærmeste sykehus?**	vohr er nairmeste sEWkeh-hooss?

Communication Essentials

Yes/no	**Ja/nei**	yah/ni
Thank you	**Takk**	takk
No, thank you	**Nei takk**	ni takk
Yes, please	**Ja takk**	yah takk
Please (offering)	**Vær så god**	varshawgo
Excuse me, please	**Unnskyld**	oonshewl
Good morning	**Mor'n**	mawrn
Good afternoon	**God dag**	go-dahg
Good evening	**God kveld**	go-kvell
Good night	**God natt**	go-natt
Goodbye	**Morn'a; (informal) ha det**	morna; hah-deh
Sorry!	**Om forlatelse!**	om forlahdelseh

Useful Phrases

I don't understand	**Jeg forstår ikke**	yI forshtawr ikkeh
Please speak more slowly	**Kan du snakke langsommere**	kan doo snakkeh lang-sawmereh
Please write it down for me	**Kan du skrive det opp for meg?**	kan doo skreeveh deh op for mI
My name is ...	**Jeg heter ...**	yI hayter
Can you tell me ...?	**Kan du si meg ...?**	kan doo see mI
I would like a ...	**Jeg vil gjerne ha en/et ...**	yI vil yarneh hah ayn/et
Where can I get ...?	**Hvor kan jeg få ...?**	vohr kan yI faw
What time is it?	**Hvor mange er klokken?**	vohr mang-eh ar klokken
I must go now	**Jeg må gå nå**	yI maw gaw naw
I've lost my way (on foot)	**Jeg har gått meg bort**	yI hahr gawt mI bohrt
Cheers!	**Skål!**	skawl
Where is the toilet?	**Hvor er toalettet?**	vohr ar toh-a-letteh

Shopping

I'd like ...	**Jeg skal ha ...**	yI skal hah
Do you have ...?	**Har du ...?**	hahr doo
How much is this?	**Hvor mye koster denne/dette?**	vohr mEW-eh koster denneh/dehtteh
I'd like to change this, please	**Kan jeg få bytte denne (dette)?**	kan yI faw bEWteh denneh (dehtteh)
Can I have a receipt?	**Kan jeg få en kvittering?**	kan yI faw ayn kvittayring
Can I try it/them on?	**Kan jeg prøve den/dem?**	kan yI pruveh den/dem
I'm just looking	**Jeg bare kikker**	yI bahreh Heekker
Do you take credit cards?	**Tar du kredittkort?**	tahr doo kredittkort
antique shop	**antikvitetshandel**	antikvitetshandel
baker	**bakeri**	bak-eree
bookshop	**bokhandel**	bohkhandel
butcher	**slakter**	slakter
cake shop	**konditori**	kohnditohree
cheap	**billig**	billi
chemist	**apotek**	apohtayk
craft shop	**husflidsforretning**	hoosfleeds-forretning
department store	**varemagasin**	vahremaga-seen
expensive	**dyrt**	dewrt
fashion	**mote**	mohteh
fishmonger	**fiskebutikk**	fiskehbooteekk
florist	**blomsterbutikk**	blomsterbooteekk
gift shop	**gavebutikk**	gahvehbooteekk
grocer	**dagligvarebutikk**	dahglivahrebooteekk
hairdresser	**frisør**	freesUR
market	**marked**	marked
newsagent	**avis-og tobakksbutikk**	aveess aw tohbaksbooteek
post office	**postkontor**	pawstkontoor
sale	**salg**	salg
shoe shop	**skobutikk**	skohbooteekk
supermarket	**supermarked**	soopermarked
toy shop	**leketøysbutikk**	layketoys-booteekk
travel agent	**reisebyrå**	raissehbewraw

Sightseeing

art gallery	**kunstgalleri**	kunnstgalleree
church	**kirke**	Heerke
fjord	**fjord**	fjord
garden	**hage**	hahge
house	**hus**	hEWs
mountain	**fjell**	fyeall
museum	**musem**	mEWseum
square	**plass**	plahss
street	**gate**	gahte
tourist office	**turistkontor**	tureestkontoor
town hall	**rådhus**	rawdhEWs
closed for holiday	**stengt på grunn av ferie**	stengt paw grewnn ahw fereeh
bus station	**busstasjon**	bewss-stashohn
railway station	**jernbanestasjon**	jairnbanestashohn

Staying in a Hotel

Have you any vacancies?	**Har dere ledige rom?**	hahr dereh laydi-eh rohm
I have a reservation	**Jeg har reservert rom**	yI hahr ressarvayrt rohm
double room	**dobbeltrom**	dobbeltrohm
twin room	**tomannsrom**	tohmanssrohm
single room	**enkeltrom**	engkeltrohm
room with a bath	**rom med bad**	rohm med bahd
shower	**dusj**	doosh
toilet	**toalett**	toh-a-lett
key	**nøkkel**	nURkkel

Eating Out

Have you got a table for...	**Kan jeg få et bord til...**	kan yI faw et bohr til...
Can I see the menu?	**Kan jeg få se menyen?**	kan yI faw say menEWen
Can I see the wine list?	**Kan jeg få se vinkartet?**	kan yI faw say veenkarteh
I'm a vegetarian	**Jeg er vegetarianer**	yI ar veggetahreeahnehr
Waiter/waitress!	**Hallo! Unnskyld**	hallo oonskEWl
The bill, please	**Regningen, takk.**	rining-en takk
beer	**øl**	URl
bottle	**flaske**	flaskeh
buffet	**koldtbord**	kawltbohr
cake	**kake**	kahkeh
children's portion	**barneporsjon**	barneporshohn
coffee	**kaffe**	kaffeh
cup	**kopp**	kopp
fork	**gaffel**	gaffel
glass	**glass**	glass
knife	**kniv**	k-neev
menu	**meny**	menEW
milk	**melk**	melk
open sandwich	**smørbrød**	smURrbrUR
plate	**tallerk**	tal-ark
receipt	**kvittering**	kvittayring
schnapps	**akevitt**	akevitt

serviette	**serviett**	sarvi-ett
snack	**smårett**	smawrett
soup	**suppe**	sooppeh
spoon	**skje**	shay
sugar	**sukker**	sookker
tea	**te**	tay
tip	**tips**	tips
waiter	**kelner**	kelner
waitress	**serveringsdame**	sarvayringssdahmeh
water	**vann**	vann
wine	**vin**	veen
wine list	**vinkart**	veenkart

Menu Decoder

ansjos	anshoos	anchovies
baguette	bagaitt	French stick
blåskjell	blaw-shayll	mussels
bringebær	bringe-bair	raspberries
brød	brUR	bread
dyrestek	dEWrestek	roast reindeer
eddik	eddikk	vinegar
elg	ailk	elk
fenalår	fehna-lawr	cured leg of mutton
fisk	feesk	fish
flatbrød	flaht-brUR	'flat bread' (leaf-thin crispbread)
flyndre	flEWndre	sole
fløte	flURteh	cream
fårikål	fawreekawl	lamb and cabbage stew
gaffelbiter	gahffel-beeter	small fillets of herring soaked in marinade
geitost	geytost	sweet, brown goats' cheese
gravlaks	grahv-lahks	cured salmon
grovbrød	grURv-brUR	wholemeal bread
grønnsaker	grURnn-sahker	vegetables
hellefisk	hellefisk	halibut
hummer	hummer	lobster
hvalbiff	vahlbiff	whale steak
hvitvin	veetveen	white wine
høns	hURns	chicken, poultry
is	ees	ice cream, ice
jordbær	joordbair	strawberries
kalv	kallv	veal
karbonade	karbonahdeh	minced beef steak
kjøtt	HURtt	meat
kjøttkaker	HURttkahker	minced beef balls
kneipbrød	k-neyp-brUR	crusty wheaten bread
knekkebrød	k-nekke-brUR	crispbread
kokt	kookt	boiled, poached
koldtbord	kawltbohr	cold buffet
krabbe	crahbbe	crab
kreps	krepss	crayfish
kveite	kvaiyteh	halibut
kylling	HEWlling	chicken
laks	lahks	salmon
lam	lamm	lamb
makrell	mahkrel	mackerel
melk	mailk	milk
mineralvann	mineralvann	mineral water
multer	mEWlter	cloudberries
mørbrad	mURbrUR	sirloin
okse	ookseh	beef
oksestek	ookseh-steek	roast beef
ost	oost	cheese
pannekaker	pannekahker	large thin pancakes
pariserloff	pareewser-loff	French stick
pinnekjøtt	pinne-HURtt	salted, dried side of lamb
pisket krem	piskett kraim	whipped cream
poteter	pootaiter	potatoes
pølser	pURlser	frankfurter sausages
rakørret	rahk-URret	fermented trout
reinsdyr	rainsdEWr	reindeer
reke(r)	rehker	prawns
ris	rees	rice
rogn	rogn	roe
rugbrød	rewgbrUR	rye bread
rødspette	rURdspetteh	plaice
rødvin	rURveen	red wine
røkelaks	rURkelaks	smoked salmon
rømme	rURmmeh	soured cream
rå	raw	raw
saus	saws	sauce
sei	saiy	coley
sild	seell	herring
sjokolade	shokolahde	chocolate
skalldyr	skall-dEWr	shellfish
skinke	shinkeh	ham
skjell	shayll	shells
smør	smURr	butter
smørbrød	smURrbrUR	open sandwich
saus	saws	sauce
stekt	stehkt	fried, roasted
sukker	sookker	sugar
suppe	sooppeh	soup
surkål	sewkall	sauerkraut
svin	sween	pork
syltetøy	sewlte-tURj	jam
søt	sURt	sweet
torsk	tawshk	cod
tyttebær	tEWtte-bair	cowberries or lingonberries
tørr	tURr	dry
vafler	vahfler	waffles
vann	vann	tap water
varm	vahrm	warm, hot
vilt	veellt	game
vin	veen	wine
øl	URl	beer
ørret	URrett	trout
østers	URsters	oysters

Numbers

0	**null**	nooll
1	**en/ett**	ayn/ett
2	**to**	toh
3	**tre**	tray
4	**fire**	feereh
5	**fem**	fem
6	**seks**	seks
7	**sju/syv**	shoo/sEWv
8	**åtte**	awtteh
9	**ni**	nee
10	**ti**	tee
11	**elleve**	elveh
12	**tolv**	tawll
13	**tretten**	tretten
14	**fjorten**	fyohrten
15	**femten**	femten
16	**seksten**	sisten
17	**sytten**	sutten
18	**atten**	atten
19	**nitten**	neetten
20	**tjue/tyve**	HOO-eh/tEWveh
21	**tjueen/enogtyve**	HOO-eh-ayn/ayn-aw-tEWveh
22	**tjueto/toogtyve**	HOO-eh-toh/toh-aw-tEWveh
30	**tretti/tredve**	tretti/tredveh
40	**førti/førr**	fURrti/fURr
50	**femti**	femti
60	**seksti**	seksti
70	**sytti**	sURtti
80	**åtti**	awtti
90	**nitti**	neetti
100	**(ett) hundre**	hoondreh
110	**hundre og ti**	hoondreh aw tee
200	**to hundre**	toh hoondreh
300	**tre hundre**	tray hoondreh
400	**fire hundre**	feereh hoondreh
1,000	**(ett) tusen**	toossen
10,000	**ti tusen**	tee toossen

Time

today	**i dag**	ee-dahg
yesterday	**i går**	ee-gawr
tomorrow	**i morgen**	ee-mawern
this morning	**i morges**	ee-morges
this afternoon	**i ettermiddag**	ee-ettermiddag
this evening/tonight	**i kveld**	ee-kvell
late	**sent**	saynt
early	**tidlig**	teeli
soon	**snart**	snahrt
later on	**senere**	saynereh
one minute	**et minutt**	et minoott
two minutes	**to minutter**	toh minootter
quarter of an hour	**et kvarter**	et kvartayr
half an hour	**en halv time**	ayn hal teemeh
Sunday	**søndag**	sURndag
Monday	**mandag**	mandag
Tuesday	**tirsdag**	teerssdag
Wednesday	**onsdag**	ohnssdag
Thursday	**torsdag**	tawrssdag
Friday	**fredag**	fraydag
Saturday	**lørdag**	lURrdag

Transport Map of Oslo

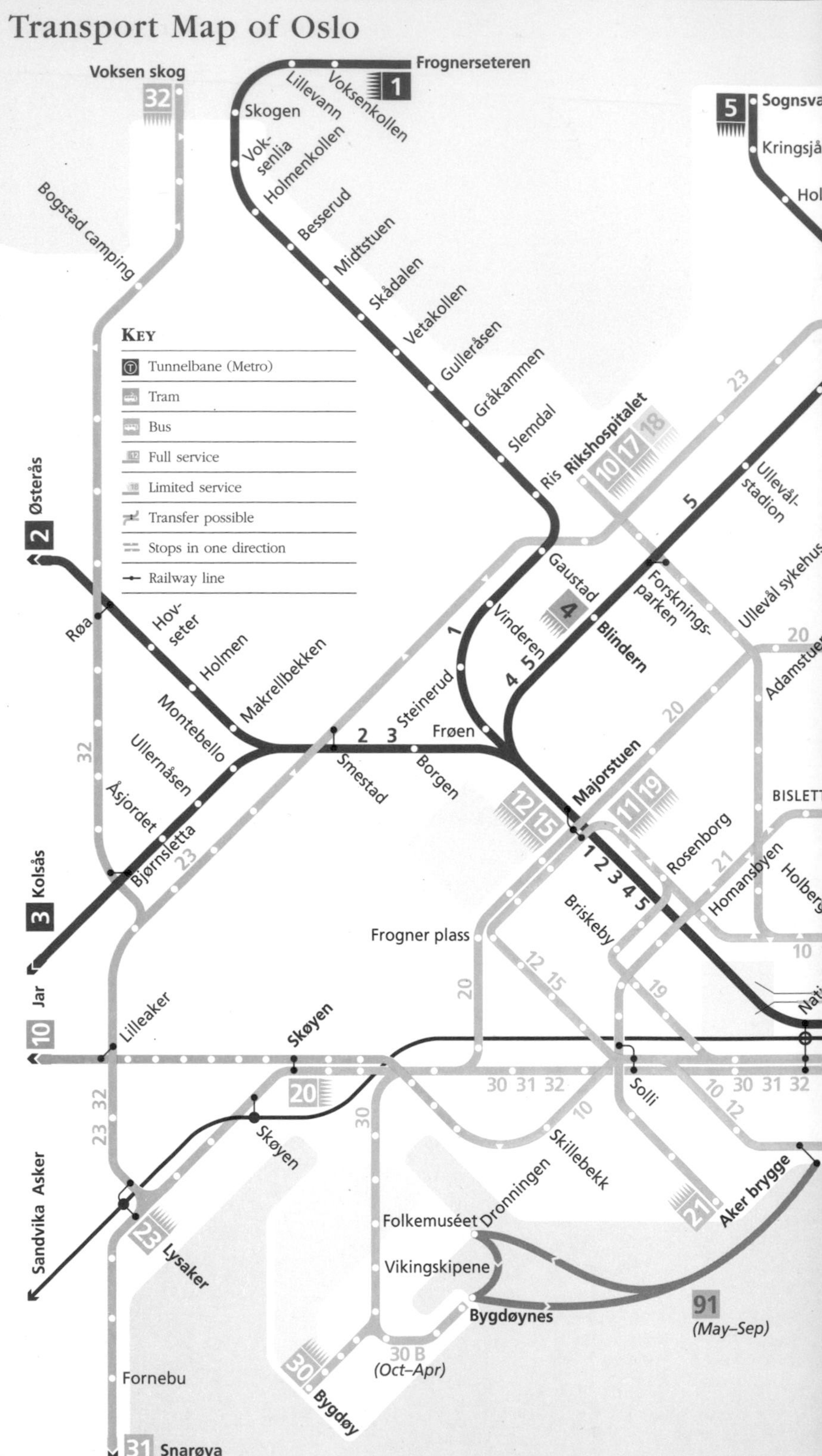

Voksen skog
Frognerseteren
Lillevann
Voksenkollen
Skogen
Vok-senlia
Holmenkollen
Besserud
Midtstuen
Skådalen
Vetakollen
Gulleråsen
Gråkammen
Slemdal
Ris
Rikshospitalet
Sognsvann
Kringsjå
Bogstad camping
KEY
Tunnelbane (Metro)
Tram
Bus
Full service
Limited service
Transfer possible
Stops in one direction
Railway line
Østerås
Røa
Hov-seter
Holmen
Makrellbekken
Montebello
Ullernåsen
Åsjordet
Bjørnsletta
Kolsås
Jar
Smestad
Steinerud
Frøen
Borgen
Vinderen
Gaustad
Blindern
Forsknings-parken
Ullevål-stadion
Ullevål sykehus
Adamstuen
Majorstuen
BISLETT
Rosenborg
Homansbyen
Briskeby
Frogner plass
Lilleaker
Skøyen
Solli
Skillebekk
Dronningen
Aker brygge
Sandvika Asker
Lysaker
Folkemuséet
Vikingskipene
Bygdøynes
(May–Sep)
30 B
(Oct–Apr)
Bygdøy
Fornebu
Snarøya